SECOND LANGUAGE TASK-BASED PERFORMANCE

Second Language Task-Based Performance is the first book to synthesize Peter Skehan's theoretical and empirical contributions all in one place. With three distinct themes explored in each section (theory, empirical studies, and assessment), Skehan's influential body of work is organized in such a way that it provides an updated reflection on the material and makes it relevant to today's researchers. Also in each section, an early publication is matched by at least one later publication, followed by a newly written commentary chapter, the combination of which provides the important function of offering a wider-ranging discussion. This book is an invaluable resource for researchers interested in second language task-based research or SLA more generally.

Peter Skehan is an Honorary Research Fellow at Birkbeck College, University of London, and has taught at universities in the UK, Hong Kong, and New Zealand. He is interested in second language acquisition, particularly task-based performance, language aptitude, and language testing. He is a recipient of the International Association of Task-Based Language Teaching Distinguished Achievement award.

Monroe C. Gutman Library
Graduate School of Education
Harvard University

Second Language Acquisition Research Series
Susan M. Gass and Alison Mackey, Series Editors

The *Second Language Acquisition Research* series presents and explores issues bearing directly on theory construction and/or research methods in the study of second language acquisition. Its titles (both authored and edited volumes) provide thorough and timely overviews of high-interest topics, and include key discussions of existing research findings and their implications. A special emphasis of the series is reflected in the volumes dealing with specific data collection methods or instruments. Each of these volumes addresses the kinds of research questions for which the method/instrument is best suited, offers extended description of its use, and outlines the problems associated with its use. The volumes in this series will be invaluable to students and scholars alike, and perfect for use in courses on research methodology and in individual research.

Second Language Task-Based Performance
Theory, Research, Assessment
Peter Skehan

For more information about this series, please visit:
www.routledge.com/Second-Language-Acquisition-Research-Series/book-series/LEASLARS

Of related interest:

Second Language Acquisition
An Introductory Course, Fourth Edition
Susan M. Gass with Jennifer Behney and Luke Plonsky

Second Language Research
Methodology and Design, Second Edition
Alison Mackey and Susan M. Gass

SECOND LANGUAGE TASK-BASED PERFORMANCE

Theory, Research, Assessment

Peter Skehan

NEW YORK AND LONDON

First published 2018
by Routledge
711 Third Avenue, New York, NY 10017

and by Routledge
2 Park Square, Milton Park, Abingdon, Oxon, OX14 4RN

Routledge is an imprint of the Taylor & Francis Group, an informa business

© 2018 Taylor & Francis

The right of Peter Skehan to be identified as author of this work has been asserted by him in accordance with sections 77 and 78 of the Copyright, Designs and Patents Act 1988.

All rights reserved. No part of this book may be reprinted or reproduced or utilised in any form or by any electronic, mechanical, or other means, now known or hereafter invented, including photocopying and recording, or in any information storage or retrieval system, without permission in writing from the publishers.

Every effort has been made to contact copyright holders. Please advise the publisher of any errors or omissions, and these will be corrected in subsequent editions.

Trademark notice: Product or corporate names may be trademarks or registered trademarks, and are used only for identification and explanation without intent to infringe.

Library of Congress Cataloging-in-Publication Data
A catalog record for this title has been requested

ISBN: 978-1-138-64275-1 (hbk)
ISBN: 978-1-138-64276-8 (pbk)
ISBN: 978-1-315-62976-6 (ebk)

Typeset in Bembo
by Apex CoVantage, LLC

For my grandchildren
Ruben, Isaac, Søren, Isla, Josh, Carwyn, and Oliver

CONTENTS

Illustrations ix
Acknowledgements xii

1 The Road to This Book 1

PART I
Theory 7

2 A Framework for the Implementation of Task-Based Instruction 13

3 Modelling Second Language Performance: Integrating Complexity, Accuracy, Fluency, and Lexis 35

4 Limited Attention Capacity and Cognition: Two Hypotheses Regarding Second Language Performance on Tasks 55

5 Reflections on Part I, Theory 83

PART II
Empirical Work 125

6 The Influence of Planning and Task Type on Second Language Performance 129

7	Self-Reported Planning Behaviour and Second Language Performance in Narrative Retelling	154
8	Lexical Performance by Native and Non-Native Speakers on Language-Learning Tasks	189
9	Reflections on Planning	206
10	Empirical Work With Tasks	233

PART III
Testing and Assessment — 253

11	Tasks and Language Performance Assessment	257
12	Models of Speaking and the Assessment of Second Language Proficiency	275
13	Reflections on Assessment	286

References — *317*
Index — *333*

ILLUSTRATIONS

Tables

2.1	Task Sequencing Features	27
2.2	Methodological Stages in Implementing Tasks	29
2.3	Factors Influencing Task Implementation	32
3.1	Comparison of Native and Non-Native Speaker Pausing on Three Tasks	38
3.2	Lexical Sophistication (Lambda) and Task Type for Native and Non-Native Speakers	40
3.3	Unavoidable Lexis and Task-Based Performance	42
3.4	The Levelt Model Linked to Influences on Second Language Performance	50
4.1	Task Research, the Levelt Model, and Performance	62
5.1	Studies Researching Performance Effects of Number of Elements and Planning	103
5.2	Performance Influences Linked to the Stages of Speaking	120
6.1	A Framework for Task Implementation	133
6.2	Design of the Control and Experimental Groups	139
6.3	Task Order Across the Groups	139
6.4	The Effects of Practice on Accuracy	141
6.5	The Effects of Practice on Complexity	142
6.6	F Values for Fluency and Task Type	143
6.7	Mean Scores for Fluency and Planning Condition	143
6.8	Complexity, Task Type, and Planning Condition	144
6.9	Syntactic Variety Measures	144
6.10	Error as a Function of Task Type and Planning Condition	145

7.1	Profile of the 48 Selected Participants	159
7.2	Frequency Data for All Codes	164
7.3	Performance Measure for Participants	166
7.4	Frequency and Error-Free Clause Mean Scores: Lexical Code 1—General Retrieval	168
7.5	Codes Associated With Greater Accuracy	169
7.6	Codes Associated With Higher and Lower Subordination Scores	170
7.7	Codes Associated With Differences in AS-Clause Boundary Pausing per 100 Words	172
7.8	Codes Associated With Differences in Mid-Clause Pausing	174
7.9	Lexical Sophistication Linked to Coding	176
8.1	Distribution of Ten-Word Chunks With Infrequent Words	192
8.2	Example Distributions and Associated Lambdas (λ)	192
8.3	Overview of the Studies	195
8.4	A Comparison of the Lexical Performance of Native and Non-Native Speakers	197
8.5	Pearson Correlations Between D and Lambda in Different Studies	198
8.6	Influence of Planning on D for Native and Non-Native Speakers	201
8.7	Influence of Planning on Lambda for Native and Non-Native Speakers	201
9.1	Cycles of Speaking	227
10.1	Independent Variables and Structural Complexity	237
10.2	Cross-Task Correlations Across Four Studies	245
11.1	Overview Description of the Six Studies	261
11.2	Familiar Information, Fluency, and Accuracy	265
11.3	Accuracy, Complexity, and Fluency on Dialogic vs. Non-Dialogic Tasks	267
11.4	Structured and Unstructured Narratives	269
11.5	Complexity of Outcome and Task Performance	270
11.6	Complexity Measures for Tasks Requiring Transformation and Tasks Not Requiring Transformation Under Different Planning Conditions	271
11.7	Summary of the Effects of Task Characteristics on Complexity, Accuracy, and Fluency	271
12.1	The Levelt Model of First Language Speech Production	276
12.2	The Levelt Model and Task Performance	280
13.1	Summary of Task and Task Condition Effects on Performance	292
13.2	Summary of Task Condition Effects on Performance	292
13.3	Types of Influence on Second Language Task Performances	298
13.4	Level of Difficulty Linked to Conceptualiser and Formulator Influences	300

Figures

11.1	A Model of Oral Test Performance (Skehan, 1998)	258
13.1	A Model of Task-Based Spoken Language Testing	306

ACKNOWLEDGEMENTS

Peter Skehan and the Publisher would like to thank the copyright holders and publishers of the original articles for granting us their permission to reproduce the following articles in this volume:

Chapter 2. A Framework for the Implementation of Task-Based Instruction

Originally published as: Skehan, P. (1996a). A framework for the implementation of task-based learning. *Applied Linguistics*, *17*(1), 38–62. Oxford University Press. Reproduced with permission of Oxford University Press.

Chapter 3. Modelling Second Language Performance: Integrating Complexity, Accuracy, Fluency, and Lexis

Originally published as: Skehan, P. (2009a). Modelling second language performance: Integrating complexity, accuracy, fluency and lexis. *Applied Linguistics*, *30*, 510–532. Oxford University Press. Reproduced with permission of Oxford University Press.

Chapter 4. Limited Attention Capacity and Cognition: Two Hypotheses Regarding Second Language Performance on Tasks

Originally published as: Skehan, P. (2015). Limited attentional capacity and cognition: Two hypotheses regarding second language performance on tasks. In M. Bygate (Ed.), *Domains and directions in the development of TBLT: A decade of plenaries from the international conference* (pp. 123–155). Amsterdam: John Benjamins. Reproduced with permission of John Benjamins.

Chapter 6. The Influence of Planning and Task Type on Second Language Performance

>Originally published as: Foster, P., & Skehan, P. (1996a). The influence of planning and task type on second language performance. *Studies in Second Language Acquisition*, *18*(3), 299–324. doi:10.1017/S0272263100015047. Reprinted with permission of Cambridge University Press.

Chapter 7. Self-Reported Planning Behaviour and Second Language Performance in Narrative Retelling

>Originally published as: Pang, F., & Skehan, P. (2014). Self-reported planning behaviour and second language performance in narrative retelling. In P. Skehan (Ed.), *Processing perspectives on task performance* (pp. 95–128). Amsterdam: John Benjamins. Reproduced with permission of John Benjamins.

Chapter 8. Lexical Performance by Native and Non-native Speakers on Language-Learning Tasks

>Originally published as: Skehan P. (2009b). Lexical Performance by native and non-native speakers on language-learning tasks. In B. Richards, H Daller, D.D. Malvern, & P. Meara (Eds.), *Vocabulary studies in first and second language acquisition: The interface between theory and application* (pp. 107–124). London: Palgrave Macmillan. Reproduced with permission of Palgrave Macmillan.

Chapter 11. Tasks and Language Performance Assessment

>Originally published as: Skehan, P. (2001). Tasks and language performance. In M. Bygate, P. Skehan, & M. Swain (Eds.), *Researching pedagogic tasks: Second language learning, teaching, and testing* (pp. 167–185). London: Longman. Copyright © Taylor & Francis. Reproduced by permission of Taylor & Francis.

Chapter 12. Models of Speaking and the Assessment of Second Language Proficiency

>Originally published as: Skehan, P. (2009c). Models of speaking and the assessment of second language proficiency. In A. G. Benati (Ed.), *Issues in second language proficiency* (pp. 202–215). London: Continuum. Reproduced by permission of Bloomsbury Publishing Plc.

1
THE ROAD TO THIS BOOK

My career in applied linguistics didn't start with an interest in tasks. At the very beginning, I had a post at the University of Birmingham, in a unit concerned with English for Academic Purposes. I had studied economics (as part of a dual honours degree), and was working with groups of Iranians who were studying economics but whose English was not of a sufficient level for the courses they were doing. So initially my focus was on the specialist language that they needed, drawing upon what I had studied of economics, linked to my previous experience as a language teacher. This was done in an EAP unit headed by Tim Johns and Tony Dudley-Evans, at a time when EAP had immense vitality as a sub-field within applied linguistics. So my earliest publications actually concerned how team teaching (with subject specialist and language specialist working in tandem) could best be organised.

But I was also working on a PhD on foreign language aptitude, at Birkbeck College, University of London. So in parallel to the focus of my day job, I was capitalising on the other part of my dual honours degree—psychology. This had, in fact, been followed by a Master's in psychology at the University of Western Ontario (and more about this can be found in Skehan, 2013). I was particularly interested in the role of memory in foreign language aptitude. Another facet of my work at Birmingham was that my head of department, John Sinclair, wanted to introduce an MA in applied linguistics, and so, on the basis that I had studied psychology and knew more about statistics than other people in the department (and the bar was not particularly high), I was tasked with teaching language testing. So most of these early interests were somewhat thrust upon me.

Not that they were uninteresting, but my individual focus, from amongst them, was definitely foreign language aptitude. I continued to research this area for the next decade, after I obtained my doctorate. But it was undeniable that there was hardly anyone else, at that time, who was interested in aptitude (a situation which is now very changed). I needed, in other words, to cast around and find more sociable areas of applied linguistics within which to work! My interest was raised by the interchange between Rod Ellis (Ellis, 1987) and Graham Crookes (Crookes, 1989) on the impact of planning on second language performance. At that time, the move was taking place from discussing communicative language teaching to using the term 'task-based learning' and the exchange between them seemed central to the way not simply that tasks could be discussed, but also, how tasks could be researched. The exchange was extremely suggestive as to how different lines of research could be pursued which (a) considered potential differences between tasks, (b) explored an additional variable, planning, in its effects on tasks, and (c) raised issues as to how to conceptualise and measure performance on tasks.

The debate between Ellis and Crookes was the catalyst which stimulated a whole new research area, one which was central to second language acquisition research at the time, and one which had a community of active researchers. But there were some other major influences. First of all, I was, by this time, working at the Polytechnic of West London, which became Thames Valley University. We formed there the Centre for Applied Linguistic Research, and this Centre, through the UK Research Assessment Exercise, attracted funding. Some of that funding was used to employ Pauline Foster as my research assistant, and this in turn led to research grants from the Economic and Social Research Council. The funding, and having Pauline as a research colleague, enabled several research studies to be done. CALR also attracted doctoral students, one of whom, Uta Mehnert, also did distinguished work in the task-based field. This activity was maintained after a move to King's College, London, where Parvaneh Tavakoli did a PhD with me. So my initial interest in tasks expanded and was supported, and I had the immense good fortune to work with excellent colleagues and doctoral students. My interest in the task-based area was firmly cemented.

Subsequently I moved to a post at the Chinese University of Hong Kong and I continued to be fortunate in the work that I did with tasks. This was in two ways. First, the Hong Kong system offered scholarships to doctoral students and while I was there I was able to supervise a very talented group of young researchers, all interested in aspects of task performance: Gavin Bui, Dai Binbin (Amy), Christina Li, Sheila Luo, Zhan Wang, and Edward Wen. It was a wonderful experience supervising such a talented bunch, but it was also really useful because we managed, as a group, to conduct fairly coordinated research, as indicated in the 2014 volume that I edited (Skehan, 2014a). But second, the Hong Kong Research Grants Council was a wonderful source of funding (and I shouldn't forget the internal funds offered by Chinese University). This money enabled me to conduct far more research than I would otherwise have been able to do, to develop my interest in tasks. It also enabled me to work with the research assistants I was able to appoint, Francine Pang, Sabrina Shum and my former doctoral students, Zhan Wang and Christina Li.

These are all the background influences to my interest in tasks. They provide a context for the set of articles and chapters on task research which are reprinted here. It has been interesting and rewarding to work in an area which has grown considerably in breadth and vitality during that period. For my part, the attraction is the way the area unites a concern for theory, a connection with psycholinguistics more generally, and the prospect of pedagogic relevance. The theory (in my case) relates to performance rather than acquisition (although extensions to acquisition, not covered much here, are not difficult to achieve), and the enduring fascination as to how we can communicate as effectively as we do. Psycholinguistics is represented by the existing models of first language speaking, and how productive it is to apply them to the case of second language performance. Allied to this is the consequence, for second language performance, of working memory and attention limitations which provide the background to the way second language use can proceed. Finally the connections to pedagogy are not at all difficult to make. The days of an exclusive focus on grammar in language teaching are now long gone (I hope!) and the challenge is to find teaching techniques which produce effective learning which translates into effective communication. The need to use tasks then becomes central.

But allied to these different motivations is the need for a balance between theory and empirical research. One of the attractions of the task area is that there are, essentially, two pressures to conduct empirical research. If theory is to be useful, it has to make testable predictions, and this requires empirical research. But pedagogy, similarly, looks to research justification for any claims that are made which might impact upon classrooms. My original training (in psycholinguistics, at the University of Western Ontario) was very much directed in this way, and so the confluence of all these forces seemed ideal to me. A training in research methods and statistics, an interest in psycholinguistics more broadly, and then an eye for pedagogic relevance seems to lead inexorably to the need to do task research!

The set of interests also connects with the structure of this book. There are three main sections, and these are concerned with theory, empirical research, and assessment. I have to admit that I am, basically, ambivalent about theory, or more exactly, its immediate role in shaping research. Obviously, it is desirable, but I also think that theory needs a solid empirical base as its starting point. I doubt that task research has quite achieved this level. So I am drawn to the use of frameworks, which are below the level of theory or even hypothesising. Frameworks attempt to systematise what is done, so that there is greater prospect of cumulative progress. The 1996 article from *Applied Linguistics*, reprinted here in the theory section, epitomises this. It attempts to structure the way research might be done, and data collected, but it attempts to be relatively neutral with respect to theory. Yet theorising and the precision and prediction that accompanies it are desirable, and so the later chapters in the section on theory do try to go beyond such a more limited starting point. The purpose of the two remaining contributions to the section therefore is to explore just how ready we now are to theorise about second language task performance.

The second major section of the book is concerned with empirical research. Two articles on planning are included, followed by one which focusses on lexis. Then, there are two 'reflections' chapters, one on planning and one on empirical research itself, on the actual measures of second language task performance. I have included planning because it seems to me one of the success stories of task research: we now understand much more about consistencies in performance and also the processes which occur during planning. It is also an interesting example of harmony between quantitative and qualitative approaches. Then the reflections chapter on measures of second language performance also tries to draw attention to progress, but in this case in understanding the measures that can be used, and consistencies in their functioning, and options which are available.

The final section focusses on testing and assessment, and includes two articles, one from 2001 and the other from 2009. They are both concerned with the same broad question: does task research have anything to say that is relevant to the testing of speaking? Naturally I argue that it does, although, as the section indicates, there can be some legitimate doubts about this. The 'Reflections' chapter tries to justify the claim of relevance, and basically argues that task-based research may have a lot to contribute in characterising the notion of 'ability for use', as a mediator between underlying competences and actual performance.

I have published a range of pieces over the years, and so one might think that the existence of these books and articles would be enough! But I have felt, and this was an idea originally encouraged by Rod Ellis, that bringing together and reprinting a selection of this material might have its value. One justification for this might be to juxtapose more highly cited publications with material that is less known, to try to bring out connections between these various writings (and this principle does apply to a limited extent). But in thinking of how such a collection might be put together, it occurred to me that it might be more revealing if, within the different sections just described (theory, empirical work, assessment), I juxtaposed something early and something late.

Fundamentally, I am hopeful of progress in the field, and one way of bringing this out might be to compare something from the beginning of my interest in task research and then something more recent (where 'beginning', of course, doesn't go back that far!). This device can then become a structure to bring out more clearly where progress may have been made. Consequently the first section, on theory, includes three articles, from 1996, 2009, and 2015. These have a pleasing twenty-year span. The second section contains articles from 1996, 2009, and 2014, which might imply the same nicely separated choices. In fact, this is a little more complicated, in that the 1996 and 2014 inclusions do have the focus of planning research, but the 2009 chapter is actually about the different area of empirical research with tasks. They do, though, provide the starting point for discussion of a range of empirical results. An additional striking feature here is that all three chapters in this section have a collaborative nature. The two chapters on planning are jointly authored, and this reflects the way they were, indeed, joint ventures. In each case I was a research grant holder and my co-author was the actual data collector as well as vital participant in the research. The other chapter, on lexis, is single authored but really draws fundamentally on the joint research I have done with Pauline Foster, and even relies, in part, on the data she collected for her PhD since this was based on native-speaker baseline data. Really the conclusion is simple: research is a joint activity and the jointness of the chapters in this section simply follows from that.

The third section includes articles from 2001 and 2009, the smallest time interval in any section. There is also a chance element here. I haven't done any direct research on language testing (despite my earlier interest in this area), and so I have only written on it when I have been invited to contribute something. In each case the chapter comes from an edited book, and I was responding to a need in that book to produce something on testing. So what I attempted to do in each case was take what I knew from the task research area and then try to apply it to assessment.

In a way, the remaining aspect of the book, which I have mentioned, but not covered explicitly yet, is the most important. Each section is followed by a reflections chapter (or in the case of the Empirical Work section, two reflections chapters!). These reflections chapters, or epilogues, are where I try to develop how, in my view, changes have occurred, and what the nature of these changes is. The epilogues (sometimes quite long), try to go beyond the individual chapters and articles, and most ambitiously, make claims about progress. Immediately, of course, I will contradict myself! Progress, in my view, is least evident in the first section, on Theory, not least because claims about theory can only be limited and provisional. They don't amount to much more than saying that our understanding of tasks themselves is now deeper, and that we have some clearer hints about the areas where research effort might be focussed. With a spoiler alert, I would claim that thinking about the conditions under which tasks are done has been more rewarding, and that linking second language task research to a model of first language speaking, that of Levelt, has paid dividends, to a much greater extent than has research into task characteristics themselves. The latter seems to me to be beset with lack of consistency and lack of clear findings.

Regarding assessment, in other words jumping from the first to the third section, the epilogue claims that task research has huge potential relevance to testing, in several areas. Understanding task characteristic and task condition influences is very important, as is a greater appreciation of how measurement of second language task performance (through complexity, accuracy, fluency, and lexis) might influence ratings of spoken performance. But the greatest potential, in my view, is in using what we have learned about tasks and task conditions to gain inroads into defining what the construct of ability for use might mean. My assumption is that there are underlying competences, but that, overlaid on these, and mediating them as far as actual performance is concerned, is the capacity to mobilise, to access underlying resources, and to solve communicational problems and breakdowns. As the Testing and Assessment epilogue argues, task research is suggestive as to how such an ability for use can be defined.

But if the specific goal of progress is to be claimed, the most convincing reflections chapters, in my view, are those in the second, empirical research section. The two relevant chapters are concerned with first planning and then second measures of second language task performance respectively. In each case, I would argue that considerable progress has been made. In the area of planning, we now have a range of findings which allow a powerful set of generalisations to be claimed as to the effects of planning. We have also seen progress in the research methodologies that are used to investigate planning, with a blend of quantitative and qualitative techniques. We are reaching a deeper understanding of what happens in planning and how we can use this knowledge to have an impact on pedagogy. Regarding the measurement of second language task performance, a great deal has been learned over the last twenty years. There are options as to the measures which can be used. If the major approach has been to explore complexity, accuracy, lexis, and fluency, in each case we are clearer about what each of these constructs represents and how its different facets can be measured. There may have been a great deal of ground-clearing in this work, but it has paid dividends. Future researchers may therefore be in a more secure position in the measures that they use.

PART I
Theory

Introduction

The two articles and one book chapter in this section are nicely spaced (1996, 2009, 2016), and reflect my views on the theoretical underpinnings of task performance. The first, from *Applied Linguistics* in 1996, was an attempt to be broad in perspective and programmatic in nature. Task research, at this point, was gathering momentum, but seemed to me prone to individual studies which might not cohere. Instead they reflected the preoccupations and contexts of many individual researchers, and as a result, risked the danger of fragmentation. I felt there was a need to take a wider view, to provide a framework for research, and to make links to underlying psycholinguistic theory and also to pedagogy. I was attracted to the term 'framework' since it is relatively neutral, theoretically, and only provides a general and inclusive structure within which research studies can be located and then linked to one another. I did not feel that the research results available at that time justified any stronger term than this.

There was also the point that I wanted to find a perspective which provided an alternative viewpoint to the Interaction Hypothesis. I had nothing against this hypothesis at all (although I had, and still have doubts about how much interaction can contribute 'on the fly' to developing underlying interlanguage systems). But my interest was performance, primarily, and it seemed to me that Graham Crookes's (1986) work, especially, had shown how performance itself could be rewarding as a research target. So this was what was uppermost in my mind when writing the 1996 article. I wanted to explore how research into second language task-based performance could be given a more secure underpinning.

From the range of material reprinted in this volume, and also the three reprinted articles in this section, the 1996 article has the greatest focus on pedagogy. This, perhaps, is the moment to add a few words on that subject, since it will not be developed elsewhere. The emphasis, in the first section, as just indicated, is on performance. But there are potential pedagogic links which can be clarified. First of these is that a greater understanding of performance can lead to more effective pedagogic work to achieve balance between the different areas of complexity (structural and lexical), accuracy, and fluency. One would like learners to make progress in all three of these areas, but it may be the case that some learners prioritise one or two at the expense of other areas. It may also be that certain tasks push learners in particular directions, e.g. fluency-oriented tasks. So one pedagogic advantage of researching tasks is for teachers and pedagogues to be better equipped, through knowledge of tasks and task conditions, to address any imbalances in the different dimensions of performance.

There is also the claim that there is an implicit pedagogic sequence built into the performance areas. New language and extension of an existing system connects with greater structural complexity. Such new language may initially be used haltingly and be error-prone. But as time passes, this new language may be automatised to some degree, and though still halting, be less error-prone. Then, as the new language becomes more automatised, accuracy and speed of production may be possible, and a more fluent performance results. In this view, the central value of tasks would be to foster this process of automatisation, and to ensure that new language is converted into usable and non-attention-demanding language. Knowledge about task characteristics, as well as the influence of task conditions, would be at the heart of how this is achieved.

But this still leaves unaccounted for the issue where new language might come from. One source might be task and condition influences which promote complexity. Planning would be the clearest example here, since it is associated consistently with greater structural complexity. But I find more convincing the idea that tasks and task conditions have, as their main role, that of making new language salient, or perhaps more realistically, the *need* for new language to be made salient—as Gin Samuda says 'creating the need to mean' (Samuda, 2001, p. 139). In effect, this is 'noticing the gap' (Swain, 1995, p. 129). Then, the vital point is to consider what happens next. In that respect I have argued in various places (and this includes the 1996 article) for the importance of the post-task stage in task-based work.

What might be termed the weak form of this is a post-task activity which nudges the second language speaker not to forget form. Following suggestions by Tony Lynch (2001, 2007), in Skehan and Foster (1997), Foster and Skehan (2013), and Li (2014) this possibility has been researched. Initially (Skehan & Foster, 1997) the goal was to use the anticipation of a post-task (consisting of a public performance of the same task) to lead to an increase in accuracy. It was reasoned that the anticipation of using the same or similar language while doing the actual task in the higher-stakes context of the public performance would cause learners to think more about avoiding error. This hypothesis was confirmed, but only in a limited way. More recently, in two later studies (Foster & Skehan, 2013; Li, 2014), the post-task for learners was modified. They had to transcribe a recording of their actual task performance. In this case the hope was that anticipating having to transcribe one's own errors would lead learners, during the actual task, to prioritise accuracy more because of their awareness of what was to come. This post-task operationalisation did have a stronger effect on accuracy, and also, unpredicted and to a lesser extent, on complexity. Requiring second language speakers doing tasks to subsequently transcribe some of their performance seems to push them to direct attention to form, whether in avoiding error or in using more advanced language. It appears to be the anticipation of transcribing one's own task performance which pushes second language speakers to divert attention in this way.

But a stronger form of the use of a post-task stage for pedagogy is to turn one of the old precepts of language teaching virtually on its head. Presentation-practice-production (the three 'Ps') becomes *production*, followed by *language focus* (i.e. a variant of presentation), and only then *practice*. This is a version of the approach advocated by Jane Willis. The key in using tasks in this way is that they will make language salient. The need to do the task, if the task and task conditions are well designed, will push the learner to be more aware of the language which is needed, and then, if that language need is recorded or retained, it can become the focus for important language work at the second or language-focus stage. In other words, noticing the gap and then very importantly retaining what has been noticed as a gap. This language work can be concerned with explication, analysis, extension, integration or whatever. The important point is that it is personal, and has arisen for a particular language learner as a result of task-generated need. Such focussed language work could then lead into more practice-oriented and consolidation activities at the final stage. Centrally, this is not boring repetitive practice, but rather a form of continued focus and consolidation of language which has been made personally salient in the task.

I have developed these ideas in Skehan (2007) and Skehan (2013), and tried to address some difficulties that ensue. In those publications I have argued that where pedagogy is concerned, the major opportunity that tasks provide is the salience of the language need that they catalyse (as argued above). This in turn leads to interesting questions regarding the ways the task-generated language can be retained and exploited, since simple memory is unlikely to be adequate. But there are also issues of the way a number of potentially important areas of language can be chosen between (since, in a class of learners different 'salient' language will emerge for different learners) and resolving this issue becomes a new part of a teacher's skills. The central point, though, is that there is a means of using tasks to generate a productive focus on new language.

The discussion of pedagogy has been a slight diversion. Returning to the reprinted articles in this first section, there is a different emphasis in the remaining two. In their way each is more focussed, and less wide-ranging than the 1996 publication. The 2009 article has a strong performance emphasis. First, it attempts to incorporate lexis into the 'default' range of measures of second language performance, to supplement the insights that come from structural complexity, accuracy, and fluency (and these performance areas were the focus of the special issue of *Applied Linguistics* from which this article comes). Secondly, and more importantly, the article contained an attempt to draw upon the Levelt model of first language speaking in a more systematic way, to try to account for second language speech. Following Kormos's (2006) broad-ranging discussion of the Levelt model, the article reprinted here tried to tease out implications specifically for the task-based area. Unlike the 1996 article, it was able to draw on a significant body of research, so that the range of extant findings could shape the nature of the discussion provided. As a result, the role of theory was considerably greater in this later article.

An interesting feature, as far as the last of the three publications in this section is concerned (Skehan, 2016), is the observation that one of the changes from 1996 is that twenty years later, the field of second language performance research had developed a fair degree of autonomy. Of course, there is still an important pedagogic connection for this research, and of course, there are links to acquisition and interlanguage development (and associated theorising). But there is also a great deal of interest in the nature of performance itself, and of the constructs, interrelationships, and measurement of complexity (structural and lexical), accuracy, and fluency. The structure of second language performance is also a prominent aspect of any comparison between the Limited Attention Capacity approach (which I espouse) and Peter Robinson's Cognition Hypothesis. This issue figures slightly in the 2009 publication (Skehan, 2009a). It becomes even more important in the last chapter in this section.

This final contribution comes from a book of plenaries, edited by Martin Bygate, and based on talks given to the international Task-Based Learning and Teaching conference over the last fourteen years. It is the written version of the plenary I gave, in a Point-Counterpoint debate with Peter Robinson. One of the points that Peter Robinson made in his talk at the TBLT conference was that the Limited Attention Capacity approach is a post hoc account. It provides a framework which can be used to explain a set of results after they are found, often by invoking notions of trade-off between different performance areas. In contrast, a strength of the Cognition Hypothesis is that it makes predictions, which can be falsified, particularly regarding the relationship between accuracy and complexity as these are affected by task complexity.

The point about my approach having a post hoc quality is entirely fair. The Limited Attention Capacity approach is indeed very serviceable in accounting for results after the event. In some ways a positive feature of this is that it is a good framework for generating research, and then research results can help in subsequent theory development. But of course this serviceability is a reflection of weakness and lack of explanatory power, as well as limitations on falsifiability. Part of the motivation for the 2009 and 2016 chapters was then to address the criticism of post hoc limitations. The final chapter of the section tries to set out the principles underlying the Limited Attention Capacity approach in a way more obviously related to making predictions (which is possible, up to a point). It tries to draw on the advances that come from (a) the greater range of research results now available, and (b) the clarity that extending the Levelt model provides. The chapter critiques the Cognition Hypothesis, as well, finally, as suggesting ways in which the Limited Capacity approach and the Cognition Hypothesis might come together in certain circumstances.

2
A FRAMEWORK FOR THE IMPLEMENTATION OF TASK-BASED INSTRUCTION[1]

Introduction

In recent years a number of researchers, syllabus designers, and educational innovators have called for a move in language teaching towards task-based approaches to instruction (Prabhu, 1987; Nunan, 1989; Long & Crookes, 1991; Crookes & Gass, 1993a, 1993b). Yet there are a number of critiques of task-based instruction that could be made (Sheen, 1994), and it is also unclear how such an approach could be implemented. The present article will examine the critiques, reviewing the theory and research that suggests limits and qualifications for task-based approaches. It then proposes a framework to enable teachers to implement task-based instruction on a more systematic and principled basis.

At the outset, it is helpful to examine some preliminary questions relating to tasks and task-based instruction. Although a number of definitions of task exist (see e.g. Nunan, 1989), for present purposes a task is taken to be an activity in which: meaning is primary; there is some sort of relationship to the real world; task completion has some priority; and the assessment of task performance is in terms of task outcome. Of course, translating these criteria into reality is not always a straightforward matter. Most activities combine a number of priorities, and it is a fine judgement to claim that the communication of meaning is a primary goal for any particular task, or to assert that a task has a real-world relationship. Classrooms are classrooms, but even so, a task which requires personal information to be exchanged, or a problem to be solved, or a collective judgement to be made bears a relationship to things that happen outside the classroom in a way that

---

Originally published as: Skehan, P. (1996a). A framework for the implementation of task-based learning. *Applied Linguistics, 17*(1), 38–62. Oxford University Press. Reproduced with permission of Oxford University Press.

separates these activities from doing, for example, a transformation exercise. One could make similar points about the other two components of definition that are offered here (task completion and task outcome assessment), but the point is that such a concept of task has sufficient focus to enable it to be a viable component for what goes on in classrooms.[2] Long and Crookes (1991) discuss a further quality of tasks: that they have a clear pedagogic relationship to out-of-class language use, in that needs analyses should clarify how students will need to use language in real life, and task design should ensure that classroom tasks bear a developmental relationship to such non-classroom activity. For this article, such a quality is regarded as desirable, but difficult to obtain, and the more restrictive approach to characterising tasks will be used. Similarly, there will be no discussion of the interesting possibility that students could be involved in the negotiation of which tasks are used, and how they are used (Breen, 1987). The approach taken here is to try to develop a framework which will help the teacher to better understand the tasks s/he is using, and to sequence and implement them more effectively.

One can, on the basis of these task characteristics, identify strong and weak forms of the task-based approach. A strong form would argue that tasks should be the *unit* of language teaching, and that everything else should be subsidiary. In this view, the need to transact tasks is seen as adequate to drive forward language development, as though second language acquisition is the result of the same process of interaction as first language acquisition (Wells, 1985). A weak form of task-based instruction would claim that tasks are a vital part of language instruction, but that they are embedded in a more complex pedagogic context. They are necessary, but may be preceded by focussed instruction, and after use, may be followed by focussed instruction which is contingent on task performance. This version of task-based instruction is clearly very close to general communicative language teaching. It could also be compatible with a traditional presentation, practice, production sequence, only with production based on tasks (as defined above), rather than more stilted and guided production activities (Littlewood, 1981).

If we turn next to research studies into task-based learning, a range of approaches are evident. Candlin (1987) discusses criteria by which tasks may be analysed, basing the categories used on an essentially data-free account of task properties, an approach developed by Nunan (1989) and Skehan (1992). Pica, Kanagy, and Falodun (1993) take a slightly different perspective, relying on research studies more directly. They analyse tasks in terms of interactional patterns and requirements, (i.e. how involved each participant needs to be), as well as the sorts of goals that underlie the tasks-to-be-transacted, (e.g. one-way vs. two-way).

A number of studies have been more specific in their analyses of tasks, positing particular contrasts or dimensions as the basis for characterising tasks. Prabhu (1987) argues in support of reasoning gap tasks; Duff (1986) contrasts divergent and convergent tasks, arguing that the latter engage acquisitional processes more effectively; and Berwick (1993) contrasts two dimensions—experiential-expository, and didactive-collaborative. There have also been studies of the participants within tasks such as Yule, Powers, and Macdonald (1992) on "hearer" effects and Plough and Gass (1993) on participant (and task) familiarity. Brown, Anderson, Shilcock, and Yule (1984) have also investigated various task design features, in an attempt to establish task difficulty on an empirical basis. They propose that static tasks (e.g. description) are easier than dynamic tasks (e.g. narration) which in turn are easier than abstract tasks (e.g. opinion giving) and that the number of elements, participants, and relationships in a task makes it more difficult. There have also been studies of processing influences on tasks. Tarone (1985) has shown that attention to form has a clear effect on accuracy of performance. Ellis (1987) reported an interaction between the engagement of planned discourse and different forms of the past tense under different task conditions. Crookes (1989) reported greater complexity and lexical variety for tasks done under a planning time condition, but, interestingly, no greater accuracy. Foster and Skehan (1994) report an interaction between opportunity to plan and task type. These research studies are individually revealing, but do not currently provide the basis for more general perspectives on task-based instruction. They do, though, play a part in the wider framework which is proposed below.

Problems and Assumptions in Task-Based Learning

Approaches to instruction which make meaning primary, such as task-based instruction, obviously have considerable appeal in terms of authenticity and linkage with acquisitional accounts of the course of language development. But there are pitfalls with such an approach, generally stemming from the consequences for form of putting such an emphasis on meaning. These pitfalls need to be understood if task-based approaches are to be properly exploited.

Learners (and native speakers) will place great emphasis on communicating meanings but not necessarily worry about the exact form that they use (Kess, 1992). In this respect, Grice (1975) has made clear that maxims for conversation make for a considerable processing burden because of what is *not* said. To spell everything out in complete and well-formed sentences would soon empty rooms, and get oneself classified as a boring pedant. Much adult conversation is elliptical and incomplete in surface form, heavy in the assumptions it makes about background knowledge being the basis for the implicatures that are made about intended meaning, speaker attitude, let alone propositional meaning (Wilson, 1994). It goes against the grain, in other words, to do more than use form as one element or pressure in native-speaker communication, where the major emphasis will be on the satisfactoriness of the flow of the conversation, not the correctness, or completeness, (or the usefulness for interlanguage development amongst learners) of what is said.

Further, if we now turn directly towards learners, two other consequences of such an emphasis on meaning become apparent. There is natural and unavoidable use of strategies of *comprehension* (Clark & Clark, 1977) in that non-deterministic and non-exhaustive methods are used to recover intended meaning, with the success of this operation often being dependent on only partial use of form as a clue to meaning (Anderson & Lynch, 1987). In other words, processing language to extract meaning does not guarantee automatic sensitivity to form, and the consequent pressure for interlanguage development which is assumed by supporters of the Input Hypothesis (see Skehan [1992] for further details). Further, there is widespread use of *communication* strategies. These, too, help the learner succeed with meaning while having the consequence of sometimes by-passing form. Cognitive and linguistic communication strategies, that is, Kellerman (1991) can be used to handle communicative pressure, but in so doing remove the automatic engagement that would be required to constantly stretch interlanguage and lead to change. Worst of all, in this regard, is the possibility that reliance on comprehension and communication strategies when meanings need to be communicated under pressure will be *too* effective. What this could mean is that "solutions" to communication problems become proceduralised and re-used on other occasions (Skehan, 1992). This would be desirable if the solutions in question led to interlanguage development, but it is equally likely that they will not, since there is little to justify the "on the fly" improvisations that are involved being part of a desired route for change. Their proceduralisation could then become a stumbling block for change in the future.

There is, though, an even more deep-seated problem—the possibility that much communication is lexical in nature. Regarding first language acquisition, Skehan (1992), following Peters (1983, 1985); Nelson (1981); Bates, Bretherton, and Snyder (1988), suggests that initial progress is lexical in nature, but then the initial stock of lexical items becomes syntacticised. Most important, though, the language system which is developed in this way then becomes *relexicalised* (Skehan, 1992), i.e. language which is analysable and has been analysed is actually stored as a repertoire of lexical items. Most centrally of all, the unit of storage is now no longer the word, but can consist of multi-word units (Peters, 1985) which, when used, are processed as a single item. The cost of such a system is that multiple storage is necessary, since each multi-word item requires separate storage as a unit. The gain, however, is considerable since during ongoing language processing such a larger unit can be processed as a whole, releasing resources for other aspects of the speech planning and execution required (Bygate, 1988).

Such a lexical interpretation of language performance has been argued in recent years by both linguists and psychologists. Bolinger (1975), for example, proposes that the idiomaticity of language has been vastly underestimated, and that much language processing is hardly creative at all, but relies upon familiar memorised material. Pawley and Syder (1983) argue that speech is planned a clause at a time, and that language users rely on lexicalised sentence stems, (of which they have thousands at their command), as they improvise their way, joining together such elements to produce connected discourse. Naittinger and De Carrico (1992) similarly argue for the importance of lexical units in speech production.

These analyses imply that language users have available dual modes of processing (Widdowson, 1989). When accessibility and time pressure are paramount, a lexical mode of communication will be relied upon, which draws upon a capacious, well-organised, and very rapid memory system. In contrast, when exactness or creativity matter, analysability and a concern for form, for syntax, and for planning, will predominate (Sinclair, 1991). Armed with these two possibilities, the language user can switch between the two modes to take account of whatever processing demands are most pressing. Skehan (in press, a) argues that "ability for use" (Widdowson, 1983) can best be understood as the capacity which marshalls processing resources in this manner in order to achieve communication.

If we relate the discussion in this section to task-based approaches to instruction, what this means is that tasks themselves, given their defining properties of meaning primacy, outcome evaluation, and realism, may well predispose those engaged in task completion to engage in a mode of communication which does not prioritise a focus on form, either in terms of using linguistic elements to achieve precision or to achieve accuracy. As a result, it may not be possible to rely on a task-based approach to automatically drive interlanguage forward. Instead, it is likely that it will teach learners simply how to do tasks better, to proceduralise strategic solutions to problems, and to engage in lexicalised communication. These conclusions suggest that it is necessary, if task-based approaches to instruction are to be viable, to devise methods of focussing on form without losing the values of tasks as realistic communicative motivators, and as opportunities to trigger acquisitional processes. Prior to discussing a framework which may achieve this goal, however, it is necessary to try to situate task-based instruction within a theoretical viewpoint more grounded in contemporary psychology—an information-processing perspective.

Cognitive Approaches to Language Learning

In recent years there have been a number of studies which have clarified the theoretical basis for a cognitive approach to language learning. These have concerned the nature of what is learned; the role of consciousness; the role of performance factors; and the way in which attention impacts upon learning. We will examine each of these in turn.

One method of addressing the question of *what* is learned is through laboratory studies of artificial languages (though see Van Patten [1994] for a critique of the relevance of such research). In the learning of such structured material, the issue is whether progress consists of the induction of underlying abstract rules following a process of (possibly implicit) restructuring (Reber, 1989; McLaughlin, 1990), or the learning of exemplars, i.e. specific, contextually coded items which may contain structure, but which are learned as chunks (Carr & Curren, 1994). The former interpretation regards development in terms of the growth and complexity of the underlying system involved, while the latter is more concerned with the accumulation of exemplars, and their utility in performance.

The connection with natural language learning here is clear. The rule-based interpretation would imply that interlanguage development would be the result of the restructuring that occurs with linguistic material (McLaughlin, 1990), motivated by the continued operation of a Universal Grammar or by other cognitive processes. The exemplar-based interpretation, in contrast, would argue for development as being the accumulation of useful chunks of language, i.e. in earlier terms, language as formulaic items. Most interestingly of all, in this regard, is that Carr and Curren (1994), following Matthews, Buss, Stanley, Blachard-Fields, Cho, and Druhan (1989), interpret findings in this area as being most consistent with a dual-mode of processing, in which there is evidence for both structured learning and exemplar-based learning, but with the operation of both modes combining in a synergistic manner to yield results, and degrees of learning, that are more than simply the sum of the parts. The parallel with the use of a *re*lexicalised repertoire of language (Skehan, 1992) is clear.

Schmidt (1990, 1994) discusses the role of consciousness in language learning. He distinguishes between several senses of this term, such as awareness, control, and attention. In this section we will discuss consciousness as awareness, moving on to consider the other two senses in the sections on fluency and attention. For Schmidt (1990, 1994) consciousness has considerable importance in language learning. There is accumulating evidence (see review in Carr & Curren, 1994) that explicit learning of structured material is generally superior to implicit learning, suggesting that awareness of the learning itself and of what is to be learned confers advantages. Schmidt (1994) suggests that, for example, awareness enables more efficient solutions to the "matching" problem (Klein, 1986), i.e. noticing the gap between one's current language system and the language one encounters. Similarly Schmidt (1994) proposes that awareness may enable learners to appreciate better the instruction they are receiving, especially the correction that is being given. Awareness may also (Karmilloff-Smith, 1986) make it easier to transform and recombine material, to restructure, in other words, as the structure of material is more available, and other organisational possibilities become clear. Finally, awareness may help learners operate the sort of dual-mode systems outlined above, where the learner/language user may need to combine rule-based systems and exemplar-based systems during ongoing performance. In this respect, one interesting possibility is that on occasions where rule-based systems are used for the generation of language, the *products* of such activity can themselves become exemplars and then retrieved and used *as exemplars* on subsequent occasions (cf. the earlier discussion on relexicalisation; Peters [1985]; and discussion below). Clearly, consciousness-as-awareness would be of considerable help in this process.

This possibility takes us into the need to discuss fluency, and the ways in which consciousness-as-control may operate. Schmidt (1992) provides an extensive review of psychological mechanisms underlying fluency in foreign language performance. In general, there seem to be three ways of accounting for the development of fluency: accelerating models, restructuring models, and instance models. The first approach simply suggests that there is a natural sequence in which initial declarative knowledge becomes proceduralised (Anderson, 1989) or automatised (Schiffrin & Schnieder, 1977) so that essentially similar processes are used, but more quickly and with less need to use mental resources to control them, i.e. the same steps are followed, but more quickly and efficiently and probably less consciously. Restructuring approaches (Cheng, 1985; McLaughlin, 1990) regard improved performance as the result of using better algorithms so that performance is better organised. One assumes, following this approach, that restructuring, when it occurs, is rapid and immediately available to sustain improved performance (fluency in this case). Instance-based approaches (Logan, 1988; Robinson & Ha, 1993) regard fluency as performance which is based not on rules which are applied more quickly or on rules which are more efficiently organised, but on contextually coded exemplars which function as units. Such units (which may be significantly longer than a word) are the product of previous rule applications which are now stored in exemplar form, and so require far less processing capacity because they are retrieved and used as wholes. On this view (Peters, 1985; Schmidt, 1992) learning is the result of instance creation, and performance (and the ensuing fluency) the result of instance use.

We will assume here that the restructuring model is not very relevant to second language learning *fluency*, although it is to interlanguage development in general. (It seems more suited to cognitive learning of a more general nature when insight and new algorithms are what lead to problem-solving efficiency.) More important for present purposes are the two other accounts. The first, the proceduralisation model, concerns an interplay between declarative knowledge and the fluency which arises from proceduralisation, with the cost that less control is available over such material. The contrasting approach, instance theory, portrays the relationship between the rule-governed part of the system and the fluency-oriented component differently, giving the latter a greater degree of autonomy.

It is the latter interpretation which is taken to be relevant to foreign language learning even though the proceduralisation account has merit. This is so largely because an instance-based interpretation fits in more effectively with the dual-mode account of structured learning presented earlier, as well as with a syntactic-lexical contrast in natural language learning. It also provides an interesting theoretical interpretation of the phenomenon of fossilisation, in that one can now regard such an outcome as the premature product of a rule-based system which is then made available as an exemplar in future language use. There is no requirement, in other words, that what are created as exemplars are correct. In beneficial circumstances rule-created exemplars may be supplanted by other exemplars which are created when the underlying rule-based system has evolved more. But if the underlying system does not so evolve, and if communicative effectiveness is achieved, the erroneous exemplar may survive and stabilise, i.e. become a syntactic fossil.

Finally, we need to consider the role and functioning of attention, the final meaning of consciousness mentioned earlier. In information-processing terms, attention is a process, and is capacity-robbing (Van Patten, 1994). One chooses to attend to some things at the expense of others, and the choice of attentional direction, as well as the use of attentional resources themselves, have costs as far as the processing of potential foregone material is concerned. Attention, that is, has both a control function for further processes, and also a direct effect in terms of the focus of conscious attention at any one time (Schmidt, 1994). Pursuing the information-processing perspective, we can consider that, in foreign language learning and performance, three stages can be distinguished: input, central processing, and output (Skehan, 1994). We will examine the role of attention in the first two of these, the third having been covered in the discussion on fluency.

Regarding input, Van Patten (1990, 1994) has shown that meaning is primary when attentional resources are limited. He argues that under such conditions there is attention to form only if it is necessary for the recovery of meaning. On the other hand, form can be attended to, even if it is not crucial for meaning, if there is no pressure on attentional resources, i.e. if there is spare attentional capacity. Schmidt (1990) argues similarly for the importance of noticing as a means to channel attentional capacity so that input can become intake. He proposes that various factors, e.g. salience, traces of previous instruction, and task demands (i.e. control of attentional capacity on the part of the task designer) will make it more likely that attention will be directed to form, but that the central issue is that this noticing occurs and that the spare attentional capacity which is involved is directed so that it attends to important aspects of form. The challenge for the task designer is then to engineer situations in which this is more likely to occur with learners.

Essentially, the effective use of attentional capacities during input is intended to create a situation in which input can become intake, and effective processing of material can be triggered so that the implications of existing input for interlanguage development can be exploited and acted upon. In this respect, we are now concerned, in Schmidt's (1994) terms, with consciousness as focal attention, with the need to commit attentional resources to the material which is being processed. Carr and Curren (1994) propose that focal attention of this sort does help in the learning of structured material. They suggest that if material is simple and unambiguous, there is no great advantage for explicitness. But if material is more complex and ambiguous (as they characterise natural languages), explicitness confers an advantage. In particular, Carr and Curren (1994) suggest that focal attention of this sort enables more effective parsing of material and richer coding, with such processes being helpful for language development. Focussed attention of this sort does not need to lead to the ability to consciously articulate underlying rules for the language being learned, but it is important that there is a self-awareness about the task of learning which is being faced. In this respect, Van Patten (1994) offers the analogy of learning to improve a backhand in tennis. One may not benefit from an exposition of the underlying physics, or of the metalanguage of tennis strokeplay, but it may be helpful to give one's full attention to the backhands one is playing, and even to benefit from "input to intake" hints from a coach, along the lines of: "think about your footwork". In language, too, attention can be directed without this direction necessarily involving detailed explanations of rules. The issue, centrally, is that limited capacity is being focussed in the area which is most helpful, with the possibility that what then happens triggers implicit processes. Generalisations in data which might otherwise be missed become more accessible with the structuring of the learning experience that is involved.

Goals in Task-Based Instruction

This discussion demonstrates that task-based approaches to instruction are currently in a transitional position. There are clear reasons for the adoption of task-based approaches, principally associated with their potential engagement of acquisitional processes; there is underlying psycholinguistic research which, to some extent is supportive; and there is a range of specifically task-based second language research which is helpful in evaluating this type of instruction. On the other hand, there are arguments, both linguistic and psychological, why a focus on meaning may not engage such acquisitional processes; there is psycholinguistic evidence which argues for a clear role for explicitness and consciousness, for the manipulation of attentional focus, and for the existence of dual modes of processing, structural and exemplar-based. This discrepancy places proponents of task-based instruction in a difficult position, since while it is clear that there are advantages to using such an approach, it is difficult to know how strongly to argue this position, and how exactly to implement such instruction. A necessary step, therefore, is to draw on the preceding discussion to set appropriate goals for task-based approaches.

It is relatively easy to identify, as a general goal in foreign language learning, that of becoming more native-like in one's performance,[3] on the grounds that most people have such views about the levels of competence and performance that they would like to achieve. Within this general goal, however, it is proposed that it is useful to separate learner goals into three main areas: accuracy, complexity, and fluency. The first of these, accuracy, is concerned with a learner's capacity to handle whatever level of interlanguage complexity s/he has currently attained. Complexity, and its attendant process, restructuring, relates to the stage and elaboration of the underlying interlanguage system. Fluency, finally, concerns the learner's capacity to mobilise an interlanguage system to communicate meanings in real time.[4]

To take the first of these goals in more detail, accuracy relates to a learner's belief in norms, and to performance which is native-like through its rule-governed nature. Such a goal is desirable for a number of reasons: inaccuracy *could* impair communicative effectiveness; it could stigmatise; it could fossilise; and finally self-perceived inaccuracy could be demoralising to the learner. Turning to the causes of inaccuracy, one is that the underlying interlanguage system is inadequate, or transitional, such that the language which has been produced *is* grammatical, but to an incorrect system which needs to change further (Ellis, 1994) (see below). One could speculate that the tendency to be inaccurate on this basis relates to how well established the particular part of the interlanguage system is. But it also possible that inaccuracy is the result of the competence-performance relationship, and of the way in which communicative pressure has led to an error being made which, under other circumstances, would not be: a lapse, in Corder's (1981) terms. And of course, we cannot ignore the possibility that inaccuracy may itself be targeted as desirable, for whatever reasons the learner is motivated by (Trevise & Noyau, 1984)!

The reverse side of this coin is to consider what *promotes* accurate language use. Clearly, the use of well-integrated aspects of the interlanguage system will be helpful here, i.e. a sort of conservative communication strategy, in which what is well-known is used, and what is not is avoided (Schachter, 1974). Learners who dislike risk-taking will, presumably, be drawn to accuracy because of a reluctance to use language they are not sure of. A similar effect will result from a greater concern, on the part of the learner, to be correct, to conform to target language norms, and to value them as important. But other factors are also likely to have an impact, such as the effectiveness with which attentional resources are mobilised, and the processing capacity which is available given other aspects of communicative pressure, i.e. the more attention is diverted elsewhere, the less attention is available for form and accuracy (Van Patten, 1990; Van Patten & Cadierno, 1993).

In this regard, we need to turn to the next goal that has been proposed for language learning—complexity/restructuring. Restructuring is concerned with the process by which the interlanguage system becomes more complex, elaborate, and structured (McLaughlin, 1990); maybe more efficient and less circumlocuitous in communication (Cheng, 1985); more consistent with input data and more native-like (Cook, 1994). It requires a learner who explicitly accepts such developments as goals and who is driven, by whatever means, to achieve them. More complex interlanguage systems are desirable since they reflect acquisition having taken place, and will enable a greater degree of acceptance as a speaker of the language concerned. Equally important, such IL systems should enable greater precision in communication (Swain, 1985), and greater communicative efficiency in face of difficult performance circumstances. They should also make it more likely that more complex ideas will be expressed effectively (Swain, 1995).

If we examine why restructuring may to some extent *fail to occur*, a number of reasons present themselves. There may be a lack of interest on the part of the learner either in the goal of becoming more native-like or simply in making the effort to change and re-organise an interlanguage system. There may also be impoverished input (or instruction), such that necessary conditions for restructuring are impaired. But there might also be problems even if the above two problems are not present. For example, learners may prefer not to take risks, relying on less elaborate interlanguage systems which are adapted to communicate meanings in such a way that interlanguage is not pressured for change (Schachter, 1974). Such a conservative strategy would promote accuracy at the expense of complexity. Equally, there may be pressure to communicate which does not provide adequate time for restructuring to occur, since processing resources have to be excessively committed to achieving certain communicative outcomes. In such cases, it is likely that solutions to communicative problems will be proceduralised, and exemplar-based learning will occur (Schmidt, 1983, 1992).

Reversing the above analysis makes it clear how restructuring can be more likely to be achieved. There needs to be an interest in achieving native-like performance, and possibly an interest in change more generally. There also needs to be helpful input, both explicit and implicit. It is also important that interactive opportunities, e.g. tasks which need to be transacted, will have a stretching influence on interlanguage, in that precision of expression should be integral to their completion (Swain, 1995). It would also be helpful if there were time to engage restructuring processes, and to attend to things other than immediate communication pressures. Finally, it would help if there were support for restructuring, through sequencing of teaching activities, through relevant preparation (Crookes, 1989), and through appropriate post-task activities (Willis & Willis, 1988; Skehan, 1992).

We can turn finally to fluency, the last of the three goals outlined earlier. Fundamentally, this consists of the capacity to mobilise one's linguistic resources in the service of real-time communication, i.e. to produce (and comprehend) speech at relatively normal rates, approaching (but not necessarily identical to) one's own native-language speech rates. In particular, one would look at features such as rate, pausing, reformulation, hesitation, redundancy, and the use of lexical units (Bygate, 1987) to establish the level of fluency which has been achieved. It is assumed that to achieve this goal requires a capacity to use implicit knowledge systems in actual performance (Schmidt, 1992).

Adequate levels of fluency are desirable if one wants to be acceptable as a worthwhile interlocutor (Schmidt, 1983). Poor fluency will lead to difficult (and less frequent) patterns of interaction and further opportunities for learning (Larsen-Freeman & Long, 1991). It will also lead to dissatisfaction, as it becomes difficult to express interesting ideas in real time and the normal orchestration of conceptualisation, planning, and execution (Levelt, 1989). From a learning perspective, fluency is also desirable to the extent that it integrates, as implicit knowledge, the results of emerging and developing restructuring, and makes accessible the lexicalised products of the operations of the restructuring in actual communication (Carr & Curren, 1994). More questionably, the sort of fluency which represents the proceduralisation or lexicalisation of transitional forms which are incorrect, and whose consolidation may compromise future development, may be undesirable. It may represent communicative progress, but of a type which makes later restructuring more difficult.

Given these perspectives, we next need to examine what promotes (a) lack of fluency, (b) undesirable fluency, and (c) effective fluency. *Lack* of fluency is clearly more likely when the speaker does not value fluency, but instead is more drawn towards other goals, such as accuracy, or precision and complexity of speech. It is also more likely when there has been insufficient opportunity for the proceduralisation of language, and for the development of an adequate repertoire of exemplars (formulaic units) to sustain the pressures involved in real-time communication. This, in turn, besides being accounted for by individual differences factors (Skehan, in press, b), is likely to be the result of inadequate opportunities to make language production automatic in the necessary manner. *Undesirable* fluency is likely to result from excessive proceduralisation, perhaps resulting from the use of Strategic Competence to solve communicative problems. Such "solutions" are what are automatised and compromise future interlanguage growth. Excessive pressure to communicate, that is, may result in transitional forms fossilising as accessible exemplars which are easy to use, appear to have communicative effectiveness, but are incorrect.

Finally, it can be proposed that *effective* fluency is achieved when previous restructuring becomes automatised or becomes a (correct) exemplar. In such a case, the pressure to achieve fluency comes at the right moment *after* restructuring has occurred. This implies a capacity to engage in cycles of analysis and synthesis on the learner's part (Klein, 1986), with the former focussing on restructuring, and the latter on fluency (Skehan, 1992). The former is necessary to keep a system open, and capable of change. The latter is vital if the system so developed is not to be simply a rule-system which has to be applied anew in each communication, but instead is made accessible (Widdowson, 1989), lexicalised, and automatised. In other words, desirable fluency implies a capacity to operate a dual-mode system, in which well-organised exemplars are available to respond to real-time pressures, but a rule-based system can still be accessed when the need for precision or creativity arises (Carr & Curren, 1994). Coming from a corpus-based linguistic perspective, essentially the same claim is made by Sinclair (1991) in his contrast between the idiom principle and the open-choice principle: the former concerns the way choices are reduced in the service of real-time communication, while the latter principle is what enables the language user to access a greater range of lexical choice when this is appropriate.

If we ask how such a level of beneficial fluency can be achieved, it is clear that there have to be opportunities to create exemplars in context which can then be retrieved in later communicative encounters. This implies giving learners communicative problems to solve at the right level of processing difficulty, i.e. avoiding excessive processing demands which would disrupt performance, while also avoiding non-challenging tasks which do not extend ability for use. In this way learners are more able to bring to bear the effects of recent restructuring, but at the same time achieve a level of fluency. For this to happen with any consistency, it is important that cycles of activity are organised so that there is a balance between a focus on form and a focus on communication (Van Patten, 1990; Skehan, 1992).

Now, though, that we have discussed accuracy, complexity, and fluency somewhat separately, it is important to examine their interrelationships. A focus on accuracy makes it less likely that interlanguage change will occur; more likely that speech will be slow; and probably consumes a considerable portion of attentional resources. A focus on complexity and the process of restructuring increases the chances that new forms will be incorporated into interlanguage systems; promotes risk-taking; and requires attention being devoted to the new forms of language which are being assembled (Foster & Skehan, 1994). Finally, a focus on fluency will lead to language being produced more quickly; to an emphasis on accessibility (Bygate, 1988); and with lower priority being attached to getting language right, or to the use of new forms.

If we consider the processing implications of having these three goals, it is clear that there is not sufficient capacity for learners to devote resources to each of them so that they can be met simultaneously. As a result, decisions about the prioritisation of attentional resources have to be made during communication and learning, leading us to need to explore the consequences of allocating attention in one direction, and not another (Van Patten, 1994). Performance is likely to prioritise fluency, and relegate restructuring and accuracy to lesser importance. A focus on development, on the other hand, is likely to prioritise restructuring, with accuracy and fluency being more secondary. Further, to the extent that such learning is cumulative, cycles of restructuring, followed by an emphasis on accuracy and fluency, may be followed by contingent, developmental cycles of further restructuring, as a particular interlanguage sub-system is progressively complexified.

We now need to consider how the three goals of accuracy, complexity-restructuring, and fluency have been addressed in language teaching methodology, i.e. what decisions are explicit or implicit in existing approaches to pedagogy. A conventional presentation, practice, production sequence tacitly assumes that change will come about through the presentation phase, and this will be translated into accuracy and fluency through the succeeding practice and production stages (Rivers, 1981). Following the earlier discussion, we have seen that there are problems with this approach. It assumes that "restructuring" can be equated with whatever the teacher (or the syllabus writer) deems to be worth presenting, and ignores the findings of systematicity that have emerged through second language acquisition research (Ellis, 1994). It similarly assumes that the teacher's plan can be cumulative, with units chosen and sequenced on non-acquisitional grounds (Breen, 1984). Further, it generally assumes that there is a linear sequence to learning the units of language: when they are covered, they are learned, and do not require cyclical revisiting and extension. Finally, there is the problem that the practice model which underlies the development of habits in such a "3Ps" approach, has been itself widely discredited (Stern, 1983). So, although there is a sense in which the three terms of restructuring, accuracy, and fluency could be associated with presentation, practice, and production, the match is, on examination, clearly inappropriate.

A task-based approach, in contrast, may achieve the goal of restructuring, if it is assumed that interaction opportunities have an "extending" influence on interlanguage development, and engage acquisitional processes. But we have seen that there is also the possibility of over-prioritisation of attentional resources towards fluency, so that the proceduralisation of a lexicalised competence emphasising accessibility is at the expense of complexity-restructuring and of accuracy. To overcome the difficulties of achieving such conflicting goals, task-based instruction needs to find ways of balancing attention allocation. The next section addresses this issue.

Task-Based Instruction: Avoiding the Dangers

The linguistic analysis presented earlier highlights the meaning-driven nature of much communication, and the problems this poses for interlanguage development. The studies from cognitive psychology and psycholinguistics reinforce this meaning-driven nature of communication, and link it to (a) the relevance of a limited capacity attentional system in which meaning is prioritised for the consumption of scarce resources, and (b) how a dual-mode system may be used to ease the processing burdens that are the consequence of the limited capacities, such that a rule-based system is often implicated, but when processing demands are high, a lexically-organised system comes into operation. Finally, the task-based learning research is relevant, but not in a systematic way. Proposals are accountable to such research but given its incomplete nature, it cannot be the *guiding* basis for proposals on task-based instruction.

What is proposed in the remainder of the article is a framework to address these problems. Although it is consistent with underlying disciplines and research findings it contains an essentially speculative component, in that it tries to provide an organisational framework which can guide pedagogic decisions, and which can structure the ways in which task-based instruction is implemented. It also provides a framework to which existing research can be related, and which could be useful for decision-making, and organising future research. The underlying themes for this discussion are that task-based learning should work towards a constant cycle of analysis and synthesis; that this should be achieved by manipulating the focus of attention of the learners; and that there should be balanced development towards the three goals of restructuring, accuracy, and fluency. In practical terms, how these aims can be achieved in task-based learning can best be discussed in terms of the traditional categories of syllabus, i.e. sequencing of tasks, and then methodology, i.e. implementing the tasks which have been chosen.

Sequencing Tasks: Syllabus Considerations

A fundamental tension in communicative language teaching is that it tries to bring together form and meaning (Van Patten, 1990) in that the learner has to have something worthwhile to say. But if there is something worthwhile to say (a) content may become of primary importance, and (b) concern with content will consume attentional resources (Van Patten, 1994). It is imperative, therefore, that tasks are sequenceable on some principled criterion, since the basis on which tasks are ordered will be a reflection of what attentional resources they require.

Developing this general approach, the following scheme is proposed for such task sequencing, drawing on previous work by Candlin (1987) and Nunan (1989): in brief, the scheme contrasts formal factors (Code Complexity) with content (Cognitive Complexity) and pressure to achieve communication (Communicative Stress). Code Complexity is concerned with traditional areas of syntactic and lexical difficulty and range and will not be pursued further here. Cognitive Complexity is concerned with the content of what is said, and relates to the conceptualisation stage of Levelt's (1989) model. It distinguishes between the two areas of *processing* and *familiarity*. Processing is concerned with the amount of on-line computation that is required while doing a task, and highlights the extent to which the learner has to actively think through task content. Familiarity, in contrast, involves the extent to which the task draws on ready-made or pre-packaged solutions. It is implicated when all that is required is the accessing of relevant aspects of schematic knowledge if such knowledge contains relevant, already-organised material, and even solutions to comparable tasks, e.g. sensitivity to macrostructures in narratives.

Communicative Stress concerns a group of factors unrelated explicitly to code or meaning, but which do have an impact upon the pressure of communication. *Time Pressure* is perhaps the most straightforward: it concerns how quickly the task has to be done, and whether there is any urgency in the manner in which it is done (Bygate, 1987). Some tasks have a time limit, while others can be done

TABLE 2.1 Task Sequencing Features

Code Complexity
Cognitive Complexity
   Cognitive processing
   Cognitive familiarity
Communicative Stress
   Time pressure
   Modality
   Scale
   Stakes
   Control

at the speed the learners choose. *Modality* simply concerns the speaking/writing and listening/reading contrast. It is assumed that speaking leads to more pressure than writing, and listening more pressure than reading (Ellis, 1987). *Scale* refers to a range of factors associated with task-based approaches to teaching. It includes the number of participants in the task, the number of relationships involved, etc. (Brown, Anderson, Shilcock, & Yule, 1984). *Stakes* depend on how important it is to do the task, and, possibly, to do it correctly. If the process itself is the main thing, and there are no consequences that follow from task completion, then stakes are low. If, on the other hand, it is important not to make mistakes while doing the task, then the stakes are high (Willis, 1993). Finally, *Control* refers to the extent to which the participants within a task can exert an influence on the task and on how it is done. Task goals can be negotiated, or if participants can ask clarification questions to reduce the speed of the input they receive, then one can conclude that control is higher, and task difficulty correspondingly lower (Pica et al., 1993).

The purpose of having a system such as this is that it allows tasks to be analysed, compared, and, best of all, sequenced according to some principled basis. The rewards, if tasks are well-chosen, are:

- *an effective balance between fluency and accuracy*. Prioritising fluency as a goal will emphasise lexicalised language production, strategic language use, and the primacy of meaning. Accuracy as a goal will require analysis, rule-focus, and attention directed to computation. It is difficult to achieve each of these goals simultaneously, but at least tasks of appropriate difficulty will give learners some chance of directing balanced attention to each of these areas (Schmidt, 1990) and operate a dual-mode system (Carr & Curren, 1994).
- *the opportunity for previous restructuring to be applied*. By enabling attentional spare capacity, there will be some chance that previous restructuring can be incorporated into ongoing language use (Swain, in press) and a wider repertoire of language be supported (Crookes, 1989; Foster & Skehan, 1994).

In contrast, bad task choice will probably lead to the opposite outcome. Tasks which are too difficult are likely to over-emphasise fluency, as learners only have the attentional capacity to convey meanings, using production strategies (Faerch & Kaspar, 1983), lexicalised language, and making meaning primary (Bygate, 1988). The result is that accuracy is seen as less important, or at least, less feasible (Ellis, 1987). Similarly, embryonic restructuring, which needs to be integrated carefully into more fluent performance, will not have sufficient attentional capacity to allow it to be exploited (Schachter, 1974). Finally, there is the contrasting danger that if tasks are too easy, they will present no challenge, and are not likely to extend any other goals of restructuring, accuracy, or fluency in any effective way.

Implementing Tasks: Methodology

It is also important to consider how tasks, once chosen, are actually implemented. One can distinguish three major stages in such a methodological implementation. These are shown in Table 2.2. The general purpose of the *pre-emptive*, or pre-task activities is to increase the chance that some restructuring will occur in the underlying language system, and that either new elements will be incorporated, or that some re-arrangement of existing elements will take place (Foster & Skehan, 1994). Within this general purpose, there are two more specific aims. First of all, pre-task activities can aim to teach or mobilise or make salient language which will be relevant to task performance. This can be attempted in a number of different ways. One, the most traditional, would be an approach which simply tries to set up the relevant language for a task, in which case one is essentially dealing with some form of pre-teaching, whether explicit or implicit. More radically, pre-task concern with language may not try to predict what language will be needed, but instead give learners a pre-task to do, and then equip them with the language that they need (Prabhu, 1987; Willis & Willis, 1988). On this view, the task itself would be the primary factor, and task completion would be the aim that would dominate.

The second major type of pre-task activity would be to ease the processing load that learners will encounter when actually doing a task, releasing more attention for the actual language that is used (Van Patten, 1994). The result will be that more complex language can be attempted (Crookes, 1989) and greater accuracy can be achieved as well (Foster & Skehan, forthcoming). A range of activities can be used to reduce cognitive complexity in this way. The cognitive familiarity of the task can be altered by pre-task activation sessions, where learners are induced to recall schematic knowledge that they have that will be relevant to the task they will do. The cognitive processing load during the task to come can also be influenced by a number of procedures. Learners could observe similar tasks being

TABLE 2.2 Methodological Stages in Implementing Tasks

Stage	Goal	Typical Techniques
Pre-Emptive Work	Restructuring – establish target language – reduce cognitive load	Consciousness-Raising Planning
During	Mediate Accuracy and Fluency	Task Choice Pressure Manipulation
Post 1	Discourage Excessive Fluency Encourage Accuracy and Restructuring	Public Performance Analysis Testing
Post 2	Cycle of Synthesis and Analysis	Task Sequences Task Families

completed on video, or they could listen to or read transcripts of comparable tasks (Willis & Willis, 1988). Learners could similarly be given related pre-tasks to do (Prabhu, 1987) so that they have clearly activated schemas when the real task is presented. Finally, and very importantly, learners could be asked to engage in pre-task planning (Crookes, 1989), either of the language that they will need to use, or of the meanings that they want to express (Foster & Skehan, 1994). Then they can devote more attention to how they are going to carry out the task, and can thereby produce more accurate, complex and fluent language (Foster & Skehan, 1994; Foster & Skehan, forthcoming).

The main factor affecting performance *during* the task is the choice of the task itself, with the goal (see Table 2.1) being to target tasks which are of the appropriate difficulty. Tasks, that is, should not be so difficult that excessive mental processing is required simply to communicate any sort of meaning. If they do, it may produce a reliance on ellipsis, context, strategies, and lexicalisation (see above) which reduces the pedagogic value of a task-based approach. Nor should tasks be so easy that learners are bored, and do not engage seriously with the task requirements, with the result that no gain is made in terms of stretching interlanguage or developing greater automaticity (Swain, 1985).

But in addition to task choice, as discussed in the section on syllabus, there are implementation decisions that teachers can make to alter the difficulty of a given task, and manipulate the way in which attention is directed. As regards the *code* itself, teachers can be explicit immediately before the task is done as to whether they want accuracy to be stressed, or whether they want specific structures to be used, (i.e. a pressure to conformity in structure choice [Willis, 1993]). As regards *cognitive complexity*, there are ways of making a task less or more difficult. To achieve the former, visual support could be provided, such as a diagram, which can ease the amount of material that learners need to keep in mind while responding to the task itself. To make tasks more difficult, surprise elements can be introduced which do not match learner expectations of what the task will require, e.g. additional evidence in a "judge" task.

But perhaps the major area for adjustment while tasks are being completed is in the area of stress (or communicative pressure). Pressure manipulation can be based on the communicative stress factors mentioned earlier in the section on sequencing, i.e.

- time
- modality
- scale
- stakes
- control

Since the operation of these factors was described in that earlier section, no additional coverage will be provided here. The point is simply that they are susceptible to variation, with consequent impact on communicative pressure.

Finally, we need to look at post-task activities. The assumption made here is that learners' knowledge of what is to come later can influence how they approach attention-management during an actual task. The central problem is that while a task is being done, the teacher needs to withdraw, be non-interventionist, and allow natural language acquisitional processes to operate (Brumfit, 1984). But then, the danger is that communication goals will be so predominant that lexicalised communication strategies will become so important that the capacity to change and restructure, to take syntactic risks, and to try to be more accurate, will not come into focus as serious goals, and worthy of attention during the intensity of task completion (Skehan, 1992). Post-task activities can change the way in which learners direct their attention during the task (Willis & Willis, 1988; Tarone, 1983). They achieve this by reminding learners that fluency is not the only goal during task completion, and that restructuring and accuracy also have importance.

Drawing on Table 2.2, two phases of post-task activities can be used. In "Post 1", the more immediately linked to the teaching which has just occurred, three general post-task activities can be mentioned: public performance; analysis; and tests. With the first of these, public performance, learners will be asked, after they have completed a task in the privacy of their own group to repeat their performance, publicly, in front of some sort of audience. The audience could be the rest of a learning group, (who themselves may also have been doing the same or a similar task, and who could equally well be asked to engage in the public performance), the teacher, or even a video camera, so that the performance could be played back later, with even the participants themselves required to watch. In this way, the knowledge while the task is being done that a task may have to be re-done publicly will cause learners to allocate attention to the goals of restructuring and accuracy where otherwise they would not. In this way, a concern with syntax can be infiltrated into the task work without the heavy-handedness of teacher intervention and error correction.

There are also other post-task aspects of task-based learning which are important, as shown in "Post 2" from Table 2.2. One must examine task sequences, task progression, and generally how sets of tasks relate to one another, and to the underlying and more important goals which are driving forward instruction. For example, there may be reasons to repeat tasks, with the idea that learners will be more effective with the analysis and synthesis goals that the task was meant to embody. Similarly, there may be parallel tasks. Such tasks are likely to be similar to one another in some important respect, but at the same time contain new elements which are sufficient to engage the interest of the learner (Plough & Gass, 1993). Perhaps most generally of all, it is useful to think in terms of "task families", where a group of tasks resemble one another and may well have similar language or cognitive demands (Candlin, 1987). In this way, learners will be clearer about the goals of such task groups, and there will be less tendency for discrepancies to arise between teachers' and learners' views about task requirements.

These various methods of analysing tasks, in terms of syllabus and methodology, are brought together in Table 2.3. This table shows how the three major stages

TABLE 2.3 Factors Influencing Task Implementation

Stage Goal	Code Complexity	Stress	Cognitive Complexity
Pre-emptive Restructuring • establish target language • reduce cognitive load	Pre-teach Consciousness-raising Practice • conventional • parallel tasks • rehearsal of elements	–	Processing Observe Solve similar tasks Plan • cognitively • linguistically Familiarity Activate
During Mediate accuracy and fluency	Accuracy focus Conformity pressure	TASK CHOICE Time Modality Scale Stakes Control	Support available Surprise elements • additional • conflicting
Post 1 Increases accuracy Encourages restructuring Discourses excessive synthesis	Public performance • teacher • group • camera Degree of analysis Testing		
Post 2 Cycle of synthesis and analysis	The task sequence • repeating • parallel tasks Task families		

of task implementation, together with the associated goals in each case, cross-referenced with syllabus design factors. In this way, it is possible to see how systematic decisions can be made regarding the change which it is intended should occur in learners' interlanguage systems. One aspect of this table which should be noted in passing is that it suggests that the syllabus-methodology distinction is still relevant, even for task-based learning. Nunan (1993) argues that this is not so: because we learn to communicate by communicating, we cannot so easily separate the target from the means of achieving it. The discussion in the last few pages, however, suggests that while we cannot pretend to offer a comprehensive sequence of tasks, there are methods of analysing tasks, both for difficulty and for type, and that as a result, we can try to work with syllabus units in a well-defined and principled way. Similarly, viewing task implementation in terms of the three phases of *pre*, *during*, and *post* clearly indicates where methodological choices are relevant in task-based learning, that these choices take as input the units from a syllabus specification, and that the choices themselves are methodologically motivated. So it is argued that the syllabus-methodology distinction can still be relevant, provided that a framework such as that advocated here is used.

Conclusions

Task-based learning is an area which has grown in importance enormously during the last ten years, and can now be approached from a number of perspectives. The present paper has taken a processing-pedagogic viewpoint and its main ideas are:

- Task-based learning, a current vogue in communicative language teaching, contains dangers if implemented without care. In particular, it is likely to create pressure for immediate communication rather than interlanguage change and growth. In the process, it may encourage learners to use excessively and prematurely lexical modes of communication.
- It is possible to draw on cognitive psychology and second language acquisition research, at least of the sort that emphasises processing factors, to propose a framework which avoids or at least minimises these dangers.

Task-based learning is an attempt to address one of the dilemmas of language teaching: how, on the one hand, to confront the need to engage naturalistic learning processes, while, on the other, to allow the pedagogic process to be managed in a systematic manner. The proposals outlined in this paper contain partial but not complete solutions to this dilemma. The paper accepts that language learning is not any sort of simple, linear, cumulative process. Instead, learners must be able to develop their interlanguage systems in more complex ways, through cycles of analysis and synthesis: revisiting some areas as they are seen to require complexification; learning others in a simple, straightforward manner; developing others by simply relexicalising that which is available syntactically, but which need not be used on such a basis. The proposals presented here attempt to offer such systematisation as is possible within such a complex situation. It attempts, that is, to structure the freedom which learners need to have! It does so, above all, by trying to address the issue of attention, or learners' capacities to focus their attention. In this way, it is hoped that, however inexact our understanding of language learning, the greatest chance is being created for naturalistic mechanisms and processes to come into play.

Clearly this analysis is more programmatic than based on a range of completed studies. The framework which was presented in Table 2.3 is an attempt to synthesise what is known about the influence of task variation on learning and performance. Some parts of this table are supported by empirical work. In other places, this is much less true. The table, that is, attempts to be consistent with the evidence that is available, but goes beyond it to try to establish a more general, and therefore useful, framework. But in other ways, what the table does is to demonstrate how much research is needed to investigate the claims that it makes. If it serves any function in addition to that of utility, it has to be that it provides some sort of organisational framework which can stimulate research, and within which future research can be located.

(Revised version received April 1995)

Acknowledgements

The author would like to thank Antony Bruton, Graham Crookes, Pauline Foster, and three anonymous reviewers, who read earlier versions of this article. Needless to say, any remaining errors or shortcomings are the responsibility of the author.

Notes

1 The author would like to thank Antony Bruton, Graham Crookes, Pauline Foster, and three anonymous reviewers, who read earlier versions of this article. Needless to say, any remaining errors or shortcomings are the responsibility of the author.
2 As an *Applied Linguistics* reviewer pointed out, this represents a narrow interpretation of what a task is. The justification for this, which should become clearer as the argument develops, is that the narrower approach draws upon acquisition research more directly, assuming that interlanguage development is a key goal for pedagogy, particularly in relation to the development of spoken language ability.
3 Although it is recognised that to accept this goal makes a number of assumptions, accepted here for expository purposes, but challengeable on a number of grounds. First of all, there is the issue of what native-like means. There is also the issue that many language learners may have other models of competence that they aspire to, rather than a *particular* native-speaker version. Finally, there are learners who reject a native-speaker model completely or partially, which complicates the picture considerably.
4 Again, for expository purposes, the concentration here is on what Bachman and Palmer (in press) would term Organisational Competence, and does not concern their Pragmatic Competence.

3

MODELLING SECOND LANGUAGE PERFORMANCE

Integrating Complexity, Accuracy, Fluency, and Lexis

Introduction

There are a range of approaches to accounting for performance on language-learning tasks. It is useful therefore to set out the assumptions that underlie the analysis presented in this article. First, it is assumed that attentional capacity and working memory are limited. This is a fairly standard account from contemporary cognitive psychology, with a long tradition of relating working memory operations to attentional availability (Miyake & Shah, 1999; Baddeley, 2007). Secondly, if one relates this general account of attentional limitations to second language performance, some specific consequences follow. Successful performance in task-based contexts has often been characterised as containing:

- more advanced language, leading to *complexity*
- a concern to avoid error, leading to higher *accuracy* if this is achieved
- the capacity to produce speech at normal rate and without interruption, resulting in greater *fluency*

If performance in each of these areas, complexity, accuracy, and fluency (CAF), requires attention and working memory involvement, then committing attentional resources to one may have a negative impact on others. In particular, one can propose that there is a tension between form (complexity and accuracy), on the one hand, and fluency, on the other. Then, within form, one can contrast

Originally published as: Skehan, P. (2009a). Modelling second language performance: Integrating complexity, accuracy, fluency and lexis. *Applied Linguistics*, 30, 510–532. Oxford University Press. Reproduced with permission of Oxford University Press.

attention directed to using challenging language in performance (complexity) relative to conservative, less advanced language, but a greater level of accuracy (Skehan, 1998). One could portray these tensions in the form of a Trade-off Hypothesis, which would predict that committing attention to one area, other things being equal, might predict lower performance in others.

To express the trade-off hypothesis in this way, though, is to propose a default position, which simply argues that there are constraints on performance which have to be accounted for, post hoc, on a case-by-case basis. If the trade-off hypothesis said no more than this, then it would indeed be, as Robinson (2008) claims it is, vacuous. For the hypothesis to have substance, more needs to be said about the precise ways in which the performance areas enter into competition, and what influences there are which mediate this competition. Explicating the nature of the competition for attentional resources, and how it can be overcome will be one of the central aims of the present article. As we will see, one can address this issue at a theoretical level, and also by examining available empirical findings. A brief account of previous research helps set the scene for the contributions of the present article. The focus is on the independent variables in task-based performance which have systematic influences on CAF.

Earlier research within a complexity-accuracy-fluency framework supported generalisations such as the following:

- accuracy and fluency, but not complexity, tend to be raised in personal information exchange tasks;
- there is higher complexity, but lower accuracy and fluency, on narrative tasks; and
- pre-task planning produces greater complexity and fluency.

These findings are broadly consistent with a trade-off interpretation, since they suggest higher-level performance in two out of three areas, but not typically in all three.

This earlier research, operating with an underspecified characterisation of task types, gave way to finer-grained approaches, showing systematic influences of task characteristics and task conditions. The newer research studies (e.g. reviewed in Skehan [2001]) offered generalisations such as:

- tasks based on concrete or familiar information advantage accuracy and fluency;
- tasks containing clear structure advantage accuracy and fluency;
- interactive tasks advantage accuracy and complexity;
- tasks requiring information manipulation lead to higher complexity; and
- strategic (pre-task) planning advantages complexity and fluency, and occasionally accuracy; and

- post-task conditions such as public performance or transcription of one's own performance raise accuracy.

This research is supportive of a trade-off hypothesis to the extent that it indicates that simultaneously advantaging all three (CAF) performance areas is unusual. It is also clarifying, in that most 'two influence' results do indeed suggest that fluency can be accompanied by either accuracy or complexity, but not both. The research, though, is limited in that while it offers generalisations, and indications consistent with attentional limitations, the explanatory force of these accounts is lacking.

It is the purpose of this article to address these issues, and to offer a theoretically motivated and empirically grounded account of complexity, accuracy, and fluency in second language performance. The article is organised in four main sections, two somewhat preliminary and empirical, and two more theoretical. First, new measures of task-based performance will be discussed. It is proposed that it is essential to be more sophisticated in the measurement of fluency, and vital to incorporate some measure of lexis into task performance. Progress in each of these areas is important to understand the psycholinguistics of second language speech production and the interrelationship between the performance areas. Secondly, there are emerging generalisations which go beyond those given above. We now have additional interesting claims that can be made about the effects of task characteristics especially. In particular, there are findings of accuracy–complexity relationships, results which might pose some problems for any trade-off-based account (Skehan, 1998), and, contrastingly, provide support for the Cognition Hypothesis (Robinson, 2001b).

This more empirical and descriptive coverage leads to the third section, more theoretical in nature, and which explores the plausibility of trade-off and cognition accounts of these generalisations. It will be argued that it is task characteristics and task conditions, in particular combinations, which predict accuracy–complexity correlations when they occur, and that it is not task complexity, *per se*, as Robinson argues, that accounts for this relationship. Fourthly, as a broad explanatory framework, Levelt's model of speaking is used to organise the research findings, and to locate the different effects within the Conceptualiser and Formulator stages of the model.

New Measures of Task Performance

Researching task performance, and measuring complexity, accuracy, and fluency is a relatively recent aspect of applied linguistics, arguably starting with Crookes (1989), but there is clear scope to develop additional measures. Here the focus will be on two measures of *general* performance, specifically of fluency and lexis.

Regarding fluency, a range of measures are available, broadly examining:

- breakdown (dys)fluency, indexed by pausing;
- repair (dys)fluency, indexed by measures such as reformulation, repetition, false starts, and replacements, as well as measures of filled pauses and pseudo-filled pauses; and
- speed, with measures such as syllables per minute.

One can also use higher-order measures such as length-of-run, as an indicator of automatisation in language performance (Towell, Hawkins, & Bazergui, 1996; Towell, 2002; Towell & Dewaele, 2005).

An interesting feature of the measurement of fluency is to compare second language speakers to first language speakers, who, of course, also pause (see Skehan and Foster [2008] and Skehan [in press], for more extensive discussion of this issue). It has been argued (Davies, 2003) that what distinguishes native and non-native pausing is more likely to be *where* pauses occur rather than that they occur. Davies (2003) suggests that it is fruitful to distinguish between pauses that occur mid-clause and those that occur at the ends of clauses, especially at Analysis of Speech (AS) boundary points (Foster, Tonkyn, & Wigglesworth, 2000). From a database of first (Foster, 2001a) and second (Foster & Skehan, 1996a) language learners doing identical tasks, this issue was investigated to explore how the two groups contrast. The relevant data are shown in Table 3.1.

The personal task here (and all tasks involved pairs of students) was to explain to one's partner how to get to one's home to turn off an oven that had been left on. The narrative task was to make up a story which linked a series of pictures which had no obvious storyline, but which did have common characters. The decision-making task was to agree (as if a judge) the appropriate sentence for a series of crimes (where the crimes generally had extenuating circumstances).

TABLE 3.1 Comparison of Native and Non-Native Speaker Pausing on Three Tasks

	Personal Task		*Decision-Making Task*		*Decision-Making Task*	
	− Plan	+ Plan	− Plan	+ Plan	− Plan	+ Plan
Native speakers						
AS pauses	2.8	1.4	4.2	2.1	3.6	0.8
Mid-cl. Pauses	1.1	1.3	*1.3*	2.6	1.6	0.4
Ratio: AS-to-Mid	(2.5)	(1.1)	(3.2)	(0.8)	(2.3)	(2.0)
Non-native speakers						
AS pauses	1.6	1.5	*3.9*	1.4	*3.7*	1.6
Mid-cl. Pauses	2.6	2.1	3.8	4.8	4.8	2.7
Ratio: AS-to-Mid	(0.6)	(0.7)	(1.0)	(0.3)	(0.8)	(0.6)

Significances are shown through italicisation.

Those without planning opportunities had to complete the task once they had understood instructions, while those with planning opportunities were given 10 minutes to prepare, during which time they could take notes, but these notes were taken away before the actual performance.

Pre-task planning is similar in its effects with native and non-native speakers for AS-clause (Analysis of Speech) boundaries—planners generally pause less (with univariate tests used, following MANOVAs). Interestingly, native speakers, in two out of three cases, pause *more* than non-natives at this point under the non-planning condition. Native speakers, in other words, seem to regard AS-boundaries as a natural place for on-line planning. The figures for mid-clause pausing, though, are very different. Here the native speakers pause very clearly less mid-clause, in fact, hardly at all, whereas for non-native speakers, this is the more frequent pause location. The difference between the two groups is shown even more clearly if one computes the AS-to-mid-clause ratio, shown in parentheses in Table 3.1. Five of the six native speaker ratios are above unity (with one marginally below), where five of the six non-native speaker ratios are below. If native speakers are taken to indicate a baseline level of performance, the natural place to pause is an AS-boundary, and that sufficient on-line regrouping can be achieved with such pausing (one also assumes that pauses located at this point are advantageous for interlocutors). The non-native speakers, in contrast, seem to have pauses thrust upon them, in the middle of what become turns lacking in smoothness, probably as they are required to handle unforeseen lexical choices. These findings suggest that, to make sense of CAF, the characterisation of fluency needs to become subtler and deeper.

The last few paragraphs have proposed measurement improvements for an established performance area. But there is another area, lexis, which has been strikingly absent in task research. This is a serious omission. The lexis-syntax connection is vital in performance models (Skehan, 2009b) such as Levelt's, and lexis represents a form of complexity that has to be assessed in second language speech performance if any sort of complete picture is to be achieved.

Generally, research into lexical measures (Daller, Van Hout, & Treffers-Daller, 2003) distinguishes between text-internal measures (so called because the text itself is sufficient for their calculation) and text-external measures (which require some sort of general reference material, usually based on word frequency). The former is typically measured through some sort of type-token ratio (TTR), but with the qualification that since TTRs are strongly related to text length, there has to be a correction made. A generally acceptable measure is D, as calculated by the VOCD subprogram within Computerised Language Analysis (CLAN) (MacWhinney, 2000), as an index of lexical variety (Malvern & Richards, 2002; Richards & Malvern, 2007).

In contrast are measures of what is called lexical sophistication (Read, 2000). These take frequency lists from corpus analysis and then compute how many words defined as difficult (on the basis of lower frequencies) are used in a text.

40 Theory

The most well-known measure of this sort is Laufer and Nation's Lexical Frequency Profile (1999). At the time the research reported on here was being done, the Laufer and Nation approach lacked spoken language corpus-based frequency lists. Accordingly, another approach was used, following Meara (Meara & Bell, 2001; Bell, 2003). This uses a Poisson distribution (a distribution appropriate for events which have low frequency levels). A text, for example the transcribed performance of someone doing a task, is divided into ten-word chunks, and then, for each ten-word chunk, the number of 'difficult' words is calculated. (Difficult is usually defined in terms of a threshold frequency; in the present case, this was 150 occurrences or fewer per million words.)[1] The number of ten-word chunks which contain no difficult words, or one difficult word, or two difficult words, and so on, is calculated. Then a statistic, lambda, is calculated, which represents the best fit of the distribution of numbers of difficult words. In other words, it is assumed that the higher the level of lambda, the greater the ability of the speaker to mobilise a wider vocabulary, drawing on less frequent words (see Skehan, 2009b for further details). In pilot studies with this measure, it was established that D, the measure of lexical variety, and lambda, as a measure of lexical sophistication, did not correlate (Skehan, 2009a). In addition, the value of D was not particularly revealing regarding task effects. Accordingly, we focus here on the findings related to lambda. The relevant values are shown in Table 3.2.

Planning opportunities make a big difference to the speaker's capacity to mobilise less frequent words. With the exceptions of the non-native speaker narrative and the native speaker personal task comparisons, the lambda scores in each case are significantly higher for planners than non-planners (and are in the predicted direction for the non-significant results). All four significant results generate effect sizes which are large (judged through Cohen's d). Planning time enables speakers, whether native or non-native, to make different lexical selections (the TTR, D, did not generate similar significant differences for planning). In addition, there are major task differences, with the narrative task generating the highest values

TABLE 3.2 Lexical Sophistication (Lambda) and Task Type for Native and Non-Native Speakers

	Personal Task		Narrative Task		Decision-Making Task	
	− Plan	+ Plan	− Plan	+ Plan	− Plan	+ Plan
Native speakers	1.27 (0.27) ($N = 13$)	1.47 (0.27) ($N = 14$)	1.46 (0.41) ($N = 16$)	1.95 (0.52) ($N = 13$)	0.76 (0.13) ($N = 14$)	0.94 (0.25) ($N = 18$)
Non-native speakers	0.94 (0.28) ($N = 16$)	1.15 (0.23) ($N = 11$)	1.00 (0.25) ($N = 12$)	1.18 (0.36) ($N = 11$)	0.54 (0.25) ($N = 14$)	0.79 (0.24) ($N = 15$)

Standard deviations are given in the first line of parentheses in each cell, cell sizes in the second.

for lambda (and the largest effects for planning), and the decision-making tasks generating the lowest.

This pattern is repeated with different narrative and decision-making tasks, as reported in Skehan and Foster (2008). It is interesting that the narrative task is the most input-driven, and the least negotiable. It seems to require the use of difficult-to-avoid lexical items. The decision-making task, in contrast, is the most negotiable, and also interactive. Speakers do not pack their contributions here with as many less frequent words.

One final aspect of these performances is interesting. With the native speakers, there is a positive correlation between lambda and structural complexity, indexed by subordination. The correlations are 0.43 with the personal task ($p < 0.05$), 0.57 for the narrative ($p < 0.001$) and 0.21 for the decision-making (not significant). With the non-native speakers, this correlation is negative (as, for them, is the correlation between lambda and accuracy). The contrast is intriguing. For native speakers, making more demanding and less obvious lexical choices does not cause problems. Consistent with the Levelt model, it even seems to drive syntax to some degree, as these lexical choices are more likely to require more complex syntactic clothing. But for non-native speakers, it seems more likely that making more complex lexical choices derails syntax in two ways—making it less complex and also less accurate—as problems occur through the additional difficulties that arise from lexical retrieval. The attention consumed here poses problems for the way more complex syntax is used, and also for avoidance of error. All these measures relate to Levelt's Formulator stage, implicating lemma retrieval and the assembly of the current utterance. They also enable us to explore the role of lexis as a driving force for syntax, as we will see below.

Wider Analyses of Task Influences

It is also possible to propose additional generalisations to those offered earlier. Three will be covered here. The generalisations are interesting in their own right, but they also illustrate the usefulness and relevance of the Levelt model. They also bear upon rival claims of the Trade-off and Cognition Hypotheses.

The first generalisation concerns information manipulation and organisation. In earlier research, it was argued that the need to manipulate and reorganise information leads to a pressure to produce more complex language. For example, Foster and Skehan (1996a) used a narrative task in which learners were required to devise a story to link a series of pictures which contain common characters but no obvious storyline. This task contrasts with most narratives (Ortega, 1999) which simply provide a series of pictures (often in cartoon format) or a video (Skehan & Foster, 1999) and simply require retelling. The task requiring the development of a storyline (Skehan & Foster, 1997) requires the speaker to create the storyline itself which links the pictures, and so necessarily requires manipulation and arrangement. The task in question generated higher complexity scores than other, 'pre-organised' narratives. This result raised the possibility that other forms of information manipulation might also lead to higher complexity scores. One such could be the need, within a narrative task, to integrate foreground and background information if the story is to be told effectively. Consequently, Tavakoli and Skehan (2005), using a conventional narrative telling based on a series of organised pictures, also included a picture series which required such integration. This picture series generated significantly higher complexity scores. This finding has been replicated by Foster and Tavakoli (2009) who show that the need to make connections between picture elements is a dependable way of increasing language complexity. Information manipulation and integration seems to require more extensive Conceptualiser use, which is reflected in a more complex pre-verbal message, and this, in turn, leads to the need to formulate more complex language. Task design, in other words, can influence the level of language complexity appropriate for a particular task.[2]

Next, we consider a generalisation based on the impact of lexis on other performance areas. It concerns the way that other dimensions of performance are affected when a task makes it difficult to avoid using less frequent lexical elements. Relevant data from a series of studies is shown in Table 3.3. The table covers three studies and reports results for narrative and decision-making tasks, in two cases, and a narrative only in one. Skehan and Foster (1999) used a video-based narrative, but the other two studies used picture series for the narratives. The decision-making tasks were a Judge task (agree on the appropriate sentences for a series of crimes), in Foster and Skehan (1996a), while Foster and Skehan (forthcoming) used an Agony Aunt task (agree on the advice to give to the writer of a letter to an Agony Aunt).

A narrative is necessarily input-driven, and unforgiving in what needs to be covered. More interactive, decision-making tasks allow greater latitude. Unavoidability, or at least, infrequency of lexis is taken to be reflected here in the lambda figures. These show a clear difference between narrative tasks on the one hand, and decision-making tasks, on the other. Narratives seem to push second language speakers (and first language speakers, Skehan, 2009b) into using less frequent lexis,

TABLE 3.3 Unavoidable Lexis and Task-Based Performance

Study	Narrative			Decision-Making		
	Lambda	Mid-clause-pauses	EFC	Lambda	Mid-clause-pauses	EFC
Foster & Skehan, 1996a	1.14	4.52	0.56	0.65	3.82	0.60
Skehan & Foster, 1999	1.66	7.32	0.45	–	–	–
Foster and Skehan (forthcoming)	1.45	4.23	0.54	0.48	3.49	0.68

EFC = Error-Free Clauses

presumably as they are responding to the events within the narrative. Decision-making tasks, in contrast, although purposeful, for example agreeing on advice to Agony Aunt letters, enable different methods of expression as speakers take different routes to expressing their positions. The differences in lambda scores are dramatic and give clear indications of the consequences of task requirements.

More interesting is the potential impact of the need to mobilise less frequent lexis on other aspects of performance. We will examine the findings first, and then relate them to psycholinguistic functioning. Using the data from Skehan and Foster (1997) the lambda scores correlated with accuracy at −0.48 (personal task), −0.23 (narrative), and −0.23 (decision-making). Although the second and third correlations are not significant, the results taken together suggest that there is a weak negative relationship. Regarding lambda and fluency (mid-clause pausing), the correlations are 0.57 (personal), 0.36 (narrative), and 0.20 (decision-making). The first two correlations are significant, and suggest that the higher the lambda scores, the more mid-clause pausing there is. In other words, the need to retrieve rarer lexical items seems to have a cost in terms of how error can be avoided and a smooth flow of speech maintained—such retrieval creates processing demands and consumes attentional resources. Achieving accuracy is thereby compromised, an interesting finding in that one would imagine that more complex tasks (cf. Robinson et al., 2009) would be associated, other things being equal, with the use of more sophisticated lexis (Read, 2000). Interestingly, the highest value of lambda, 1.66, (and the lowest accuracy value, 0.45) is with the video-based narrative (Skehan & Foster, 1999). Hence, there may be important differences within narratives also which are dependent on performance conditions.

These results, too, fit within the Levelt model. In the Levelt model, the Conceptualiser delivers the pre-verbal message to the Formulator, which then has to undertake the process of lemma retrieval that can subsequently drive syntactic encoding (since the syntactic information is stored in the lemma). With native speakers, this lemma retrieval proceeds smoothly, enabling parallel processing (as the Formulator deals with previous Conceptualiser cycles, while the Conceptualiser simultaneously attends to the current cycle). Native-speaker mental lexicons are extensive, and well-organised. Accordingly, the demands the pre-verbal message makes are met without undue difficulty. In contrast, the pre-verbal message developed by the non-native speaker arrives at a Formulator equipped with access to a smaller mental lexicon and with significantly less organisation and elaboration. The result is that the pre-conditions for smooth parallel processing are not met, and the Formulator stage is more effortful, often requiring repair and replacement. Pre-verbal messages which require more difficult lexical items make greater demands on this mental lexicon and the operation of the Formulator as an automatic process is particularly disrupted. If we assume that accuracy is the consequence of attention being available for Formulator operations, then needing to access more difficult lexical items will be particularly hard to handle.

The third area for cross-study generalisation concerns task organisation. Organisation will be defined here in relation to macrostructure of component elements, often involving schematic knowledge, or simply knowledge of text structure. This can be operationalised in a number of different, but related ways. This could simply be a story with a clear beginning, middle, and end. It could also be a schematic structure, or well-known 'script', such as visiting the doctor. Or it could be a discourse structure, such as Labov's analysis of narratives. All of these have in common that the details of what is being done at any one moment fit in easily to the wider macrostructure, so that less processing is required during speaking. Early examples of research studies exploring this are Foster and Skehan (1996a), with the need to instruct someone on a familiar journey one makes, as well as Skehan and Foster (1997) with cartoon picture series with a clear beginning, middle, and end. Subsequently, Skehan and Foster (1999) compared video-based retellings (of Mr. Bean stories) contrasting a structured narrative (following the well-known restaurant script) with a less-structured story (a chaotic round of Crazy Golf).

More recently, Tavakoli and Skehan (2005) attempted to operationalise structure more predictively. Picture series were analysed into four levels of structure, operationalised in terms of the number of individual pictures (other than first and last) which could be exchanged without impairing the storyline. The more structured picture series followed a problem–solution pattern (Hoey, 1983). The levels did not generate an ordered four-step scale, but there was still a clear distinction between unstructured and structured performances. Tavakoli and Foster (2008) used a similar research design and reported the same structured–unstructured contrast. Both studies deliver the same general performance. The degree of structure in a task does not tend to influence subordination-based measures of complexity (with an exception to be covered below), but it does consistently have a positive impact on fluency and accuracy. It appears that the support of having a wider macrostructure enables the speaker to operate within helpfully limiting parameters. Conceptualiser-outcome, that is the pre-verbal message, is the basis for communication, but the ideas that need to be expressed fit into the wider structure fairly clearly, and so do not take much attentional capacity. The consequence is that more attention is available for ongoing performance, and so the performance dimensions which are more affected by this immediate, Formulator-linked attention, benefit. These, it seems, are more likely to be fluency and accuracy. We can recap these three generalisations as follows:

- Need to organise and integrate more demanding information
- Need to retrieve and make available more difficult lexis
- Capacity to draw on clear macrostructure

– Pressure on Conceptualiser and push for greater language complexity
– Pressure from pre-verbal message, difficulties for lemma retrieval, and pressure on Formulator
– Easing of Conceptualiser and release of attention for Formulator operations

In the introductory section, generalisations from earlier task research were presented, and these were portrayed as (a) consistent with a limited capacity view of attention, and (b) suggesting a default contrast between certain performance areas. These generalisations lack theory and predictive power. The last two sections, though, on new measures and new generalisations, have shown the centrality of lexis, the need for subtler measures of fluency, and have started to make contact with the Levelt model of speaking. The Conceptualiser stage seems to be influenced by the ideas that need to be expressed. Any influences which push for the need to formulate more complex ideas raise the importance of this stage, and lead to increases in the structural complexity of the language which is used. The integration of foreground and background information exemplified this. Lexical Formulator influences will impact upon the way the pre-verbal message interfaces with mental lexicon access and lemma retrieval. In this case, involvement of a mental lexicon that can handle the demands of the pre-verbal message will be associated with the capacity to produce fluent and accurate language through parallel processing. More demanding lexical pressures with second language speakers will disrupt this process and impair harmonious real-time parallel speech production, with delays, a need for repair, and heavy attentional demands. The difficulties of narrative tasks, and the lexical demands they make, illustrate this. Both these processes involve pressures on the resources a speaker has available for second language performance. But the third area, structure, reflects a more supportive influence. Here greater structuring in a task can ease attentional demands, and enable the speaker to channel attention to immediate performance. The result is that more attention is available for ongoing Formulation, and consequently the areas the Formulator is responsible for, accuracy and fluency, are more effectively handled. So we see that within the constraints of limited attentional capacities, difficulties manifest themselves in a non-random manner—the stages of speech production give us some insight into which CAF areas are affected by which influences.

Complexity–Accuracy Relationships: Trade-Off and Cognition

The generalisations from previous sections provide new ways of explicating trade-off effects while linking performance to a model of speech production. But the sharpest challenge for a trade-off account, and where it differs most clearly from the Cognition Hypothesis, is where and why it predicts a correlation between accuracy and complexity in performance. In addition to this Trade-off vs. Cognition Hypotheses contrast, this specific relationship is revealing with respect to CAF relationships more generally; how these dimensions can be accounted for theoretically; and what sorts of influences can be manipulated to raise or lower performance in each of the two areas.

We have seen that a trade-off interpretation proposes that the 'natural' tension when resources are limited is between accuracy and complexity. This contrasts with the Cognition Hypothesis, which proposes that task complexity will be associated with increases in complexity and accuracy. A key issue, therefore, is what the evidence is regarding situations where complexity and accuracy are simultaneously advantaged. As it happens, researchers within the Cognition Hypothesis framework have very rarely provided evidence of this sort, with many studies reporting raised accuracy, but no increase in complexity (Gilabert, 2007a; Kuiken & Vedder, 2007, 2008b; Michel et al., 2007a). There is even the possibility that the accuracy effects themselves are due to lexical, rather than syntactic—morphological differences (Kuiken & Vedder, 2008a), and they seem to have greater importance in narrative, but not interactive tasks (Michel et al., 2007b). Ishikawa (2007) does report significant effects for specific accuracy measures (although general accuracy measures do not reach significance), and for complexity. This, then, is an important study but it involves written, not oral performance, and is effectively also a study of planning, since 5 minutes preparation time was given, that is we do not know if these results would apply to a non-planning condition. Gilabert (2007b), too, presents data supportive of the Cognition Hypothesis. Three tasks were used, and although no complexity scores are given, he does report greater accuracy for narrative and instruction-giving tasks, where, interestingly, task complexity was operationalised in different ways. The lack of complexity scores, though, means that this study can only provide limited evidence in favour of the Cognition Hypothesis.

In this section, we will discuss three studies which do actually report joint accuracy–complexity effects. The first of these studies investigated different types of planning (Foster & Skehan, 1999). The planning was either solitary (as in most previous studies), or group-based, teacher-led (and focussed on either content or language). General planning effects were found comparable with other studies (and see Ellis this issue). But the teacher-led planning was particularly interesting, because in this condition both complexity and accuracy were raised, unlike the other planning conditions. This result suggests that planning has more than one function (Ortega, 2005). Ellis (2005b), for example, discusses distinctions between planning-as-rehearsal and planning as-complexification (as well as on-line planning). What seems to be happening is that teacher-led planning was able to combine these different aspects of planning, and so both complexification and rehearsal were handled more effectively. The result was that planning-as-complexification led to greater levels of language complexity, while planning-as-rehearsal was associated with increases in accuracy. The two, frequently competing, areas can go together therefore, but they are mediated by planning opportunities of a particular kind, in this case orchestrated by the teacher, with the result that attentional limitations during the subsequent task performance are eased. Carefully organised planning was used, in other words, to overcome normal performance constraints.

Another study which reports a joint accuracy–complexity effect is Tavakoli and Skehan (2005). Several variables were manipulated in this study, but the focus here is the effect of task structure, in the context of a narrative retelling. Task structure yielded results following predictions, which is greater fluency and accuracy. But the joint raising of accuracy and complexity in one of the tasks (structured, and with a need to integrate foreground and background information) was particularly interesting. A tentative post hoc interpretation was that there was a need to incorporate not simply the 'driving' storyline embodied in foreground information, but also to bring into play background information from earlier pictures in order to make sense of the events in later pictures in the story. This might account for the way both accuracy and complexity were raised. Tavakoli and Foster (2008) and Foster and Tavakoli (2009) built on this post hoc interpretation to design studies specifically aimed at manipulating these two variables. They confirmed the findings: both accuracy and complexity were raised when there was a structured task which also required the integration of foreground and background information.

Hence, two performance areas can be jointly affected, but their raised levels are the result of separate influences. Structure tends to lead to a greater accuracy. Information manipulation leads to greater subordination-based measures of syntactic complexity. Each influence is a task design feature, but they seem to be able to operate additively. When this happens with a picture series that is both structured and requires information integration, complexity and accuracy are both raised. This set of studies suggests that under supportive conditions the constraints of limited attentional capacity can be overcome to some extent. The key issue regarding the Cognition Hypothesis, though, is that a task which is simultaneously structured and information integrating cannot be regarded as a more complex task (as the Cognition Hypothesis requires). In other words, it is not task complexity per se which drives the joint increases in these performance areas: it is the separate but additive impact that each of the influencing variables has.

The final study concerns the effects of a post-task condition. Skehan and Foster (1997) explored whether learners' knowledge while doing a task that they might be required to re-do the task publicly later would lead them to prioritise accuracy. The results provided limited support for this hypothesis. In a subsequent study (Foster and Skehan, 2013), they used a different post-task operationalisation, the need to transcribe 1 minute of one's own performance. This was a more personally applicable and more language-related implementation of a post-task activity. In addition, accuracy was measured slightly differently focussing on the length of clause that could be accurately handled rather than the proportion of error-free clauses (see Skehan & Foster, 2005 for discussion). In this subsequent study, a significant accuracy effect was found for both decision-making and narrative tasks. This suggests that learners can prioritise attention to particular areas. The post-task condition induced changes in attention management on the part of second language speakers.

But the second of these post-task studies (Foster and Skehan, 2013) proved even more interesting. For the decision-making task, not only did the post-task condition produce significantly higher accuracy, it also produced significantly higher language complexity. This was unpredicted, but very interesting. At first sight, this finding is supportive of one of the central predictions of the Cognition Hypothesis—a simultaneous effect on accuracy and complexity. It should be recalled, though, that the Cognition Hypothesis proposes both that (a) raised accuracy and complexity are brought about by greater task complexity, and that (b) this joint increase in performance is not constrained by attentional limitations. As a first point, we have to consider whether doing a task with a post-task activity such as transcription can be regarded as making the task more complex. This is difficult to see. It is the same task that is being done, after all, and the change in task performance seems to be the result of an interpretation by the task participants of what they should do.[3] The participants seem to be the ones, in other words, who shift their goals and prioritise certain performance areas. It also seems to be the case that they need to prioritise attention in this way—the baseline performance from control groups suggests that this is not a natural thing to do with such task. This is, in other words, a manipulated effect.

This result poses problems for both the Cognition Hypothesis and the Trade-off Hypothesis, and what we need to do is explore how serious these problems are. For the Cognition Hypothesis we have already explored the dissociation between task complexity, on the one hand, and accuracy–complexity relationships, on the other. The results therefore appear to support one aspect of the Cognition Hypothesis but without involving its central tenet—that it is task complexity which simultaneously drives structural complexity and accuracy. Turning to a trade-off account, the results suggest that the (empirically founded) generalisation that accuracy and complexity rarely go together, and that this reflects the consequence of limited attention, may not always apply. But there is a complicating issue to be addressed in this regard. Research so far which bears upon the Cognition Hypothesis has sought to explore whether significant effects can be found simultaneously for accuracy and complexity. If such effects are found then support is inferred for the Cognition Hypothesis.

But one could apply a stronger test here than simply the demonstration of joint experimental effects. This is because one cannot assume from such effects that group effects are mirrored at the individual level. It is also possible that one can obtain significant effects for both performance areas where each effect is accounted for by different participants. In other words, to support the Cognition Hypothesis, not only does one need to establish experimental effects—one also needs to demonstrate that there is a correlation between performances in the two areas. If we examine correlations between accuracy and complexity in Foster and Skehan (2013), the results are that complexity and accuracy correlate at 0.26 for the decision-making task (not significant, but one has to take account of the small sample size of only 16), and negatively, at −0.13 for the narrative task. The post-task condition did seem to work in orienting participants towards form, but different participants seemed to gravitate to different aspects of form. Some emphasised structural complexity and some emphasised accuracy, but in general there was no suggestion that both areas were advantaged together. This sits comfortably with a trade-off account because it appears that at the individual level, prioritising accuracy or complexity is the norm.

Applying the Levelt Model to Second Language Task Performance

The findings which have accumulated over the last 20 years or so about second language task performance are extensive and provide a foundation for theorising about the influences on such performance especially through connections with the Levelt (1989, 1999) model of first language speaking. It is important, though, to try to systematise the discussion of this potentially relevant model, and to try to identify patterns in the influences on second language performance. In that respect a first approach is represented in Table 3.4, which organises a range of task-based findings in terms of the model.

In the centre of the table, the influences are organised following three major stages from the model: Conceptualisation, Formulation: Lemma Retrieval, and Formulation: Syntactic Encoding (all shown in bold). These three stages provide a good structure for locating the range of influences that are available and which have been described in previous sections. Next, though, we need to distinguish the influences shown on the left-hand side from those on the right-hand side. On the left are influences which do one of the two things (but both of which add to the difficulty of a task). First, some influences may complexify the performance that results. All the influences shown at the Conceptualiser stage fall into this category. They lead to the speaker developing a message which is more demanding of cognitive resources, and which requires more active working memory use during speech production. But second, we have the influences which are relevant at the Formulator stage. These generally have the effect of pressuring performance. At the lemma access stage, it is proposed that two related influences are important: the need to use less frequent lexis and the non-negotiability of the task. Each of these creates pressure because the learner is forced to do something difficult during on-line speech production and wrestle with the problems that come from more effortful and slower access to the information stored in lemmas. In other words, both influences are concerned with the way that an easy route cannot be taken because task demands do not allow flexibility. As indicated earlier, the Levelt model, applied to the first language case, presumes a well-organised and elaborated lexicon. When second language speakers need to access more difficult lemmas, or when they cannot be flexible to ease their processing problems, ongoing Formulation is disrupted, and it becomes very difficult to sustain parallel processing (Kormos, 2006; Skehan, 2009b).

TABLE 3.4 The Levelt Model Linked to Influences on Second Language Performance

Complexifying/Pressuring		Easing/Focussing
	Conceptualiser	
• Planning: extending		• Concrete, static information
• More complex cognitive operations		• Less information
• Abstract, dynamic information		• Less complex cognitive operations
• Greater quantity of information		
	Formulator: Lemma Retrieval	
• Need for less frequent lexis		• Planning: organising ideas
• Non-negotiability of task		• Dialogic
	Formulator: Syntactic Encoding	
• Time pressure		• Planning: rehearsing
• Heavy input presence		• Structured tasks
• Monologic		• Dialogic
		• Post-task condition

A different set of pressuring influences are associated with the syntactic stage of Formulation (although in fact they would also have an impact on lemma retrieval, or at least, the time available for lemma retrieval and information extraction from the lemma). They concern the on-line pressures that the speaker has to deal with, and include particularly the time pressure under which speaking has to take place, as well as the amount of input that is received by the speaker preparatory to (or even during) speaking. The former, which connects with Ellis's (2005b) concept of on-line planning, is an index of the amount of time the speaker has to access material, to build syntactic frames, and to regroup as necessary. Influencing this amount of time is the need to deal with input, if relevant. Monologic tasks do not present any different or additional difficulties—they simply represent the task type which combines the different pressuring conditions, since they are likely to contain significant quantities of input, especially if a narrative is involved, and especially a video-based narrative retelling, and they are also likely to have to be done under pressuring conditions, since there may simply be a time limit or a quantity of language which has to be achieved, or there may be the need to keep up with a video. It is interesting, in passing, that this analysis of pressuring conditions would be associated with Robinson's (2001a) 'here-and-now' condition, which he claims to be the less complex. It may be that while there is a difference between 'there-and-then' and 'here-and-now' regarding complexity, since the 'there-and-then' condition does require memory, in contrast, it is less input-dominated and more negotiable as a result. In other words, there is something of a genre difference between the two conditions which significantly complicates their comparison.

Conceptualiser operations may be more difficult with the 'there-and-then' condition, but Formulator conditions may be eased.

We turn next to the right-hand side of Table 3.4. Here we have influences which either ease the task or alternatively focus attention in a particular area. Regarding Conceptualisation, the issues mainly affect the information contained in the task, particularly the quantity and the nature of the information. Concrete, static information is seen as being easier to deal with, and retrieval less demanding than manipulation and transformation. So tasks using such information types, and requiring such information manipulation processes are seen as less demanding for Conceptualiser operations. Essentially these are the reverse of some of the features shown on the left-hand side which complexify Conceptualiser operations.

There are also beneficial, easing influences on Formulator stages, although since many of these function by making more attention available, it is more difficult to separate the lemma retrieval and syntactic building stages. We saw earlier that planning can function to complexify ideas. It can also work, rather differently, to organise ideas. In this case, pre-task work can help to identify ideas and their interrelationships and thereby prime lexical elements so that they can be retrieved more effectively when the Formulator stage arrives. The pre-verbal message, in other words, has made certain lemmas more salient, and then their access is smoothed. We have also seen that dialogic tasks have a beneficial influence on performance. Here it is assumed that interaction confers two benefits on lemma retrieval. First, more globally, the fact that interaction is occurring means that while one's interlocutor has the floor, one has more time to regroup, to replan, and to prepare the ground for the message one will utter very soon. In other words, the process of lemma retrieval is given more time to work. But secondly, there is the issue that one's interlocutor can provide useful scaffolding and priming opportunities so that one's own task can be eased because one's interlocutor has done some of the hard work (Skehan, 2009b).

There are comparable favourable influences on the syntactic stage of the Formulator. First, again, we have planning, where on this occasion pre-task planning time is directed at syntactic operations. Learners may prepare syntactic frames, sentence fragments, or even complete sentences, that is, they may rehearse (Ortega, 2005). These may or may not be retrieved at relevant points during performance, but they are generally helpful preparation for what happens during speech and help the speaker avoid error. There is also the benefit for syntactic encoding of having more time available, and here the evidence on structured tasks is relevant. If speakers do not have to plan so actively for the wider macrostructure content of what they are saying, they can focus more on the detail and have attention available for syntax building (Bygate, 2001).

There is another possible influence with interactive tasks. It may be that the presence of an interlocutor makes more salient the need to be precise and to avoid error. In other words, the immediate presence and reality of the person who is being spoken to, coupled with tasks which require precise information, may lead to error avoidance.[4] This is similar to the effect of a post-task activity, but for completely different reasons. In this second case, it is awareness of one's own performance, and its greater salience in terms of formal structure, which leads to an attentional prioritising that pays more attention to error. But with both of these influences, we have a Formulator (and possibly monitoring) activity that is concerned with the surface of the language which is produced, and which leads the speaker to try to avoid making syntactic mistakes.

The discussion has been around complexification, pressuring, easing, and focussing as influences on the different stages of the Levelt model. These four categories of influence have been instantiated through existing task research findings. But it is also important that the Levelt model connects with the performance areas that are the focus of this special issue. The proposals made here are that complexification links mainly to the Conceptualisation stage and then structural and lexical complexity. Pressuring, easing, and focussing are more relevant for the Formulator, and then, accuracy and fluency. It is to be hoped that future research can extend the categories of influence by identifying additional salient variables that extend this picture, and fine-tune the functioning of the influences covered here.

Conclusions

There are three broad conclusions to draw from the material presented in this article—that complexity, accuracy, and fluency are important dimensions of second language performance but that they need to be supplemented by measures of lexical performance; that trade-off accounts of findings can account for the results that have been obtained even where accuracy and complexity are simultaneously raised; and that the Levelt model is a useful framework for theorising this performance.

Regarding the first, it is clear that CAF provide an important touchstone for considering and comparing different models of second language performance. These dimensions are revealing as to the ways task characteristics and task conditions impact upon performance, and seem to capture how second language speakers adapt to different speaking demands when faced with different communication problems. But it is clear that one also needs to consider lexical performance, and so the range of measures needs to be widened to cover this additional area. Of course, one can debate whether it is better to consider lexis as a separate area, or whether it is sufficient to include it within complexity, so that structural complexity and lexical complexity would be considered to be different aspects of this same performance area. The contrast in correlation between lexical sophistication and structural complexity for non-native and native speakers is intriguing in this regard. For native speakers, indeed, complexity may be more unidimensional in that lexical complexity and structural complexity go hand in hand, but for non-native speakers, the two areas do not seem to be integrated so well. Research at other proficiency levels between the ubiquitously studied low intermediates and native speakers is vital in this regard.

But the research reviewed makes it clear that measures of CAF bear upon hypotheses regarding second language performance, and how we can understand the Trade-off and Cognition Hypotheses. Evidence has been reviewed, which shows clearly that trade-off accounts are only part of the picture, and that in some ways, understanding how attentional limitations constrain second language performance is only the starting point. We have seen arguments that the Cognition Hypothesis is not automatically needed to account for cases where complexity and accuracy come together. Alternative accounts, totally compatible with attentional limitations being overcome through judicious task manipulation and task conditions, are satisfactory in accounting for the results reported. Identifying more contexts and conditions that generate raised performance in structural complexity, lexis, accuracy, and fluency, and accounting for such simultaneous influences will provide a more stringent test of the claim that attentional limitations are fundamental.

That brings us to the utility of the Levelt model. There are several advantages to using this model in relation to second language performance. Even so, and somewhat paradoxically, it should be made clear that it may also be limited in its direct appropriateness. The model portrays a modular, parallel process for speech production. What we know is that second language speakers, depending on conditions and proficiency level, often operate in this way with difficulty. A major reason for this difficulty is the difference between first and second language lexicons, in terms of size, elaborateness, and organisation. These differences cause difficulties for second language speakers regarding modular parallel processing (Kormos, 2006), leading them to 'shift down' to more serial processes on occasions. Despite this, however, the model is still extremely useful. This applies because it can be linked to what happens as second language proficiency increases (even though there is a dearth of research examining what happens as proficiency grows in relation to the performance areas of complexity, accuracy, lexis, and fluency). We can use the model, and comparisons of native and non-native speaker performance, to give us a handle on how second language speakers change as their proficiency grows, and the ways in which they come to approximate first language speakers. But there is another point of relevance to the model. It separates speech production into more conceptual areas and into more linguistic areas. When studying the second language speaker, it would seem useful to retain this distinction, and then to explore how it is relevant for a differently equipped second language speaker in terms of mental lexicon use. Essentially the framework allows us to distinguish between factors that address the complexity of tasks, since these relate more to the Conceptualiser stage, and factors which affect the way expressions are actually built, since these will impact more on the Formulator stage. In other words, one can propose that certain influences, for example type of information, operations upon information, connect with the pre-verbal message which is developed, while other factors, for example task structure, presence of a post-task activity, are concerned with the amount of attention available, and its focus, when a message is actually expressed. In this way, one can relate limitations in working memory capacity to how the two stages may or may not function smoothly and effortlessly. This may also be relevant to establishing task difficulty for assessment purposes (Skehan, 2009c). One needs to distinguish the complexity of the pre-verbal message from the difficulties that arise from the expression of that message subsequently. It is vital in this regard to have measures of complexity, lexis, accuracy, and fluency, because they capture the different facets of performance that have to be rated. There is no absolute standard of task difficulty, because task difficulty is going to be affected differently by these two major stages in speech production.

Acknowledgements

The author would like to thank the editors of this special issue of Applied Linguistics as well as three anonymous reviewers for comments on an earlier version which have strengthened the contribution considerably. The author would also like to thank the Research Grants Commission, Hong Kong SAR, for the support, through Grant No. 450307, that made the preparation of this article possible.

Notes

1 An anonymous reviewer pointed out, entirely fairly, that frequency is a useful but dubious criterion for difficulty. In defence of this approach, one can only point to the workability of this criterion as a surrogate measure in lieu of an acceptable, more valid alternative.
2 An anonymous reviewer is unconvinced by the strength of this claim, and suggests that the connection between task design features, Conceptualiser operations, and subsequent language complexity may be more complicated than is proposed here. Further research on this entirely valid point would be interesting.
3 Or, as an anonymous reviewer points out, of the criteria for performance.
4 An anonymous reviewer pointed out, though, that this must depend a lot on the interlocutor. It can also be argued that with tasks where precision of expression and outcome are not so prominent, interlocutors can rely on one another to solve problems, not only of meaning, but also of form.

4

LIMITED ATTENTION CAPACITY AND COGNITION

Two Hypotheses Regarding Second Language Performance on Tasks[1]

Introduction

This chapter is slightly unusual, in that it is 'twinned' with the chapter by Peter Robinson, and was originally part of a plenary presentation intended to compare the two accounts we provide of second language task-based performance. But prior to setting out the main focus for the chapter, the comparison of the two approaches, some contextualising remarks are needed.

Early task research developed out of pedagogic and research concerns. Pedagogically, an interest in tasks represents a development of the move, several decades ago, towards communicative language teaching, with an emphasis on meaning which contrasted with previous structural orientations. In parallel, there was a greater realisation of the need for empirical research to investigate the claims which might be made regarding alternative pedagogic activities, and so many researchers, such as Long (1985), argued strongly that asserting the usefulness of some pedagogic activity was not sufficient—there also needed to be data to test, and hopefully corroborate the claims which were made.

The most influential early guiding theory was the Interaction Hypothesis, which proposed that tasks were more effective because they were useful catalysts to provoke the sort of personalised feedback that arises naturally through interaction. The central concern was to explore how tasks might lead to more interaction and feedback, and then more feedback, it was proposed, would lead to greater

---

Originally published as: Skehan, P. (2015). Limited attentional capacity and cognition: Two hypotheses regarding second language performance on tasks. In M. Bygate (Ed.), *Domains and directions in the development of TBLT: A decade of plenaries from the international conference* (pp. 123–155). Amsterdam: John Benjamins. Reproduced with permission of John Benjamins.

acquisition. Consequently research studies explored possible task design features which might generate more feedback, such as two-way tasks, or convergent tasks and so on.

But relatively soon the context for task-based research broadened, and interest grew in task performance in its own terms. Although there was still a strong research tradition which explored feedback (in the shape of negotiation of meaning, and recasts), many researchers became interested in how tasks might have a systematic effect on the sort of language that was used, often conceptualised in terms of language complexity, accuracy, and fluency. Such research also explored the impact on performance of a range of performance conditions, such as what happens before the task is done (such as planning) or while the task is actually in progress (such as time pressure).

It is against this background that the present chapter needs to be understood. With the growing interest in performance, the need emerged to theorise that performance, and to have a deeper understanding of the major task and task condition influences upon it. The range of findings is expanding all the time, and the two approaches represented here are an attempt to systematise and explain why second language performance is structured the way it is, and why the different influences work in the way that they do.

The Limited Attention Capacity (LAC) Hypothesis: Underlying Principles

In some ways, 'hypothesis' dignifies what we are talking about here, since we are more concerned really with general operating principles for second language task performance. The theory to underpin this account has yet to arrive, and as Peter Robinson remarked (reasonably) in the original plenary presentation, there is a danger that a Limited Attention Capacity account could be vacuous by providing a framework for post hoc interpretation, without making actual predictions ahead of time. (We will see later that predictions are, in fact, possible.) It is worth saying at the outset, though, that I prefer the term Limited Attention Capacity to the term 'Trade-off'. This latter term implies that trade-offs between performance areas are pervasive and unavoidable. One of the things this chapter will try to do is bring out how the effects of limited attention capacities can be overcome, and the need for trade-off circumvented. Given this background discussion, it is useful at the outset to set out some of the principles that are central to a LAC account.

Principle One: Working memory, and attention, are limited: The assumption that this is the case is taken from contemporary cognitive psychology, and is, I would claim, consistent with the vast majority of theorists and research (Baddeley, 2015). There have been debates over the years about what the capacity of working memory is, with Miller's (1956) original speculation of seven (plus or minus two) revised downwards by people like Nelson Cowan (2015) to more like four or five units. In general, a fractionated view of working memory also has some consensus (Baddeley, 2015), with a central executive (which 'supervises' other working memory operations and which also is important for access to long-term memory), supplemented by various buffers (phonological, visuo-spatial, and more recently episodic). If one regards working memory as a sort of workspace for the solution of processing problems, then working memory also limits the amount of attention that is available, with any 'free' attention depending on the demands on other aspects of the working memory system. For example, failing, while driving, to attend to what one's passenger is saying because of challenging traffic conditions may be very excusable on this basis (except to the passenger). It is, of course, possible that at any one time the maximum capacity of working memory is not used, but then working memory can only expand up to its (quite limited) maximum.

Principle Two: Performance can usefully be measured in terms of Complexity, Accuracy, Lexis, and Fluency[2] (CALF): There are two aspects to this principle. First, there is now sufficient evidence to argue that these performance areas are distinct from one another (Skehan & Foster, 1997; Tavakoli & Skehan, 2005), and that one can characterise performance in profile terms, as a result. In other words, elevated complexity might not be associated with elevated accuracy, or fluency. Many task researchers have taken to using these areas (or at least, complexity, accuracy, and fluency, but often not lexis) as the most appropriate indices to assess task performance. Second, I assume that if there is some degree of independence between these areas, then a limited processing capacity might mean that there is competition between them for resources (or more properly, and see below, between the stages of speech production). Following from this, raised complexity, say, might be associated with lower fluency, or raised accuracy with lower complexity. In practice, these interrelationships become empirical questions. I would offer the generalisation, though, that complexity and fluency go together quite frequently, and accuracy and fluency also. The least likely combination (though not impossible, by any means) is raised accuracy and complexity (Foster & Skehan, 2012).

Principle Three: Task characteristics and conditions influence the nature of task performance, separately and in interaction: If attention and working memory are limited, and if complexity (structural and lexical), accuracy, and fluency compete for such resources, the question arises as to which areas win out in this competition, and what variables are most influential. Essentially LAC research has been preoccupied with this question, and its applications for pedagogy. A starting assumption was that empirical generalisations are needed to prime any theorising that is done. Going along with this, it is proposed that there is a lot to do to establish a set of dependable findings which are worth theorising over. In that respect LAC research focusses on task characteristics, on the one hand, such as the impact of task structure (Foster & Skehan, 2012), and then the conditions under which tasks are done, on the other, such as the effect of planning (Foster & Skehan, 1996a; Skehan, 2014b). In addition, there are studies which look at the interaction between different task characteristics and different conditions, such as task structure and time perspective (Wang & Skehan, 2014). In the later section on evidence supporting the LAC position, these claims are expanded and justified at greater length.

Principle Four: A limited attention capacity account can be related very effectively to Levelt's model of first language speaking: Levelt (1989, 1999) proposes a model of speaking in which, for the first language case, one can view speaking in terms of three broad stages, Conceptualisation, Formulation, and Articulation, with an associated process of monitoring. It is important to say, first, that the stages are modular and encapsulated, so that each does its work and then transmits information to the next stage, while simultaneously embarking on new work appropriate to its stage (see Kormos, 2006 for a much fuller account of this model applied to second language speaking), in a process that continues iteratively while speaking takes place. The first stage, broadly, is concerned with ideas, context, and stance and outputs a pre-verbal message to the Formulator stage. This second stage takes the pre-verbal message, and accesses the mental lexicon for appropriate lemmas which then become the basis for syntax building, and articulatory preparation. Articulation itself then takes the output of the Formulator and prepares actual speech.

I assume that, broadly, the same stages and processes apply to the second language case, but with some important differences. That the same stages apply is vital, since they imply that the Conceptualisation stage will be concerned with ideas, while the Formulator will engage with the details of language, lemma retrieval, information extraction from the lemma, and then syntax building based on the contents of the lemmas retrieved. The implication is a degree of separation between conceptualisation, first, and then detailed language construction, second. A major difference between first and second language speaking is the differences in the first and second language mental lexicons. In the first language case, such lexicons are extensive, but equally important, well-organised, with rich entries, often with multiple storage of the same 'item' as it also fits into formulaic language (Skehan, 1996). In the second language case, the speaker has to contend with a much smaller mental lexicon, which poses difficulties enough. But in addition, it is likely that the entries in the mental lexicon are more superficial in nature, and may lack extensive meaning links, collocational information, and features that enable the lemma to be incorporated effectively in syntax building. As a result, even when a lemma is present, that presence may be partial and less accessible, compared to a native speaker level (Schur, 2007).

Two major implications (at least) follow from this analysis. First, Conceptualisation and Formulation need to be considered separately in the L2 case. It is assumed that L2 speakers fundamentally are not different from L1 speakers in their ability to conceptualise, (except that ongoing communication may siphon off attentional resources from this stage because of the problems elsewhere in the speech production system). However, Formulation is a much more vulnerable stage in L2 speech production since it is underpinned by less rich mental lexicon resources and less automatic syntax-building processes. Second, there are issues of parallel processing. The modular, encapsulated nature of the L1 speech production stages means that the system is generally very efficient, with different stages working on different speech production challenges at the same time. Parallel function, implied by this modularity, is the norm, and is achievable, essentially, because the demands made on the mental lexicon by the pre-verbal message are met routinely due to the fact that that lexicon is extensive, elaborate, and well organised. In the second language case this is not so, and the demands of pre-verbal messages can exceed what the second language mental lexicon can deliver (with this, obviously, becoming less important as proficiency increases). When such problems occur (and of course, real time is implacably proceeding), the parallel speech production process is derailed, and it becomes serial in nature as greater demands are made on limited attentional resources to repair the problems being encountered at the Formulator stage. In other words, the division in attentional resources that is required to 'power' the Conceptualiser, Formulator, and Articulator is no longer feasible because the Formulator has become so demanding. According to this interpretation, then, serial processing results, and it becomes more difficult for the second language speaker to regain parallel processing.

Principle Five: Task difficulty: What is clear by this point is that the LAC position is founded on psycholinguistic processing, and so one judges influences on performance in terms of these processes. What is being argued for is the need to consider Conceptualisation and Formulation/Articulation as distinct from one another in the way they impact upon task difficulty. In other words, the factors that push for more demands at the Conceptualisation stage may not be the same as those which push for greater demands at the Formulation/Articulation stages. In the former case, Conceptualisation, we are dealing with issues which require more cognitive operations (Skehan, 1996), perhaps connected with:

- more unfamiliar, abstract information (vs. more familiar, concrete information);
- more complex manipulation of information (vs. less complex manipulations);
  - number of steps;
  - transformation of material;
  - linkage of different pieces of information;
  - need to justify assertions, and respond to challenges;
- decisions on perspective and stance;
- likelihood of pre-task planning opportunities used to handle ideas.

Whereas if we switch to considering Formulation (we will not pursue the under-researched area of Articulation factors, though see Wang [2009] for discussion), we are more likely to focus on:

- the lexical demands that a task may make;
- the degree of structure in the task;

60 Theory

- likelihood of pre-task planning opportunities used for rehearsal and organisation;
- opportunities for on-line planning;
- general time pressure conditions;
- familiarity with the task in question, through previous engagement with the task, such as when a task is repeated;
- working memory demands while the task is being done;
- opportunity for negotiability of what is to be done during a task.

Clearly, this viewpoint introduces complications. Most challenging here is the possibility that tasks can vary independently in difficulty between these two areas. So there may be tasks which are demanding conceptually, but not so demanding regarding linguistic resources or in terms of performance conditions.[3] And of course, the opposite may well be true also. Another complication is that one can analyse what might appear to be the same thing, so that it appears at more than one stage. Planning is a clear example of this. If pre-task planning time is used to deal with the ideas in a task and introduce greater complexity to what will be attempted, then one would have to regard the task as more difficult at the Conceptualiser stage. But if such planning time is used (successfully) to rehearse, or to mobilise relevant lexis, then one might argue that it eases subsequent Formulator operations, and makes the task easier at that stage. A third complication with difficulty is how one measures performance. If we use structural complexity, accuracy, lexis, and fluency, there is no one overall measure available to enable us to chart how changes in the task impact upon performance, since we may see elevated performance in one area linked to lower performance in another. The different performance areas cannot be guaranteed to move in concert, and so to make judgements about task difficulty one would have to nominate which of them is the touchstone for difficulty in cases where one, perhaps, is raised, and others not. Would it be complexity, or accuracy, for example?

Evidence and Theory

Task Research and the Levelt Model: General Outline

The Limited Attention Capacity approach is based on relatively little theory (although what there is will be discussed later). Its central tenets are simple, and draw on the preceding principles quite closely. It is argued that limited attentional capacity, when applied to a second language speaker with a limited and less elaborate second language mental lexicon, can nonetheless be based on an extension of the Levelt model of first language speaking to the second language case. If this is done, the key issue is the contribution of different task and task condition variables to second language task-based performance, where this performance is measured in terms of complexity, accuracy, lexis, and fluency. Such variables can be investigated on a case-by-case basis (and through interactions between them) to establish generalisations about their effects on CALF. However, to be convincing, insights need to be related to the Conceptualiser and Formulator stages in speech production. Skehan (2009c) proposes that one can look at groups of such variables as:

> Complexifying: where the effect of a variable is to make the task at hand more complex in nature, and so increase the amount of work done by the Conceptualiser, for instance in the case of planning used to complexify the ideas in a task (Pang & Skehan, 2014).
> Easing: where the effect of a variable is to make the work of the Formulator easier to manage, less demanding of attentional resources, and more likely to support parallel processing, such as in structured tasks (where the clear structure reduces the amount of Conceptualiser work, releasing more attention for the Formulator) (Skehan & Shum, 2014); or a task which is less demanding lexically (Skehan, 2009b).
> Pressuring: where the effect of a variable is to make the work of the Formulator more difficult to manage, more demanding of attentional resources, and more likely to force serial processing, for instance via time pressure (as when on-line planning opportunities are not available) (Ellis & Yuan, 2005).
> Focussing: where speaker goals, typically accuracy, can be influenced, for example where post-tasks are anticipated, since the post-task condition induces second language speakers to focus attention on particular areas of performance (Foster & Skehan, 2013).

The advantage of looking at performance influences in the above terms is that these higher-order categories (complexifying, pressuring, etc.) connect more easily with the stages from the Levelt model of first language speaking. They also show how sets of variables can impact on the same stage of the sequence of speaking, sometimes with the same variable having impact at more than one stage. These relationships are shown in Table 4.1 (adapted from Skehan, Bei, Li, & Wang, 2012).

Conceptualiser Influences

The central column in Table 4.1 shows that the entries in this table are linked to the stages from the Levelt model. Then the headings in the leftmost and rightmost columns, following the previous discussion, show the major headings grouping the task characteristic and task condition variables. It is important to say that each entry is based on research findings, and so it is important to review the relevant evidence.

Following the structure of the table, some Conceptualiser operations increase linguistic complexity in performance. The need to engage more complex

62 Theory

TABLE 4.1 Task Research, the Levelt Model, and Performance

Complexifying/Pressuring Influences	Stages of the Levelt Model	Easing/Focussing Influences
Complex cognitive operations • linking information • transforming information Complex information type • abstract • poorly structured Planning: extending Non-negotiable tasks Structured tasks	Conceptualiser	Concrete/static Less information Familiarity of information Easier cognitive operations Task repetition
Infrequent lexis Non-negotiable task	Formulator: Lemma retrieval	Planning: organising Negotiable tasks Familiarity of lexis Dialogic Task repetition
Time pressure Heavy input pressure Monologic	Formulator: Syntactic Encoding	Planning: rehearsing Structured tasks Dialogic Post-task condition Supported on-line Task repetition

cognitive operations exemplifies this. Tasks which push speakers to link information, e.g. foreground and background information in a narrative, as in Tavakoli and Skehan (2005), Tavakoli and Foster (2008), and Foster and Tavakoli (2009), raise subordination scores. Similarly tasks which require speakers to transform information, as in Skehan and Foster (1997) also lead to greater structural complexity. Structured tasks, (discussed further below), originally predicted only to influence the Formulator, now appear, if they have a problem-solution structure, to raise subordination scores also, suggesting that the complexity of the causal relations within such narratives is the basis for the raised structural complexity scores. The type of information that underlies a task also has an impact (Skehan, 1996). Foster and Skehan (1996b) showed that more concrete and familiar information is associated with greater fluency and accuracy only, while more abstract information makes a task more difficult (Brown et al., 1984). The impact of familiarity has been extended in work by Bui (2014) who links greater familiarity to raised lexical performance, operationalised in his study with a measure of lexical sophistication (Meara & Bell, 2001). Bui (2014) reports that producing a narrative in a familiar area of content gives access to richer, and more appropriate lexis.

Staying with the Conceptualiser stage, the remaining influences from Table 4.1 concern the conditions under which a task is done. Pang and Skehan (2014), following Ortega (2005), and using a qualitative methodology, report first of all that pre-task planning time can be associated with different processes. One of these, planning-as-extending, concerns second language speakers using the planning time to focus on ideas to complexify the story to be told in a task, by interpreting the demands of the task more ambitiously. In these cases, the greater use of planning time to extend ideas is then associated with greater structural complexity in the performance of the task. In other words, the planning time is used to change the task that is being done, and to push the speaker to take more risks and say more linguistically complex things.

Another claim that can be made about Conceptualiser operations, albeit tentatively, is that non-negotiable tasks (where the speaker has less choice about what is to be said, as in a narrative) can have a damaging effect on Conceptualiser operations. This is particularly the case if there is also time and input pressure. The central problem is needing to encode relatively fixed ideas, especially where this has to be done quickly where the speaker cannot shape what is to be said very much. (The converse is also true—scope to negotiate and shape, especially with less input and more time available, ease Conceptualisation.) This analysis is something of a revised presentation of Robinson's time perspective (here-and-now vs. there-and-then). Wang and Skehan (2014) contrasted a here-and-now video narrative retelling condition with a there-and-then condition. They report a considerable increase in structural complexity for the there-and-then condition, and interpret this as a reflection first of the lack of remorseless input pressure—since in the there-and-then condition, the video has already been seen—but second there is also the opportunity for the speaker, in this condition, to be selective about what will be spoken about, and also to shape the story. In this way, the speaker may adapt what will be said, and even play to their strengths by using lexis and syntax that they have confidence in, and perhaps have used before. If they have time, they can remember language they have used in the past, and use it again, exploiting the greater time available to elaborate where possible, and achieve greater language complexity. The result in Wang and Skehan (2014) was clearly raised complexity. Interestingly, since this study also had plus-or-minus structure as another independent variable, the structured there-and-then condition combination produced easily the highest level of language complexity, suggesting that this condition enabled repackaging and also exploited the potential for structure (and greater complexity therefore) in the story.

One final influence may be relevant for Conceptualiser use and that is repetition. Earlier research (Plough & Gass, 1993; Bygate, 2001) has shown that delayed repetition has a beneficial effect on performance, but more recently, using the CAF framework, Wang (2014) has shown that *immediate* repetition produced huge effect sizes with structural complexity scores. The question then becomes one of asking whether this is due to Conceptualiser operations, or work at the Formulator stage which impacts on structural complexity. We cannot be sure at present, but it can at least be proposed that attempting to tell a narrative pushes learners to familiarise themselves with events, and with the lemmas required to tell the story. Then the repeated performance allows them to manipulate the events of the story a little more freely, and to be able to explore alternative methods of saying what happened (Skehan, 2014b). If this concerns issues like stance, or organisation of ideas, then we can reasonably conclude that it is the Conceptualiser stage that is implicated. (We will discuss the important influence of repetition on the Formulator stage below).

What is interesting in this analysis of Conceptualiser operations is the division between task characteristic effects and task condition effects. Each has a part to play, but there are interesting contrasts. The evidence on task characteristics suggests that task design has an influence on how ideas are marshalled and organised, particularly how the relationship between ideas may be structured. Hence with structure and information organisation (foreground, background) the Conceptualiser has to wrestle with the expression of causality (with structure) and the relationship between different elements in a story (information organisation). Regarding task conditions, there is more focus within task conditions on processes such as changing ideas, or complexifying them; or in finding different ways to organise ideas; or of choosing which ideas to express. Characteristics and conditions seem like different routes to a relatively common destination, but with differences in flavour. But the important point to finish with is that Conceptualisation work can come from either source, and if we are to discuss task complexity, we need to include more than a set of characteristics—we also need to include the conditions under which the task is done. There are a range of interesting findings already on the effects on performance of different task characteristics and conditions, but it is clear that there is considerable scope to gather more empirical data to clarify how they relate to Conceptualiser operations.

Formulator Influences: Lemma Retrieval

Moving on in Table 4.1, the Formulator stage in speech production has a lemma retrieval stage followed by a syntax-building stage. The table shows them as separate, which they are in principle, but it is often difficult to allocate an influence unambiguously to one or the other. We can start with the impact of lemma retrieval since this is slightly more distinct. Skehan (2009b), summarising effects across a range of studies, suggests that less frequent lexis is associated with lower levels of performance regarding structural complexity and accuracy, and that, in contrast to native speaker performance, use of less frequent lexis correlates either not at all, or even negatively with structural complexity and accuracy scores. In other words, needing to retrieve less frequent lemmas seems to cause processing problems. This post hoc summary of research was not confirmed, however, by the one study (Wang & Skehan, 2014) which manipulated lexical frequency directly, and which showed effects for mid-clause pausing (a component of breakdown fluency), and lexical demands, but no effects on accuracy or complexity. The Wang and Skehan study is also analysed in terms of a task condition influence—that of degree of negotiability in a task. There is a clear difference in performance between their here-and-now and there-and-then conditions, with the former being significantly lower. Skehan (2014b) interprets this as following from the way input in the here-and-now condition cannot be negotiated—the video whose story is being retold has to be addressed as it unfolds. As a result, the events, and the associated lexis and perhaps contingent syntax, have to be worked with, even when they are difficult. In contrast, the there-and-then condition does not have remorseless and unavoidable input, and so speakers are able to make choices about the details of what they say. There is a lower likelihood therefore that people will be tripped up by particular lexical (or syntactic) items. In other words, the Formulator stage has greater flexibility regarding lemma choices, and so deficiencies in the second language mental lexicon can be avoided.

Three more factors are likely to have a particular impact at the Formulator: Lemma Retrieval stage, and these will each be interpreted positively, that is, as having an easing influence on performance (though in each case there is a contrasting condition, which will be briefly mentioned). Earlier it was mentioned that planning subsumes a number of processes. This applies to lemma retrieval in two ways. First, where planning is used for retrieval of likely words to be used in the actual performance, that is, planning-as-rehearsal, the retrieval during planning, if it can be retained and used in actual performance, will enable lemma retrieval, even comprehensive retrieval of many lemma features, to become less burdensome, with the result that actual performance requires less attentional resources and can proceed more smoothly (Pang & Skehan, 2014). Second, where planning is used for organisation, the subsequent performance, if this planning is retained, can create 'space' to enable the speaker to have more time to allocate to lemma retrieval. It will, in other words, create conditions akin to those with structured tasks, and enable the speaker to be clear about the 'big picture' and as a result, be able to mobilise more attention for the details of what is being said (Wang & Skehan, 2014).

Dialogic tasks are also likely to have a beneficial impact on lemma retrieval, relative, that is, to monologic tasks. First of all, dialogic tasks, by their nature, involve turn-taking, and this means that while one's interlocutor is speaking, there is time to engage in a form of on-line planning and at the same time as one is listening to one's interlocutor, or pretending to listen, one can be preparing for the next turn, and perhaps anticipating the lemmas which will need to be retrieved (and also possibly engaging in some Conceptualiser work). But if one does listen to one's interlocutor, it may be that s/he might use some very useful lemmas that one would not have thought of otherwise, lemmas which might then be activated, together with rich information about lemma features, thus conferring a considerable advantage to how well one will perform at one's next turn. In contrast, a monologic task provides neither of these advantages. There is no time to prepare while one's interlocutor is speaking because there is no interlocutor! And equally, there is no useful language to 'steal' because in a monologic task, one could only steal from oneself (Foster & Skehan, 2013).

The major influence on more effective lemma retrieval, however, is the opportunity for repetition. Earlier we saw that this is associated with huge effect sizes regarding language complexity. In Skehan (2014b) I argue that repetition is different from pre-task planning. In planning, where words are retrieved to be used later, what is retrieved is rather shallow, whereas when there is repetition, the original performance forces a deeper level of processing which prepares the ground much more effectively for the second performance (Bygate, 2006). The first performance pushes the second language speaker not simply to retrieve a vague form of the lemma, with incomplete information: it also raises awareness of additional information, such as syntactic implications, or collocational information, and so on. The repeated performance, next, benefits from this much richer information and performance is eased and enhanced enormously.

Formulator Influences: Syntactic Encoding

When we turn to the Formulator: Syntactic Encoding stage, some of the factors influential at the earlier Formulator stage are also relevant. The monologic vs. dialogic contrast applies similarly as far as greater on-line time is concerned while the interlocutor is speaking. But where the interlocutor's language is 'borrowed' this would also apply to syntax. In addition, it is possible that interlocutors might jointly push themselves to greater ambition in what is said, and also, possibly, to greater precision because of the obvious presence of the interlocutor (Foster & Skehan, 2013). Planning-as-rehearsal can apply in the same way with sentence frames and syntax as it did with vocabulary retrieval during planning (and indeed, in this case, would have to flow from the lemma retrieval which has occurred during the earliest stages of planning). Heavy input pressure and non-negotiability of task will also have similar effects, depriving the speaker of time to take stock and plan on-line, as well as giving unavoidable language problems to confront, rather than allowing time to orient the production to linguistic areas in which the speaker feels more comfortable. Finally, repetition has similar effects on syntax generation as it did with lemma retrieval, although here we are dealing with the consequences of that superior lemma retrieval for syntax building itself. The repeated performance is able to take the traces of syntax building from the original performance and capitalise on performance which was only partially realised, both by producing more complex language (as earlier failures are overcome) or by achieving higher levels of accuracy (as the error from the first performance is corrected). In the first case speakers may be able to extract more information from a lemma and realise its implications more fully in the way a syntactic frame is built. In the latter, the speaker can draw on the problems noticed in the first performance to monitor more effectively and avoid the erroneous form. What is interesting is that the syntactic encoding stage, analysed in this way, sees two major performance areas both benefit (Wang, 2014).

There are a couple of influences on the syntax-building stage, though, which are more distinct in their relevance at this point in the speech production process. First, there is the influence of post-task conditions. A series of studies have explored this possibility. Skehan and Foster (1997) showed a significant effect on accuracy of requiring some participants to engage in a public performance of a task that they had just done in (private) pairs. Here it was anticipation of the threat of a possible public performance that influenced the accuracy of performance during the earlier actual task. However, in Skehan and Foster (1997), three tasks were used: a personal task, a narrative, and a decision-making task, but only one, that last of these, yielded significance. Accordingly Foster and Skehan (2013) used a different post-task operationalisation, the need to transcribe one's own performance, to explore whether this different post-task activity would be more effective in causing participants to focus on form. It was, with both a decision-making and a narrative task, achieving significance in each case. (The narrative was used because it had shown the least effect in the previous study, and so was considered the most stringent test of the new operationalisation.) Interestingly, the decision-making task also generated significance for a measure of subordination, as an index of structural complexity. Subsequently, Li (2014) has confirmed and extended these results, showing a general accuracy effect, but then additional more specific effects of different transcription conditions (individual vs. group transcription; transcription with and without revision). Now we can generalise from these studies and claim that if learners know that there is a post-task to come, and they take this post-task activity seriously, they can be induced to allocate attention to form. Initially we (Skehan & Foster, 1997) thought this anticipation would link with a wish to avoid error only, but now it appears that under supportive conditions (an interactive task) it can impact upon language complexity also. In passing it should be noted that accuracy and complexity scores in these studies do not show strong patterns of intercorrelation—it appears that the participants who achieve higher accuracy are not those who achieve higher complexity. The 'nudging' of form that takes place (Lynch, 2007) seems to be towards one performance area or the other, not so often both for the same individual. This is consistent, of course, with limited attentional capacities having an important role, linked perhaps with individual disposition towards accuracy or complexity.

The other influence which seems most directed to the Formulator: syntactic encoding stage is that of what can be termed supported on-line planning (Ellis, 2005b). The basic claim with on-line planning (Ellis, 2005b) is that less pressured conditions enable the speaker to plan while speaking, since time is available to 'regroup' even while speaking is taking place. Wang (2014) researched on-line planning, on the basis that the operationalisations of on-line planning in Ellis and Yuan (2005) may not have guaranteed the level of time pressure that was assumed in order to prevent on-line planning or to facilitate it. Using more controlled operationalisations, with slowed versus normal speed video narratives for retelling, she showed that in a 'strict' on-line planning condition, there was no effect on accuracy in performance. In other words, more relaxed speech production conditions were not associated with greater accuracy. However, if the on-line planning condition was preceded by the opportunity for pre-task planning, accuracy was raised. Skehan (2014b) interprets this effect as supporting the claim that on-line planning is effective (i.e. beneficial Formulator conditions are being created) but it has to be accompanied by relevant Conceptualiser work. The pre-task planning engages the Conceptualiser, and the pre-verbal messages which are created have more substance, and then the on-line conditions, and effective Formulator work, enable the effect on higher accuracy to manifest itself.

After this survey of the evidence, it is worth restating the heart of the approach taken. Fundamental are the stages in a model of speech production, first or second, and what these stages are influenced by. Then the challenge is to explore how external influences can affect the internal psycholinguistic processes at Levelt's three stages where, in the second language case, attentional and memory limitations have a much greater impact on the smoothness with which the Formulator stage, in particular, can operate because the second language mental lexicon and associated syntactic encoding processes are less developed than the first. This leads to the problem that what is essentially a parallel process in first language speaking often becomes a serial process in the second.

The LAC approach does not view second language speech production through the lens of an over-arching theory, and so there is no all-encompassing prediction of how performance will be influenced. That is because such production is influenced by many factors, and one can only understand such speech production by attempting to integrate these diverse influences within a wide and accommodating framework. But that is not to say, first, that anything goes, or second, that predictions cannot be made. Regarding the first, a LAC interpretation of performance does not mean that any set of results can be accommodated by invoking notions of attention having been allocated to a raised dimension of performance and then 'siphoned off' from lowered areas. It only means that there are limited amounts of attention, and then the interest in research studies is to explore how these limitations play out with performance and performance dimensions, and how these limitations can be overcome. The research which has been surveyed demonstrates how productive this approach can be. Indeed, the most interesting aspects of research within a Limited Attention Capacity framework explore how attentional limitations can be overcome or circumvented, and how multiple performance areas can be simultaneously raised through the joint action of these different influences. It is assumed that this is difficult, but not impossible, as a number of studies attest (Tavakoli & Skehan, 2005; Foster & Skehan, 2013; Wang & Skehan, 2014), and will be discussed below, in an evaluation of the evidence relevant to the Cognition Hypothesis.

Predictions also come naturally to the LAC approach, and at two levels. First, given the range of extant studies, there are many predictions which are based on previous research. If a study involves planning, for example, or interactivity, or structured tasks (and all of these have been researched most intensively by LAC-oriented researchers), then predictions can be made in future studies based on these previous findings. Skehan and Shum (2014) and Li (2014) are examples of this where predictions were made (and confirmed) on the basis of existing research, and where additional variables were incorporated to extend our understanding of second language task performance. But second, and more interestingly, top-down predictions can be made with specific studies about novel research designs because they follow from the sort of speaking-model-generated analyses covered earlier. At a general level, if we assume limited attention and a key role for lemma-driven Formulation, one could predict that as proficiency develops, and the second language mental lexicon grows in scale and organisation, the consequences of limited attention will change. The richer mental lexicon will not be so pressured, and as a result performance will improve, but, more interestingly, trade-offs between performance areas may diminish, and tensions between, for example, accuracy and complexity reduce. More specifically, one can use new combinations of variables from a framework such as that shown in Table 4.1 to make predictions about the interactive effect of such combinations. Tavakoli and Foster (2008), for example, showed that if task structure and information integration were involved, they produced a joint effect on complexity and accuracy. Similarly Wang and Skehan (2014) designed a study to combine task structure and time perspective, showing that the combination of structure and a there-and-then condition also produced raised accuracy and complexity. Wang (2014) showed how predictions could be made by linking Leveltian stages in speaking to task conditions, showing that Conceptualiser and Formulator lead to raised performance if they work in harmony. As we learn more about the effects on task performance of a range of different variables, we will be able to make more and more predictions of this sort, and explore whether the limited attention account is falsifiable, in whole or in part.

The Cognition Hypothesis

The focus in this chapter has been on the Limited Attention Capacity approach to accounting for task performance. But it is, as from the original plenary on which this chapter is based, in counterpoint to the Cognition Hypothesis, and so this section, more briefly, will look at this alternative position, especially where the two approaches illuminate one another. The Cognition Hypothesis discusses task complexity factors, task condition factors, and task difficulty (or learner) factors. Each in turn has a further division into two categories (resource-directing vs. resource-dispersing; participation vs. participant; affective vs. ability variables, respectively). We will examine these in reverse order, since it is the first, task complexity, that is the most relevant for the present comparison, and so it will be saved for last!

Robinson (2011a) does not talk about task difficulty as inherent in a task, but rather focusses on how different learners may respond to a particular task differently. Hence for him, difficulty arises from ability and affective factors on the part of the learner in interaction with the actual task. Clearly I agree learner factors have a major impact on task performance, and indeed, two learners may respond in different ways to the same stimulus material. But it does seem to me misleading to define task difficulty in this way, and not to have any sort of construct which speaks to a general difficulty or difficulty level from the task itself. This would depend on Conceptualiser, Formulator, and Articulator factors. Robinson's task complexity seems to relate to only the first of these since it emphasises the quantity and nature of the information in the task and the operations and processes performed on such information. There is little reference to performance conditions themselves. My preference for task difficulty would include them all (while accepting the usefulness—indeed necessity—of having some index of complexity from the first alone). That does not mean at all that learner factors should be deemphasised (and they are, in fact, one of the major under-researched areas in task-based approaches). But one could use something like item response theory (from language testing) to try to locate both tasks and learners on one scale of difficulty, where each of these could be located much like test items and test takers (Revesz, 2009). In this way, there might be something to say about general task difficulty, even if it would be mediated, in all cases, by particular learner factors.[4]

Moving on to the task condition (interactional) factors, divided as they are into participation and the participant, these present interesting lists of potential influences on task performance. Some arise out of a negotiation of meaning perspective, and the variables that have emerged in that sub-literature. Slightly surprisingly, perhaps, given the participant emphasis, there is nothing to capture what might be termed the participant engagement potential of the task, something that might have a strong impact on the amount of attention mobilised, and the nature of the performance generally (although perhaps it could be argued that task motivation is relevant here, even though I interpret task motivation as what is brought to the task by the speaker from outside, so to speak, rather than arising from involvement in the ongoing task). But apart from this, the list of influences constitutes an interesting program for research, and one which would fit in equally well to the Cognition or LAC Hypotheses, as, in fact, would the list of learner factors which are outlined.

The key category of variables, however, is that of Task Complexity, and the cognitive factors of resource-directing and resource-dispersing variables. Resource-directing variables are the central and most interesting part of the Cognition Hypothesis. Robinson (2011a) argues that with each pair of resource-directing variables (+/- here-and-now; +/- few elements; +/- spatial reasoning; +/- causal reasoning; +/- intentional reasoning; +/- perspective taking) one value is associated with a more complex task and the other with a simpler task. More deeply, these variables are all assumed to reflect some construct of task complexity. Further, the more complex value for the variable is seen as pushing for simultaneous higher linguistic complexity *and* accuracy (and lower fluency) in performance, following the assumption that attention expands to meet the demands made upon it by the more complex value. The second language speaker, that is, responds to the challenge of the more complex task by raising their level of performance in terms of accuracy and complexity, and at the expense of fluency. It is also the case that the raised game is directed at form, whether this relates to complexity or error avoidance, and this is what justifies the term resource-*directing*, with this directing often being to form-in-general (Michel, 2011), but in some studies, to specific forms relevant to the resource-directing dimension (Revesz, Sachs, & Mackey, 2011).

Resource-dispersing variables, on the other hand, although cognitive, and although posited to impact on performance, do not have this attention-directing quality, and 'disperse attention over many linguistic and non-linguistic aspects of the task that need to be handled simultaneously' (Robinson, 2011a, p. 17). The variables do have values that are more performatively complex, such as lack of planning opportunity, lack of prior knowledge, multi-tasking, but these do not impact upon form selectively, or noticing, or interlanguage development, but rather influence level of control and fast access to resources, in Bialystok's (1994) terms.

The Cognition Hypothesis is wide-ranging, and so contains many variables which could generate research studies. But the key contrast, as indicated earlier, is between the categories of resource-directing and resource-dispersing task complexity variables, which are posited to have common effects within each of these categories, and different effects across categories. The first problem, therefore, is that task complexity is currently rather under-specified, and the variables enumerated above are little more than a list. There may be links to first language acquisition work, but conceptualisations, and putative common influences on task complexity, need to be re-established in different domains. So, for the second language domain, there is no over-arching characterisation of complexity, and as we have seen in earlier sections (and also below), there are alternative analyses possible for the features under this heading, such as time perspective. It seems to me that, at the moment, individual task complexity features need to be researched, and if they generate the predicted results, they can be considered to generate greater task complexity (a somewhat circular argument). The lack of certainty that this will happen weakens the construct of task complexity considerably, in that aspects of overt language performance are taken as evidence of constructs of the underlying task. There is an emerging trend to use task-external measures to explore the construct of task complexity, such as introspection (Tavakoli, 2009), stimulated recall (Kim, 2013a), time estimation (Baralt, 2010; Malicka & Levkina, 2012), and eye-tracking (Revesz, Sachs, & Hama, 2013). These techniques offer some promise in avoiding charges of circularity when claims of task complexity are made, although there may well be considerable methodological challenges to overcome before they can be used dependably in task research.

But there is also the problem of the distinction between resource-directing and resource-dispersing features. The research studies conducted from a LAC perspective are strongly suggestive that two resource-dispersing features have been mis-analysed. Planning, as we have seen, is not monolithic, and could mean planning-as-extending, or planning-as-organising, or planning-as-rehearsing. The first of these essentially increases the conceptual demands of tasks (and so should be resource-directing), while the third is also focussed on form, but in this case more towards accuracy. A similar analysis could be presented regarding task structure (another resource-dispersing variable in the Cognition Hypothesis). We have seen that the original LAC predictions for structure were for raised accuracy and fluency because Formulator operations were eased. But additional research has shown that task structure can also be associated with greater structural complexity, as speakers respond to a problem-solution structure and produce more complex language to reflect this. In other words, task structure, in this analysis, seems to meet the criteria for resource-directing variables rather than resource-dispersing. In the following section, more extended analyses of planning and structure will be provided from a LAC perspective, so nothing more will be said here. But the central point is clear—the resource-directing vs. resource-dispersing distinction initially appears to be clear, but on further probing it is obvious that the separation between factors which underpin this distinction are nothing like as clear-cut as they are presented as being.

To sum up this section analysing the resource-directing and resource-dispersing variables, there appear to be two sorts of problem. First, there is the lower-level problem that the lists of what is included under each heading type are not convincing, and analysis of various of them raises doubts about whether they are correctly located. But at a higher level, it is unclear what the construct of task complexity entails, other than a list of potential factors. It comes across that more research is needed to establish whether there is a viable construct involved, and how it might be operationalised (Revesz, 2014). Until this is done, it may be premature to make claims about how task complexity might influence performance, and better to research individual variables to see what impact they have.

Then, of course, there is the issue of evidence. The Cognition Hypothesis is clearer and bolder than the LAC hypothesis in this regard: it predicts that increasing task complexity along resource-directing dimensions will raise the conceptual demands of tasks which in turn will push second language speakers to raise linguistic complexity *and* accuracy, with lowered fluency, as their attention is directed to form and as that attention expands to respond to the challenges the speaker faces. It is important to note that the Cognition Hypothesis predicts a joint raising of these two performance areas. To me this suggests two corollaries. First, it is not enough for a resource-directing variable to cause complexity *or* accuracy to be raised—*both* need to be higher. (Occasionally one sees studies which show raised complexity only, or raised accuracy only, and it is claimed that this is consistent with the Cognition Hypothesis. In fact, such a finding would be irrelevant to the

Cognition Hypothesis, not least because almost any approach to tasks will relate some understanding of task complexity to increased language complexity.) But second, it seems to me that the raised complexity and accuracy need to be operative at the individual level, that is, the same individuals should show increased complexity and accuracy, not that some participants in a study show raised complexity and others show raised accuracy, even if this produces significant effects in both performance domains. In other words, it is important to show that when there is a joint raising of these performance areas, there is also a correlation coefficient of some magnitude to reflect the individual increase.

During the last twenty years, a great deal of research has been conducted to explore Cognition Hypothesis predictions, research which has been reviewed elsewhere (Ellis, 2011; Skehan, 2014b) and which has generated some book-length edited publications (Garcia-Mayo, 2007; Robinson, 2011a). This is not the place to offer another review, but it is important to make some points. First, clear support for the Cognition Hypothesis is very rare (Ellis, 2011). What is much more typical is that one performance area, such as complexity, is raised, but important others, for instance accuracy, are not. This is even true in the volume devoted to the Cognition Hypothesis (Robinson, 2011a), where several studies exemplify this. Second, an important meta-analysis of Cognition Hypothesis work (Jackson & Suethanapornkul, 2013) suggests that, across the range of studies included, there are small positive effect sizes for accuracy and fluency, but nothing for complexity, again failing to confirm the central claim of the Cognition Hypothesis. In any case, this predisposition, if there is an effect, for it to concern accuracy, does seem curious to me. If there was going to be one effect, I would have expected it to be for language complexity, since I assume that factors such as reasoning demands, or perspective taking would have increased the likelihood of more subordination, or even more words per clause (Norris & Ortega, 2009). Thus the conclusion of this meta-analysis seems very important to me in suggesting that some revision of the hypothesis may be necessary. All in all, then, despite the considerable amount of research which has now accumulated, the supportive evidence is, to say the least, slender.

Interestingly, and returning to the central Cognition Hypothesis claim, there are some supportive studies, in the sense that a joint raising of complexity and accuracy at the group level is reported, but most of these have been conducted by what one might term LAC researchers! For example, Tavakoli and Skehan (2005), Foster and Skehan (2013), and Wang and Skehan (2014) all report joint increases in complexity and accuracy. So, on the face of it, there are supportive results for the Cognition Hypothesis. However, alternative interpretations are possible and even convincing, for these results. First, there is the possibility that other variables act together to produce the jointly raised results. Tavakoli and Skehan (2005) ascribe the joint accuracy–complexity effect to task structure (accuracy) and planning (complexity) working together, that is a joint influence of two 'resource-dispersing' variables. Foster and Skehan (2013) interpret the joint effect finding with a decision-making (but not a narrative) task to a post-task condition (which raises accuracy) and interactivity (which raises complexity), a result confirmed by Li (2014). Wang and Skehan (2014) attribute their joint effect to task structure (accuracy) and a there-and-then time perspective, with a lack of pressured, non-negotiable processing (complexity). Importantly, in none of these studies can it be convincingly argued that the condition which produces the jointly raised accuracy and complexity can be analysed as having greater task complexity along resource-directing dimensions (the driver for the Cognition Hypothesis), e.g. how can a post-task condition raise task complexity? Equally importantly, the studies hardly ever generate significant correlations between accuracy and complexity scores, suggesting that some participants show raised performance in complexity, some accuracy, but rarely both at the same time. In other words, the findings that accuracy and complexity are jointly raised at the group level are not matched by the findings at the individual level. All in all, then, the Cognition Hypothesis urgently needs some supportive evidence if it is to continue to be regarded as credible.

Contrasts Between the Approaches

Now that both approaches have been covered, we can move on to examine contrasts and similarities between them. Some of these have been implicit in the preceding discussion, but now they can be brought into clearer focus.

Hinterland

Perhaps the clearest difference between the Cognition and LAC Hypotheses is their 'hinterland'. The Cognition Hypothesis relies strongly on a linguistic analysis of performance (Givon, 1985), and then supplements this with a view of memory functioning which does not view memory and attention limitations as significant (Sanders, 1998). From the first of these influences comes the proposition that speakers respond to task demands, and 'up their game' when the task is more conceptually complex, pushing for precision and accuracy, to do justice to the task complexity, and also using more complex language for the same reason. This analysis relies on a particular view of memory functioning. Although working memory may be regarded as limited in size, attention is seen as expandable, and drawing on multiple resource pools (Wickens, 2007), although the detail of the functioning of these multiple resource pools, and how they enable attention to expand, is not made clear.

The LAC Hypothesis does not have much to say about the linguistic basis for speech production. Instead it relies upon a model of first language speaking (Levelt, 1989) which is generalised to the second language case (de Bot, 1992; Kormos, 2006). Then, for underlying psychological processes, it assumes a limited capacity system, in which working memory has a maximum size, as do attentional resources. In the first case, LAC makes the same assumptions as the Levelt model about stages of speech production (Conceptualisation, Formulation, Articulation), associated processes such as monitoring, and the importance of a mental lexicon (although in this case, smaller, less elaborate, and less organised). Conceptualisation is concerned with the ideas to be expressed, the use of context, and the development of stance, and outputs the pre-verbal message. (This is likely to be the greatest focus for responding to task complexity.) Then the Formulator and Articulator address the problems of clothing the pre-verbal message in the second language. It is here that one of the major differences between first and second language speaking becomes salient—the way the parallel processing typical of the first language case becomes serial, as Formulator operations encounter difficulty and consume attentional resources as they try to address and recover from the difficulties which stem from the less rich second language mental lexicon. So with hinterland, then, the two approaches seem a long way apart, each owing allegiance to distinct underlying disciplines and theorising.

Analysing Influences Upon Performance

This focus on the internal processes of the stages of speech production leads to some different analyses of second language performance (and essentially, predictions), compared to the Cognition Hypothesis. Three examples can bring this out. Planning is shown in several places in Table 4.1, reflecting the way that the planning process can be more than one thing. Planning time can be used to reanalyse a task, to make it more complex, or to transform the ideas that it contains (Pang & Skehan, 2014). In this case planning relates to the Conceptualiser stage, and indeed increases task complexity through the nature of the speaker preparation. But alternatively, planning can be used to organise the task, perhaps even to impose structure upon what will be done during the task. In this case, the planning time is used not so much to change the ideas that will drive the task forward (i.e. general task complexity is unaffected), but more to provide a discourse framework that enables the speaker to execute the task (and recover from any difficulties encountered) more efficiently. Here, the planning activity bears fruit during the Formulator stage. Another possibility (Ortega, 2005; Pang & Skehan, 2014) is that planning time is used to rehearse either lexis or morphosyntax. In this case, the speaker, during planning time, may prepare exact language which is to be used during the task proper. Very clearly, this too is directed at more efficient Formulator operations (with the assumption, of course, that what is 'rehearsed' in this way is actually retained and transferred to the task itself. The final point to make here about planning derives from the qualitative studies which have been done. This is that planning is two-edged, in that good things can flow from what is done in pre-task planning, but equally, the speaker can inadvertently engage in planning behaviour (planning 'large', planning detailed form), which qualitative studies (Pang & Skehan, 2014) have shown to be associated with lower performance. All in all, here, the point is that one cannot treat planning as a monolithic invariant category—it subsumes a set of processes, processes which can only be illuminated if they are related to a psycholinguistically based model of speaking.

A second example of this approach concerns task structure. A range of studies have now been conducted, all of which suggest that greater task structure has a beneficial impact on performance, regarding fluency (almost always), accuracy (fairly consistently), and in more recent studies language complexity. Skehan (2014b) analyses these effects as connected to three things. First, as a basic interpretation, the clear structure clarifies what the Formulator stage has to accomplish. The structure shapes the 'broad lines' of a task or a narrative, and then the speaker is 'licensed' to focus on the details, on the surface of local-level language. Hence the greater accuracy and fluency possibly because of the greater amount of attention available, since less Conceptualiser work needs to be done. Second, the existence of task structure means that when, despite the support, things do go wrong, and a parallel mode of processing is replaced by effortful serial processing, it is easier to use the structure, and its 'staging points' to relaunch a parallel mode rather than flounder around, trying to catch up. In a restaurant narrative, for example, well-attested parts of the restaurant script, such as being greeted, then seated, following by being given the menu, ordering food and so on, could be such staging points and the basis for relaunching the narrative after any local difficulties. Again, in this case, the Formulator is able to function more effectively, and accuracy and fluency benefit. But finally, and linking with findings which suggest a connection between task structure and greater language complexity, there is also the point that structure in the task is likely to be matched by greater complexity in the language which is used. This would probably apply most clearly with tighter structure, such as problem-solution (Winter, 1976; Hoey, 1983), since sentence frames used in such a discourse structure would be likely to be more subordinated and have more complex clausal structure. So we see with this variable also that one can portray language consequences that flow from task features through the stages of a speech production model. It also brings out that analysing task structure in terms of task complexity, that is, that structure makes a task less complex (Long, 2015, p. 244) is misplaced—this does not reflect at all the way the detailed influences on Conceptualiser *and* Formulator stages operate, and the empirical results on the effects of structure on performance. Structure can lead to more potential for greater task complexity and more conceptualisation, but then also ease performance conditions and Formulator pressures.

The third and final example concerns one of the central Cognition Hypothesis variables, time perspective, which contrasts here-and-now with there-and-then tasks. The Cognition Hypothesis analyses the there-and-then condition as generating greater task complexity, on the basis that there are memory as well as conceptual demands during speech production, compared to a lack of memory demands during the 'easier' here-and-now condition. But a limited attention capacity analysis would be quite different here. The there-and-then condition does indeed create a memory burden. On the other hand, it has the considerable advantage that it is not dominated by input, which can be the case under the here-and-now condition. In addition, the there-and-then condition allows the speaker, in the absence of dominating input, to be more selective about what is said, that is, to negotiate what the task consists of. These two factors, lack of input domination, and scope to renegotiate the task, make for less pressure on resources while the task is being done. Input domination pushes the speaker to commit resources to handle the latest input that needs to be processed, and leads to a mode of communication which is very stimulus dependent. Working memory cannot be cleared before new input arrives and has to be handled, so while material does not need to be retained, as in the there-and-then condition, both central executive and buffer systems in working memory are fully committed. Scope to renegotiate the task means that there is not the same input dependence, and so the details of each aspect of the input do not automatically have to be responded to. The speaker can therefore use the freedom to select some things to communicate to reorganise what is to be said, and even increase its complexity. (This analysis of the here-and-now compared to there-and-then focusses on influences where processing factors are emphasised. Bygate [personal communication] points out that there may be other influences which make the here-and-now condition more challenging, such as negotiating deictic reference under information gap conditions.)[5]

The point with these three analyses is that a LAC approach is more flexible in accounting for the operation of salient variables in second language speech performance. Using the stages of the Levelt model as the spine of the account brings out that variables such as planning or structure are relevant at more than one stage in the speech production process. To categorise an influence as directing or dispersing imposes something of a straightjacket and prevents any comparable analytic flexibility. In Cognition terms, it is clear that some of the time planning and structure are resource directing, and at other times, resource dispersing. Taking the more psycholinguistic approach makes it easier to see this. Similarly, with time perspective, an account more linked to memory functioning, including the totality of the memory system, enables a radically different perspective, since it highlights the role of working memory operations, and the implications that pressuring working memory through input demands have for the level of second language performance that results. Not to do this will inevitably produce an incomplete picture.

Acquisition

For clarity, it is also worth contrasting the two approaches with respect to acquisition and development. The Cognition Hypothesis, where it focusses on resource-directing tasks, is not simply a proposal regarding performance; it also makes claims regarding acquisition and development. Robinson (2011a) argues that resource-directing tasks are more likely to generate feedback and recasting for learners, and that these conversational moves will foster acquisition. He also proposes that resource-directing tasks, by their nature, introduce a focus on language, and that this connects with Bialystok's (1994) views on analysis, as opposed to control (Robinson, 2011a, p. 17). This often applies to specific language forms, and so, unlike LAC which focusses on more general measures, there is an attempt, on occasions, to link specific tasks to specific language. In other words, the Cognition Hypothesis attempts (laudably) to integrate acquisition and performance.

The LAC approach, in contrast, is essentially an account of performance, and in itself, has little to say about acquisition. It explores how tasks and task conditions can have an impact on general areas such as language complexity (morphosyntactic and lexical), accuracy, and fluency. As such it downplays acquisition, and no LAC studies have had much of an acquisitional orientation. The only way in which any claims about development might be made is through proposals for the general performance areas of complexity, accuracy, and fluency also having a potential acquisitional sequence. Complexity could be the result of new and more advanced language being used, but not in an especially controlled way, since it may be produced with error and haltingly. But then this new language could be proceduralised, or become implicit, to some degree, but with an ability to achieve control only under supportive production conditions (cf. on-line planning). One would then view the final stage of acquisition as being when the new language can be used without error and in real time with a good semblance of fluency. This sequence (which would be followed many times as more and different target language enters the interlanguage system) would suggest that performance can be an important aspect of the way in which acquisition proceeds (Skehan, 2014b).

This is not to say that acquisition has not been discussed from within an LAC approach, but such discussions have focussed on an expanded post-task stage within instruction. In Skehan (2013), I propose that one can explore different activities which contribute to acquisition but which take place after the task proper has been completed. We saw earlier that one type of post-task activity is when anticipation of the later activity (e.g. transcription of one's own performance) causes the earlier actual task to be done differently (and generally, more accurately). But a different and more extended post-task stage, following Willis (1996), would be to use the language which has been made salient earlier, during the pre-task or task stage, and capitalise upon it as the basis for acquisition and change. In other words, it is assumed that the earlier performance will have raised awareness of gaps or insufficiencies or previously unrealised complexities in the L2 which can then be addressed, in a more focussed manner, at the post-task stage (Willis, 1996; Lynch, 2001; Bygate, 2006; Skehan, 2013). The task (or even pre-task) may have created an opportunity—the post-task provides scope for focussed and even sustained, explicit treatment of the language which has come into prominence, language which may well be timely in relation to the learner's developmental position. These proposals are discussed at greater length in Skehan (2013, 2014b).

Scope for Resolution?

Fundamentally, following the discussion in the last section, it is difficult to see how the two positions, Cognition and Limited Attentional Capacity, can be reconciled. Major influences on the two approaches are very different from one another, one emphasising a more linguistic approach (Givon, 1985), and the other psycholinguistic (Levelt, 1989, 1999). Their views of memory and attention contrast very clearly. They do agree that tasks are a useful unit to explore performance, and they agree that the complexity of a task is an important influence on performance, sometimes leading to a focus on language, and sometimes less so. Some of the categories of analysis are also quite similar to one another, especially in how these relate to task performance. The Cognition Hypothesis resource-directing category, especially if one removes time perspective (for reasons given earlier, and also because it seems qualitatively different to the other examples in this category) does seem quite close to the earlier LAC section examining influences on the Conceptualisation stage in the Levelt model (and Robinson (2011a) does discuss Levelt in relation to the Cognition Hypothesis). LAC, though, seems to have a wider range of factors which push for more conceptualisation work, although the Cognition Hypothesis resource-directing factors (from e.g. Robinson [2011a]) are pretty much included. But the various factors are interpreted very differently, and the two approaches also differ in the relative importance they attach to tasks themselves and to task conditions, with Cognition emphasising task characteristics (at least with respect to resource-directing variables), and LAC ascribing at least as much influence to task conditions.

But there are a couple of areas where some closer alignment may be possible. First, I would argue that attentional resources may not be constant, a central point for the Cognition Hypothesis. But I do not regard attention as expandable, so much as something which may not always be used to its maximum possible. Many tasks one gives learners are not totally engaging, and may sometimes, frankly, be a bit boring. It may be the case that something like 'task engagement' (Bygate & Samuda, 2009) is an important influence here. Maximum task engagement would mean that participants are more likely to use as much attention as they can, whereas lower task engagement may mean that there are unused resources. Whether (a) the maximum use of resources would translate into simultaneously greater accuracy and complexity is an empirical issue, and (b) whether task complexity is what might have an impact on task engagement is something that has yet to be established. But at least this possibility holds out some hope of resolution between the two positions.

But the final area seems to me more promising. Given the many variables which have been explored by task researchers, it is curious that level of proficiency has not come much into prominence. In a way, from a Cognition Hypothesis perspective, it may not be obvious how this is important—resource-directing tasks should have the same effect at different proficiencies. But from a LAC perspective, one might anticipate some changes. The point was made earlier that second language task performance, through mental-lexicon-based pressure on the Formulator, may become serial in nature rather than the desirable parallel process it might be. But as proficiency increases, one assumes that the second language mental lexicon becomes larger, more organised, and more elaborate, and therefore, more capable of handling the problems the pre-verbal message gives it. If lemmas are retrieved more quickly and if the morphosyntactic information they contain is also retrieved and can be acted upon, it may be that the tension between accuracy and complexity is reduced, and these two performance areas are more integrated. In this case, and rather curiously, if one takes on the rather perverse task of using a limited attention capacity framework and then applying it to the Cognition Hypothesis(!), this might suggest that the Cognition Hypothesis may become more convincing as second language proficiency increases.[6] Researching with low-intermediate or intermediate participants (the most typical in most studies) may not, therefore, be the most supportive group to work with in Cognition Hypothesis research. It will be interesting to see in the future if proficiency, as a variable, comes more into focus, and whether it provides grounds for bringing the two hypotheses closer together. Certainly the study by Malicka and Levkina (2012) is encouraging in this regard, since they report results suggesting that accuracy and complexity relate more strongly in the higher proficiency group of the two groups in their study.

Concluding Remarks

The final thoughts to this chapter have to emphasise two caveats which apply equally to Cognition and LAC, and which qualify a great deal of what has been discussed earlier—the issues of task complexity and performance measurement. That there is so much uncertainty associated with each of these hampers any claims which are made, from either position.

Task complexity is, of course, central to the Cognition Hypothesis, but figures often with the LAC approach too. Although Cognition holds out the prospect of clarifying task complexity, as we have seen, the attempt is fraught with difficulties, and the Cognition Hypothesis proposals only amount to a list of possibilities for research. What we need, in the future, is a clearer account of what the construct of task complexity consists of (Revesz, 2014), what the dimensions of that complexity are, and how they can be measured (Sasayama, 2014). Only then will we be able to make any claims about task complexity effects. Even then there might be problems. One might argue that task complexity will have a systematic impact on performance, such that greater complexity has greater effects. It would seem to me that this is an assumption only. It may be that greater task complexity is not consistently associated with greater language complexity and that contextual effects mediate its operation, a claim which can only be assessed empirically once we have greater understanding of what task complexity is.

Turning to measurement, one might claim that our field is young, and so we have to expect initial investigations to have limited measurement techniques. Assuming that complexity (structural and lexical), accuracy, and fluency are the dimensions we are interested in, there is certainly considerable scope for improvement, and I will mention three areas. First there is an urgent need for standardisation of measurement, to ensure comparability across studies. At present there is considerable cross-study variation. Second we need to understand any sub-dimensions of existing constructs so that we know how the measures within any particular area interrelate. For example we generally accept that there are sub-dimensions of fluency (breakdown, repair, speed) or of lexis (diversity, density, sophistication) but we need to know how these sub-dimensions interrelate. In this way we can evaluate the particular variables and measures used in a research study more effectively. Third, we need to be clear about which measures are appropriate for which constructs. Areas like structural complexity (with subordination, words per clause, words per phrase, and even developmental measures) and accuracy (with measures such as error-free clauses, errors per 100 words, length of clause without error) may be reasonably clear. But then there are issues such as error gravity, and even inconsistent placement of particular measures (repair as part of fluency, or repair as part of accuracy) which are ready for careful reconsideration and clarification. Until analysis makes progress, claims in the field generally, and certainly comparisons of Cognition and LAC, will be seriously compromised.

Notes

1 The author would like to thank Andrea Revesz, Martin Bygate, and two anonymous reviewers, whose comments improved the chapter considerably.
2 These are not the only aspects of performance that could be measured, but they are the most frequent. Undoubtedly other areas, such as discourse complexity, or task outcome (Revesz, personal communication), will become more common in the future.
3 One example might be the puzzle of the old woman on one bank of a river with a wolf, a goat, and a cabbage, and who needs to use a boat to get all parties to the other side, where the boat can only transport two things at a time (including the woman). Yet, if left alone together the wolf will eat the goat, and the goat will eat the cabbage. Another example would be a narrative where a set of pictures with no obvious storyline has to be woven into a convincing story. In each case the language required is not that difficult, but the thinking is more demanding.
4 Revesz (personal communication) points out that identifying the dependent variable here might constitute an interesting and difficult problem in itself, and go beyond CAF measures, including also, possibly, task completion rates and measures of cognitive load.
5 A reviewer points out that time perspective might still be a viable and interesting variable within the Cognition Hypothesis, but that it would need to be operationalised

differently, so that influences such as memory burden and input domination are more carefully controlled. Then the central comparison would only be of time perspective.
6 A reviewer proposes that the two positions can be reconciled if it is assumed that the Cognition Hypothesis is considered to address the connection between functional and linguistic demands that a task may pose, while the Limited Attentional Capacity approach can capture the nature of L2 learners' language use, which is effortful and attention-demanding.

5
REFLECTIONS ON PART I, THEORY

Introduction

This epilogue to the reprinted articles in the first section of the book tries to reflect upon the articles, and then assess where they might have taken us. The first part of the chapter stays close to the reprinted articles themselves, and offers ideas that seem relevant now to what each of them tried to achieve. Then a second section explores the basics of second language speech. This is relevant to this chapter, and also is foundational for the rest of the book. A third section presents a wider-ranging analysis of tasks, their characteristics and their nature, and is followed by a very brief account of task conditions. All of this leads into a final section on tasks, conditions, and models of speaking. The basic theme of these final sections is that, surprisingly, tasks themselves can be considered to be disappointing in how they have influenced the performances that they catalyse. On the other hand, much more optimistically, task conditions are seen to be more usable, and to link with psycholinguistic theorising about the nature of second language performance.

Three Articles: What Did They Say? How Did They Evolve?

In 1994–1995, when I wrote the 'Framework' article (Skehan, 1996), I was something like five years into an interest in tasks within second language teaching. I had already started conducting empirical studies in this area (with Pauline Foster as my co-researcher), but what I felt was lacking was some broader account of how tasks in second language research related to the wider theoretical context, on the one hand, and to more direct pedagogic activity, on the other. The overarching aim was to provide a framework, for myself as well as for others, so that one could combat the danger of individual research studies which, while possibly good in themselves, did not fit in easily to a wider context and produce cumulative progress. Important influences, at this stage, were the substantial literature on the Interaction Hypothesis (Long, 1996), the pedagogically oriented publications of David Nunan (1989), the range of interesting studies in the two Crookes and Gass volumes (1993a, 1993b), and analyses of tasks such as those of Graham Crookes (1986) and Chris Candlin (1987).

Regarding theoretical context, the focus of the article, then, was tasks themselves, and I proposed a tripartite contrast between the language needed by a task; the psychological underpinning of the tasks; and the conditions under which the task was done. Language, the first of these, broadly followed Candlin (1987) and it was proposed that tasks which required more complex and varied language (syntax, morphology, lexis) would, other things being equal, be more difficult to do. Conditions, the third in the above contrast, were discussed in a rudimentary way. The focus was only on time pressure (speed of speaking, urgency), modality, scale (the number of participants and the number of relationships involved), the stakes (the importance of being accurate and avoiding mistakes), and control (in this case meaning the negotiability of the task and the scope for the participant to shape or even change the task). This discussion of conditions was largely speculative, although many of these characteristics will be discussed and related to research studies in this book, since they have figured in the subsequent literature.

This leaves the second contrast in the set of three, the task itself and indeed the major thrust was on the ideas that a task revolves around, and how these ideas could be accessed. I made a major distinction (for me, at least) between 'ready-made' solutions to the ideas within a task, and tasks requiring active computation. In the first case the emphasis is on memory, and a capacity to recall relevant material which can be used with little modification. This might simply involve information that is relevant to a task, but it could also involve having done a similar task before, or having solved a particular type of problem before. Occasions where such a response might be possible could be linked to a capacity to draw upon memorised (or exemplar-based) language. Above all, here, there is the possibility that thinking is not under particular pressure, and there can be a focus on performance itself, on the surface of language. In contrast there are tasks which require active thinking or computation when faced with task demands. In such cases the task introduces new material which must be processed, for example when directions have to be given in a map task (where a pair of participants are unable to be looking at the map at the same time, or when some sort of problem has to be solved, as in discussions where the level of punishment has to be agreed for a crime of some sort). Faced with these demands language has to be composed afresh, a degree of unpredictability may be involved, and so the thinking demands are greater.

Framing these discussions in the 1996 article was a view that attentional capacities are limited and that this has important consequences for second language performance. The 'ideal' situation of being able to attend to everything was assumed not to exist, and instead the assumption was that directing attention towards one area, e.g. the thinking required to do a computation-oriented task, might be at the expense of other areas, e.g. the language used to express such thoughts. This general assumption was not developed at that time in any detail to explore exactly how the different dimensions of performance would be influenced by the interaction of task demands and attentional limitations.

Regarding pedagogic activity, the possibilities were discussion of task sequencing; the problem of task selection (and what might constitute a 'good' task); and task implementation. Very little was said about the first of these, task sequencing. Rather, there was an emphasis on the principles that should guide task selection. Most important, in this regard, was the suggestion that there are dangers in using tasks which promote excessive fluency, and that a major goal would have to be to engineer a focus on form. There was also a distinction between restructuring, and a concern for new language and change, and accuracy, with a focus on using a given repertoire without error. So the major concern was the potential to analyse any individual task in these terms, rather than try to decide which tasks were easier than others or should come first or second or whatever in any teaching sequence. But then, even though task conditions and implementation were not extensively discussed theoretically or empirically, it was conditions which figured more prominently in the implementation of these pedagogic principles. It was suggested that things could be done before a task to promote restructuring, to manage actual task-as-process, through task choice and the manipulation of pressure. Then two post-task stages were proposed. The first, associated with post-task activities such as public performance, analysis, and testing, was intended to discourage an over-enthusiastic intention to get a task done at the expense of form. The second post-task approach, also designed to push people to think beyond a task performance in itself, was to embed a task in a wider sequence of related tasks, so that doing one task would have a natural relationship to doing later tasks. Both these stages were intended to promote a focus-on-form, in a general way. They tried to influence how attention worked within a task (to ensure that form was not forgotten), and then to exploit any form that had been noticed within the task by providing opportunities for re-use. Later I co-published (with Gavin Bui, Christina Li, and Zhan Wang) an article titled 'The task is not enough' (a feeble play on the title of a James Bond film current at the time) which tried to convey exactly this idea—something more has to happen in the implementation of task that ensures that form is not forgotten.

It is interesting to reflect on what was not in focus in the 1996 article, given the way the field has developed since. First, there was no real grounding of any claims in relation to a model of second language speaking. Although the distinction between thinking and performing was clearly there, there was no explicit reference to Leveltian stages of Conceptualisation and Formulation, or any detail of psycholinguistic operations with a model of speaking. Nor was there any systematicity in the treatment of task conditions. Some, as we have seen, were mentioned, but there was a random, and certainly non-empirical quality to this section. Recognition, obviously, that how a task is done has importance, but no linkage to any body of work which could illuminate consistencies in performance as a result of such differences. Indeed there was little concern with performance itself. Following Crookes (1989) there was an acceptance that many studies of task-based performance measured complexity, accuracy, and fluency, but these three areas were explored as much through a sense of history and convenience as following theory or educational linkage. Curiously, there was very little discussion of pre-task planning. Although I was involved in planning research at the time, and although planning was mentioned as a pre-task option, it was not developed, and in common with much of the article, there was little connection with research studies. How that situation has changed! And finally, there was no mention of the Cognition Hypothesis. That was still in the future, and so the debates that have taken place since had no traces in this early, 1996 publication.

At the time of the 1996 article, which was intended to be somewhat programmatic regarding research into task-based performance, there was not that much actual research! There were important studies but these tended to be small in number if one does not include the fertile literature on the Interaction Hypothesis. So the article had to try to make the best of things, given the relatively slender empirical foundation. By 2009 this situation had changed markedly, and there was an extensive research literature and many studies available. So the context for the later article was very different, and indeed, the article introduced some different emphases. One important aspect of the context was that the article appeared in a special issue of *Applied Linguistics*, edited by Alex Housen and Folkert Kuiken, with the theme of Complexity, Accuracy, and Fluency in second language task-based performance. So it may seem fairly obvious, therefore, that the article was concerned with CAF. It had to be! The existence of the special issue (and a preceding conference in Brussels [Van Daele, Housen, Kuiken, Pierrard, & Vedder, 2008]), with a CAF focus, indicated that these performance areas had achieved some impact in the research field in their own right. So my contribution to the special issue played a part in this wider goal of exploring why these performance areas were of interest and how they could best be measured. This reflected their widespread (though not universal) use in the task field, with the consequent need to subject them to some scrutiny (and see Chapter 10, at the end of Part II, on empirical work with task measures). It also perhaps reflected the way the three areas were seen as having some independence from one another, as functioning in distinct ways (Tavakoli & Skehan, 2005) such that raised performance in one does not automatically mean that other areas will be raised. Most challenging of all, perhaps is the possibility that there are acquisitional links, following the sequence complexity and initial (hesitant) interlanguage change being followed by greater control, less error, and more accuracy, with this leading later (for any particular language feature) to even more automatised control and greater fluency. Interesting indeed that what was originally a practical response to detecting change in different experimental conditions within task-based research had developed a degree of autonomy and interest in its own terms (Housen, Kuiken, & Vedder, 2012)!

The later article (Skehan, 2009a) did, then, try to capture my viewpoint on CAF, but it also attempted a little more than that. First of all, it extended the conceptualisation of performance to include lexis, in conjunction with Skehan (2009b). Since that time explorations of the lexical aspect of performance have become more common (e.g. in Jarvis and Daller [2013]), but at the time there was little work which included a concern for the words that are used within a task. The article argued that, in addition to the more established measure of lexical diversity (i.e. a corrected type-token ratio, corrected for text length, that is [Malvern & Richards, 2002]), there was also a need to assess lexical sophistication, the capacity to draw upon less frequent words. The empirical data suggests, first of all, that these two measures, lexical diversity and lexical sophistication, frequently do not correlate—they seem to capture different aspects of lexical performance. One can, of course, argue that they are each facets of what might be termed lexical complexity, with this a counterpart to structural complexity, the form of complexity most typically measured in task research. Even so, it has to be said that lexical and structural complexity do not typically correlate either! So we are dealing with an aspect of performance whose functioning is a little unclear. We will return to this in Chapter 10.

Second, the article tried to incorporate, at a fundamental level, the importance of the Levelt model of first language speaking (Levelt, 1999), applied to the second language case (Kormos, 2006). In particular the article tried to bring out how different influences on task-based performance, as indexed by CAF, or rather CALF (complexity, accuracy, *lexis*, and fluency) measures, would be related to the different stages (Conceptualisation, Formulation, Articulation) of the Levelt model. This work was complemented by a parallel chapter (Skehan, 2009c) which tried to organise the different influences on task performance into the more superordinate categories of Complexifying, Easing, Pressuring, and Focussing, and then related these to different stages of the Levelt model. This was the most important theoretical contribution (well, in my view) of the 2009 article. Task-based performance necessarily involves having something worthwhile to say, which implicates Conceptualisation, and then the means to say it, which requires the Formulator and the resources that it draws on. Then, exploring second language learners' response to tasks can be illuminated by focussing on ideas and language resources separately.

The third major change from 1996 was to incorporate discussion of the wider theoretical issues that contrasted my own approach to that of Peter Robinson's Cognition Hypothesis special issue (Robinson, Cadierno, & Shirai, 2009). It gave me an opportunity to refer to my approach as the Limited Attentional Capacity approach. One way or another, prior to this, my approach was often referred to as the Trade-off Hypothesis. I felt that a label such as the Limited Attention

Capacity (LAC) approach was a truer reflection of what I was trying to get at. Trade-off implies a degree of inevitability that if one area is advantaged, then it must be at the expense of another (with this often being interpreted as accuracy pitted against complexity). I think it is more accurate to regard limited attention as functioning as a constraint. The constraint has consequences for performance, but then the purpose of research is to explore how the constraining effects of limited attention can be minimised or even totally combated. The focus of research then becomes the study of the range of different task and condition effects as these relate to CALF. The assumption is that these effects are separate, but that one can draw upon this range of effects to raise different CALF aspects, such as combining planning opportunities (a consistent raiser of complexity) with a structured task (aimed at increasing accuracy). The broad intention is to 'nudge' performance dimensions in desired directions through knowledge of task research effects and in so doing to overcome the constraints of limited attentional capacity. This, of course, contrasts with the Cognition Hypothesis, which proposes a distinction between resource-directing tasks (e.g. through constructs such as time perspective, reasoning operations, number of elements) which are hypothesised to raise complexity and accuracy simultaneously, and resource-dispersing tasks (e.g. characterised through constructs such as planning time, or structure) which impact on performative dimensions of tasks, but which do not have any direct resource-directing impact. Here the two approaches are mentioned to bring out how the landscape had changed between 1996 and 2009. By this latter date, there were (at least) these two characterisations of second language performance (the Cognition Hypothesis and the Limited Attention Capacity approach) which merited discussion, a considerable change relative to the situation in 1996, when the emphasis was on devising a programmatic approach which might stimulate and organise research which could, only later, be the basis for theorising.

There was, in other words, something of gulf between the 1996 and 2009 articles. The final article in this section appeared in a collection of plenaries from the biennial Task-Based Language and Teaching conferences. It is the result of a Point-Counterpoint plenary, with Peter Robinson and myself. The plenary took place in 2009, but the chapter was written for the 2015 publication. As a result, it extends the 2009 article, but in a more general way, rather than a radical development. The ideas emerging in the 2009 article were simply formalised in the first section of 2015. The five principles for the LAC approach are, as we have seen:

- working memory and attention are limited;
- CALF is useful for measurement in research studies and to characterise performance;
- task characteristics and task conditions influence performance separately and in combination;
- the Limited Attentional Capacity approach fits well with the Levelt model if this is extended to cover the second language case;

- task difficulty needs to be approached differently for the Conceptualisation and Formulation stages of the Levelt model in second language speaking.

Essentially, these points simply present, more succinctly, the argument of the 2009 article, and also the discussion in the last page. In addition, one can go beyond these five principles and argue that if one bases claims on the broad trends in research results, task condition studies and research have suggested stronger and more consistent influences on performance than have task characteristic research. This was covered in more detail in Skehan (2016) and is discussed further below. This is an interesting (and perhaps slightly surprising) claim, and a non-obvious generalisation (to me) to emerge from the task literature.

The coverage of the underlying principles of LAC was, though, the first part of the chapter, but since the origin of the work was the Point-Counterpoint discussion from the TBLT Conference, the discussion necessarily moved on to a consideration of the Cognition Hypothesis and how it relates to the Limited Attention approach. Of course, the Cognition Hypothesis has moved on since then, and Robinson now discusses the SSARC model (which contains the Cognition Hypothesis). SSARC (stabilise, simplify, automatise, restructure, complexify) is more wide-ranging and goes beyond the focus on performance that is implicit in the CH, whereas LAC is, really, mostly concerned with performance (albeit with occasional insights regarding acquisition).

LAC and the CH do contrast in several ways. Principally the view of attention is different, in that LAC, as indicated already, assumes important constraints which need to be overcome where possible, while CH sees attention as expandable when resource-directing tasks push second language learners to focus on form, in such a way that accuracy and complexity are both raised. LAC, in contrast, is comfortable with both these performance areas being raised, but sees this as the result of separate task and condition factors which combine to produce this effect. The earlier, reprinted chapter clarifies the detail of this argument from a LAC perspective, as well as my suggestion that proficiency level might be an important variable to bring the two approaches more closely together, in that the consequences of limited attention should be mitigated as proficiency increases. The second language mental lexicon will be more impressive and as a result second language performance will come to resemble first language performance more, enabling speakers to respond to the challenges contained within tasks in more native-like ways. But this is, largely, research which remains to be done.

A point that I will raise here, but which is of general significance, is to ask why second language speakers should be accurate. Although the CH makes interesting predictions in this regard, the empirical research which is available is not particularly supportive of the claim that tasks can be linked to raised accuracy. In fact, and more generally, across the task-based performance literature, I think it could be claimed that accuracy is the most difficult performance area to influence. Planning, for example, that most robust of variables, has less effect on accuracy than it has on any other area, (though perhaps Rod Ellis's 2009 review counters this view slightly). So one can ask, with genuine curiosity, what motivates second language speakers to be more accurate, with this not being as trivial a question as one might think.

The obvious first answer, of course, is that speakers *want* to be accurate, partly because they have been taught that this is an important goal, and partly because individuals will simply want a sense of achievement with one of the most stereotypical aspects of good second language performance. This is undoubtedly an important and general factor, but perhaps more general and vague than precise and effective. Set against this, of course, is some evidence that all learners do not accept this interpretation of what second language development is. The literature has, for example, the well-known case of Richard Schmidt's Wes, whose goals, expressed in terms of the Canale and Swain (1980) framework, emphasised discourse and strategic effectiveness rather than accuracy. So not all speakers may value accuracy as much as teachers (and researchers) do.

This caveat, though, may not have that much importance for the vast majority of second language learners and speakers, although there may nonetheless be variation in how important the goal of accuracy is for most speakers. A more serious impediment to prioritising accuracy is the nature of second language communication itself. If one gives learners a task to do, then task outcome, necessarily, has some importance. The very idea that a task has value and is worth accomplishing may predispose the learner to focus on meaning. In that respect, since the task will be driven by ideas, it seems more natural that goals such as complexity (both structural and lexical) and fluency are important for most learners. If the ideas in the task are not adequately expressed, the task outcome will be unsatisfactory. These goals are unavoidable. But accuracy and error avoidance do not have the same inherent desirability, since inaccurate language can often be perfectly communicative. So once more it is worth asking what factors would, other things being equal, lead to greater accuracy.

Inevitably, from a LAC perspective, one answer has to be adequate attentional capacity for monitoring. As we will see below, the Levelt model has an important role for monitoring, and it seems reasonable to argue that one of the main things that is likely to be monitored is error and accuracy. The model has provision that at certain points in the speech production process the embryonic message can be accessed and modified if appropriate. Here it is assumed that tasks and task conditions which provide easier and less demanding attentional demands will be consistent with more monitoring. Hence tasks based on more familiar information, or containing structure may allow monitoring to take place when otherwise it wouldn't. So notwithstanding any pressure to simply get a task done, lower attentional demands may enable more monitoring and therefore greater accuracy.

A different influence on accuracy might come from what could be termed 'directed attention', although such a phrase seems to me to overstate the claim that is being made, and perhaps something like 'nudged attention' would be fairer!

A series of studies are relevant here. Skehan and Foster (1997), Foster and Skehan (2013), and Li (2014) all used a post-task condition in an attempt to induce anticipation by the second language speaker of the post-task to come. The intention in doing this is to push the speaker while doing the actual task to pay more attention to avoiding error, and thereby increase accuracy. Skehan and Foster (1997) used the 'threat' of a public performance of the same task that was done in what could be termed 'pairwork privacy', and demonstrated that this produced a significant accuracy effect, but only for a decision-making task (and not for a personal information exchange task or a narrative, though the results, arithmetically, were in the predicted direction). Foster and Skehan (2013) and Li (2014), following suggestions by Lynch (2007) operationalised the post-task condition as the need to transcribe some of one's own performance. This produced significant accuracy results for each task used (a decision-making and a narrative task with also a complexity effect for the decision-making task). There was nothing about any of the tasks here, or any other conditions which caused attention to be augmented or supported. What seemed to happen is that, within existing attentional resources, the awareness, the anticipation of the post-task led the speakers to direct more attention to monitoring the surface of their performance so that there was less error. It seems, in other words, as if performance priorities can be 'nudged' to some degree, and the performance area which is normally the most difficult to influence, accuracy, can be enhanced in this way.

The final influence specifically on accuracy has to be the task itself. We have seen already that tasks which do not make excessive attentional demands are associated with greater accuracy. But in addition to that, there is the possibility that greater accuracy may be integrally important for some tasks. The Cognition Hypothesis certainly argues for this, suggesting that task complexity pushes second language speakers to boost attention and respond to the task complexity by focussing on form and raising structural complexity and accuracy. Similarly, Ellis (2005b) advocates the use of tasks where language itself is the focus of the task as in Ellis, Tanaka, and Yamazaki (1994), with, in this case, a focus on lexis. Finally interactive tasks may push learners to be more accurate, because awareness of the interlocutor may push the speaker to be more listener-aware, and consequently try to avoid error as a means of achieving greater precision.

In an optimistic frame of mind, I would want to believe all of these 'nudges' towards accuracy are effective. Unfortunately, the evidence is not entirely supportive! For example, a meta-analysis of Cognition Hypothesis studies (Jackson & Suethanapornkul, 2013) reported only a small accuracy effect in general (and of course, following arguments earlier, there may be task-condition-linked interpretations of these effects). The language-related tasks that Ellis reports provide stronger evidence, but there is the disadvantage that such tasks are not the most typical of all tasks, and might be considered to be only on the borders of 'taskiness'. Finally, the evidence for interaction tasks promoting accuracy is patchy. Some studies are supportive, and perhaps one can offer the generalisation that these are tasks which require greatest engagement. But interactive tasks, generally, are variable in their effects on accuracy.

Possibly the analyses here have to be extended to go beyond broad characterisations of task complexity and to explore particular characteristics which specifically lead to a push for precision where accuracy contributes to that precision. At present we have not devised the research designs to bring this out. For now, the earlier discussed possibilities (lower attentional demands, familiar information, and directed attention) seem a better bet for raising accuracy.

The Basics of Second Language Speech

Now that the three reprinted chapters have been covered and commented upon, it becomes possible to see where these publications have taken us, and how one might effectively theorise second language task-based performance. Prior to that, though, an offstage presence needs to come centre stage to provide a framework for the discussion which follows. This is, of course, the Levelt model of first language speaking (Levelt, 1989, 1999).

At a basic level the model proposes three broad stages in first language speech:

- Conceptualisation
    - Developing the ideas to be expressed.
- Formulation
    - Accessing lemmas in the mental lexicon;
    - Using the information in these lemmas to build syntax, morphology, and phonological foundations.
- Articulation

The model targets the first language case, and so it is expedient to start by exploring its functioning in first language speech, when things are going well. Ideas are developed and then the ideas may be related to the current context of speech for packaging for appropriateness (e.g. saying enough, but not saying too much; taking account of what interlocutors already know), as well as stance to the other speakers, with all this leading to the development of the pre-verbal message. This is what feeds into the Formulator which then builds the utterances which will be produced, through lemma retrieval and through rich information extraction from the lemmas that are retrieved (information which may not be just syntactic, but also morphological and phonological as well as collocational, discoursal, and so on). It is the lemma-based information which drives the Formulator's work in building syntactic frames. The Formulator then outputs a schema which is ready for conversion to speech through the operation of the Articulator, since this phase has the phonological equipment to produce connected sound.

Monitoring of these processes takes place and enables modification at certain well-defined points.

When things are going well the three stages operate in parallel, in a modular fashion. That is to say, the Conceptualiser 'delivers' its pre-verbal message and the Formulator gets on with its task while simultaneously the Conceptualiser is embarking on the next set of challenges to produce another pre-verbal message. The Articulator also gets on with its task, dealing with the output of the Formulator, while the Formulator, in turn, gets on with the latest 'arrival' from the Conceptualiser. In this way, while time passes, action and output do not get hung up, and so a fairly continuous flow of speech results. In the first language case, this is possible because each component in the system, most of the time, makes 'reasonable' demands on the other components, and so each functions modularly and efficiently. Fundamental to this is that the Formulator, when dealing with the pre-verbal message, accesses mental lexicon resources which are fit for purpose (usually). The mental lexicon is extensive, well-organised, and rich. As a result, the information associated with each lemma is quickly and comprehensively accessible, and so syntax and general utterance building can proceed, seemingly effortlessly (and below the level of consciousness). This is even possible when input demands are high and the quantity of input that has to be processed, for example, from other speakers, is high, and even when the pressure of speech is also great. The mental lexicon is impressive and underpins this rapid and efficient communication system. Of course, this does not always work perfectly. Considerable thinking demands can cause problems and need to be solved before fluent communication is resumed. Similarly, there may be gaps in the mental lexicon which require some attention. It can also be the case that monitoring requires changes when a message is reformulated while speaking. Then also there may be feedback, verbal and non-verbal, from an interlocutor, which requires modification. But most of the time, somewhat amazingly, this system operates seemingly effortlessly and effectively and in real time.

The situation with the second language speaker is interestingly different. The heart of the difference is the less advanced state of the *second* language mental lexicon. Ideas may be generated and manipulated equally well, but the demands they place on the second language mental lexicon can be, and often are, excessive. The second language mental lexicon (SLML) is:

- smaller, with the result that there are no lemmas at all in some or many areas;
- less rich, so that the range of syntactic, morphological, discoursal, collocational information is not available even if a lemma is present in some form;
- less extensive, so that the multiple meanings of words are less likely to be available;
- less organised, so that connections and associations between lemmas are less available, and priming opportunities are reduced;
- less accessible, and likely slower, so that more effort is required to dig out the information that is contained in particular lemmas.

Effective and natural communication, as with native speakers, presupposes good balance between the different stages (Conceptualisation, Formulation, Articulation). In this case there is what might be termed component balance. The Conceptualiser makes demands of the Formulator, but because of the quality of the first language mental lexicon, these demands are reasonable, and are met. As we move to the second language case, the relationship between Conceptualiser and Formulator changes. In this case it may well be that the Conceptualiser makes demands which exceed what the Formulator can deliver in time for a normal rate of fluency. Beyond that, it may now be necessary for the Conceptualiser to consider, in addition to its normal tasks, what the implications are for the second language mental lexicon of the demands that are being made. In other words, the Conceptualiser may have to develop 'foresight' skills to anticipate problems 'downstream' as it were, thus adding to the attentional demands placed upon the system. All of this is the consequence of the smaller, less rich, less organised, and less accessible mental lexicon which is unable to access lexical material and build syntactic frames in the way ongoing communication presupposes.

A considerable strength of the Levelt model is that it proposes modularity as a basic principle of operation. In other words, the different stages are encapsulated and proceed fairly independently of one another. This is what enables a parallel mode of processing in that Conceptualiser, Formulator and Articulator can be working simultaneously, but on different phases of the message that is being conveyed. The analysis that has just been presented, bringing out the contrast between first and second language speaking, makes it clear that successful modularity and parallel processing can come under threat in the second language case (often) and the first language case (occasionally). This happens when a particular stage, most often the Formulator, encounters difficulty, and has to solve a problem of some sort, needing to retrieve rich lemma information more slowly, or to compensate in some way for the non-existence of a particular lemma and information which might have been stored in a lemma (and would be in one's first language) but isn't. In these cases, the below-consciousness functioning of the Formulator is disrupted, and more conscious attentional focus is required. Worse, these attentional demands may have consequences which spill over to the other stages of speech production to the extent that the parallel processing which is the desirable norm cannot be sustained. As a result, a more serial mode of processing has to be resorted to. Similar consequences would follow if the Articulator encountered difficulty because of the lack of resources to access phonological material. In this case, one stage of speech processing consumes all attentional resources, so that the other stages, effectively, have to stop until the difficulties are overcome. Then the speaker has the challenging task of rediscovering the thread of speech.

The Levelt model, of course, has been well covered in the second language performance literature, notably by Kormos (2006), and so one might wonder why so much space has been devoted to it here. The reason is that it provides a very helpful clarifying framework which enables deeper understanding of second language task-based performance, of the variables which have proved effective, and those that have not. The essential principles are:

- promoting effective Conceptualiser-Formulator balance is the key;
- this leads to the important corollary: one needs to explore what factors enhance C-F balance and what factors create difficulties.

These simple points are remarkably productive in synthesising quite a lot of existing task research. To illustrate this, and make the discussion less abstract, a capsule study is very clarifying.

Wang (2014): Strategic and On-Line Planning in Task-Based Narrative Retellings

Wang (2014) explored the separate and joint functioning of strategic (i.e. pre-task) and on-line planning, as these have an influence on video-based narrative retellings (of Mr. Bean stories). She wanted to develop insights from Ellis and Yuan (2005) that on-line planning, i.e. the planning that can take place during performance when there are less pressured processing conditions, can selectively advantage accuracy, in contrast to the range of studies of strategic planning which consistently show advantages for complexity and fluency. In addition, she wanted to use a tighter operationalisation of the on-line planning condition itself than had been the case in the Ellis and Yuan studies. To that end she used slowed vs. normal speed videos of Mr. Bean to control more carefully exactly how much time was available in the on-line condition. (This is what had not been carefully controlled in the Ellis-Yuan studies.) When she did this she found that the on-line condition in her study was not associated with an increase in accuracy. However, when the on-line condition was preceded by a strategic planning condition, accuracy was raised, and indeed, the two conditions seemed to operate synergistically. This leads to the conclusion that what is necessary for higher-level performance is not simply more time to plan on-line, but also the opportunity to prepare for the ideas and the actual performance through strategic planning.

If we relate these results to the discussion of Levelt presented earlier, the interpretation is clear. The key issue is Conceptualiser-Formulator balance, and in Wang (2014) we seem to have conditions which have promoted that. The strategic planning has supported Conceptualiser use (and as a result there is raised complexity of language) while the on-line planning was helpful for Formulator use (and so accuracy was raised). What becomes interesting then is to see that in the condition where strategic planning only was available, complexity was raised, thus advantaging the Conceptualiser, while in the on-line only condition, no raising of performance occurred. In this case it seems as if the more generous time conditions for speaking did not facilitate greater accuracy: for that to occur the conjoint influence of things to say (Conceptualiser work following from strategic planning) and time to say those things (Formulator work following from on-line planning) was needed. The strategic planning provided the input, and then the less pressured time conditions enabled more effective monitoring also, so that not only was second language mental lexicon access more easily handled, but in addition there was enough spare capacity for scrutiny of the potential output and some degree of modification of that output. After all, in the first language case, monitoring is concerned largely with the appropriateness of what is being said. In the second language case, such considerations are still operative, but in addition there is a need to monitor for error, for syntax, for morphology, for lexical choice, and so on.

The point of the capsule study is that it nicely illustrates how an account of a task-based study, through the framing of the Levelt model, makes sense and is illuminating. What I move on to do now is to discuss a range of task findings in the same light: exploring how the different stages of speech production are relevant to the interpretation of results, and how the ideal goal of good Conceptualiser-Formulator balance might be promoted or might be impeded. The underlying theme is that analysis of task variables through speaking stages and an exploration of implications that they might have for Conceptualiser-Formulator balance can be surprisingly helpful. The areas to be covered are planning and repetition; and selective attention (though it should be said that planning is covered much more extensively in Chapter 9).

Planning: The scene-setting capsule study has taken us some distance here, but at the same time there is quite a lot more to say. First it is important to broaden the concept of planning and to think more in terms of readiness (Bui, 2014) or preparedness (Skehan, 2014a). As Skehan (2014a) argues, planning is a subset of a number of things which put the speaker in a position to communicate more effectively, and these include using time to plan about something new (and this is, of course, the most common implementation of planning in the literature); or talking about something which relates to one's personal experience, or from one's life, including educational experience; or speaking about something which has been spoken about before, or which someone else has spoken about before. All of these prepare the speaker, to some degree, and so while the typical planning study, which provides X minutes (usually 10) of planning time constitutes one interpretation of preparedness, there are others, and merely to list them in this way clarifies how much more research can be done in this domain.

Relating these different forms of preparedness to the stages of speaking is worthwhile. Drawing on one's previous experiences clearly gives the Conceptualiser an easier task to perform. The ideas are familiar and are organised, and so the communicational challenge is concerned with selection and presentation. In addition, if it is the case that the same material has been spoken about before, then Formulation is likely to be eased also, since relevant lemmas are more likely to be familiar and to have been retrieved in the past. These forms of preparedness contrast with the typical way preparedness is operationalised, which takes something new, such as a decision-making problem or a narrative retelling, and gives the speaker time in order to prepare. There is time to get ready, but the task itself may have little connection to the personal experience of participants. Given these circumstances, Ellis (2005b) clarified the ways that second language speakers might use this time. There might be a focus on the content of the task, on the ideas and on their organisation as participants try to mobilise ideas for this new conversational challenge. In this case, the emphasis is on Conceptualiser operations. But there may also be rehearsal, as speakers try to anticipate the language that will be required in the task and try to foreground that language. Here they will be relying on guesswork, since they may not have spoken on this topic before. So when pre-task planning of this sort is focussed on, it does seem to present a very particular challenge.

Additional insights regarding planning behaviour come from more recent research. Pang and Skehan (2014), following Ortega's (1999, 2005) qualitative research on planning, gathered retrospective think-aloud data on second language speakers (L1 Putonghua or Cantonese) who had had planning opportunities before completing narrative, picture-story tasks. They were able to show that the sorts of behaviours reported by the participants fell neatly into an analysis system which conformed with the Leveltian stages. But in addition, they related the retrospective data to actual performance. The planning was the typical research design approach: 10 minutes, accompanied by notes which were taken away prior to the actual performance. Several unanticipated findings emerged. Foremost amongst these was the issue of memory. Planning at a considerable level of detail, and engaging in extensive rehearsing, was counter-productive. The problem was that speakers simply did not remember the detail of their preparation. Memory for what was planned, in other words, emerged as a very important factor. Interestingly, focussing on the larger picture, and avoiding detail, in other words, being more concerned with ideas, were self-reported planning behaviours which more clearly connected with elevated performance.

However there is a fine line for planners here. Planning over-ambitiously was associated with lower performance on the task itself, and it seemed that an important metacognitive aspect of planning concerned the speaker's self-knowledge and capacity to take on realistic planning challenges, given their level of ability. Those who were unrealistic then produced impaired performances. The conclusion seems to be that while planning is a favourable influence on performance, and one of the successes of the research literature, with important implications for pedagogy, it is, for all that, two-edged. There are circumstances when it can go wrong and make things worse. Insight into this possibility can go a long way, perhaps through the training of planning, to avoiding this pitfall. For now, though, it has to slightly temper the general clean bill of health that planning has.

The beginning of this discussion of planning was at pains to point out the wider concept of preparedness, of which planning is a particular example. Another example of preparedness is exemplified by task repetition, where here, obviously, the focus is on the second, repeated performance. The first performance acts as a particular type of rehearsal for the second, and so when the repeated performance is required, the residue of the first performance can be drawn on. Wang (2009, 2014) showed that an immediate repetition condition was associated with higher complexity and accuracy in performance, at high significance levels and with large effect sizes.

So an effective method of 'preparation' is to do the same thing again. Recall that in Pang and Skehan (2014), planning as rehearsal was vulnerable to memory problems: the rehearsal may have taken place during the planning period, but it was not necessarily retained for the actual performance. Bear in mind that this form of planning activity essentially aims at Formulator operations. The purpose of the rehearsal planning is to ease access to the second language mental lexicon while the task is under way later so that lemma retrieval is easier, and lemma information can, more readily, be used to build actual utterances. In theory, strategic planning should be able to achieve this, but we have seen that it is vulnerable to memory effects. Much happens during the planning period, and not all of this is available for later use. Fading and interference may compromise retention. This functions as the first limitation of planning.

But there is a second and this is illuminated by processes involved in repetition. Strategic planning can be used to anticipate relevant information and prime it, to some degree (Foster & Skehan, 1996a). But it may well be the case that this form of rehearsing linguistic elements is superficial, and possibly satisfied with a relatively shallow level of retrieval. The broad phonological shape of the lemma may be all that is retrieved, without the additional information that is potentially retrievable and which is necessary when language is actually going to be built. In contrast, when we have an original performance followed by a repeated performance, the first performance is likely to confront the speaker with the need to access a lemma in a deeper manner, as its implications for syntax building, for example, also become important. This activity may, of course, be successful, so that the more deeply processed information becomes available for the repeated performance. But it may also only be partially successful, in that lemma retrieval processes take place but the speed of communication prevents what might only be partially retrieved lemma information (e.g. syntactic information about word order, or collocational information) from being acted upon. But there are traces of this partial retrieval; these may be in a greater stage of activation in the repeated performance. Then the preparatory work, with its potential, can be realised more effectively. Planning may cause some priming to occur, but this may not be put to the test of actual use. Repetition creates the circumstance where the deeper priming that has occurred because of actual use can be exploited. The key is that there is greater depth (and therefore greater memorability) of activation that takes place during the first performance.

To sum up, these analyses of planning, filtered as they have been through the speaking stages outlined in the Levelt model, provide a slightly different perspective on the effects of planning.

- the analysis provides a different perspective on the way planning may be directed at Conceptualiser or Formulator operations, leading to differences in the impact on subsequent task performance;
- there can be differences in the depth of retrieval of material and greater depth will be helpful during subsequent performance. Strategic planning may lead to shallower rehearsal which is vulnerable to retention problems, while a first performance as the method of preparation may lead to deeper engagement with lemma material which has greater potential use in later performance;
- the ideal situation is to produce situations where Conceptualiser and Formulator are both involved—things to say and then supportive conditions for saying them—and this may require the use of both strategic and on-line planning.

A much broader discussion of planning is provided in Chapter 9.

Task Structure: As with planning, but with a smaller research literature, there have been a number of studies of the impact of task structure on second language task performance, generally using the more easily manipulable narrative tasks. For the present, and following Tavakoli and Skehan (2005), structure is considered to be analysable into a fairly loose scale, perhaps starting with tasks which have a beginning-middle-end structure, then tasks where there are causal links between the different steps in a narrative account, and finishing with tasks which have a tight and complete discourse structure, most often operationalised through the Winter-Hoey problem-solution structure (with the optional Situation and Evaluation components at the beginning and the end, and with the possibility that the problem-solution heart of a story may have some recursion). In general, tasks with tight problem-solution structure have been associated with higher accuracy and mostly with higher fluency, as demonstrated in Skehan and Foster (1999), Tavakoli and Skehan (2005), Tavakoli and Foster (2008), and Skehan and Shum (2014). In addition, Tavakoli and Skehan (2005) reported increased structural complexity with a more structured task, a finding confirmed in Tavakoli and Foster (2008).

Obviously the key question here is the interpretation of these findings, and, given the thrust of the discussion, how they relate to the Levelt model. Skehan (2014a) offers three parts to such an interpretation. First, there is the issue that tightly structured tasks have the considerable virtue, from the speaker's perspective, that they provide an inherent macrostructure for the broader task. The different features within the task have a clearer relationship to the whole. The speaker may, for example, be handling the problem component, but this can be done in the awareness that there has been some scene-setting (the Situation component) and that there will be a proposed solution to the problem (and the possibility that this will be followed by an Evaluation). So current utterances fit in to a clearer view of this wider structure. As a result, the speaker requires less attention to keep track of where they are in the broader scheme of things, and the general shape of what they will have to say next. In turn, this means that they can allocate more attention to the surface of the language that they are expressing at any one moment, and perhaps because of that, achieve greater accuracy and fluency. In Leveltian terms, we have a situation in which Conceptualiser and Formulator have some degree of harmony, and can function together more easily in parallel fashion.

Second, if a task has structure, then it follows that the inter-connections of the different components of, say, a narrative, need to be described effectively if the narrative is to be done effectively. This is a case where task design itself impacts upon language. Problem-solution structure implies causal relationships between the different components of the task. Language, and this means structural complexity, has to respond to the challenge of expressing such relationships. This is, essentially, a resource-directing interpretation (though interestingly structure is categorised as a resource-dispersing factor in the Cognition Hypothesis). In relation to Levelt, the issue is that Conceptualisation is brought into prominence since what is involved is the relationship between the ideas and elements within the task. Resource-direction and Conceptualisation work together here.

Third, recall the importance attached to the contrast between parallel (the desired norm) and serial processing. In a perfect world, parallel processing (and effective modularity of the stages of speech production) would be maintained throughout communication. But when a problem is encountered, there is the need, first of all, to solve that problem, and then to get parallel processing back on track. In the first language case, problem-solving is generally so quick, and spare attentional capacity available, that this is not much of a challenge. In the second language case, one can imagine that Formulator or Articulator problems have caused the desired communication flow to break down, and so the content of other stages, principally Conceptualisation, is lost. Then, recovering the flow that might sustain parallel processing is much more difficult. In other words, one might consider the 'recoverability potential' of different tasks. If something goes wrong, how difficult is it to retrieve the situation? With structured tasks we have some basis for believing that recoverability is, at least to some degree, facilitated. A structured task will have a number of sub-sections, and so even if there are problems along the way, and a halting serial mode is used to get from the point of breakdown to the next sub-section starting, there is then the opportunity to 'kick start' parallel processing again. In addition, it is likely that along the way the speaker is less likely to be lost, and unable to find a sense of direction in the task. The existence of structure, in other words, is a very helpful crutch for the second language speaker to retrieve dynamism and flow in what is being said.

As with the section on planning, it is useful to recap how the different aspects of structure link with a Leveltian interpretation of second language performance.

- Structure and Conceptualisation
    - Structure allows larger units of thinking to proceed and then be organised and reorganised;
    - Structure allows delegation of thinking to particular sections of an overall plan.
- Structure and Formulation
    - Structure allows the speaker to concentrate on the details of the surface of language, sure the reconnections with the larger plan can occur;
    - Structure releases some attention since less attention has to be devoted to tracking the larger discourse;
    - Structure enables recovery if there are problems so that Formulator activity can regain flow;
- Most generally, Structure supports an effective Conceptualiser-Formulator balance.

Selective attention and performance: Although covered earlier, brief mention is justified of the selective attention studies. A danger with task-based approaches to developing second language ability is that tasks, if they are engaging, might induce second language speakers to get a task done, and prioritise this over other performance goals. We saw also the possibility that accuracy, in a task-based context, might be more difficult to attain as a goal than complexity or fluency. So the point of the 'anticipation' studies was to explore whether, in the consciousness of a learner doing a task, foreknowledge of a post-task to come might change the way the task itself was completed. Anticipation of the post-task is intended to nudge the speaker into realising that the task is not an end in itself, but might connect with wider performance goals. As we saw, the predictions that motivated the various studies (Skehan & Foster, 1997; Foster & Skehan, 2013; Li, 2014) were broadly supportive, but perhaps with the caveat that anticipation of a post-task activity orients learners towards form most of all specifically with decision-making (interactive) tasks. The most interesting aspect of these studies is that speakers were induced to devote attention to avoiding error and achieving higher accuracy simply through the knowledge of what would come. They were not given instructions to be more accurate—it was their own response to the experimental conditions which seemed to bring about a different prioritisation of performance dimensions. Once again it is appropriate to relate these findings to the Leveltian account of speaking. Noteworthy in this respect is that the focus is no longer on any of the stages of speaking, but rather the ancillary process of monitoring.

- Anticipation of a post-task in which the form of the language used may be important can induce second language speakers to allocate more attention to avoiding error and achieving higher accuracy;
- Anticipation may also lead, under favourable circumstances, to greater Conceptualisation work;
- The greater monitoring that takes place may have implications for fluency, lowering it slightly.

Conclusions

The point of this section on second language speech, following Kormos (2006, 2011) and De Bot (1992) has been to try to make the case that a Leveltian analysis of first language speaking is relevant for second language speaking. The challenge is to explore what the consequences are for this extension when we consider the differences between first and second language speech. Central to this is the vastly different mental lexicon in each case. The much richer first language mental lexicon has the scale, organisation, and speed to respond to the sorts of demands the Conceptualiser makes. The second language mental lexicon does not have these riches, and this has considerable impact on how well the Formulator can function (and how the Conceptualiser has to anticipate these deficiencies). The result is that the parallel processing typical of the first language case does not transfer to second language speaking, where a serial mode of communication (with all attentional resources needed by the Formulator) is more common. Part of the communication challenge then becomes recovering this parallel mode of speaking.

We have brought out these claims through brief surveys of research into planning and repetition; task structure; and post-task influences on selective attention. The planning research brings out (cf. the capsule study [Wang, 2014]) the importance of Conceptualiser-Formulator balance, with other planning research showing how this can be derailed. The linked area of repetition research demonstrates more clearly the intricacies of Formulator operations, and the centrality of lemma retrieval processes. Task structure, too, illuminates the importance of Conceptualiser-Formulator balance and also the particular importance, for the second language speaker, of recovering from communicational mishaps. Then, finally, the role of selective attention is linked to the priority second language speakers may attach to monitoring.

But these different areas were chosen for discussion because they are particularly relevant in illustrating the relevance of a Leveltian approach. Although each has been associated with considerable research, especially the area of planning, they cannot be regarded as comprehensive, or even representative. For that reason, the rest of this section will try to broaden the coverage of task-related research, first by considering tasks themselves, and then by trying to systematise the influences on second language task performance.

An Analysis of Tasks

The 1996 article, as indicated earlier, focussed primarily on tasks and task qualities, but then in 2009 the focus switched more to performance and the psycholinguistics of second language speaking, a switch whose emphasis was maintained in the 2015 publication, and indeed the discussion in this Postscript so far. We need to redress this emphasis and return next to tasks themselves. To do so I will, first of all, draw on my contribution to the 2016 *Annual Review of Applied Linguistics* special issue on task-based approaches to instruction. That publication started with a table, reproduced here as Table 5.1. The table is closely based on the work of Shoko Sasayama (2015, 2016). What she did, very instructively, is compare

TABLE 5.1 Studies Researching Performance Effects of Number of Elements and Planning

No. of Elements	Comp	Acc	Lexis	Fluen.	Planning	Comp.	Acc.	Lexis	Fluen.
Robinson, 2001b	'='	'='	+	−	Foster & Skehan, 1996a	+	+	X	+
Gilabert, 2007b	X	'='	X	X	Foster & Skehan, 1996a	+	=	X	+
Kuiken & Vedder, 2007/2008a	'='	+	'='	X	Ortega, 1999	+	+/−	X	+
Michel et al., 2007b	'='	+	+	−	Iwashita, McNamara, & Elder, 2001	'='	'='	X	'='
Révész, 2011	−	+	+	X	Yuan & Ellis, 2003	+	'='	'='	+
Sasayama, 2011	+	'='	X	X	Ellis & Yuan, 2004	+	'='	'='	+
Sasayama et al., 2012	'='		'='		Mochizuki & Ortega, 2008	+	'='	X	'='
Michel, 2011	'='	'='	+	'='	Mochizuki & Ortega, 2008	+	+	X	=
Levkina, Gilabert, 2012	'='	'='	+	−	Tavares, 2009	'='	+	X	+
Michel, 2013	'='	'='	'='	'='	Farahani and Meraji, 2011	+	'='	'='	+
					Meraji, 2011	+	+	'='	+
					Mohammadzadeh, Dabaghi, & Tavakoli, 2013	'='	+	X	=

Comp. = Structural complexity; Acc. = Accuracy; Fluen. = Fluency.

'+' indicates a positive influence; '−' indicates a negative influence; '=' indicates no difference; 'X' indicates that the dependent variable was not studied.

one example of a task feature, in this case the number of elements in a task, and one example of a conditions feature, in this case planning. As it happens, the task feature, number of elements, plays an important role in the Cognition Hypothesis as a resource-directing variable, while planning has been extensively studied with the Limited Attention Capacity framework and, as it happens, is labelled as a resource-dispersing feature in the Cognition Hypothesis. Sasayama then located studies under each heading and explored what impact could be shown, from each study, on the different areas of structural complexity, accuracy, lexis, and fluency. In this way she wanted to see the comparative degree of consistency the two examples, number of elements and planning, had shown in the literature.

Obviously, these two examples, of a task characteristic and a task condition, cannot be regarded as representative or definitive. But they do have some importance, and could reasonably be regarded as the task characteristic and task condition that have been most researched.

The major contrast here is consistency of findings. Looking through the performance effects in Table 5.1, on the left side, structural complexity does not seem to be affected by number of elements. The same is mostly the case (in six studies) for accuracy, although there are three studies which report a positive effect (and one negative). Things are more positive with lexis (five positive studies), with two showing no effect, and none a negative influence. Fluency does show some consistency with four negative effects. So, rather curiously the clearest effects are with lexis (positive) and fluency (negative), rather than the two central aspects of form, complexity and accuracy. With planning, there is slightly greater clarity. Structural complexity shows effects in nine studies, no effect in three, and no negative effects. Accuracy has five positive effects and six 'no effects'. Lexis, only represented in four studies, is unaffected in each. Finally fluency is positively influenced in eight studies and not affected in four, with no negative effects. It seems to be the case that the task variable of number of elements has little overall effect on structural complexity and accuracy, and some positive effect on lexis (lexical diversity, usually) and a negative effect on fluency. In contrast, planning has a very solid positive influence on structural complexity and fluency, a fairly positive effect on accuracy (and see Ellis's 2009 review on this), and no effect on lexis.

These are the results from this particular contrast, a task feature, number of elements and a conditions variable, planning, and the specific studies shown in the table. But what I want to do is explore whether there is something more general here, and that what we need to do is consider the possibility that it is not this particular comparison that is the issue but that tasks *generally* may often show such mixed and rather underwhelming results, and conditions similarly produce influences on performance with greater dependability.

As a starting point for this discussion, Loschky and Bley-Vroman (1993), in what one might now consider to be the early days of an interest in tasks, made a clear linkage between tasks and particular language structures. They offered a tripartite analysis of tasks, in which the relation between a task and a particular structure was:

- *natural*: in this case it was perfectly normal for a particular structure to be used with a particular task—there was no shoehorning of the structure—as when a conditional structure might be used when giving advice;
- *useful*: in this case there is a particular usefulness about using a particular structure, as when one uses modality to indicate degrees of probability or possibility (may, might) rather than what might be considered more cumbersome expressions (it is possible that);
- *essential*: in the final case the task makes the use of a target structure unavoidable. Loschky and Bley-Vroman (1993) provide the example of the use of reflexive pronouns in an 'essential' task.

Loschky and Bley-Vroman (1993) were wrestling with one of the basic issues in task-based approaches. Tasks, fundamentally, prioritise meaning, but at the same time course designers and teachers are keen to be providing instruction that is systematic and which covers what they think needs to be acquired. The tension between using tasks within instruction which meet qualities of 'taskiness' but which also achieve other pedagogic goals is still with us. The discussion, for example, of resource-directing tasks, or claims that certain task qualities lead to the salience of particular aspects of language (e.g. structure and fluency) are simply more contemporary versions of the same thing. So the problem that has to be engaged with is the relationship between the task and the language which is used, and correspondingly, the predictability of that language use, whether that language use is the need for the present perfect specifically, or the relevance of discourse markers, or simply structural or lexical complexity in general.

The generalisations which emerge from the number-of-elements studies in Table 5.1 speak to this point. The basic premise is that tasks may be worthwhile to do, challenging for learners, and stimulating for the capacity to use language, a whole range of good things. But they do not necessarily work in the way that designers or researchers intend, as the number-of-elements studies shown in Table 5.1 make clear. It is important to give some attention to why this might be so, and what different reasons may be involved.

A central problem is that if tasks are engaging and interesting things to do, second language speakers may find ways of doing them which are unanticipated. Dave Willis gave the example of a task designed to provoke the use of the conditional form, where participants were supposedly nudged to use the frame 'If I were you, I would visit X', given the prompt of travel advice to a visitor to one's own country. The outcome, despite the neatly worked out prompt, was different than what was anticipated. Speakers tended not to use conditional forms. If they did gravitate towards a particular form, it was to use the present tense! They tended to say things like: 'When I'm in X, I always go Y'. This seemed to function as a statement of fact, which the listener might or might not act upon. It was as though the use of a conditional form might function in a rather condescending way, and speakers preferred to avoid overt advice, and instead laid out possibilities which the listener could then act upon, or not, as they saw fit.

In a sense a sociocultural critique of tasks extends these points. In this view it is not simply the individual speaker who reinterprets the communication situation, as in the Willis example. Rather a pair, engaged in dialogue, will take the interaction in unforeseen directions. Coughlan and Duff (1994) and Markee and Kunitz (2013) have argued clearly along these lines, and suggested that it is a delusion to expect second language learners doing tasks to do what is expected of them. Instead they will spark ideas off one another and the ideas will flow in whatever way seems natural at the time (even wandering away from the goals of the task as set). In this viewpoint, it is hardly surprising that tasks do not work out exactly as intended—the familiar contrast, in other words, between task-as-workplan and task-as-process. The example above on using conditionals brings out the perils of what might be called 'structure trapping', and the sociocultural critique makes us even more aware of the dangers of trying to do so.

So we need to recognise that the belief that tasks might trigger the use of fairly specific language (conditionals, modality, etc.) may be overly optimistic. Both the LAC approach and the Cognition Hypothesis make links between task features and *broader* increases in CALF, where the different dimensions are assessed through generalised measures (although proponents of the Cognition Hypothesis have also made attempts to predict raised performance with specific measures, too). Predicting broader performance areas may be more realistic, and indeed there are successes. For example:

- tasks based on familiar information tend to raise accuracy and fluency;
- tasks linking background and foreground information tend to raise structural complexity;
- tasks based on there-and-then conditions tend to raise accuracy slightly, though not complexity;
- structured tasks tend to raise accuracy, as we have seen, and sometimes also complexity and fluency.

But there are also many examples where tasks, although hypothesised to impact on performance levels, do not do so, as in the meta-analysis of the Cognition Hypothesis studies which suggested that resource-directing variables do raise accuracy, but only very slightly, whereas the results for complexity and fluency are not supportive of the predictions made (Jackson & Suethanapornkul, 2013).

As a consequence of these results, it is worth probing why tasks are not dependable influences on performance, even when this is assessed through generalised CALF measures. In that respect, the study by Shoko Sasayama, mentioned earlier, has more to contribute. Earlier Table 5.1 showed the patterns of results comparing research studies exploring number of elements (NoE) and studies involving planning. Focussing on the number-of-elements studies, we saw inconsistency in the results obtained, and this, of course, leads to the question as to why this might be. In fact, Sasayama's own research probed this very point. Most NoE studies compare conditions with only one or two elements with conditions with larger numbers of elements. Many studies have comparison between just two experimental groups, such as two elements and four. Sasayama wanted to explore whether varying the number of elements systematically would lead to a clearer and more meaningful relationship and so she, with a picture narrative retelling tasks, had four levels, with respectively two, three, six, and nine elements. In this way she could hypothesise that task complexity should increase as a function of number of elements and that this should have an impact upon the complexity (and accuracy) of the language produced. The study did not, in fact, show clear relationships between the different levels and the performance measures. There was, though, a trend, but only if one compared the fewest and the most elements conditions, i.e. two and nine.

A very interesting feature is that, in addition to the straightforward quantitative research, Sasayama (2015) also gathered qualitative data, asking participants about their reactions to the different tasks. Recalling that the picture series used had one, two, four, and nine characters respectively, and that there was a clear contrast between the two- and nine-participant conditions, what Sasayama found was considerable variation in participants' reaction to the different picture series. In addition to the problem posed by the number of participants, there were other issues that caused difficulty. First of all, while there may be a trend for more participants to generate less obvious storylines, that relationship is not totally predictable. The four-participant task, involving a mother, two children, and a baby (with baby substitution being central to the story) was fairly clear in overall organisation (and could be considered structured from the earlier discussion), whereas the two- and nine-participant picture sequences caused a certain amount of confusion, as participants misunderstood what was happening in particular pictures, or didn't notice a key event in an earlier picture and so did not understand the significance of the events later in the series. As a result, participants might resort to simply describing individual pictures, or perhaps simplified the story or omitted certain elements which did not appear to fit in to the overall narrative development. In other words, the picture series, although in one sense they operationalised number of elements clearly, were responded to differentially, and other variables intruded into performance. Perhaps most clearly of all, as the number of participants increased, so did the tendency to simplify and omit in order to have a more manageable story to tell, thus undermining the very point of having more participants.

The materials that Sasayama used were drawn from Hill (1960) and Elder and Iwashita (2005), and were, basically, typical of the materials used in narrative retelling task research. The detail of Sasayama's work and the qualitative dimension of research allows us to 'look inside' in an unusual way in this particular study, but the problems are likely to be exactly the same with studies which do not contain a qualitative component—the difference is simply that much will be hidden, and inferences will be drawn from quantitative data without input from an insider's perspective on the task. So, given that there was nothing special about the materials used (and indeed they were chosen to be typical) there is something of a research design problem here. The very goals the researcher is trying to achieve, control and manipulability, become difficult to achieve because one is using a task which, by definition, gives meaning primacy, and the speaker freedom to interpret.

The argument I want to make is that what we have learned from these studies has general significance for research into task characteristics. To take on a task means that the participants have to do some thinking, some problem-solving. If there is an attempt to explore particular task characteristics, the task designer (or selector) will try to constrain performance in some way, and influence the nature of the thinking that takes place. To understand what happens in such circumstances we need to draw upon the literature in cognitive psychology as to what people do in problem-solving situations. In this respect, Kahnemann (2011) is instructive. The title of his major book *Thinking, Fast and Slow* refers to the claim that we use two modes of thinking, System 1 and System 2. System 1 is fast, operates with little or no effort, automatically. There is no sense of control with this system. System 2 requires attention, and effort, and takes on complex mental activity. It is associated with a sense of agency, choice, and concentration. Each has its uses, but this depends on the problem being solved—each is more appropriate to certain types of problem. He also characterises the operation of these systems as potentially lazy, with perhaps, a tendency to be over-reliant on the more intuitive System 1. A relevant thing he proposes for our purposes is that, following the laziness, we use the attention-consuming System 2 slightly reluctantly, and one aspect of this is that if we are faced with a complex problem, for which System 2 is required, we may frequently avoid the complexity of the problem and recast it as a simpler one. In other words, we don't answer the question as set: we create an easier one for ourselves and answer that!

Returning now to tasks that are used in research, we can see that:

- many tasks push learners towards a (reluctant) need to engage System 2;
- many tasks are decontextualised and the participants' previous lives are often hardly relevant to the problem posed by the task.

In other words, we are giving learners very difficult things to do, often under a little bit of time pressure. It is not at all surprising, in other words, if the task-as-proposed is not the same as the task-as-interpreted. Very frequently participants may respond by circumventing the task or simplifying it, or flat-out changing it (and do a simpler easier task, as Kahnemann alerts us to). It may also be the case that they misinterpret and simply fail to understand what is required. In such cases, the research design may appear to have been satisfactory, with well-constructed comparisons, but the participants themselves do something different. We saw that in the Sasayama study. I would contend that this can often be general.

But task research does exist, and it has generated a range of interesting (and robust) findings, and this seems to be slightly at variance to the above pessimistic analysis! So I would like to offer some reasons why tasks do work, and work as intended.

- Tasks can be disguised conditions: The argument to be made more forcefully later is that conditions have been more dependable generators of significant results, and so this point anticipates this later section. Structure is a clear case here (and has been analysed earlier). There we saw that structured tasks ease participant work because (a) they provide a macrostructure which means less attention has to be given to broader conceptualisation and discourse development, releasing attention for ongoing performance, and (b) they provide recovery points which enable the speaker, if there have been problems, to regain a parallel mode of speaking. Structured tasks then have advantages, but looked at in this way, the advantages occur because they facilitate effective processing, rather than pushing towards the use of language itself. They create conditions. It is then for the speaker to be oriented to the use of more advanced or more accurate language. (We have also seen that structured tasks, for example, problem-solution tasks, may also raise complexity as the interrelationships between the elements of the tasks need to be expressed. In this case, structured tasks do selectively, and more directly, influence language choice.)
- Tasks can provide freedom: A dimension of tasks that has importance (and has not been particularly researched) concerns features such as freedom for interpretation, and negotiability. Or, conversely, tasks may have tightly required elements and/or be non-negotiable. In these latter cases, what needs to be said will be tightly constrained, and have required, unavoidable features, as when specific components have to be used, or when specific goals need to be achieved. Examples could indeed be choosing a particular type of cell phone, given a range of features which might be important, some of greater priority than others; or the need to rescue people from a burning building when limited resources are available and the people to be rescued vary in urgency. In these cases, the scope for freedom, to take different routes to the same place, to find ways of playing to one's strengths and avoiding weaknesses are limited, and what has to be included, difficult vocabulary or structure or not, is clearly constrained. (This simply reminds one of the importance of routinely including native speaker data as a baseline, to try to establish what language features are feasible even for such a group.) In all these cases, the

Kahnemann proposal that when the going gets tough, our first response is to solve a different (and easier) problem is highly relevant. The decision as to whether to take on the task exactly as set, or alternatively to be creative and simplify, becomes an important one. Since different people will do different things, there will inevitably be error variance in performance attributable not to the task features but to strategies of response. To put this another way, it is important with tasks to explore potential for shortcuts that exist with tasks, since if shortcuts are readily available, it is likely that participants will take them! The first suggestion that emerges out of this discussion is that tasks with freedom (and lack of constraint) and negotiability (and lack of specific goals) facilitate higher-level performance and so if tasks of this sort are used, there will be task effects, but not necessarily for the features that were originally intended!

- Tasks may vary in clarity. We saw earlier in the Sasayama study that with four levels of participant numbers in her tasks, there was scope for misunderstanding, confusion, and circumvention. But there were tasks which had a clear storyline where the number of participants variable was not clouded by the existence of alternative influences on performance. In other words, while constructing research designs with tasks is not easy, it may indeed be possible. And it does produce effects, as Sasayama showed. If variables which guide the different conditions in a task study are carefully controlled, then indeed, the range of additional and misleading variables which exist can be handled effectively (De Jong & Vercelotti, 2015; Inoue, 2013). But it does suggest that preliminary piloting work with task materials is more difficult than has been generally realised, and it is therefore incumbent on researchers to (a) pilot materials effectively and carefully, and (b) gather qualitative data routinely to establish that comparisons which were intended were indeed operative in the actual study.

- Task engagement: Tasks vary, as indicated earlier, in terms of the extent to which they provide personal relevance and interest, on the one hand, versus tasks which are, quite clearly, experimental constructions designed to push learners into language production. Tasks which engage, which contain inherent interest, and which allow the speaker to be themselves, may lead speakers to reach a level of communicative depth and spontaneity that more manipulated tasks do not achieve. I would argue that this might lead to a greater likelihood of achieving higher complexity and higher fluency (though would be neutral about accuracy). I have argued elsewhere (Skehan, 2014c) that task engagement might be a characteristic which reduces the gap between the Cognition Hypothesis and the Limited Attention Capacity approach in a key area: the amount of attention that can be mobilised. The Cognition Hypothesis regards attention as expandable, which I do not. But I do not regard attention as operating at a constant amount which is always mobilised to the maximum for any task performance. I believe there is a maximum

which is available, but that this interacts with the task itself, in that some tasks do not provoke speakers to maximise potential attention while others are more likely to do so. And of course it is tasks which engage which are more likely to recruit as much attention as they can. This raises the possibility that tasks might be compared, and differences found and attributed to other characteristics when really all that is happening is that one tasks engages more attention than the other. An example might be the two problem-solving and interactive tasks in Foster and Skehan (1996a) and Skehan and Foster (1997) (and which were intended to be equivalent). In Foster and Skehan (1996a) the task was to agree, in pairs, on the judicial sentence for a series of crimes. In practice, participants did not particularly engage with the pros and cons embedded in each case, but instead engaged in a fairly superficial conversation about the number of years for prison sentences ('Five?', 'No, three', 'OK, Four', 'OK'). In Skehan and Foster (1997) the task was to agree, in pairs, on the advice to be given to the writers of a series of letters to a newspaper agony aunt. In this case there was much more engagement as the participants threw themselves into the task. This resulted in more complex language.
- A final thought here is that these different task characteristics are not mutually exclusive and sometimes relate to one another. Task engagement, for example, presupposes freedom within the task to relate the task to personal factors. So while each of the characteristics is distinct, they do interrelate and share sources of influence.

Tasks, broadly, are not a lost cause! There are task features which do have consistent effects, albeit at general, CALF-type levels. Undoubtedly future research will extend our knowledge about task-performance consistencies, and it may even be possible to develop a theory of task influence. But what we have at present are a number of subverting influences which have the potential to deflect task performance. The degree of engagement, the extent to which tasks are negotiable (or not), the clarity of a task, the unforeseen lexical demands, all have the potential to push actual performance away from what was (probably quite reasonably) intended. In addition, as with the variable of task structure, one can argue that consistent effects relate more to the way a particular task characteristic relates to processing, and conditions of language production, rather than the task feature itself.

A Brief Analysis of Conditions

The discussion so far has slightly questioned the dependability of the contribution that tasks and task characteristics can make to influencing performance. Correspondingly, but more implicitly, task conditions have been argued to produce more consistent relationships with performance. There is scope now to reflect on reasons which might underlie this claim, something that is developed at greater length in Skehan (2016).

In my view there are two broad reasons why task conditions produce more consistent effects in research studies—the way different conditions relate more naturally to the stages of speaking, and the way conditions often connect with flexibility and negotiability. Regarding the first of these, speaking stages, the range of conditions which have been researched (planning [strategic and on-line], repetition, post-task effects, even interactivity) all sit quite naturally with the extension of the Levelt model that has been discussed here. Research into strategic planning has shown that the Conceptualiser and Formulator stages are each advantaged. The quantitative research study results amply demonstrate this (Skehan, 2016) and then the qualitative studies (Ortega, 2005; Pang & Skehan, 2014) clarify that both preparation of ideas and their organisation, and also processes such as retrieval and rehearsal are commonly reported. So in these cases, opportunity to plan can be exploited to help natural speaking stages work better, and have an impact, usually beneficial, on performance. Earlier research into on-line planning (Ellis & Yuan, 2005) also suggested that using more relaxed time conditions was beneficial for performance. It seemed that such conditions enabled the speakers to have more attention available during actual performance, and this was channelled to Formulator operations and an increase in accuracy. Wang's (2014) subsequent research complicates this picture slightly, in that she argued that the ideal condition is a combination of pre-task and on-line planning. This, in turn, is analysable as opportunity for more effective Conceptualiser work linked to the more relaxed attentional conditions for Formulation and monitoring—something worthwhile to say, and supportive conditions to say it—in other words, good Conceptualiser-Formulator balance.

Repetition, as we have seen (and there is further discussion in Chapter 9) can also be analysed through stages of speaking. There is Conceptualiser-linkage as ideas are laid down in a first performance, and then can be elaborated or organised more effectively in the second performance. Formulator relevance is very interesting, and stems from the greater effectiveness of priming from the first performance as the need to use lemma information for syntax building pushes for more complete and deeper retrieval of lemma information. This, although maybe not used in the first performance, for time pressure reasons, then becomes available for the second.

Planning and repetition are conditions which relate to the Conceptualiser and Formulator stages, and, importantly, to their interrelationship. The next condition, selective attention, does connect somewhat with Formulator operations, but is most linked to monitoring. It appears that, where there are limited attentional resources, it is possible to influence learner priorities amongst performance dimensions, and to lead to a concern to achieve greater accuracy. Possibly surprisingly, second language speakers do seem able to make choices, and these choices can be influenced, in this case to the most challenging performance area of all—accuracy. It appears that, for second language speakers at least, engaging the capacity to monitor is variable—it can be forgotten in the hurly-burly of pressured communication, but it is also possible to foster its use.

The other general reason for the greater consistency of results with conditions of speaking concerns flexibility and negotiability. Tasks themselves are often likely to be fairly constraining, and push learners to engage in particular and unavoidable Conceptualiser and Formulator operations. Task conditions such as planning or repetition or post-task conditions have no such requirements. Instead second language speakers can interpret the opportunities they provide in whatever way the wish. They can, legitimately, transform the task to make it easier, or more difficult. They can choose to play to their strengths and away from their weaknesses, by focussing on what they know about that is relevant and where they have 'ready made' things they can say. They can try to make tasks more personally relevant. All of these possibilities exist because conditions tend to influence the 'how' rather than the 'what' in communication.

This analysis, linked to the previous section, brings out the usefulness of conditions, as opposed to tasks. The way conditions can be analysed through the advantages they confer for stages of speaking, coupled with the greater flexibility and negotiability that typically accompanies them clarifies how performance areas can be advantaged. They are a good example of Kahnemann's (2011) analyses of how System 1 and System 2, in his terms, co-exist, and how negotiability makes it easier for System 1 to be used. There may be limitations to this situation, too. Negotiability and clear linkage to speaking may have their advantages, but a consequence might well be a lack of concern for any notions of targeted form, and consequently, potential for acquisition. The emphasis, in other words, might be performance itself, rather than development and change.

Tasks, Conditions, and a Model of Speaking

Bringing together the details of the previous sections of this postscript, the central claims can be simply expressed:

- In considering the usefulness and potential for second language performance of task characteristics and task conditions, it is instructive, even vital, to relate these to a model of speaking, and to consider how thought and language can be best be supported and stimulated for second language speakers;
- More specifically, it is important to consider how an effective balance can be achieved between Conceptualiser and Formulator operations;
- Looking at tasks and task conditions through this lens is illuminating for our understanding of second language speaking and its potential for acquisition;
- On balance, tasks themselves, even though there are successes, do not generate many consistent influences on performance. In contrast, task conditions such as planning have produced a wider range of consistent results, perhaps reflecting the way condition-linked research can be argued to be more directly linked to the processes of second language speaking.

Effective communication, in the first or the second language case, requires effective thinking translated into effective use of linguistic elements, in other words, Conceptualisation and Formulation-Articulation. As we have seen, in the first language case, the richness of the mental lexicon enables the Formulator and Articulator to respond to the Conceptualiser demands that are made in real time and to sustain, mostly, a mode of parallel processing, supplemented by what might be termed non-disruptive monitoring. What we have seen is that in the second language case, the lower scale, organisation, richness, and accessibility of the second language mental lexicon do not allow the same thing to happen, and in addition, monitoring has to take on the additional function of attending to accuracy as well as the other monitoring functions which operate in the first language case. This leads to the need to explore how an effective Conceptualiser-Formulator balance can be achieved, and how task choice and task implementation conditions might impact upon this. Such an exploration forces us to think about Conceptualiser demands in more detail, and correspondingly about the nature of the operations the Formulator has to engage in. In turn, this leads to the question as to how these can be manipulated in desirable ways.

Despite the reference to the second language mental lexicon, it is important to stress that we are not simply dealing with proficiency here, or any underlying competence. The focus is on what might be more accurately termed *ability for use* (Skehan, 1995, and see discussion in Part III). The interest is in developing the capacity to access and use what is held in the second language mental lexicon, and to exploit what needs to happen in the stages of speaking more effectively. This means, essentially, findings ways, while communication proceeds, of not overloading any part of the system to the detriment of others. So the focus is on the marshalling of resources. Of course there may be other consequences which are desirable. It is possible that careful harmonious tasks and conditions can lead to automatisation of speaking, as speakers learn how to access and use the second language mental lexicon more effectively, and the way lemmas are accessed and syntactic frames are built becomes more ingrained. Similarly, there may be some scope for acquisition to occur if language made salient by the need to complete a task can be consolidated, or extended, or integrated more effectively. But the main thrust has to be here the way that speaking itself can be enhanced, and how ability for use can be developed. So the main concern is to link research findings from the task literature to the extension of the Levelt model to the second language case.

All of the task characteristics and conditions have already been covered, in the earlier reprinted chapters or in earlier sections of this chapter. The purpose of this section is to relate them, perhaps a little more thoroughly, to the stages of speaking. In addition, although it may seem a little cumbersome, positive and negative influences are separated, even though these are often different facets of the same thing. The separation does allow significant differences to be brought out more clearly.

Positive Conceptualiser Influences

The focus here is on factors which ease or which organise Conceptualiser operations.

- Tasks based on familiar information: Such tasks facilitate retrieval of information, of lemmas, or the organisation of ideas, and as a result it is more straightforward to develop a pre-verbal message. (There are Formulator advantages also.);
- Tasks which, in format, are themselves familiar: Generating language for a task is always a mixture of the broad structure of the task and the detail of expressing individual propositions. Familiar format tasks minimise the difficulty caused by the first of these, and so enable the Conceptualiser to operate with more attentional resources;
- Tasks where the ideas are part of the speaker's life, and may have been talked about before: Such tasks benefit from greater ease in recalling, in accessing previously organised ideas and language which has already been primed. There is less need for on-line computation, and so ideas can be accessed more easily. (There are Formulator advantages also.);
- Planning: Planning has several possible influences. Here the focus is on planning time used to develop the ideas that underpin a task. One consequence is that speakers develop the interrelation between ideas, and as a result Conceptualisation attempts to bring out these relationships and causes greater subordination complexity. Another is that Conceptualisation leads to larger units, so that within phrases there is greater Words-per-Clause complexity;
- Repeated tasks: As with planning, there are several possible influences. Here the focus is on the impact on the repeated task of (a) the familiarity and (b) the partial construction from the original task. Familiarity of ideas is increased through previous access, and so Conceptualiser operations can be slightly faster. In addition, the first performance, probably influenced by pressure of the need to keep speaking, may have generated partial versions of the pre-verbal message. In the repeated performance, these are primed for availability and so can be developed further, leading to greater complexity;
- Structured tasks: Structured tasks also have dual functions in their impact on the Conceptualiser. First, they make it easier to 'package' material, since the speaker has structure which can be exploited, and as a result, more clearly bring out causal connections between ideas. Second they facilitate attentional use, since they provide a macrostructure which is easier to manipulate and to retain in working memory during ongoing communication;
- Negotiable tasks: Tasks with scope for interpretation and which do not constrain or require the incorporation of particular elements enable the speaker to develop ideas more naturally and to link them over cycles of communication. The speaker can play to their strengths, with ideas that are familiar, that

may have been used before, and avoid the need to engage with the unfamiliar, or to need on-line computation. The result is that less attention is required for Conceptualisation but at the same time pre-verbal ideas are generated more quickly and at a greater level of complexity.

Negative Conceptualiser Influences

- Planning (again): There are features of planning which might also create Conceptualiser problems. The next section reprints Pang and Skehan (2014), a qualitative study of planning which related self-reported planning activities to subsequent task performance. What this showed was that memory for what is planned can be an issue, in that it does not transfer to actual performance. In fact, two areas of planning are important here. First we have over-ambitious planning where the ideas that are involved push the speaker to be a little out of their depth. This may cause the second language speaker to have to wrestle with language that they are not totally equipped to handle with the result that processing demands lead to *worse* performance as attention is used, in Formulation, that attempts, sometimes unsuccessfully, to deal with the trouble the planning has led the speaker into. Second, there is rehearsal. In this case it is likely that no serious trouble is caused, simply that the time spent rehearsing, if it is not used in performance, could be time wasted;
- Large tasks: The problem with tasks of greater scale is that cycles of communication require the Conceptualiser to operate in ongoing fashion, which means keeping track of the wider picture (one's place in the discourse, any signals, verbal or non-verbal, from interlocutors). These factors are in addition to current Conceptualiser activity at any point, and are likely to be even more burdensome in second language cases, since other stages in communication are themselves demanding of attentional resources. As a result, the additional Conceptualiser work may cause difficulty, and this may spill over into the rest of the system;
- Close reasoning tasks and tasks which require transformation of material: Such tasks make it more difficult to access ready-made solutions to problems or previously used language. Although they may lead to greater complexity (which, of course, may be a good thing), it is likely that they will lead to the Conceptualiser requiring considerable attentional resources and this will have implications for processing at other speaking stages. The manipulation of ideas that is involved is likely to absorb attention even without recourse to language. Relatively unusually, this is likely to be important for native speakers also;
- Non-negotiable tasks: Such tasks are likely to be the result of non-negotiable goals, and/or the incorporation of particular elements which have to be considered or involved as part of the task requirements. (The reasoning tasks just described are very close to this.);

Reflections on Part I, Theory **117**

- Tasks based on unfamiliar or more abstract information: The Conceptualiser problem here is simply that the ideas which are going to be expressed, and possibly manipulated are less accessible or more elusive in how they can be handled. This can create Conceptualiser problems without necessarily translating into greater complexity. It is simply that attention is being siphoned off to deal with ideas and this may be at the expense of other speaking stages.

Positive Formulator Influences

- Greater proficiency: Although it was made clear earlier that proficiency is not the major issue in discussions of ability for use, it is not irrelevant. The important thing here is that greater proficiency, other things being equal, is more likely to be associated with a second language mental lexicon which is larger, better organised, richer, and more accessible. As a result, the Conceptualiser demands which are made on it are more likely to be handled, in real time;
- Reduced time pressure: Analysed purely in terms of the Formulator, the issue here is that less time pressure gives the stages that need to be handled more time to operate. Essentially this means that lemma retrieval (required from the pre-verbal message) has more time to operate (and could compensate a little for lower proficiency) and so can occur more thoroughly. In addition more time can mean richer retrieval of more than the basic phonological shape of the lemma, and so facilitate syntax building and priming of other elements;
- Tasks with structure: Such tasks have two advantages. First, and this links with the Conceptualiser, they provide a clearer macrostructure for what is being said, and this 'licenses' the speaker, since they are surer where they are in the overall task, to devote more attention to Formulation and the surface of language. They can take just a little longer to retrieve lemma-based information, and they can also take just a little longer to build syntactic frames, as well as monitor what is being said. The results should lead to greater accuracy and greater fluency. Second, structured tasks provide recovery points. If there has been a breakdown in speaking, the beginning of the next section of the task structure might enable the second language speaker to 'kick start' production into a parallel mode, less encumbered by the difficulties of the previous section;
- Repeated tasks: The first performance is likely to have set in motion processes of lemma retrieval and at this time activated traces associated with the lemma which might not have been acted upon or incorporated in the message which was formulated. But if a task is repeated within a reasonable time interval, it is likely that they will still be available, and so richer access (and better syntax, etc.) in the repeated performance can be capitalised upon;
- Effective rehearsal: Some of the time strategic planning is used for engagement with ideas, and is Conceptualiser oriented. But time may also be devoted to

rehearsal (Ellis, 2005b) and to preparation for the actual performance of a task. In such cases, particular lemmas, particular syntactic frames may be prepared. If this is done, then the advantage is for Formulator operations, since the elements so accessed will be anticipations of what will actually be said. We also saw earlier from the study by Pang and Skehan (2014) that such preparation is vulnerable, since its usefulness for Formulator operations presupposes that it will have been remembered. Pang and Skehan (2014) showed that this is often not the case, and so for many participants in their study, planning time allocated to rehearsal was not optimally used. Even so, where it is retrieved, it is advantageous.

Negative Formulator Influences

- Time pressure: Clearly time pressure militates against effective Formulator operations. The second language mental lexicon operations that underpin effective parallel processing are vital, and if there is time pressure, it is likely that they will be often incomplete and shallow and this shortcoming will then have consequences for performance. If lemma retrieval is partial, then some real-time speaking may be possible, but if lemma retrieval is totally unsuccessful, it is likely that ongoing communication with be disrupted as alternative formulations are sought. The less the time pressure, the more likely it is that, whatever the completeness (or lack of completeness) of the second language mental lexicon, the second language speaker can muddle through;
- Tasks with difficult and unavoidable lexis: Whatever the time pressure conditions, the Formulator will encounter more difficulty in sustaining parallel processing if the specific lexical demands are greater. This will occur when what needs to be retrieved is less accessible or incomplete, which of course will often be the case with lexical items in a growing lexicon. Low frequency, or a range of other factors may come into play with this. But there is also the point that some lemmas may be more easily substituted than others. If a lemma is vital, and there is no obvious alternative, and that item is lacking, then the speaker is in some trouble. So tasks which make certain lexical items salient may cause more Formulator problems than other tasks which, even though they may require difficulty lexis, are more flexible and forgiving in their demands (De Jong & Vercelotti, 2015).

Positive Influences on Conceptualiser-Formulator Balance

- The influences already covered provide the basic account of second language speaking. They operate singly or in combination, and since some have greater impact on the Conceptualiser and others the Formulator, they go some way, collectively, to accounting for favourable and unfavourable speaking conditions. In other words, they can be used to predict when communication is more likely to be parallel and when it is more likely to be serial. Balance between Conceptualiser and Formulator, the foundation for parallel processing, is based, in a major way, on the variables covered so far in this section, and good balance is the outcome of these separate variables, acting in concert. (This approach is the nub of the distinction between the LAC approach and the Cognition Hypothesis.) But there are some occasions where there seems to be a clearer synergy in the way conditions operate which jointly have an impact on balance, and on both stages of speaking. We will cover just a few of these.

- Structured tasks: These, discussed earlier, influence the work of the Conceptualiser in two ways, easing its operations because a macrostructure is provided, so the speaker needs to allocate less attention to keeping their place in the discourse, while simultaneously providing a reason to complexify the subordination of what is to be said as the speaker tries to bring out the relationship between elements of the task when structure involves causal links. The Formulator is also eased because of the greater discourse clarity, enabling more attention to be paid to the means of expression, to the surface of language. Finally, clarity of structure enables 'pick up' points where, if difficulty has been experienced, the speaker can take up the thread again to continue the discourse flow. So structured tasks have potential Conceptualiser-Formulator balance effects;
- Strategic Planning linked to on-line planning and reduced time pressure: Again, as discussed earlier, we have two aspects of the same thing, planning, in the shape of strategic planning, which is likely to be implicated in developing the ideas that drive the pre-verbal message (and so greater complexity), and then eased performance conditions which enable the speaker to allocate more attention to Formulator processes of lemma retrieval and syntax building as well as monitoring performance, including for accuracy and error avoidance;
- Repetition: As indicated earlier, the first performance leaves traces for the second performance. Where these concern ideas, Conceptualisation, and the pre-verbal messages that have been produced, they prepare the ground for a second performance where original pre-verbal messages can be developed, made more compact (Bygate, 2001), and elaborated. Where this concerns Formulation, the partial lemma access from the first performance primes the second performance, and enables the lemma retrieval to be faster, richer and more likely to build sentence frames quickly. Both Conceptualisation and Formulation are thereby advantaged by the same activity.

Negative Influences on Conceptualiser-Formulator Balance

- Non-negotiable tasks: Some tasks have little room for manouevre and so there is little opportunity for the speaker to modify how they approach the task. For example, tasks which have clear outcome requirements linked to multiple elements are difficult to handle because they simultaneously require considerable Conceptualiser work, but they also pose problems for the Formulator since the language which has to be accessed, while not totally pre-ordained, does not enable very much discretion on the part of the speaker.

So Conceptualiser work may be halting and attention is required to ensure that all elements of the task have been incorporated, and Formulator work will similarly be demanding of attention because the lexical elements that are needed, as well perhaps as syntactic frames, have to be what they are. There is only one route to go in the task (or rather not many routes that could be taken) and as a result there is huge competition for attentional resources.

These insights can be presented more succinctly in the form of a table, as shown in Table 5.2. This table takes the first two stages of speech production, in the Levelt model, as well as their combination (which is concerned with factors which promote parallel processing by second language learners), and links them to the different general categories of processing that have been discussed: complexifying, easing, pressuring, and focussing. In doing this, a broad outline is offered about the sorts of separate influences on performance which have emerged as important. This would then be a basis for combining different influences to obtain combinations of influences on the processes of speaking.

TABLE 5.2 Performance Influences Linked to the Stages of Speaking

Speaking Stage	Complexifying	Easing	Pressuring	Focussing
Conceptualisation	Planning Repetition Structured tasks Interactive Larger-scale tasks (more elements; more reasoning; more justification)	Familiarity – information – format Easier personal relationship Repetition Structured – discourse Negotiable	Planning Larger-scale tasks Close reasoning Non-negotiable Unfamiliar – information – format	Resource-directing tasks
Formulation	Challenging lexis and syntax	Proficiency No time pressure Structured tasks Repeated tasks Rehearsal Interactive Negotiable	Time pressure Difficult language demands Narrative format	Resource-directing tasks Post-task conditions
Conceptualisation-Formulation balance and capacity for parallel processing	Strategic plus on-line planning Repetition Structured tasks	Strategic plus on-line planning	Non-negotiable Time pressure	

If the table is considered representative of what task research has achieved, a first impression is that the easing and pressuring influences are more numerous, and also are spread across Conceptualisation and Formulation. They concern the conditions under which tasks are done (such as planning and repetition) and also the content of the tasks, both the information type and the operations on that information. Complexifying influences are not so numerous, and in turn they are more focussed on the Conceptualisation stage, which is something that might be a natural situation. But if they are not so numerous, they do contain some of the major themes which have emerged, with some of the most consistent results, as with planning and repetition. The overall impression is that a range of influences can now be understood as influencing performance, for ideas (Conceptualisation) and execution (Formulation), and that these influences fall into useful and organising general categories. Finally, though, the influence which is least represented is focussing. Only two such influences are represented, and I have to admit that this portrayal represents a personal interpretation of the area. The first of these influences is labelled resource-directing. I have no problems with this label, as such, if it is taken to mean task qualities which are associated with a greater tendency to use particular language or to raise particular performance dimensions. The example of structured tasks is a good one here. Then the second focussing influence, a post-task condition, is concerned with attention manipulation, and so is Formulator-linked. The Limited Attentional Capacity approach is entirely consistent with this interpretation. Perhaps there will be scope to expand upon this column in future research.

Conclusions

Given the way this chapter started, by briefly discussing the 1996 article, I thought it might be interesting to present a sort of Report Card based on that article, primarily as a means of relating what has happened since the claims from more than twenty years ago. Recall that the purpose of the article was to present a framework that could facilitate thinking about theory and pedagogy, and that three areas were proposed as relevant to thinking about tasks: language, cognition, and conditions. I will look at each of these, in turn.

Language: The proposal that language demands would have an impact on task performance has not really been associated with much research. Instead, the focus has been on what impacts upon language in the first place, as with the sorts of complexification influences discussed in Table 5.2. Nor has Loschky and Bley-Vroman's (1993) proposal on the different levels of necessity had much influence on the design of task research studies. Perhaps the one exception to this concerns lexis, where there have been some studies. I have explored tendencies for tasks which require more difficult (operationalised as less frequent) lexis to lead to difficulties with fluency and accuracy. The first attempt at showing this (Skehan, 2009b) which was suggestive of interesting results, was not confirmed by Wang and Skehan (2014) who, in a more experimental design, did not show any spillover effects of more difficult lexis on other aspects of performance. De Jong and Vercelotti (2015) more recently have, though, shown that the need to use unforeseen lexis can have a difficult effect on task performance.

Cognition: The major distinction made in the 1996 article concerned the contrast between tasks which emphasise the retrieval of familiar and well-organised information, and tasks which required significant amounts of on-line computation. This distinction is still with us (sometimes with different labels), and is relevant to both the Limited Attentional Capacity and Cognition Hypothesis approaches. Indeed, many of the influences in Table 5.2 are, in effect, the details of this distinction, as they involve the information a task is based on (familiar-unfamiliar, etc.) and the operations carried out on that information (transformation, reorganisation, selection, and so on). This has been an important area of research to try to map out the task characteristics that most impact upon performance. (And this is where I argued, in an earlier section, that task research has not delivered anything like as much as I, for one, was expecting.) So the distinction made in the 1996 article can be claimed to link with a great deal of subsequent task research.

Conditions: What were proposed here were the areas of time pressure, modality, scale, stakes, and control. All of these have had some activity. But the most relevant thing is to talk about the areas of activity which were not given any focus in 1996. Planning was mentioned, but not centrally, and not as an area likely to generate much research. Similarly, repetition, although mentioned in relation to pedagogy, was not covered as an important task condition. The same is true regarding interactivity, and post-task work, and also the relevance of support materials when tasks are being done. All of these have generated considerable interest since, and have figured in the discussion in this chapter. But they were largely absent in this earlier article.

Even so, the areas which were mentioned have all seen some research. Time pressure has been actively researched, principally as interpreted through on-line planning (so planning, in a way, was implicit in this earlier article!). The literature on this is reasonably large now, with both quantitative and qualitative studies, and these will be covered in greater detail in Chapter 9. Modality has been an active area for research also. I think it is fair to say that most task research has concerned spoken language. But there has been work focussing on listening tasks, such as that done by Ellis and Shintani (2014), and there have also been studies of writing, such as Kuiken and Vedder (2008a) and Ishikawa (2007). There have been no major comparative studies across modality, though. Scale was mentioned in the 1996 article as part of conditions, but this variable can be equally well analysed as a task feature. This, in fact, has often been the case, as in the Cognition Hypothesis. There has been little research within the main task literature to look at stakes, in the sense that this is varied within a research study in a systematic way. But there have been some interesting studies done to take insights from task research and apply them to a language-testing context. In their way, these results present a mini-challenge to the task literature, in that they tend to show much smaller effects on performance when variables drawn from the task literature are applied to language tests. Iwashita et al. (2001), for example, found that effects which would be expected from the task literature were not duplicated when a testing context was involved. Tavakoli and Skehan (2005) did find comparable effects, and ones where planning led to low-intermediate students achieving the same level as higher proficiency students. But theirs was presented *as if* in a testing context, but the test-task was not a high-stakes test, whereas Iwashita et al. (2001) did have a more convincing test and assessment context. In Chapter 13 it is argued that the task literature has a great deal to offer to language testing, not least in the claim that test-tasks are not neutral instruments. Studies such as Iwashita et al. (2001), though, suggest that when second language speakers do tests, their approach to performance is not the same as their approach in 'ordinary' task situations, and the effects that are found in one context may not generalise to the other. This is an interesting challenge for future research.

The final task condition from the 1996 article is Control. Essentially I would argue that this is the same as negotiability. This notion has figured quite a lot in discussion (including in this chapter) and the general interpretation is that tasks which enable negotiability are likely to be easier and more personally relevant to the participants. In contrast, tasks which are not very negotiable, and a good example of this is tasks which have quite precise demands that have to be met to achieve task outcomes (e.g. often tasks involving reasoning and number of elements), are likely to prove very difficult, and as a result may lead participants to change the task. Ironically, therefore, tasks which are presented as non-negotiable may push participants into changing them! Negotiability is presented here as a (convincing) interpretation of task studies, one which links with a sociocultural view of the construct of task. But it hasn't been systematically researched, so there has to be a strong speculative component to the claims which are made. But I will nonetheless make them—I feel that the negotiability-compulsoriness dimension of tasks would be a rewarding one for research studies, and in that respect am slightly disappointed that its mention in 1996 has not really led anywhere as far as a research literature is concerned.

So if one reflects on this analysis of the 1996 article, the picture is remarkably mixed! I would say that the distinction within the cognitive basis for tasks between retrieval and familiarity, on the one hand, and on-line computation and challenging material, on the other, has stood up well, and has also generated quite a bit of insightful research. One could also say that, regarding pedagogy, the (fairly obvious) distinction between the pre-task, the mid-task, and the post-task stages has also worn fairly well. Even more broadly, a contrast between the language involved in a task, the nature of the task itself, and the conditions under which the task is done is still with us, and very influential.

This does not seem a bad evaluation at all. But in contrast to that, three telling limitations paint a rather different picture. First, the hope that we would understand tasks themselves better, and be able to analyse tasks into characteristics whose impact on performance would be consistent and clear has not materialised. Tasks are still elusive. There is more to them than we currently understand. Second, a range of the most important influences on task performance (planning, repetition, interactivity) were not really anticipated very much, or integrated into the general argument as to how tasks could be understood or used. These are serious omissions, and the occasional hints at their importance did not go nearly far enough. Third, the lack of a solid psycholinguistic grounding in what we understand about speaking was a major omission. To be able to draw on the Levelt model has contributed so much to our understanding of second language task performance since then. The account the 1996 article provided was interesting, certainly, but now is massively overtaken by subsequent research.

PART II
Empirical Work

Introduction

This second section of the book is not going to provide a general survey of empirical work with tasks, or even an account of my own work! Instead, the reprinted articles and chapters and the reflections chapters which follow focus on just two areas: planning (as an example of an independent variable) and the measurement of task performance (with a focus on dependent variables or measures). Two articles are reprinted from work that I have done on planning, and one is reprinted on the measurement of the dependent variables included in task research.

I find it interesting and appropriate that the two reprinted planning articles are joint articles, reflecting the way research is a collaborative activity, and also that the research I have done has benefited from wonderful co-researchers, with the two joint authors involved here, Pauline Foster and Francine Pang, typical of that group of talented research colleagues. There is also a considerable time gap between the two articles: 1996 and 2014, as well as a major contrast in the methodologies involved, with the first study being quantitative in nature, and the second a hybrid design with strong qualitative as well as quantitative elements.

The first of the planning articles is a major source of pride to me. It was the first empirical article on tasks that Pauline Foster and I published, and it seems to have stood the test of time fairly well (and is still cited). It focussed on planning, obviously, but it also tried to go beyond the 'one task type' approach, including a personal information exchange, a narrative, and a decision-making task. It may not be that long ago, in some ways, but one memory of the study is the large number of small tape recorders that Pauline had to carry around to gather data! How things have changed, so that now, mobile phones would achieve the same purpose far more easily and contain built-in digitisation. I think the complexity of the research design is one of the factors which has led to the study's durability. Another perhaps is the naturalness of the data collection. This took place in intact classrooms, in a school where Pauline Foster, the data collector, was herself a teacher and therefore a familiar figure. One of the claims that can be made about planning is that it is simple (and free) to use by classroom teachers, and I have spoken to teachers who have read about this research, and who have endorsed its use in actual classrooms. That the 1996 study was conducted in an intact classroom fits in with this claim that planning is a generally usable technique: the setting for this first study attests to the claim that it doesn't need a laboratory or any special equipment to do meaningful and relevant research.

The second of the reprinted studies, conducted in the second of the major research settings I have worked in with tasks, Hong Kong (or more exactly, in this study, Macao), took a contrasting approach. The first study, typical of many in the field, essentially black-boxed planning time (the standard 10 minutes, as people have emulated Crookes [1989]), and looked for quantitative relationships between planning and actual performance. This general research design has served us well, and many studies have accumulated which have given us a better appreciation of planning's effects. But it is limited, since the researcher has to infer what happens during planning, and how this might be important. The qualitative approach in Pang and Skehan (2014) changes this, since the planners themselves are able to comment on what they did. Then, as researchers, we were able to link these self-reports to actual performance. The outcome, as the reprinted article shows, was insightful and surprising, in equal measure. This study actually collected data on two tasks, a narrative (monologic) and a decision-making (dialogic) task. The reprinted article focusses on the narrative. Francine and I are still working on the decision-making data!

I am not sure I would have picked the variable of planning as likely to be so enduring. Yet more than twenty years after our first study (and thirty years since Ellis's [1987] article), it is still a vibrant source of research studies, with increasingly sophisticated research designs, and many active questions, as well as a number of established generalisations. Given this sub-literature, one of the epilogues in this section is essentially a story of planning research, and where we now are. It takes the two reprinted studies as the starting point, and surveys the range of research results which are now available. It is already quite a story, and shows that we have a deeper understanding now of what is involved in planning. In particular, the planning research has been beneficially complexified by the notion of on-line planning, introduced by Rod Ellis. The notion of on-line planning links planning research to the nature of ongoing performance, and this clarifies how processing influences have a major role. The epilogue tries to bring these aspects of planning together, and in so doing makes serious claims for progress, both theoretical and practical.

The other reprinted article, and the associated epilogue, are concerned with the nature of performance itself. In a way, the greatest interest in most research studies is the independent variables which impact upon performance, such as task characteristics (e.g. task structure, reasoning demands) or task conditions, (e.g. planning or post-task conditions). But fundamental though these concerns are, it is vital that task performance itself can be productively measured. If it cannot, then however interesting the independent variables and the associated theories, the touchstone for evaluation of claims will be, well, opaque. So measurement in capturing aspects of task performance is also important. Two aspects of performance are in strongest focus here in the reprinted chapter. First, the chapter focusses on lexical performance and how different measures of lexis interrelate and also are affected differentially, comparing native and non-native speakers. Second, the article also considers the measurement of fluency in slightly greater depth, examining whether the location of silent pauses (at clause boundaries or mid-clause) requires separate interpretation.

But another issue is important here—the role of native speaker data. When we research tasks with second language speakers, our central interest is how those tasks might make a contribution to second language performance, and, possibly, acquisition. A particular task, for example, might appear to be helpful in promoting fluency. We would like to conclude that the task itself is promoting fluency, perhaps helping the process of automatisation, and providing more supportive conditions for fluency to emerge. But if we discover that native speakers, doing the same task, also show raised fluency, this may cause us to re-evaluate the nature of the task in question. It may simply be that greater fluency follows from the task itself and its inherent qualities. It may be that no automatisation or change is taking place. The speaker is simply following task demands, whether they are native or non-native. The third reprinted article explores this issue, and compares native and non-native speakers doing exactly the same task. This approach to research, building in native and non-native groups for comparison, is not common. It is represented in Foster and Tavakoli (2009a) and Skehan and Shum (2014, 2017). It would be nice to see many more research designs which build in this comparison.

The reflections chapter on planning (described above) is a natural development of the two reprinted chapters on planning. It uses them as the springboard to discuss planning more generally, but the connection between the reprinted chapters and the reflections chapter is always (in my view) clear enough. This is much less true for the epilogue on measures of second language task performance. The reprinted chapter does provide a springboard, but I have to admit, the connection between the starting point and the discussion which follows is rather tenuous. In fact, the Reflections chapter is based on a quite a lot of data re-analysis. The data comes largely from the studies I conducted with colleagues during my time in Hong Kong. I explore the range of complementary studies to tease out the broader generalisations about performance. On this basis, the epilogue here does two things. First, it explores the different measures of complexity, accuracy, and fluency. As mentioned earlier, these three areas have become the focus for a great deal of research and publication. The discussion tries to provide a deeper understanding of these constructs. Second, the argument is proposed that the contrast between a discourse mode of processing and a clause mode has not been sufficiently appreciated and the research data suggest something of a tension between these two areas. I hadn't particularly foreseen the importance of this tension when I started to re-analyse the later data. I hope others find it equally convincing.

6
THE INFLUENCE OF PLANNING AND TASK TYPE ON SECOND LANGUAGE PERFORMANCE

Recent work applying concepts from cognitive psychology to language teaching have suggested that (a) attention and noticing are central for second language development (Schmidt, 1990, 1994) and (b) attentional resources are limited (Van Patten, 1990). Decisions have to be made about their allocation (Anderson, 1995), and decisions to attend to one area are usually made at the expense of attending to another. In the context of second language learning, the main competition for attentional resources is between meaning and form, with first priority generally being given to meaning (Van Patten, 1990).

These developments have important implications for language teaching. In recent years there has been a significant move from controlled, structured approaches to syllabus and teaching to the use of more communicative materials meant to promote interaction (Harmer, 1991). This, in turn, is seen as catalyzing acquisitional processes. One question that has arisen from this change is whether interaction should be viewed as an adjunct of traditional approaches, a more engaging version of conventional production activities (Rivers, 1981), or interaction should actually constitute the language learning experience in a more self-sufficient way. In this respect, recent proposals for task-based approaches (Long & Crookes, 1991, 1993; Prabhu, 1987) represent a clear case of the more extreme interaction-based position, as they advocate tasks as the unit of syllabus design and teaching. Tasks are defined as activities that are meaning-focused and outcome-evaluated and have some sort of real-world relationship. In other

---

Originally published as: Foster, P., & Skehan, P. (1996a). The influence of planning and task type on second language performance. *Studies in Second Language Acquisition, 18*(3), 299–324. doi:10.1017/S0272263100015047. Reprinted with permission of Cambridge University Press.

words, transacting tasks will push forward interlanguage development because the demands that tasks make will engage the very processes that lead to acquisition.

This approach to syllabus design and language pedagogy requires us to know more about the general area of task-based instruction. To try to achieve this, this article will explore two relevant areas: task analysis and task implementation. Recent proposals regarding task analysis have divided generally into (a) those emphasizing the potential of different tasks to generate patterns of language use that are deemed "better" and (b) those concerned with establishing task difficulty (Long, 1989). In the former category, Duff (1986) proposes a distinction between convergent (one answer must be agreed, e.g., on how to allocate blame in a moral problem) and divergent (disagreement, e.g., in a discussion task, is regarded as natural) tasks. She proposes that convergent tasks have a greater potential to generate negotiation of meaning, a theoretically valued form of conversational interaction. Long (1989) distinguishes between open and closed tasks, again relating the distinction to the extent to which tasks lead to greater use of conversational gambits such as confirmation checks, clarification requests, and other features that are seen as implicated in interlanguage change. Similarly, Pica, Kanagy, and Falodun (1993) propose that tasks can be analyzed in terms of the following scheme:

Interactional activity

Interactional relationship, that is, information held by different participants;
Interactional requirements, that is, required or optional participation

Communicational goal

Goal orientation: convergent or divergent;
Outcome option: one solution only, or more than one

This scheme enables tasks to be chosen that yield a "better" quality of language for acquisition, assuming that the negotiation of meaning, which would be promoted, does indeed reflect a more malleable interlanguage system and greater scaffolding and feedback at particularly opportune moments. Aston (1986) argues that such negotiation is more irritating to learners than beneficial, and Foster (1994) proposes that relatively few subjects in research studies may account for virtually all the negotiation of meaning that is found; that is, most learners do not negotiate at all!

The alternative perspective on task analysis is to propose features that enable tasks to be ranked in difficulty. Brown, Anderson, Shilcock, and Yule (1984), based on extensive empirical work, propose two dimensions for this, one concerned with type of information, the other with scale. The former refers to the increasing difficulty of tasks as they move from static to dynamic to abstract, whereas scale concerns the number of participants or objects contained in the task as well as the nature of the relationships between these elements. Even so, the tasks on which this research was based are restricted in type. Candlin (1987) proposes a wider-ranging (but speculative) scheme for assessing task difficulty, and for incorporating cognitive load, communicative stress, code complexity, clarity of task goals, and familiarity of task type. Skehan (1996) extends and slightly reorganizes this scheme into the following categories:

Language factors

Syntactic complexity and range
Lexical complexity and range
Redundancy and variety

Cognitive factors

Familiarity

Familiarity of material in the task
Familiarity of task type and discourse genre

On-line processing

Reasoning operations required
Nature of input material used in the task
Degree of organization of input material

In this way, a clear distinction is made between language and cognition, as well as the consequences for task difficulty that arise from each of these. Then, within cognitive factors, a further distinction can be made. On the one hand there is accessing knowledge sources directly, that is, drawing upon knowledge already held in memory that is relevant to completing a particular task. On the other hand there is needing to work out the answer to a task; that is, an active intellectual engagement with the task is called for because understanding the material involved, or arriving at a solution, cannot simply be based on accessing existing knowledge and using it untransformed. This scheme, too, is speculative, but it is an important motivating influence upon the present study.

Regarding task implementation, a number of studies have suggested ways in which pedagogic decisions influence performance. Ellis (1987), in a picture-story narration task, investigated the effects of engaging what he termed different degrees of planned discourse. Subjects in the most planned condition were required to write a story to a set of (coherently structured) picture prompts. A second condition required these subjects to tell the same story orally, but without access to their previous written versions. Finally, the least planned condition was one in which subjects had to tell a story orally to a new set of picture prompts.

Ellis (1987) found that accuracy on the regular (rule-governed) form of the past tense declined according to lack of planned discourse being engaged, whereas performance on the irregular (lexical) past form was hardly affected by these conditions. In contrast, Crookes (1989) reported a study in which providing subjects with pretask planning time leads to greater complexity and variety of language but no significant increases in accuracy. In this respect, Crookes proposed that the Ellis (1987) study confounded modality and planning time, rendering its results suspect. However, a problem with the Crookes study is that it is difficult to know what subjects actually did during the planning time available to them. It is noteworthy, in this regard, that the standard deviations for the measures reported tended to be higher for the planning groups for the complexity measures, suggesting that some subjects interpreted the planning instructions in different ways, using the time to prepare differently. Research attempting to influence the nature of the planning that takes place would therefore seem desirable.

Other manipulations of task conditions are also possible. Harrison (1986), for example, suggested that for testing as well as teaching it would be worth investigating the impact on performance of introducing surprise elements midtask, to explore how well different learners cope with this condition, on the assumption that it is likely to be disruptive to some degree but nonetheless typical of everyday language use. Conversely, it may be useful to explore how supporting learners with, for example, visual representation of the information required in tasks may ease processing demands and improve performance (Loschky & Bley-Vroman, 1993; D. Willis, 1990). It is also possible to introduce post-task manipulation. Here the central issue is that if one is using a task-based approach one does not want to interfere with performance midtask, because to do so would compromise one of the central defining qualities of tasks: they are meaning-focused. But a focus on form (rather than a focus on forms, i.e., form in general rather than any form in particular) is very important if language development is to occur (Doughty, 1991) because such a focus makes noticing more likely and also enables language teaching goals of accuracy and complexity (Skehan, 1992) to be pursued more effectively. To that end, it has been proposed (J. Willis & Willis, 1988) that post-task activities with a strong focus on form can have a beneficial effect on (earlier) task performance itself, provided that learners themselves make the connection between task completion and subsequent post-task activity. In this way, post-task activities, if salient in learners' attention, can infiltrate a focus on form into the earlier task completion and reduce the likelihood that the learners engaged in such task completion will allocate attention exclusively to meaning.

Based on studies such as these, Skehan (1996) proposes a framework to organize methods of task implementation that allow principled decisions to be made regarding the attentional focus and pedagogic goals of different activities. The framework is shown in Table 6.1.

The framework draws upon existing research but then elaborates a more comprehensive perspective on how task-based approaches can be implemented.

TABLE 6.1 A Framework for Task Implementation

Stage	Goal	Typical Techniques
Pretask		
Linguistic	Introduce new forms to interlanguage repertoire	Explicit and implicit teaching Consciousness-raising
Cognitive	Reduce cognitive load	Plan linguistically and cognitively
		Observe similar tasks
	Push learners to express more complex ideas	Plan
		Observe
Midtask		Use analytic scheme
Task choice	Balance difficulty of task	Introduce surprise
Task calibration	Increase or reduce difficulty	Provide (visual) support
Post-task	Raise consciousness for a focus on form	Use public performance and post-task activities

Obviously, the components of the framework constitute claims as to variables that will be important in task-based studies, and so underpinning research needs to be carried out to support or disconfirm the claims implicit in Table 6.1. We will report on research here that bears upon the role of planning as an aspect of pretask activities. Prior to that, however, we need to discuss alternative methods of assessing task-based performance and the relationship these different measures have to underlying theory.

In considering performance on tasks and following researchers such as Crookes (1989), Skehan (1992, 1996) makes a three-way distinction between complexity, accuracy, and fluency. The first two of these concern form but with a significant difference in emphasis. Complexity emphasizes the organization of what is said and draws attention to the progressively more elaborate language that may be used, as well as a greater variety of syntactic patterning. Complexity is likely to reflect a willingness, on the learner's part, to engage in restructuring as more complex subsystems of language are developed. It is also likely to be associated with greater risktaking to the extent that actual performances may be exploited to use forms closer to the cutting edge of interlanguage development.

The other aspect of form is accuracy. In this case the focus is on freedom from error, based on whatever language is used. In other words, a measure of accuracy may not reflect complexity of language and may be the result of relatively simple, well-controlled forms being used to achieve a more target-like use of language. In a sense, therefore, accuracy, as a reflection of a focus on form, may have a more conservative orientation, whereas complexity may capture a greater willingness to experiment and to take risks. Complexity, in other words, connects with change and the opportunities for development and growth in the interlanguage system. Accuracy, in contrast, concerns control at a particular interlanguage level.

Finally, we need to consider the role of fluency. Skehan (1992, 1996), following Schmidt (1990), takes fluency to reflect the primacy of meaning and the capacity to cope with real-time communication. It may therefore prioritize lexicalized language (Ellis, 1987) and the way learners, during tasks, avoid rule-based, constructed language, instead preferring to use more idiom-based language (Sinclair, 1991) to enable communication to proceed more smoothly. Fluency also reflects the effectiveness of the planning process and the way propositions can be orchestrated into effective, ongoing discourse.

It is also important to consider how each of these variables can be operationalized. A first question concerns whether to use general or specific measures. Ellis (1987) used specific measures of accuracy, such as measuring error rates with three past-tense forms. Crookes (1989), similarly, focused on use of articles and third person -s. Robinson, Ting, and Urwin (1995), in contrast, reported the use of more generalized measures for fluency (counting the number of pauses and the number of words per utterance) and complexity (calculating the number of embeddings per S-node, as well as lexical density). On occasion, clearly, specific measures are appropriate, as in the Ellis (1987) study in which the research design generated large numbers of tokens of the past tense and in which the past tense was central to the task. But when tasks do not provoke hypotheses about the use of specific forms, it would seem more appropriate to use generalized measures. Above all, such measures are likely to be more sensitive to differences in experimental conditions, detecting weaker effects because these are likely to be based on more variance. Crookes (1989) relied principally on specific measures (target-like use of the article system and of plural -s), and this may have been a factor in the lack of significance reported. Given the exploratory state of planning research, a general approach to measuring accuracy would appear more defensible at present.

But this still leaves the question of exactly which general measures should best be used. The general principle proposed is that useful variance should be maximized. To that end, as a measure of accuracy, the calculation of error-free clauses has merit. The unit involved, the clause, is relatively short, so that there is considerable scope for subjects to get moderately high scores. Clauses would also generalize across a range of different specific forms and not be dependent on any one of them. Finally, such a measure should produce good intersubject variation.

Turning to complexity, more generalized measures have been widely used, as with Robinson et al. (1995) and Crookes (1989), who used the number of subordinate clauses per utterance and per T-unit. To the extent that subordination, as an index, reflects a greater degree of internal structuring of speech, it captures a great deal of useful variance and so is a satisfactory measure. However, it can be argued that measures based on T-units ignore useful data. Hunt's (1966) definition of the T-unit (as a main clause plus embedded or attached subordinate clauses) excluded ellipsis and is therefore often unsatisfactory in dealing with spoken interaction where ellipsis quite naturally abounds. The c-unit, defined by Brock (1986) as an independent utterance providing referential or pragmatic meaning, allows for ellipsis and is thus a more sensitive measure for the spoken language. It is considered more appropriate for this study to capture complexity within the spoken language produced. But in addition to measuring complexity through subordination, one can also try to measure the range of syntactic forms used, as these reflect a capacity to draw upon a greater variety of language. If only base forms are used, such as simple present or simple past tenses, there would seem to be little impetus for interlanguage change to occur through the use of more challenging forms. To explore this possibility, it would seem worthwhile to examine measures of syntactic variety. Following Crookes (1989), we will focus on verbs and examine such areas as tense, aspect, voice, and modality.

Finally, we need to consider measures of conversational fluency. There is no generally accepted operationalization of fluency, although one can distinguish among different aspects. One is the capacity to engage in continued performance. This would suggest measures such as pauses, the total amount of silence, and perhaps repetition and hesitation as appropriate indices. Another aspect of fluency is the need to engage in more frequent repairs of breakdown in speech. This can be measured through indices of replacement, false starts, and reformulation. Finally, given arguments presented earlier, one might assess fluency through the importance of lexicalized communication. This study will not explore the last of these possibilities, useful though it would be, as there are no clear methods for establishing lexicalized units of production. Consequently, the measures used will reflect *fluency as continued performance* and *fluency as repair avoidance*.

Drawing on the preceding review, we can now formulate a number of hypotheses regarding the effects of planning on the nature of performance on language-learning tasks. These hypotheses relate to the three aspects of performance already discussed: fluency, complexity, and accuracy. The overriding hypothesis is that planning will have positive effects on performance in each of these areas, but this general claim can be broken down into several more detailed hypotheses:

Hypothesis 1: Under planned conditions, there will be greater fluency in language; that is, there will be fewer repetitions, fewer reformulations, fewer replacements, fewer false starts, fewer pauses, and a smaller silence total. This follows from the preparation that can be accomplished during planning. Ideas can be organized to enable more fluid expression, less on-line attention is needed to handle ongoing discourse processing, and lexicalized language units can have been prepared to ease processing even further.

Hypothesis 2: Under planned conditions, there will be greater complexity of language; that is, there will be a greater number of clauses per c-unit. This relates to the Crookes (1989) study. Planning can enable more ambitious ideas to be attempted and will enable the relationships between ideas to be expressed more clearly.

Hypothesis 3: Under planned conditions, there will be greater variability in language; that is, there will be a wider range in the tense, aspect, modality, and voice of verbs. This also follows from Crookes (1989). Nonplanners will need to engage in more on-line processing and, as a result, will tend to rely on a narrower range of linguistic forms. Planners will be able to access a wider repertoire of linguistic forms, partly because of freer on-line resources and partly because such forms will have been made salient from the planning phase itself.

Hypothesis 4: Under planned conditions, there will be greater accuracy in language; that is, there will be a higher proportion of error-free to total clauses. This relates to the study by Ellis (1987) in which significant differences in accuracy were found and to that by Crookes (1989) in which there was a nonsignificant trend toward accuracy, though only specific accuracy measures were used. It is proposed that under the planning condition greater accuracy will result partly from the greater attention that is available on-line (Tarone, 1985) and partly from the activity in the planning phase itself that is directed toward achieving accuracy.

Hypothesis 5: The effects predicted in Hypotheses 1–4 will all be greater when planning is carried out at a more detailed level. The motivation for this hypothesis relates to the effectiveness with which planning is directed toward task performance and to the larger standard deviations for the planners' complexity scores reported in Crookes (1989). It is proposed that more detailed planning will lead subjects to use planning time more effectively and in ways that aid subsequent retrieval of the products of planning during task performance.

Hypothesis 6: The effects predicted in Hypotheses 1–5 will all be greater for tasks that are more cognitively demanding, that is, those based on less familiar information and requiring more on-line processing. Such tasks provide a greater challenge for subjects, as they require more attentional resources to handle cognitive content and, correspondingly, provide greater scope for planning to prepare for the subsequent task performance.

Method

The study is essentially a multifactorial design, examining the effects of task choice and implementation conditions on a range of measures of language performance. We will describe the tasks themselves, the implementation conditions, the subjects, the setting, the overall research design, and then the dependent variables.

Tasks

All tasks were carried out by subjects in dyads. The three tasks used were a personal information exchange, a narrative based on pictures, and a decision-making task. The choice of these types was based on an analysis of tasks commonly used in current English language teaching textbooks. They were hypothesized to require different levels of attention on the part of the subjects, with progressively less familiar and less predictable information causing an increasingly taxing cognitive load and, as a consequence, influencing performance on the task.

The *Personal Information Exchange* task required subjects to describe to the other member of the dyad how to get to his or her home from the college that subjects were attending and then to turn off a gas cooker that had been left on. As it involved accessing information well known to the speaker and possibly already rehearsed in English, it was seen as requiring the least cognitive effort and allowing the greatest attention to language form. Moreover, it was reasoned that the nature of the task would require relatively simple linguistic forms to be used.

For the *Narrative* task, each member of the dyad had to construct a storyline from a set of five pictures that were loosely but not obviously connected and to relay their ideas to each other. This task involved encoding new, visual information into linguistic form and required some degree of imagination. It was seen as giving scope for more complex language but also demanding greater cognitive effort, therefore allowing less attention to be devoted to form.

For the *Decision-Making* task, subjects were asked to act as judges at the trials of a list of offenders and to reach an agreement with their partner on a suitable prison sentence for each. This task involved considering a lot of new information (i.e., the facts of each case), evaluating it, and then defending an opinion against any objections from the other member of the dyad. This task was considered to place the heaviest cognitive load upon the subject and to allow the least attentional resources to be given to language form. At the same time, the process of trying to reach an agreement on a series of difficult questions was considered most likely to require the use of complex language.[1]

This characterization suggests that the Personal task should be easiest and most accessible to learners and that the Narrative and Decision tasks are similar to one another in that they provide relatively low familiarity but a high computational load. Looking at these latter two tasks in more detail, one might propose that the Decision task is slightly more familiar than the Narrative task, in that the moral values relevant to each judgment ought not to be totally unknown to the subjects in the study. Conversely, one might argue that the more unpredictable interactions in the Decision task make it more difficult. It should also be the case that the Narrative task is eased through the visual and "plot" support that is involved. On balance, then, the Narrative task is judged to be easier than the Decision task.

Planning Condition

Three groups of students were involved in the study: one control and two experimental. The control group dyads did the tasks with only a brief introduction to ensure that they all understood what was required of them. The experimental dyads had the same brief introduction, followed by 10 minutes of individual planning time (as in Crookes, 1989). To maximize the chances that they would indeed engage in planning, they were asked to make notes about what they were going to say but were told that these notes would be taken away before they began to speak. The planning condition was operationalized as detailed and undetailed; that is, half of the experimental dyads received guidance on how they might use the 10 minutes to consider the syntax, lexis, content, and organization of what they would say, and the other half received no guidance and were simply told to plan. In this way, it was possible to investigate any effect that quality of planning might have on task performance.

Subjects and Setting

The subjects were 32 preintermediate-level students studying English as a foreign language six hours per week at a local college. They came from a wide variety of L1 backgrounds and were all between 18 and 30 years old, and all but three were female. They had been placed in one of four preintermediate classes on the basis of a brief interview and the standard college placement test.[2] Which of the four classes an individual student chose to join was not based on any difference in language proficiency but on a personal preference for a particular class time. The make-up of each class can justifiably be described as comparable in respect to language proficiency, age range, and L1 background. Eight subjects were selected for study in each class, although all class members were, in fact, treated in the same way. The students selected were simply those who attended during all three weeks of the study. It was only the selected students whose data were analyzed. The classes had begun three weeks before data-gathering was started. It was intended that this preresearch period would allow the classes to become established and would lead to more stable populations.

All data were collected during normally scheduled class times. The researcher, who was already familiar to some of the students, took the role of teacher and introduced the tasks as classroom communicative activities. (This was unproblematic, as each of the tasks was closely based on types commonly used in classrooms.) All data were collected using small, unobtrusive dictation machines with no external microphone, which enabled all the dyads to be recorded simultaneously and with the least disruption to normal class routines. In these ways, an authentic classroom setting was preserved as far as possible. It is argued that the use of intact classes under relatively normal conditions minimizes any effects that experimental conditions might have on subjects' performance (Foster, 1994). It makes for greater naturalness in the language produced, not least because of subjects' familiarity with one another (Plough & Gass, 1993). In addition, the inclusion of all class members in the data collection meant that the selected experimental subjects were not alerted to the fact that only their data would be analyzed. The applicability to L2 classrooms of the results of the study is therefore arguably more justified (van Lier, 1989).

Design

Of the four intact classes used in the study, two acted as controls and two as experimental groups. The experimental groups were each divided into two, and in each case half the subjects were randomly assigned the undetailed planning condition and half the detailed planning condition (see Table 6.2). As all subjects in the experimental groups had 10 minutes of planning time before the task, it was not obvious to either the detailed or the undetailed planners that others in the same class were responding to a different set of instructions as to how this time might be used.

Each class was visited on three occasions at weekly intervals and on each visit was given one of the three tasks to do. To combat any practice effect, each of the controls and each of the experimental groups did the tasks in a different order (see Table 6.3). The eventual scores for the Narrative groups, under whichever design condition, were therefore made up of subjects who had done this task in the first week of the study and others who had done it in the third week. The scores for the Decision task were similarly obtained, rendering the two conditions more directly comparable. It was assumed that if there was a practice effect of consistent strength over the three visits of the study, the Personal Information Exchange task, always completed in the second week, would be affected to the same degree as the averaged performance on the other two tasks.

As far as possible, the students worked with the same partner on all of the tasks. At each data-gathering session, all students present in the class, including those not part of the study, were recorded. In this way, subjects were protected from any special pressure that selection for recording might have had upon their performance.

TABLE 6.2 Design of the Control and Experimental Groups

Control Groups		Experimental Groups			
Class A	Class B	Class C		Class D	
No planning	No planning	Undetailed planning	Detailed planning	Undetailed planning	Detailed planning

TABLE 6.3 Task Order Across the Groups

	Control Groups		Experimental Group	
	Class A	Class B	Class C	Class D
Week 1	Decision	Narrative	Narrative	Decision
Week 2	Personal	Personal	Personal	Personal
Week 3	Narrative	Decision	Decision	Narrative

At the end of the 3 weeks, data were transcribed only for 8 subjects in each group who had attended all of the sessions and who had worked with the same partner each time, giving a total of 32 subjects. It was at this stage that the problem with the misclassified student was identified, thus reducing the total sample to 31. Another subject in a control group failed to take her turn in one of the tasks, and an experimental group dyad that had only attended for two of the tasks was nevertheless included to even up the numbers across the four groups. The data set, based on 31 subjects, is otherwise complete.

Analysis

The data were also coded for a range of dependent variables following the rationale provided in the previous section.

Fluency

Reformulations: Either phrases or clauses that are repeated with some modification to syntax, morphology, or word order.

Replacements: Lexical items that are immediately substituted for another.

False starts: Utterances that are abandoned before completion and that may or may not be followed by a reformulation.

Repetitions: Words, phrases, or clauses that are repeated with no modification whatsoever to syntax, morphology, or word order.

Hesitations: Initial phoneme or syllable(s) uttered one or more times before the complete word is spoken.

Pauses: A break of 1.0 second or longer either within a turn or between turns.

Silence total: The sum of pauses in each transcript.

Complexity

Clauses/c-units: Clauses are either a simple independent finite clause or a dependent finite or nonfinite clause. A c-unit is defined as each independent utterance providing referential or pragmatic meaning. Thus, a c-unit may be made up of one simple independent finite clause or else an independent finite clause plus one or more dependent finite or nonfinite clauses.

Syntactic variety: A collection of variables based on verb forms and identifying the tense, modality, voice, and aspect of both finite and nonfinite verbs.

Accuracy

Error-free clauses: A clause in which there is no error in syntax, morphology, or word order. Errors in lexis were counted when the word used was incontrovertibly wrong. In cases of fine decisions of appropriacy, no error was recorded.

Given the focus of the study on planning conditions with three tasks, the general approach to analysis was to perform one-way ANOVAs for each dependent variable for each task, followed by post hoc tests where *F* values justified this procedure. This approach is most revealing because it is the planning conditions that have the most complex relationship with the various dependent variables. It was also felt important to examine the dependent variables, in the groups outlined, in separate ANOVAs, rather than through a more general multivariate ANOVA. The rationale for the dependent variables presented earlier indicates the distinct role that each contributes. This claim is supported by a factor analytic study of a pooled data set from the present data set and a related study (Skehan & Foster, 1996). This analysis generated a three-factor solution, with the three orthogonal factors clearly identifiable as fluency, complexity, and accuracy, suggesting adequate independence among them.

Results

As indicated earlier (see Table 6.2), the research employed a design to counterbalance practice effects as the Narrative and Decision tasks were done in both the first and third weeks by different groups of subjects. This design does, however, enable us to probe for practice effects, as one can compare the performance of subjects who completed the Narrative task in week 1 with those who did this task in week 3, and the reverse sequence for the Decision task. The relevant data are shown in Tables 6.4 and 6.5. The results focus on the measures for complexity and error, as representative of the wider results available.

None of the complexity figures, for either task, for any of the planning conditions, showed any significant differences. In addition, it is clear from visual inspection of these means that there is no pattern in the data. We can conclude, therefore (and this is interesting in itself), that general task familiarity does not have an influence on the level of complexity achieved. The situation is slightly more complicated for the error measures. No significant differences were found, so we can conclude that the null hypothesis is sustained in this case; that is, familiarity of general task conditions does not lead to improved performance. But two factors

TABLE 6.4 The Effects of Practice on Accuracy

	No Planning	*Undetailed Planning*	*Detailed Planning*
Narrative			
Week 1 (0.60)	0.58	0.64	0.54
Week 3 (0.64)	0.64	0.69	0.61
Decision			
Week 1 (0.65)	0.61	0.70	0.70
Week 3 (0.69)	0.65	0.76	0.72

Note: Figures represent percentage of error-free clauses

TABLE 6.5 The Effects of Practice on Complexity

	No Planning	Undetailed Planning	Detailed Planning
Narrative			
Week 1 (1.36)	1.21	1.38	1.94
Week 3 (1.34)	1.22	1.57	1.52
Decision			
Week 1 (0.65)	1.20	1.41	1.55
Week 3 (0.69)	1.24	1.28	1.50

Note: Figures represent average number of clauses per c-unit

suggest that this should be a qualified conclusion. First, for every set of data, there was a higher average score for the third week's performance compared to the first, with this superiority generally being of about 0.05 error-free clauses.[3] Second, the sample sizes here were quite small, and it may well be that with larger groups significant findings might have been found, in which case one would have to relate familiarity to a slight reduction in the amount of error. In any case, given the counterbalanced nature of the research design, any trend toward a practice effect on errors does not influence the conclusions to be drawn later. As a result, we can now move on to consider the major hypotheses of the study.

Hypothesis 1 proposed that fluency will be greater under planned conditions. Relevant results are presented in Tables 6.6 and 6.7. Table 6.6 gives the separate F values for one-way ANOVAs relating the three levels of planning to each of the fluency variables for each of the three tasks. Table 6.7 gives the actual mean scores for only those comparisons revealed to be significant by the one-way ANOVAs. For example, the F value of 3.47 in Table 6.6 for the measure of total silence for the levels of planning on the Personal task reaches the 0.05 level of significance, so Table 6.7 gives the three relevant mean scores of 31.8 seconds (no planning), 19.5 seconds (undetailed planning), and 14.5 seconds (detailed planning). The figures in Table 6.6 indicate that pauses and total silence achieved significance for all three tasks, with very high levels achieved for the Narrative and Decision tasks. Otherwise, the only significant values were for repetitions-hesitations and replacements for the Decision task.

Table 6.7 provides the more detailed information for the three planning conditions for those cases where significant F values were found. The most striking result here is in terms of the number of pauses and the amount of total silence. The effects are marked and show a consistent effect for planning. In addition, it is striking that, whereas for the Narrative task the different planning conditions themselves (detailed vs. undetailed) each exerted an influence (e.g., pauses: 30.3, 15.3, 8.0), for the Personal and Decision tasks there was only an overall effect for planning versus no planning, the results showing little difference between the two planning conditions (e.g., pauses, Decision: 17.3 vs. 17.3). Perhaps linked to this,

TABLE 6.6 F Values for Fluency and Task Type

	Personal	Narrative	Decision
Replacements	1.59	0.37	4.48★
False starts	0.15	0.13	0.84
Reformulations	1.28	0.62	0.45
Passives	0.49	2.38	1.2
Repetitions/hesitations[a]	0.32	0.79	2.99★
Pauses	4.68★	9.3★★★	12.33★★★
Total silence	3.47★	17.31★★★	21.94★★★

[a] These categories, described separately earlier, were collapsed under one heading for statistical tests.
★ $p < 0.05$ ★★★ $p < 0.001$

TABLE 6.7 Mean Scores for Fluency and Planning Condition

	Pauses			Repetition-Hesitations
	Personal	Narrative	Decision	Decision
No planning	19.2	30.3	37.0	9.9
Undetailed planning	10.0	15.3	17.3	20.1
Detailed planning	11.2	8.0	17.3	17.9
	Total Silence			Replacements
	Personal	Narrative	Decision	Decision
No planning	31.8	120.3	91.4	0.56
Undetailed planning	19.5	29.3	25.8	1.38
Detailed planning	14.5	14.2	29.5	2.63

the one other result worth commenting on is that for the Decision task—in contrast to the other two, there were significant differences across planning conditions for repetition and hesitation, and for replacement (though not for reformulation) but in the opposite direction. In other words, planning was associated with more repetition, hesitation, and replacement. This combination of findings might suggest that the effects of planning, although very important, are more complex than was expected. Subjects seem to use planning time to capitalize on the use of time-creating devices (Bygate, 1987), as indexed by the effect for repetition and replacement. Such learners seem to use the planning they have done to think "on-line" and possibly to make their discourse more naturalistic. We can conclude, therefore, that Hypothesis 1 is supported for pauses and total silence. Variables such as repetition and replacement clearly merit further research.

Hypothesis 2 stated that planning would be associated with greater complexity, with complexity indexed by the ratio of clauses divided by c-units. Following the sequence used with the fluency measures, Table 6.8 shows first the F values from one-way ANOVAs for the subordination measures (e.g., 8.35 being the F value for the one-way analysis of the three planning conditions for the Personal task). Table 6.8 shows next the mean scores for the three planning conditions on this task—for example, 1.11, 1.16, and 1.26 as the three mean scores dependent on the F value of 8.35.

The results in Table 6.8 suggest a very strong effect for the planning condition: detailed planning produced significantly more subordination than undetailed planning, which in turn produced significantly more subordination than no planning.

Range tests using Duncan's procedure (Norusis, 1990) indicate that within each task all pairwise comparisons are significantly different from one another with the exception of the no planning (1.11) and undetailed planning (1.16) conditions for the Personal task, which were not. Hypothesis 2 is accordingly confirmed.

TABLE 6.8 Complexity, Task Type, and Planning Condition

	Personal	Narrative	Decision
F values			
Clauses/c-units	8.35	9.30	15.00
Mean scores			
No planning	1.11	1.20	1.23
Undetailed planning	1.16	1.43	1.35
Detailed planning	1.26	1.68	1.52

★★★ All values are significant at $p < 0.001$

TABLE 6.9 Syntactic Variety Measures

	Personal	Narrative	Decision
F values			
Nonsimple present tenses	0.06	0.10	0.80
Nonsimple past tenses	3.46★	5.12★★	1.93
Modal total	0.56	0.99	0.49
Conditional total	1.42	1.45	2.75
Mean scores for nonsimple past tenses			
No planning	0.0	0.0	
Undetailed planning	0.0	1.13	
Detailed planning	0.25	1.17	

★ $p < 0.05$ ★★ $p < 0.01$

Hypothesis 3 stated that planning would be associated with greater structural variety. The relevant results are shown in Table 6.9. *F* values are shown for the one-way ANOVAs that examined the effects of planning conditions for each variable for each task; for example, 5.12 is the *F* value for the three planning conditions for the Narrative task and the dependent variable of nonsimple past tenses. The actual mean scores for the three planning conditions are shown for the two cases (nonsimple past tenses on the Personal and Narrative tasks) in which significant *F* values were found. These mean scores are necessarily low because opportunity for use of the different structures is unavoidably limited in scope and because they are given in the form of proportion scores.

The significant results all involve use of the past tense. The measures examine the number of uses of past-tense forms other than the simple past, that is, those that could be argued to be more interesting and challenging forms, and whose use reflects learners who are more willing and able to take risks, restructure, and use forms at the borders of interlanguage competence. The results show that for the Personal and Narrative forms significance is achieved, whereas for the Decision task, in which the *F* value of 1.93 produces a probability value of only $p < 0.16$, significance was approached but not attained. The detailed mean scores then show that planning is associated with greater variety of past-tense usage. No significant differences were found for greater variety of present-tense usage (i.e., forms other than the simple present), modals, or conditionals. Hypothesis 3 therefore receives some support, but only at a fairly weak level.

Hypothesis 4 stated that planning would be associated with greater accuracy. Relevant results are presented in Table 6.10. Only one measure is presented here, the percentage of error-free clauses. The three *F* values are shown first, followed by detailed means scores.

The central finding here is that there are significant differences in the proportion of error-free clauses that were used under the different planning conditions, but these differences show a complex pattern. The *F* ratio of 5.73 for the Decision task is significant at the 0.01 level, with Duncan range tests demonstrating that the

TABLE 6.10 Error as a Function of Task Type and Planning Condition

F-values	*Personal*	*Narrative*	*Decision*	*Mean*
F values from one-way ANOVAs	2.46*	0.69ns	5.73**	
Mean error scores by planning condition by task				
No planning	0.64	0.61	0.63	0.63
Undetailed planning	0.76	0.65	0.73	0.71
Detailed planning	0.69	0.58	0.71	0.66
Mean score	0.70	0.61	0.69	

★ $p < 0.05$ ★★ $p < 0.01$ ns = not significant

no planning condition was significantly different from the two planning conditions but that the two types of planning did not produce significantly different effects. The F value for the Personal task just attains the 0.05 level of significance. Detailed tests indicate that the no planning condition and the undetailed planners are significantly different from one another. No other comparisons are significant. Significance is not attained for the Narrative task. These results provide limited support for Hypothesis 4.

Hypothesis 5 proposed that the effects of planning would be stronger as planning is carried out at a more detailed level, that is, that there would be a basically monotonic relationship over the three planning levels, with the detailed planning condition producing stronger effects than the undetailed condition, which in turn would have stronger effects than the no planning condition. This hypothesis can be explored by drawing upon the data already presented in Tables 6.6–6.10. Regarding the fluency measures of pauses and silence, the no planning group always produced the least fluency. Detailed planning only led to greater fluency than undetailed planning for the Narrative task. For the Personal and Decision tasks variation in planning produced little difference. The findings for complexity, in contrast, essentially supported Hypothesis 5 across the tasks, with the detailed planners always producing significantly greater complexity than the undetailed planners, who in turn outperformed the no planning group (with only the comparison for the no planners vs. the undetailed planners failing to reach significance). The syntactic variety results, which provided only limited support for the more specific Hypothesis 3, patterned similarly to the fluency measures, with little difference between the two planning conditions.

Finally, we need to consider the accuracy results. For each task it is noteworthy that the undetailed planners produced the most accurate level of performance. This is strikingly so in the case of the Personal task (0.76 vs. 0.64 and 0.69) and the Narrative task (0.65 vs. 0.61 and 0.58) but only marginally true in the case of the Decision task (0.73 vs. 0. 71 and 0.63). In addition, the detailed planners produced a level of accuracy that was greater than the no planning condition for the Personal and Decision tasks, but the no planning condition produced more accurate performance than detailed planning in the Narrative task. These comparisons do not attain significance in specific pairwise comparisons, but the trend in the results is clear.

Two aspects of these findings merit additional comment. First, these results contrast with those of Crookes (1989) in that here planning is associated with a greater degree of accuracy, at least some of the time. It does appear, in other words, that some of the value of having planning time available is channeled into achieving more error-free language. Second, the results also contrast somewhat with those for subordination, in which there was a monotonic relationship with planning condition and in which the detailed planners produced the most subordination on all three tasks. With accuracy, the trend is toward the undetailed planners being the most accurate. We will return to this finding; at this point, we have to conclude that Hypothesis 5 is only supported to a limited degree and that the results obtained reveal a more complex picture than was predicted.

Finally, Hypothesis 6 proposed that the effects predicted in Hypotheses 1–5 would be greater for the more cognitively demanding tasks, that is, those based on less familiar information and more cognitive processing. In the present case, this contrasts the Personal task with the Narrative and Decision tasks. Once again, the hypothesis can be explored by going over the data presented in Tables 6.6–6.10. There is some support for this hypothesis as shown by the fluency measures for pauses and total silence in Table 6.7. The fluency measures for the Personal task reduced by less than do those for the Decision task and, most of all, the Narrative, where total silence decreased from 120.3 seconds (no planning) to 14.2 seconds (detailed planning), an enormous change compared to a reduction of around 17 seconds for the Personal task (31.8–14.5).

A similar picture emerges for the complexity measures. The Personal task always produced the least subordination, perhaps reflecting the linguistic demands that were made to express directional meanings, as well as the succinctness that may result from well-organized knowledge. Furthermore, the difference between the no planning and detailed planning conditions for the Personal task is only 0.15 (i.e., 1.26–1.11). The corresponding figures for the Decision and Narrative tasks are 0.29 and 0.48, respectively, appreciably larger figures. Planning, in other words, does not operate in the same way with all tasks. It would be valuable to probe which task qualities—for example, use of less familiar knowledge or greater on-line processing—account for these differential effects.

The measures of syntactic variety were not strong, in any sense, and provide no clear support for Hypothesis 6. The use of nonsimple past tenses to refer to past time generated the only significant results. Inspection of the actual mean scores provides no supportive evidence here, and indeed the fact that the Personal task generated one significant F value when the Decision task did not seems to argue against Hypothesis 6. Similarly, the results for accuracy do not support Hypothesis 6. The greatest difference between a no planning and a planning score is that between no planning and undetailed planning Personal scores. The gain scores for accuracy on the other two tasks are lower and, indeed, the detailed planners on the Narrative produce lower accuracy scores than the no planners.

We can conclude, therefore, that Hypothesis 6, which can be broken down into subhypotheses for the different dependent variables, does not yield a unified picture. It is supported by the complexity results and partially supported by the fluency results. In contrast, the syntactic variety results do not support the hypothesis, whereas the results for accuracy, if anything, run counter to it. This mixed picture will be discussed in the next section in terms of trade-off effects that result from processing capacity limitations.

Discussion

The general perspective in this article is that attention is limited in capacity and that its use to achieve one goal can reduce the capacity remaining for the achievement of other goals. Thus, the framework proposed in Table 6.1 was intended to enable the organization of task-based instruction to minimize its dangers (excessive focus on meaning) while maximizing the chances that its advantages will be realized (accurate and complex form). The framework also generates hypotheses that are testable, and this article has focused on one phase (pretask activities) and one area within that phase (planning), as well as on the nature of the tasks themselves.[4]

Regarding task difficulty, it was proposed earlier that the Personal task would be the easiest, the Decision task the most difficult, with the Narrative closer to the Decision than to the Personal. The results obtained only partly fit into this analysis. The Personal task indeed produced much more fluent performance, as indexed by the average number of pauses and the average amount of silence, with the differential between the tasks being interestingly narrowed for the more planned conditions. This applies dramatically to the total silence figure for the unplanned Narrative task and suggests that being able to draw upon familiar, ready-encoded information does promote a greater degree of fluency and a corresponding lack of need for planning.

The pattern changes for the figures on average error. Here, the Personal and Decision tasks lead (average error proportions of 0.70 and 0.69, respectively), whereas the Narrative task produces the lowest overall accuracy level (0.61). But these rankings change when we consider the average complexity figures. The least complex language is used with the Personal task (1.18 clauses per c-unit), the Decision task produces more complex language (1.32), and the Narrative task produces the most complex language of all (1.44). But these average figures disguise some important interactions between task type and planning condition. First of all, it is noteworthy that the no planning condition produces a relatively even level of performance across the tasks. The range in scores across the tasks is only 0.03 for accuracy and 0.08 for complexity. In contrast, the two planning conditions lead to much more uneven figures. With accuracy, the Personal task and the Decision task produce clear (and fairly similar) gains, whereas the degree of improvement for the Narrative task is less marked. A contrasting picture emerges with the complexity measures. The smallest improvement shown as a function of planning is for the Personal task (i.e., the opportunity to use more time does not seem here to confer much advantage for complexity). The Decision task is influenced appreciably by planning, and the Narrative task is influenced most of all.

Generalizing from these results, what seems to be at issue here is that each of the tasks produces a pattern of results that basically reflects task properties. The Personal task generates a greater degree of accuracy without achieving much complexity. The Narrative task produces the highest level of complexity, suggesting a greater need to use precise and extending language, but this gain seems to be at the expense of accuracy, as this highest complexity measure (1.68) is associated with the lowest accuracy score (0.58). Finally, the Decision task seems to occupy an intermediate position, producing useful levels of accuracy and complexity. The accuracy level, it will be recalled, is comparable to that obtained with the Personal task (and above that obtained for the Narrative task). Complexity, in contrast, although never as great as the Narrative task, is higher than the Personal task and shows a more marked effect for planning. This suggests that the combination of task type and planning condition provides scope for complexity to operate as a viable goal without compromising accuracy.

More broadly, what seems to be happening here is that subjects were operating under some information-processing pressure: they had to allocate attention to particular goals at the expense of other goals. The pattern of results, in other words, supports trade-off effects between complexity and accuracy, a point developed more fully in Skehan and Foster (1996). Decision task subjects under planning conditions were most able to combine goals simultaneously. Other tasks seemed to lead to a greater degree of sacrifice of one goal or another. The implication, in other words, is that task selection and task implementation can lead to systematic and selective influences upon the nature of the ensuing proficiency.

We turn next to examining the effect of the planning variable in its own terms. We have seen briefly that planning has an effect upon fluency. This effect is of a monotonic nature for the Narrative task, but there is only a binary distinction for the other two tasks (i.e., the detailed and undetailed conditions do not lead to different patterns of pausing and total silence). Clearly, subjects required to wrestle with the complexity of the story to be told in the Narrative task receive additional benefit from the structure that the detailed planning condition provides. Possibly, with tasks that are most demanding cognitively, the planning suggestions provided to subjects enable them to make more inroads into a problem they might otherwise not be able to analyze so effectively. Interestingly, the one other fluency effect for planning is with the Decision task and the variables of repetition/hesitation and replacement. Planning produces more of these, rendering the discourse, in one sense, less fluent. But we interpret this finding to suggest naturalness of discourse, in that native speakers also engage in a greater use of such linguistic behaviors to enable them to cope with the problem of real time. In other words, it may be that the subjects under the unplanned condition, who would benefit most from the use of techniques to protect time for ongoing planning, are unable to exploit them. In contrast, the planned condition subjects, already favored by the experimental condition they received, are able to capitalize upon their clear ideas and language and to make things even easier by exploiting repetitions and replacements to create a natural buffer against time pressure.

The complexity and error measures make for an interesting contrast. The complexity values provide a very clear picture: the relationship is linear, and it does appear that detailed planners have responded to the suggestions given to them by producing more subordinated language. At present, we cannot say whether this is the result of incorporating more complex forms into speech consciously, or the detailed planning has reduced cognitive load to enable greater challenges to be attempted during ongoing discourse, or the effects of the (detailed) planning have been cognitive, and so pushed learners to find language to express more complex ideas. We suspect the last of these, a proposal consistent with the reactions of the subjects, who thought the Narrative task most difficult but produced the most complex language while doing it. Further research will be necessary to try to establish what the operative causal factors are.

But what is even more interesting still is that this pattern of results is not repeated for the accuracy measures. Here, the accuracy level order for the Personal and Decision tasks is no planning < detailed planning < undetailed planning, whereas for the Narrative task the order is detailed planning < no planning < undetailed planning. In all cases, though, the most accurate performance is for the undetailed planners.[5] This pattern of results was not predicted. First of all, we need to recall that the evidence on the influence of planning on accuracy is mixed. Although Ellis (1987) reported such an effect, it was for a study that focused on only one language form (the past tense, so that no complexity dimension was involved) and for which the experimental conditions (talking, alone, into a tape recorder) might be thought to favor accuracy. The most comparable study (Crookes, 1989) reported a complexity effect, but no significant differences for accuracy. A generally similar pattern of results is reported in Alvarez-Ossario (1996). So it is already striking that there is an accuracy effect in the present study, even though statistically it is not as strong as that for complexity or fluency. But even more surprising is that the detailed planners, who were expected to exploit the guiding instructions to facilitate generalized improvement, did not seem to do so.

In trying to account for the discrepancy with Crookes (1989) and Alvarez-Ossario (1996), two potential explanations present themselves. First of all, the contrast in findings may be due to the nature of the measures used. Crookes (1989) looked for specific effects on a wide range of variables, whereas the present study used a more global measure based on all contributory influences on error and correctness. Crookes (1989) seemed to be testing for specific increases in accuracy, whereas we were more interested in detecting a more generalized accuracy effect. It may simply be, therefore, that the use of a dependent variable such as error-free clauses is more sensitive to an overall accuracy effect, a proposal perhaps consistent with the weaker finding in this area than for complexity. A second explanation, however, focuses on the tasks themselves. Crookes's (1989) tasks, for example, a LEGO assembly, were classroom tasks and did not have much connection with the subjects' real lives. They were, quite simply, devices for the transmission of neutral and arbitrary information. The tasks in this study contrast with these to some degree. This is clearly the case with the Personal and Decision tasks. In the first case, students described an aspect of their actual lives, whereas in the second they had to draw upon their own system of values and beliefs. There is evidence (Tarone, 1985) indicating that discourse salience can influence the level of accuracy on a task, particularly when syntax and morphology have discoursal value to signal meaning. Although this is, of course, speculative, it may be the case that subjects are drawn toward a greater degree of precision and accuracy when they can use planning conditions to invest the language they use in tasks with more personal significance. In passing, it should be noted that the Narrative task is less effective at meeting this criterion of real-world connection, as there is obviously an arbitrary, detached quality to producing an imaginary story based on a set of (relatively) unrelated photographs. It is relevant, in this respect, that the changes in accuracy were least for this task, with even a reduction of accuracy level for the detailed versus the undetailed planners. In any case, the two explanations for the discrepancies in research findings are post hoc and will have to await further research directed specifically at this issue before they can be resolved.

Even so, two points remain that do require discussion: the nature of the relationship between the accuracy and complexity results, and the precise role of detailed and undetailed planning. In reality, these points can be accounted for together. What seems to be happening is that the goals of complexity and accuracy compete for limited information-processing resources and that what is achievable depends on the precise allocational decisions made. Certainly the joint levels of accuracy and complexity achieved by the undetailed planners reflect progress being made toward both goals simultaneously (as well as toward fluency). In that respect, the psycholinguistic resources available seemed to cope adequately with the pressures that had been manipulated. But the next condition, detailed planning, seemed to lead to a level of pressure too great for subjects to cope with all aspects of performance, with the result that prioritizing decisions had to be made. Consistent with Crookes (1989), complexity became the preeminent goal, but accuracy suffered to some degree, reducing to a point midway between the undetailed and nonplanning conditions for the Personal task, below the no planning conditions for the Narrative task, and only slightly inferior to the undetailed planning for the Decision task.

Turning finally to the explanation for the excessive pressure on processing resources that is produced by the detailed planning condition, the most plausible account would seem to be that detailed planning causes subjects to structure their subsequent task contributions in a more ambitious manner. This may have been in terms of propositional content and discoursal development, such that the planning time was channeled into the production of more complex ideas, which then pushed learners to levels of syntax beyond their level of comfortable control or, alternatively, whose execution was so demanding on available resources that, through the prioritization of more interesting ideas, accuracy was squeezed out. Alternatively, the detailed planning time was used to access more "cutting edge" language that, precisely because of its developing nature, was less controlled. Further research will have to probe which of these interesting alternatives was the more powerful influence.

Conclusion

Two broad implications can be drawn from the research reported here. First of all, there is the issue of the framework within which research can be most usefully conducted in the area of task-based instruction. This study has drawn on the framework from Table 6.1, which suggests a number of factors, organized as pre-, mid-, and post-task stages, that may influence the balance struck in task-based instruction among goals of fluency, complexity, and accuracy. It has shown that pretask activities can have a significant impact on the ways that tasks are done. But what the framework also does is suggest other areas that can be researched to produce a better overall understanding of how tasks can be most effectively used pedagogically. Simply building on the present results, it is clear that, interesting though they are, and immediately useful as they may be for pedagogic decisions, they raise as many questions as they provide answers. Although it seems likely that trade-off attentional effects are central, the exact patterning of results was not completely predicted, and it is clear that additional research is now urgently necessary into the precise effects of planning time on the competing goals of complexity and accuracy, especially. Planning time has a major impact, but it would seem that if we could learn more about this area it would be possible to predict more effectively the exact balance between these different goals. In this way, it would be possible to set longer term pedagogic goals in which cycles of synthesis and analysis are engaged and areas of interlanguage are developed and then integrated into fluent performance. To achieve this, clearer operationalizations of planning time, as a construct, are necessary, as well as the use of research methodologies, such as immediate retrospection, that provide more detailed information on which planning operations were undertaken and what the differential effects of such operations might be.

The framework from Table 6.1, however, encompasses more than simply pretask activities. It also suggests that midtask and post-task activities are important. Skehan and Foster (1996) researched post-task activities, and this research suggests that the knowledge or threat that a post-task repeat public performance of the task being done is likely to be required increases the focus on accuracy. The framework also suggests that midtask manipulations may also influence the balance among the goals of fluency, complexity, and accuracy. Research into the injection of surprise elements, or the use of different degrees of visual support, may well be productive (Foster & Skehan, 1996b).

Finally, the three tasks used in the present study—a Personal Information Exchange task, a Narrative task, and a Decision-Making task—yielded interestingly contrasting results. These three tasks were chosen because they vary the importance of background knowledge and general familiarity, on the one hand, and inherent structure, on the other. The results obtained were consistent with the hypothesized task properties. But these conclusions are based on just three tasks. It is also important to conduct research on other examples of these three task types, as well as on other task types, and to explore the predictability of the language characteristics associated with such tasks. This is essential if one is to be able to use tasks whose worth can be predicted in advance rather than only observable after task completion. In this way, perhaps, a library of tasks, of known qualities, can be drawn upon as a resource by the teacher interested in task-based instruction. These issues are explored more fully in Skehan and Foster (1996).

Acknowledgment

The authors thank four anonymous SSLA reviewers whose comments on an earlier draft of this article were very helpful. We also thank the staff and students at Richmond Adult and Community College for their considerable cooperation. Without them the research reported here would have been impossible. Finally, thanks are also due to the Centre for Applied Linguistic Research at Thames Valley University and to the Economic and Social Research Council, whose financial support was crucial in enabling the research to proceed.

Notes

1. Before the study proper began, a number of candidate tasks were piloted at a neighboring college in order to determine for each of the three types which task was the most productive of language and the most enjoyable to do. In this way, the risk of basing the research project on unpopular and unproductive tasks was reduced.
2. Subsequently, one subject had to be discarded when it was realized that the college had not applied its own selection policy to him. Despite a low test score, he had been placed in one of the four groups simply for scheduling convenience reasons. When the lower level of his performance was noticed, his results were removed from the data set.
3. In any case here, even if there were an effect that has not been detected in the present study, the underlying cause may be task familiarity, or simply improvements in proficiency over time. The students were following courses of instruction, and it may be that this instruction was having an effect. Even so, it must be borne in mind that the effect, in such a case, was on accuracy, not on complexity.
4. See Skehan and Foster (1996) and Foster and Skehan (1996b) for studies on post-task and during-task influences, respectively.
5. This pattern of results has been replicated in a subsequent study (Foster & Skehan, 1996b).

7

SELF-REPORTED PLANNING BEHAVIOUR AND SECOND LANGUAGE PERFORMANCE IN NARRATIVE RETELLING

Introduction

Early Publications on Planning

What we think of as contemporary second language planning research started with two publications (Ellis, 1987; Crookes, 1989), which demonstrated the importance of the opportunity to plan before doing a second language task, and which disagreed in ways that are still interesting and influential. In the quarter century since Ellis's publication, the field of second language planning research has grown enormously, and has produced many research articles. A great deal has been found out regarding the effects of different planning conditions (Mehnert, 1998; Skehan & Foster, 1997); the impact of planning with different proficiency levels (Wigglesworth, 1997; Tavakoli & Skehan, 2005); the relevance of different task factors (Michel et al., 2007b; Tavakoli & Foster, 2008); the time perspective under which tasks are completed (Robinson, 2011a); the time when planning occurs, with a contrast between pre-task or strategic planning compared to on-line planning which takes place when time is available while speaking is taking place (Ellis, 2005a) (see other chapters in Skehan, 2014). As a result, we are now in a much better position to predict what the impact will be on performance of manipulating different task features and different task conditions. Indeed, an index of the success of these developments is that we have competing accounts of what produces the different effects which have been reported. Whereas Skehan (2009a) argues that limitations in attention frequently lead to trade-offs between

---

Originally published as: Pang, F., & Skehan, P. (2014). Self-reported planning behaviour and second language performance in narrative retelling. In P. Skehan (Ed.), *Processing perspectives on task performance* (pp. 95–128). Amsterdam: John Benjamins. Reproduced with permission of John Benjamins.

different areas, and that careful task choice and use can mitigate the impact of these trade-offs, Robinson (2001b, 2011a), through the Cognition Hypothesis, analyses attention differently, as less limited, and proposes that task difficulty can push for different aspects of performance (complexity, accuracy) to be simultaneously raised.

The nature of performance itself has been the focus for much research, reflecting a wider interest in second language performance dimensions. Following Crookes (1989), task researchers have usually focussed on the dimensions of complexity, accuracy, and fluency. More recently measures of lexis have also started to become more common in task research (Skehan, 2009b). Essentially, these four aspects of performance are regarded as distinct, so that one or two might be raised, while the others are not. This connects with one of the most interesting debates on the effects of planning: whether it impacts on all areas of performance, or only on complexity and fluency. Some researchers, including Crookes (1989) and Ortega (2005), argue that planning raises these two areas only, whereas others, notably Foster and Skehan (1996a), argue that planning can also have an impact on accuracy.

Some experimental studies have tried to address some of the disagreements (see for example Wang [2014] and Bui [2014, Chapter 3]), as do studies by Michel et al. (2007c) and Revesz (2009). Their hope has been to design studies in such a way as to tease out differences and predictions from theoretical positions which will resolve disagreements. Such research has been useful, but so far, not definitive. In reflecting on this it is important to point out that the vast majority of studies on planning have been quantitative in nature. Hypotheses have been framed, data collected, coded, and scored, and quantitative techniques have been used to explore the match or mismatch between hypotheses and results. Next, interpretations of the experimental conditions and their effects in relation to the results have been put forward, hence the claims about Cognition, Trade-off, accuracy versus complexity effects, and so on. What has been strikingly absent is any tradition of qualitative research used to gain insights into what happens during the period when planning is undertaken. Researchers seem to have been keener to try to infer the mental processes of participants from quantitative patterns, rather than to discover what the participants themselves have to say.

The major exception to this comes from two studies by Ortega (1995, 1999), and the broader account she published of this work (Ortega, 2005), where she herself wonders why there had been so little qualitative research in this area. Several years later, it is even more striking that this state of affairs has not really changed, particularly given that qualitative studies have the potential to unlock a great deal in relation to debates within the literature. They can provide insights into the aims learners have during the planning period, the processes they try to engage in, and their satisfaction subsequently with the activities they have engaged in. The present research tries to redress this situation and report qualitative data on planners' activities, an endeavour which, if nothing else, will add to Ortega's initial work.

Ortega's Research Into Planning

First, though, Ortega's research is worth reviewing, because it does make major contributions to our understanding of what learners say about what they do during planning. She used narrative retellings of picture stories from Hill (1960) as the basis for her research. The participants in her studies were learners of Spanish at the University of Hawaii. Her first study involved learners she characterises as low intermediate, and the second study focussed on advanced learners. Participants first listened to a tape recording of the story in their L1 (not a typical approach in the task literature). Then, following a planning period, learners provided their own narrative account, after which they were engaged in retrospective interviews, in which they were probed about what they had done while planning. An important aspect of this research is the coding scheme that was developed to work with the data. A strong influence here were schemes developed to taxonomise learner strategies, particularly O'Malley and Chamot (1990), but also Oxford (1990). The categories in these two schemes were supplemented by examination of the transcripts of the retrospective interviews, which enabled further categories and themes to emerge in their own right. The coding system ultimately used was a mixture of the existing learner strategies schemes (consisting of 34 categories), and the additional categories which achieved salience in the transcripts, generating a further six new codes.

Ortega (2005) reports that retrieval and rehearsal strategies were particularly important with her participants. She also reports that the advanced group had more of a balance in their use of these two strategy types than the low-intermediate participants, with these latter using more retrieval strategies. She also reported that a range of monitoring strategies were used, such as production monitoring, although this was less effectively done with the lower-proficiency participants. In the main, her participants felt that planning was helpful. This was partly because it gave them more time to organise, to formulate thoughts, to solve lexical problems, to practise and rehearse. Writing notes was also regarded as helpful, enabling the formulation of thought, helping lexical retrieval and lexical choice, and also helping to monitor grammar. There were, however, some reports of planning not being helpful. One reason proposed was that the narrative tasks were rather easy, and did not need much planning. There were also reports of lack of transfer from planning to actual performance. Many of these points are prescient with respect to the results to be reported here.

Ortega (2005) makes two more general points which have importance. First, she draws attention to individual differences. She contrasts communicatively oriented participants and those more focussed on form, and argues that participants brought this predisposition to the way planning time is exploited. Second, she draws attention to issues deriving from the presence of a listener. Participants were put in pairs, with one as speaker and the other as listener. Both participants were 'valued' in the encounter, but in fact, it was only the data from the speakers which was used. However, the speakers were clearly aware of the listener as an important factor in the encounter. Ortega (2005) reports this had a major impact on performance, with speakers reporting thinking of how to use planning time to make content more accessible, of how they could retrieve easier vocabulary, and how they could avoid more advanced grammar. There was also a reluctance to self-correct and even a willingness to slow down delivery in order to make comprehension easier for the listener.

Motivation for the Present Research

An earlier pilot study carried out by the researchers (Pang & Skehan, 2006) was their first attempt to find out what learners planned before doing a speaking task. The planners, undergraduates at a university in Hong Kong, were asked what they did during the 10-minute planning time they were allowed, what they prioritised, and whether the planning activities helped them in performing the actual task. The retrospective interviews (generally conducted in Cantonese) were translated, transcribed, and coded. A preliminary coding scheme was developed from the codes and categories which emerged through a process of iteration. This preliminary coding scheme was very revealing, demonstrating the viability of using a model of speaking (Levelt, 1989) as the basis for the categories of codes which were developed.

Against this background of previous research, we can now outline the reasons which motivated the present research. First, it is desirable to gather qualitative data in more settings with different participants to clarify the robustness and replicability of extant findings and generalisations. Second, there is the coding scheme. Ortega (2005) based hers on the work of O'Malley and Chamot (1990) and Oxford (1990). There was a stage in which coding categories additional to those derived from these two schemes could emerge. However, in Ortega's final coding scheme (Ortega, 2005, pp. 84–85) the number of 'emergent' categories is not large in relation to the total used (as noted above), so that most of the coding category headings are those from O'Malley and Chamot (1990). A difficulty here is that these systems target *learning* rather than speaking strategies, and so they may not be totally appropriate. In particular they are not based on any theory of speaking, either first or second language (Levelt, 1999; Kormos, 2006). There would seem scope, therefore, to use an emergent category approach from the beginning, but to have in mind while categories emerge the possibility of relating them to a model of speaking, such as Levelt's, which has been applied to the second language case (De Bot, 1992; Kormos, 2006; Skehan, 2009a). In this way, from retrospective interviews, one could look for comments which might relate to the different stages in the Levelt model (Conceptualisation, Formulation, and Articulation), as well as associated processes such as monitoring. At the same time, one could also explore whether and how far Levelt's proposals on the functioning of a mental lexicon have relevance for the reports which are gathered.

A third motivation for the present research is that there is no research we are aware of that explores the relation between participants' reports on what they did during planning and their subsequent performance. Ortega's work gives us excellent insights into what participants say they do during planning, and also what they say about how effective they think their planning was, but we have no information about whether the reports on planning are associated with success or failure. This is important to the extent that the planning literature is centrally concerned with trying to establish linkages between planning and performance, with performance generally conceived of in terms of complexity, accuracy, fluency, and lexis. Indeed, the debates within the literature are less about the desirability of planning (because in the main, researchers assume its value), but rather how different interpretations of planning, perhaps with different tasks, can impact upon different aspects of performance. So, to gather retrospective data on planning, and to link this to performance, would relate to wider debates within the planning literature. For instance, such data might shed light on which planning behaviours are most effective, in such a way that one could make relevant suggestions for pedagogic intervention, and even offer suggestions for how more effective planning could be trained. This, too, would go beyond planning as being a rather monolithic and crude pedagogic option, and suggest how it could be fine-tuned and targeted more effectively.

Method

Research Questions

This background generates two fairly straightforward research questions. It is inappropriate, given the exploratory, qualitative nature of the proposed research, to put forward research hypotheses and predictions. Instead the two general questions are:

1 In the context of planning ahead of a narrative task, is a coding scheme based on categories which emerge from the data consistent with models of speaking?
2 Is frequency of use of the emergent categories related to different levels of performance on a narrative task, particularly in terms of complexity, accuracy, fluency, and lexis?

Research Methodology

Participants and Setting

The participants were selected from a university in Macao. Five hundred and sixty-seven students who took English courses in the English Centre were invited to take a listening comprehension test, which included a short conversation, a long conversation and a short talk, with 50 questions in total. Cronbach's Alpha for this test is 0.82. Students who got marks between 15 and 24 were considered to be low-intermediate EFL learners, and those who got marks higher than 34 as high-intermediate EFL learners for this study. In total 48 students were selected to participate in the study including 24 high-intermediate and 24 low-intermediate EFL learners, with 24 male and 24 female learners, and 24 students majoring in Language and Communication and 24 in Business Administration (see Table 7.1).

The researcher met each dyad of participants in an individual room. She briefed the two participants that they would have 10 minutes to plan a picture story individually and would take turns to tell the story in English for about 2 minutes to each other (see the instructions in Appendix 7.1). The listener could not see the pictures and was told to ask at least one question after the story was told. All storytellings were audio-recorded. When participants finished telling the story, the researcher interviewed each student individually about what they did during the 10-minute planning time. The retrospective interview questions, trialed in the pilot study mentioned earlier, were intended to collect planning activities in a range of areas including words, grammar, ideas, story structure. The interview was conducted in Mandarin or Cantonese Chinese and was audio-recorded.

Tasks

Selecting interesting and appropriate story pictures for this study was a challenging process. Given the success of the Shaun the Sheep video narrative retellings (Wang & Skehan, 2014), it was decided to adapt the video stories as the basis for making a cartoon series. A wide range of Shaun the Sheep episodes were initially identified. These were then scrutinised by the researchers and reduced to seven. The seven selected episodes were converted into picture story series, and these were each evaluated by around 10 MA TESOL students. Based on the ratings of the story series given by the graduate students in terms of clarity, humour, and depth, four picture series were selected to be used in the pilot study. The two

TABLE 7.1 Profile of the 48 Selected Participants

		Male	Female	Remarks
High Intermediate	Language and Communication	6	6	Dyads: 2: M+F, 2: F+F, 2: M+M
	Business Administration	6	6	Dyads: 2: M+F, 2: F+F, 2: M+M
Low Intermediate	Language & Communication	6	6	Dyads: 2: M+F, 2: F+F, 2: M+M
	Business Administration	6	6	Dyads: 2: M+F, 2: F+F, 2: M+M
	Subtotal	24	24	

aims of the pilot study were to trial the retrospective interview questions, and to select two story pictures for the present study. Fourteen students from the same university in Macao participated in the pilot study. Two picture series were finally selected based on the following criteria: amount of useful retrospection about planning, variety of self-reported planning behaviour, and ratings by the participants (clarity, humour, depth, and difficulty in completion). The pilot also enabled a decision to be made about the length of planning time to be used. The two selected story pictures adopted in this study each had 19 pictures in total and were printed in colour for use in the research sessions.

Procedures

The Retrospective Interviews (RIs) of the 48 participants were audio-recorded. All the 48 digitally recorded RIs were transferred to computer as MP3 files. They were transcribed (and translated at the same time) using Soundscriber, to facilitate control over the sound file during transcription. The prompts for these interviews are shown in Appendix 7.2.

The data handling for the narrative performances followed the procedures used in most of the chapters in Skehan (2014), and therefore does not need to be discussed in great detail. A broad transcription was made of each sound file. Transcriptions were segmented into Analysis of Speech (AS) units, and copied to contain two identical lines for each AS unit. The first line was then coded following CHAT conventions (MacWhinney, 2000), and represented as the CHAT tier. The second line was coded following TaskProfile conventions, containing clausal segmentation, error coding, measurement of pauses longer than 0.40 seconds, and coding for a range of repair types (reformulation, repetition, etc.). In addition, the length of time taken, at millisecond level, for each AS turn was recorded as a third line. These codings enabled TaskProfile to generate all the measures required in the present study (for a fuller discussion of performance codings, see Skehan, 2014b, Chapter 1).

Performance Measures

Five performance measures were used in this study. Complexity was measured using the subordination measure described in Skehan (2014b, Chapter 1): the total number of clauses was divided by the total number of AS units, generating an index with a minimum value of 1 (no AS unit contained anything other than a matrix clause, with no subordination), with most values falling between 1 and 2. Accuracy was measured as the proportion of clauses that were error-free, and in this case, although the data was coded for gravity of error, the measure which was actually used, on the basis of effective discrimination, was that based on all errors (rather than only serious errors, as in Skehan and Shum [2014]). Fluency was measured by two indices, both of pausing: pauses per 100 words at AS boundary points, and pauses, again per 100 words, which occurred mid-clause. Skehan (2009b) has shown that pauses at these two locations need to be considered separately. Finally, lexical sophistication was measured as the Lambda score, the index which captured the extent to which the contribution of the speaker contained less frequent words (see Skehan [2014b] for a more detailed account). These five measures constitute a basic set of those described more fully in Skehan (2014b).

Segmenting the Retrospective Interviews

After the transcriptions of the retrospective interviews (RIs) were completed, the segmentation of the 48 RIs was undertaken. There are different methods to segment such qualitative data, such as grammatical-based, idea-based, and activity-based approaches. The activity-based method was applied in this case, because the main purpose in analysing the RIs is to examine the types of planning activities ESL speakers would engage in before telling a picture story. Furthermore, using the activity-based approach to segment the RIs allowed the feasibility of building an RI corpus which might result in more sophisticated analysis of the segments both qualitatively and quantitatively.

First Coding: Constructing the Coding Scheme

The first task was to code each segment, that is, each *RI unit* (the term used in this study) as a CODE, to represent a planning activity. There were several influences on this stage. These included an earlier pilot study (Pang & Skehan, 2006) based on different narrative tasks and participants, but which had generated a provisional coding scheme. The Ortega (2005) scheme was also examined and was kept in mind as relevant. Finally, the first author's initial recognition of emerging planning activities when doing the earlier transcription and segmentation of the RIs had sensitised her to the sorts of behaviours which had been reported.

The provisional Coding Scheme consisted of little more than a list of codes with a provisional description of each of them. Although the codes and the categories were preliminary, they created an initial framework for coding the data in this study by taking advantage of the similar features of the participants, tertiary Chinese non-English major students in the pilot study and in this study. The 48 RIs were coded using the method of constant comparison (Strauss & Corbin, 1990). That is, the researcher attempted to closely examine and re-examine each RI unit, compare for similarities and differences, and ask questions about the planning activities reflected in the retrospective interviews. In addition, every effort was made to ensure the coding system was sensitive to the variety of planning activities the ESL speakers might use. Detecting all the planning activities reported by each participant (either reported directly by the participants or inferred from the interview) was the starting point for this.

162 Empirical Work

Having constructed the provisional Coding Scheme and having coded the 12 RIs in the previous pilot study, the first author became more sensitive throughout the investigation to the possibility of any emergent planning activities. The view is that the more exhaustive the analyses, the more realistic they would be with respect to the planning activities used by both groups of speakers, the high-intermediate and the low-intermediate groups. Therefore, in constructing the Coding Scheme, no quantitative criterion was used; that is, regardless of the frequency with which a planning activity occurred, it was incorporated into the Coding Scheme. For example, the following three planning activities are included in the Coding Scheme although they only occurred once: (A) 2. *Macro planning plan sequence: Look at pictures one by one, then describe*; (D) 6. *Lexical choice: Advanced words*; (E) 8. *Lexical: Planned but not used/correctly used*; (see Appendix 7.3).

This first pass through the 48 RIs to develop coding categories took a significantly longer time than was anticipated. This is not only because of coding the data itself (as it would have taken much less time if a fixed, established coding scheme had been used) but also because the final Coding Scheme underwent an iterative process of multiple revisions. The action of examining, re-examining, comparing, and asking questions challenges the RI units themselves and the method of coding the RI units continually. In other words, how to match an RI unit to a code subtly *and* how to code all RI units consistently created considerable complexity.

The first coding of all the 48 RIs resulted in the identification of 42 planning activities (i.e., 42 codes). This Coding Scheme included: the codes of the planning activities, a description of each code, and an appropriate example, demonstrating the planning activity. As a brief example of the scheme in operation, the code "*Connect the pictures to develop the story plot*" (described as "*Try to connect or structure the pictures to develop the story plot*") is the result of conceptualising an RI unit "*I emphasized on the plots. I considered how to connect the pictures to make the story better.*"

The next stage was to explore whether any order could be brought to the codes. It proved possible to organise the entire set of 42 planning *activities* (i.e., the codes) into five groups reflecting their functions. These were (A) Macro planning; (B) Micro planning; (C) Lexical and grammar planning; (D) Metacognitive planning, and (E) Post-task perception and evaluation. The last category will not be pursued further in this chapter, for reasons of space. This first Coding Scheme was not intended to be a complete representation of all possible planning activities. Nevertheless, it does represent an exhaustive list of the planning activities the participants used to prepare for telling a story from a series of pictures.

Second Coding: Real Coding

The 48 RIs were coded a second time based on the final Coding Scheme (shown in Appendix 7.3). During the first coding, while the Coding Scheme was evolving, an RI unit that was examined after a code had been added or deleted might be coded differently to an RI unit coded earlier although both exemplified the same concept. Therefore, the second coding was regarded as the *real* coding, which would be the basis for the quantitative analysis and the associations with actual performance.

At this point, the first author's theoretical familiarity and sensitivity had grown significantly from coding the 12 RIs in the previous Pilot Study (Pang & Skehan, 2006) and the coding of the 48 RIs during the first coding. This sensitivity helped in distinguishing the slightly different concepts between closely related codes and therefore made it easier to detect examples of codes in use, and also to make final decisions with some RI units which were close to falling between two codes or even three codes. For example, the concept is very similar for the two codes: (D) 5. *Metacognitive: Rehearse: Memorisation* and (D) 8. *Metacognitive: Memorisation* and so the actual RI unit needed to be closely re-examined with coding sensitivity to decide which one was appropriate in any particular case.

Finally, all the coded retrospective interviews were incorporated within an Excel file. The same codes were grouped together, and as a result the same RI units could be re-examined and compared to see whether they fitted into each code so that final revision of the coding system could be undertaken. In addition, at this stage, the description of each code was modified to reach its final form.

Results

Basic Quantitative Analyses

Table 7.2, below, shows the raw values for each of the coding categories that emerged from the retrospective interviews. Each line gives one of the coding categories (and the fuller version is provided in Appendix 7.3), together with the raw frequencies for the lower-proficiency group and the higher proficiency group, as well as the entire group. This shows the number of times a given coding was made. So, for the first line (*Macro planning: plan sequence: scan then describe*), in the low proficiency group, no one coded zero (i.e., no one failed to report this planning behaviour), so that the table shows that all 24 lower-proficiency participants reported using this behaviour. This contrasts with the first of the Micro Planning Behaviours: *Understand pictures in detail*. Here, five participants (still with the low proficiency group) did not report using this behaviour, ten participants reported it once, seven reported it twice, two reported it three times, and no one in this group reported using it four or more times (although in the high proficiency group there was one participant who reported this behaviour four times). These raw values have been reported, rather than averages or percentages, because they communicate the situation more effectively.

The table gives a general picture of the frequency with which different codings were found for the participants. Not a great deal will be said about these figures at this stage, since more discussion will be provided when we link coded behaviours to actual performance. Even so, a number of points are worth making. First, there

TABLE 7.2 Frequency Data for All Codes

Number of mentions	Low Prof. 0 1 2 3 4	High Prof. 0 1 2 3 4	Total 0 1 2 3 4
Macro Planning			
Plan sequence: Scan, then describe	0 24	0 24	0 48
Plan sequence: Look at each picture, describe	23 1	24 0	47 1
Micro Planning			
Understand pictures in detail	5 10 7 2 0	10 6 4 3 1	15 16 11 5 1
Plan general things	16 8	12 12	28 20
Plan small details	8 14 2	2 12 10	10 26 12
Plan how to tell the story	8 11 4 1	12 9 3 0	20 20 7 1
Plan how to express oneself better	13 7 4	13 7 4	26 14 8
Think of ideas beyond the pictures	17 7	10 12 2	27 19 2
Organise the ideas developed from pictures	17 6 1	14 8 1	31 14 2 1
Connect the pictures to develop the story	14 9 1	6 12 4 2	20 21 5 2
Lexical and grammar planning			
Lexical: general retrieval	12 12 0	7 12 5	19 24 5
Lexical Choice: Appropriate words	21 3	19 3 2	40 6 2
Lexical Choice: Simple words	16 7 1	20 4 0	36 11 1
Lexical Choice: Connective words	17 6 1	12 12	29 18 1
Lexical Choice: Personification words	24 0	22 2	46 2
Lexical Choice: Advanced words	24 0	23 1	47 1
Lexical Choice: Variety of words	23 1	21 3	44 4
Lexical Choice: Accurate words	24 0	19 5	43 5
Lexical Compensation: Approximation	21 3	21 3	42 6
Lexical Compensation: Circumlocution	15 6 2 1	15 7 2 0	30 13 4 1
Lexical: No or little concern	19 5	23 1	42 6
Grammar: General use considered	18 5 1	19 5	37 10 1
Grammar: Correct use of tense	17 7	15 9	32 16
Grammar: No or little concern	12 12	11 13	23 25
Metacognitive Planning			
Rehearse: General	9 15	16 8	25 23
Rehearse: To be accurate	18 6	17 6 1	35 12 1
Rehearse: To be fluent	15 9	13 11	28 20
Rehearse: To be logical or clear	24 0	19 4 1	43 4 1
Rehearse: To help to memorise	24 0	22 1 1	46 1 1
Take notes to help plan	16 7 0 1	15 7 2 0	31 14 2 1
Take notes: No need	11 13	13 11	24 24
Memorisation	24 0	22 2	46 2
Try to be aware of the listener	3 18 2 0 1	6 11 3 4	9 29 5 4 1

is the issue of discrimination and whether there is variation between participants in the use of a particular code. If the goal were simply to characterise self-reported planning behaviours, this would not be important. They are what they are, and it is the patterns amongst them which would be of interest. But if we are to link such behaviours to performance, it is helpful if there is dispersion. On these grounds, then, both of the macro behaviours (the two *Plan sequence* behaviours), as well as several of the lexical codings, (e.g., *Advanced words*, plus one or two of the metacognitive behaviours) are problematic, since effectively only one value is reported, with this often being zero or one, indicating that the behaviour is simply not reported by the vast majority of the participants. A second point which stands out is the connection with proficiency level. Several of the codes show interestingly different patterns for the low and high proficiency students. For example, the Micro Planning Behaviour *Connect the pictures to develop the story* sees fourteen of the low proficiency participants code '0', while only six of the high proficiency participants code in this way. One wonders, therefore, if this behaviour is facilitated by students' higher levels of proficiency.

The Codes and the Levelt Model

We can now discuss the different codes in relation to the Levelt model of speaking. The broad categories are Macro Planning, Micro Planning, Lexical and Grammar Planning, and Metacognitive Planning. Both Macro and Micro Planning are concerned with Levelt's Conceptualiser stage, and with the speaker's processing of the ideas that are going to feed into the pre-verbal message. These codes vary in focus (pictures, ideas, outside the ideas, manner of expression) and also in scale (local versus general) but they are all concerned with thinking. Lexical and Grammar planning are much more focussed on performance, and are, fairly obviously, linked with the Formulator stage in speech production (though Formulation processes clearly take place in relation to prior conceptualisations). Several of the codes are clearly concerned with lexical retrieval, others are focussed on grammar and the building of syntactic frames. Yet others involve a mixture of the two, both lexical and grammatical, and are also implicated in Formulation processes that are anticipated, such as handling difficulty in communication. The one higher-order coding category which straddles Leveltian stages are the Metacognitive codes. Here we have some which are concerned with Conceptualisation, where the focus is on ideas, or on the communication as part of a speech event with a listener present. There are a number of codes concerned with rehearsal, and these seem directed at Formulator operations (although even here, one is concerned with a form of cognitive monitoring). In any case, it is not difficult to link the coding categories which emerged with aspects of the Leveltian analysis of speaking.

Quantitative Data

Table 7.3 shows the performance results for the participants. The data is shown for one measure of accuracy (error-free clauses), one of complexity (subordination), two pausing measures (number of pauses at AS boundaries per 100 words, number of pauses mid-clause, per 100 words), length of run, and Lambda, so covering accuracy, complexity, fluency, and lexis. The measures are given for the entire group, and then also for low and high proficiency participants. In this case, significance values are also given, based on between-subjects t-tests. The Length of Run measure is only given to provide a limited degree of comparison with Ortega (2005) who used a very similar index. For all values in this table the N is 48 overall, with 24 low proficiency participants and 24 high proficiency participants.

We will first consider the general values in this table. There are now a wide range of studies (including in Skehan, 2014) which use the set of measures shown in the table, and so one can relate the values shown here to the wider literature. In this respect, the values for accuracy are relatively low (although there may be issues here with Chinese L1 EFL learners of English, they are somewhat lower than those reported by research conducted in a UK context). The values for fluency are fairly normal for the sorts of narrative retellings involved here, and are low, if anything, relative to other research studies. The remaining values, though, are in fact higher than is normally reported. The subordination values for tasks of this sort are usually a little lower, possibly more in the 1.4 to 1.5 range for planned performances. Similarly, the Lambda values, as an index of lexical sophistication, are definitely higher than is typical, probably around 0.2 to 0.5 above what one normally finds (Skehan, 2009b). Finally, the length of run values are also clearly higher than the norm, since one often sees values here of 3 or 4 rather than the 5.42 and 6.12 shown for the two groups. Indeed, these values approach those

TABLE 7.3 Performance Measure for Participants

Performance Measure	Total Group Mean (St.Dev.)	Low Profic. Group Mean (St.Dev.)	High Profic. Group Mean (St.Dev.)	Significance Low vs. High Proficiency
Error-free clauses	0.40 (0.16)	0.34 (0.14)	0.47 (0.15)	0.002
Subordination	1.66 (0.30)	1.62 (0.26)	1.69 (0.33)	0.410
AS boundary pauses	3.38 (1.26)	3.57 (1.48)	3.20 (0.99)	0.31
Mid-clause pauses	3.64 (1.98)	4.07 (2.34)	3.21 (1.48)	0.14
Lambda	1.85 (0.26)	1.80 (0.27)	1.91 (0.26)	0.15
Length of run	6.12 (1.42)	5.42 (1.0)	6.82 (1.44)	0.001

found with native speakers. If one makes a rather tentative comparison with Ortega's (2005, p. 84) 'words within one intonation contour' index, one would estimate that the participants in this study are between her two groups, and perhaps closer to her advanced group. In all, one could characterise these performances as lacking in accuracy, but lexically rich and complex.

Turning to the comparisons of the low and high groups, it is surprising how few significant differences are reported. In fact, there are only two, for accuracy and for length of run, although each of these comparisons reaches quite a high level of significance. So the advanced group is more accurate (consistent with Bui [2014]), and they produce 'smoother' language, producing units of speech which are longer. In contrast, with fluency and with lexical and structural complexity, there are no significant differences. It is noteworthy that in all these cases, the high proficiency group produces arithmetic means which indicate a higher level of performance, but none of these comparisons actually reach significance. But one important point does need to be made here regarding the accuracy contrast. In the next section we are going to turn to the associations between self-reported planning behaviours and actual performance. For structural complexity, for lexical sophistication and for fluency, we shall treat the two proficiency groups as effectively one group, given the lack of significant differences found. But the two groups have to be considered differently for accuracy. As we will see, this poses a problem for interpretation. If certain coded behaviours are associated with higher levels of performance and also discriminate between the two proficiency groups, we cannot tell whether these behaviours are 'enabled' by the higher proficiency, or whether they contribute to that higher level of performance. We will return to this problem below.

Frequency of Reported Planning Behaviour and Performance Levels

We turn next to exploring the relationship between the different coded behaviours and performance in the narrative retellings. To this end, every code (with its values of 0, 1, 2, 3 for the use of that code) was related to performance in terms of accuracy, complexity, fluency (both pausing measures), and lexical sophistication. For example, Lexical Code 1, *General retrieval* tallied as 19 individuals with 0 occurrences, 24 with 1 occurrence, and 5 individuals with 2 occurrences. These three values (0, 1, 2) and the associated participants were then examined for mean error-free clauses scores, as shown in Table 7.4. These figures, based on Lexical Code 1, suggest that there is some association between the use of this behaviour during planning and level of accuracy, in that greater use of this code seems to be associated with greater accuracy. It should be made clear that, given the exploratory nature of this study, and the strong reliance on qualitative data, these figures are only presented descriptively, to gain some insight into what is associated with higher performance.

TABLE 7.4 Frequency and Error-Free Clause Mean Scores: Lexical Code 1—General Retrieval

Code	Number of Reports	Mean Error-Free Clauses Score
0	19	0.37
1	24	0.41
2	5	0.45

The same descriptive procedure was followed with all the codes used in this study. For each code, number of uses of a code was the basis for calculating a mean score for those individuals who used the code that often, and then frequency of use was related to the mean performance score (accuracy, complexity, fluency, lexis) involved. Finally, for the different performance areas, all codes which seemed to have some association with performance were brought together (whereas codes which generated no such relationship were not included). Table 7.5 presents the findings for the error-free clauses measure, both positive and negative. The first two columns give information about the coding involved, and fuller information is provided in Appendix 7.3. The third column shows whether there is a linkage to proficiency, and the fourth column shows the distribution of coding frequency (0, 1, 2, etc.) and also the mean error-free clauses score associated with each frequency.

Only the relations with error-free clauses have been shown here, and the other performance areas are covered in the tables which follow. It may be, therefore, that codes appear in more than one table, if a particular code has a relationship with more than one performance area. Intriguingly, one or two codes have positive associations with one performance area and negative associations with another. For example, LE1, *Lexical General retrieval*, the first coding shown in Table 7.5, and with a positive relationship, also has a negative relation with mid-clause pausing (negative, that is, with greater fluency, in that LE1 is associated with *more* mid-clause pausing). In any case, and setting aside proficiency linkages for the moment, it appears that higher accuracy scores are obtained when more focussed behaviour is involved, whether this is rehearsing specific words or rehearsing in a more targeted way. *Rehearsing (note-taking)* linked to structure (Meta2) is beneficial, consistent with focussed behaviour within planning being effective. In contrast, lower accuracy is associated with planning leading to problems, either through lexical difficulties or with over-extension in what is attempted. It is interesting that these suggest the potential for planning to be two-edged: it can lead the speaker into trouble, as well as be helpful, depending on how the planning time is used.

Table 7.6 below shows the comparable information for the Subordination measure. Once again the linkage with proficiency level is shown, but it should be borne in mind that there was no significant contrast here between the two proficiency levels.

Self-Reported Planning Behaviour 169

TABLE 7.5 Codes Associated With Greater Accuracy

No. CODE	Description of CODE	Proficiency Linkage	Performance Influence	
Positive				
LE1: Lexical: General retrieval	Try to remember the words used in the task	Yes	Distrib: EFC:	19–24–5 0.37/0.41/0.47
LE8: Lexical choice: Accurate words	Try to use accurate words	Yes	Distrib: EFC:	43–5 0.40/0.46
Meta2: Comment on notes: Structure clear story	The notes taken are helpful to structure a clear story	No	Distrib: EFC:	35–12–1 0.38–0.47–0.54
Meta3: Rehearse: Fluent	Rehearse to be fluent	No	Distrib: EFC:	28–20 0.36/0.47
Meta4: Rehearse: Logical or clear	Rehearse to check whether what is planned is logical or clear	Yes	Distrib: EFC:	43–4–1 0.39/0.55/0.50
Mic8: Connect the pictures to develop the story plot	Try to connect or structure the pictures to develop the story plot	Yes	Distrib: EFC:	19–21–5–2 0.35/0.43/0.43/0.56
Negative				
Le10: Lexical compensation: Circumlocution	Use a few words or another way to replace a word which cannot be recalled	No	Distrib: EFC:	30–13–4 0.43/0.38/0.27
Mic5: Plan how to express better	Plan how to describe the story more vividly, interestingly, or clearly, etc.	No	Distrib: EFC:	26–14–8 0.43/0.38/−0.37

An obvious first remark here has to be that the number of positive and negative associations is somewhat reversed for those with accuracy. There, positive associations predominated. Here we find quite a few more negative connections than positive. Regarding the positive influences, it does come across that ideas lead the way when subordination increases, and grammar takes a back seat. It also

TABLE 7.6 Codes Associated With Higher and Lower Subordination Scores

Positive

Le14: Grammar: No/Little concern	No or very little concern about grammar use	No	Distrib: Subord:	23–25 1.62/1.69
Mic3: Plan small details	Plan small details, such as detailed description	Yes	Distrib: Subord:	10–26–12 1.6/1.62/1.78
Mic4: Plan how to tell the story	Plan how to tell the story in general	Yes	Distrib: Subord:	20–20–7–1 1.65/1.63/1.72/1.89
Mic7: Organise the ideas developed from the pictures	Try to organise the ideas developed from different pictures to have a clear story plot	No	Distrib: Subord:	31–14–2–1 1.63/1.7/1.72/1.63

Negative

Le2: Lexical choice: Appropriate words	Choose appropriate words for telling the story	No	Distrib: Negative Subord:	40–6–2 1.68/1.58/1.56
Le4: Lexical choice: Connective words	Choose to use some connective words	Yes	Distrib: Negative Subord:	29–18–1 1.71/1.58/1.37
Le7: Lexical choice: Various words	Try to use various words to talk about the same thing	No	Distrib: Negative Subord:	44–4 1.67/1.46
Le8: Lexical choice: Accurate words	Try to use accurate words	Yes	Distrib: Subord:	43–5 1.67/1.58
Le9: Lexical compensation: Approximating	Use a word similar in meaning to replace the word which can't be recalled	No	Distrib: Subord:	42–6 1.67/1.53
Le12: Grammar: General use	Think of general use of grammar	No	Distrib: Subord:	37–10 1.68/1.62
Le13: Grammar: Tense	Think of the use of correct tense	No	Distrib: Subord:	32–16 1.7/1.57

Positive

Mic2: Plan general things	Plan general things, such as describing the general plot of the story	Yes	Distrib: Subord:	28–20 1.69/1.61
Mic5: Plan how to express better	Plan how to describe the story more vividly, interestingly, or clearly, etc.	No	Distrib: Subord:	26–14–8 1.69/1.63/1.59
Mic8: Connect the pictures to develop the story plot	Try to connect or structure the pictures to develop the story plot	Yes	Distrib: Subord:	19–21–5–2 1.71/1.64/1.56/1.5

appears that organising, and going from big to small, is a good strategy to raise subordination. The literature on tasks suggests that task structure is generally a good thing, and that earlier findings that accuracy was advanced by structure have now been extended to suggest that complexity is also affected. The results in this section are that if learners can use planning time to bring their own structure to the narrative retelling, this seems to raise the subordination measure. The negative influences do seem to have a common quality here. It is over-ambition. This could be over-ambition in lexical choices, or over-ambition generally in what can be done during planning time. This seems to be associated with performance being damaged to some degree, particularly with regard to complexity. In addition, it seems as if those who focus on grammar do so at the expense of complexity, at least as indexed by subordination.

Next, we turn to the two measures of fluency, AS pauses and mid-clause pauses. They are treated separately, mainly because while there is a certain amount of overlap in the associations found, mostly the two fluency measures are influenced by different things, and in one case a code is negatively associated with one, and positively associated with the other, as we shall see. The information for AS pauses is given in Table 7.7. A slight difference in this compared to the other tables is that where there is a relevant mid-clause pausing association, that too is shown. The same thing is done in Table 7.8, since AS pause information is shown in a table focussing on mid-clause pauses. In this way, the two tables provide separate information on these two aspects of dysfluency, but also facilitate interpretations of shared influences, such as *Lexis 14*, in the positive section of Table 7.8, or discrepant influences, such as *Lexis 8*, in the negative section of the same table. Note also that greater fluency is indexed by *lower* pausing scores.

TABLE 7.7 Codes Associated With Differences in AS-Clause Boundary Pausing per 100 Words

Positive				
Le7: Lexical choice: Various words	Try to use various words to talk about the same thing	No	Distrib: AS pausing:	44–4 3.41/3.07
Le10: Lexical compensation: Circumlocution	Use a few words or another way to replace a word which cannot be recalled	No	Distrib: AS pausing	30–13–4 3.62/2.96/3.06
Le11: Lexical: No/ Little concern	No or very little concern about vocabulary.		Distrib: AS pausing	42–6 3.42/3.16
Le14: Grammar: No/Little concern	No or very little concern about grammar use	No	Distrib: AS pausing Positive, Mid-pause:	23–25 3.88/2.93 4.22/3.10
Meta4: Rehearse: Logical or clear	Rehearse to check whether what is planned is logical or clear	Yes	Distrib: AS pausing	43–4–1 3.44/2.88/3.05
Mic3: Plan small details	Plan small details, such as detailed description	Yes	Distrib: AS pausing Positive, Mid-pause:	10–26–12 3.68/3.27/3.37 5.25/3.43/2.77
Mic7: Organise the ideas developed from the pictures	Try to organise the ideas developed from different pictures to have a clear story plot	No	Distrib: AS pausing	31–14–2 3.53/3.16/2.16
Negative				
Le2: Lexical choice: Appropriate words	Choose appropriate words for telling the story	No	Distrib: AS pausing	02/06/40 3.34/3.54/3.72
Le4: Lexical choice: Connective words	Choose to use some connective words	Yes	Distrib: AS pausing Negative, Mid-pause:	29–18 3.15/3.65 3.54/3.79

Positive				
Le8: Lexical choice: Accurate words	Try to use accurate words	Yes	Distrib: AS pausing Positive, Mid-pause:	43–5 3.35/3.69 3.8/2.26
Le12: Grammar: General use	Think of general use of grammar	No	Distrib: AS pausing	37–10 3.18/4.0
Le13: Grammar: Tense	Think of the use of the correct tense	No	Distrib: AS pausing Negative, Mid-clause:	32–16 2.98/4.19 3.18/4.56
Mic6: Think of ideas beyond pictures	Think of more ideas beyond the pictures	Yes	Distrib: AS pausing Positive, Mid-pause:	27–19–2 3.32/3.42/3.93 3.82/3.49/2.6
Mic8: Connect the pictures to develop the story	Try to connect or structure the pictures to develop the story plot	Yes	Distrib: AS pausing Negative, Mid-pause	19–21–5–2 3.17/3.48/3.58/ 4.08/3.37/3.99/ 3.93/2.36

AS pauses, clearly, are at a natural pausing point in speech, as evidenced by native speakers pausing at this point also (Skehan, 2009b). But the issue with them, with second language speakers, is when pausing at this point is greater than would be typical of native speakers. The data here are consistent with this interpretation, as indexed by the native speaker data given in Skehan (2009b). Once again, we can consider the positive influences, that is, those that lead to less pausing at this point, and negative influences that lead to more pausing, separately. Regarding the content of what is said, it appears that AS pausing is reduced when ideas are organised, and so speakers embark on more extensive contributions. With lexis, what comes across here is that it is important to be resourceful and flexible with words, and that if one is, pausing is reduced. Perhaps going along with both these points, it seems to be advantageous for this aspect of fluency if one rehearses and works small (presumably so that what is prepared transfers from planning to performance more easily). Finally, it seems beneficial for fluency if the speaker avoids a focus on form. Most of the negative influences on AS boundary fluency are the reverse of the positive influences. Being fixed and inflexible with words is not good for fluency, as one might expect. Being very concerned with form, similarly, leads to more AS pausing. And finally, it seems harmful for fluency if the speaker tries to be ambitious and fancy in what they say.

A final note on these results is the degree of correspondence between AS pausing and mid-clause pausing. Two positive codes are shared (Le14 [*don't worry about grammar*] and Micro3 [*plan small details*]), as are three negative codes (Le4 [*use*

174 Empirical Work

connective words], Le13 [*think of the correct tense*], and Micro8 [*structure the pictures*]). Surprisingly, two codes diverge. Le8 (*try to use accurate words*) and Micro6 (*think of ideas beyond pictures*) are negative for AS pausing and positive for mid-clause pausing, which is, to say the least, intriguing.

We turn next to Table 7.8, which shows the data for the influences on mid-clause pausing. For the positive influences here, the general theme seems to be one of avoiding specific sources of difficulty, of avoiding the areas which might cause difficulty. These, of course, include avoiding preoccupation with form, but more *generally* the strategy seems to be to find paths where difficulties are less likely. There is certainly a sense of anticipating difficulty so as to be better prepared

TABLE 7.8 Codes Associated With Differences in Mid-Clause Pausing

Positive				
Le3: Lexical choice: Simple words	Choose to use simple words	No	Distrib: Mid.Cl.Pausing:	36–11–1 3.95/2.67/3.26
Le8: Lexical choice: Accurate words	Try to use accurate words	Yes	Distrib: Mid.Cl.Pausing: Negative: AS:	43–5 3.8/3.26 3.35/3.69
Le9: Lexical compensation	Use a similar word to that which can't be recalled	No	Distrib: Mid.Cl.Pausing:	42–6 3.71/3.14
Le14: Grammar, little concern	No or very little concern about grammar use	No	Distrib: Mid.Cl.Pausing: Positive: AS:	23–25 4.22/3.10 3.88/2.93
Mic3: Plan small details	Plan small details, such as detailed description	Yes	Distrib: Mid.Cl.Pausing: Positive: AS:	10–26–12 5.25/3.43/2.77 3.68/3.27/3.37
Mic6: Think of ideas beyond pictures	Think of more ideas beyond the pictures	Yes	Distrib: Mid.Cl.Pausing: Negative: AS:	27–19–2 3.82/3.49/2.6 3.32/3.42/3.93
Negative				
Le1: Lexical: General retrieval	Try to remember the words used in the task	Yes	Distrib: Mid.Cl.Pausing:	19–24–5 3.22/3.94/3.82
Le4: Lexical: Connective words	Choose to use some connective words	Yes	Distrib: Mid.Cl.Pausing: Negative: AS:	29–18 3.54/3.79 3.15/3.65
Le13: Grammar: Tense	Think of the use of correct tense	No	Distrib: Mid.Cl.Pausing: Negative: AS:	32–16 3.18/4.56 2.98/4.19

Positive				
Meta2: Rehearse, accurate	Rehearse to be accurate	No	Distrib: Mid.Cl.Pausing:	35–12 3.52/4.12
Meta7: No need to take notes	There is no need to take notes	No	Distrib: Mid.Cl.Pausing:	24–24 3.48/3.8
Mic8: Connect pictures to develop story	Try to connect or structure the pictures to develop the story plot	Yes	Distrib: Mid.Cl.Pausing: Negative: AS:	19–21–5–2 3.37/3.99/3.93/2.36 3.17/3.48/3.58/4.08

when it does occur (as perhaps it inevitably will), and this is allied to a sense of what to do when that difficulty arises. There is also a (grudging?) willingness to be pushed to be more ambitious, but only when this does not take the speaker into waters which are too uncharted. The negative influences are also interesting. First of all, there is the possibility that one can be pushed too far. Once again, being too fancy does not seem to be a good influence. Similarly, (and this chimes with other performance areas), focussing on form, and being general, seem to have some costs in terms of mid-clause pauses. Finally, and perhaps surprisingly, taking notes can contain dangers, perhaps because this too leads speakers to go beyond their abilities.

The final area to be considered is that of lexical sophistication, as indexed by the value Lambda. The relevant data are shown in Table 7.9 below. Perhaps the first thing to say here is how disappointingly small this table is. It would have been nice to have a range of positive and negative associations between coded planning behaviours and lexical performance, similar to other performance areas. In the event there are only two positive influences and two negative, which seems remarkably slight. Even they are not terribly revealing. Positively, we have a focus on words and the desirability of being general with ideas. Negatively, there is the behaviour of avoiding lexical difficulty, of being (too) unambitious, and of relatively unfocussed rehearsal. There may be connections here with other areas—level of achievable ambition is relevant, as is the issue of generality-specificity, although here the influence is positive for generality for ideas, and negative for rehearsal. The most we can draw from this is that there does seem to be a specific attraction or rejection of words for different participants.

Discussion

In this discussion section we will first explore convergence and contrast with Ortega (2005). Then we will examine successes and failures within the present coding scheme in terms of its broader categories, notably the macro and lexico-grammar categories, and then move to relate this data to dimensions of

TABLE 7.9 Lexical Sophistication Linked to Coding

Positive

Le8: Lexical choice: Accurate words	Try to use accurate words	Yes	Distrib: Lex.Sophist.:	43–5 1.83/2.02
Mic5: Plan how to tell the story	Plan how to tell the story in general	Yes	Distrib: Lex.Sophist.:	20–20–7 1.83/1.87/1.92

Negative

Le3: Lexical choice: Simple words	Choose to use simple words	No	Distrib: Lex.Sophist.:	36–11–1 1.9/1.73/1.59
Meta1: Rehearse, General	Rehearse what is planned to say (and hopefully remember better)	Yes	Distrib: Lex.Sophist.:	25–23 1.91/1.68

performance (complexity, accuracy, fluency, lexis) as well as the Levelt model. We will finish by briefly discussing debates in the planning literature, as illuminated by the present study, and then make some suggestions for training and pedagogic applications.

The coding scheme developed in the present research has proved usable and illuminating. It contains the broad categories of Macro Cognitive Codes, Micro Cognitive Codes, Lexical and Grammar Codes, and Metacognitive Codes. This 'packaging' may contain a number of similar elements to those in Ortega (2005), but their arrangement is sometimes different. The major change is the introduction of Macro and Micro Codes. Some of the detailed codes here relate to Ortega's metacognitive strategies, since they concern organisational planning and various forms of attentional focus, (though, they do not emphasise monitoring and evaluation as much as she does in relation to the Metacognitive codes). Also the present scheme has a number of lexical and grammar planning codes, which in principle connect with cognitive strategies. However, here the overlap with Ortega's scheme is not extensive. In fact, our system treats rehearsal as part of metacognitive planning (on the basis that there is self-awareness involved), whereas Ortega includes it as a form of cognitive strategy. Our rehearsal codes are also more explicitly linked with aspects of performance, which can be closely associated with different stages of Levelt's model.

We now shift focus a little and consider how the codes are associated with differences in performance. Here we have some interesting contrasts. The two Macro codes (Table 7.2) were of little help in the analysis, in that they totally failed to discriminate between participants. (As a result, there was no scope for any association with performance to emerge.) In contrast, the Micro planning codes were far more successful, though only one (Micro1) had no connection with performance. The other seven discriminated, and also had associations with different performance areas, with a tendency to link with complexity (Table 7.6) and pausing, both AS pausing (Table 7.7) and mid-clause pausing (Table 7.8). Turning to the Lexical and Grammatical codes, their contribution was more mixed, with two lexical codes yielding nothing. The remainder, though, did make some contribution to the associations with performance. The lexical codes had associations with all performance areas, both negative as well as positive, although fluency (Tables 7.7 and 7.8) was the commonest area to crop up. Interestingly, the three grammar codes, which all revealed associations with aspects of performance, were consistent: they showed no relation to accuracy (Table 7.5), and showed negative relationships with subordination (Table 7.6) and pausing (Tables 7.7 and 7.8)! Finally, the metacognitive codes were a mixed bag. Around half either failed to discriminate or had no connection with performance. The focus here is on rehearsal, and while this was important for accuracy (the most consistent sub-area to have this connection: Table 7.5), other metacognitive codes, such as involving notes, or memorisation, or being aware of the listener, had little to provoke discussion. Clearly these results suggest that some areas of reported planning behaviour are more rewarding than others.

We turn next to exploring in greater depth why codes were associated with performance success. We will propose five wider principles which seem to subsume the more detailed codes which have been discussed so far. The principles are:

- build your own structure
- avoid trouble, and be realistic
- handle trouble when it occurs
- plan small or specific (versus plan general)
- avoid grammar focus.

The principles emerged from a close scrutiny of Tables 7.5 to 7.9, from which wider generalisations seemed warranted. These generalisations were based on the specific codes which were associated with stronger and weaker performance. The generalisations always subsumed the separate codes into the more general principle concerned. Interestingly, four of the five principles cut across the performance areas, and so they are proposed as general principles for good use of planning time, though they manifest themselves in different performance areas in different ways. Only the fifth is directly connected with any particular performance area. In fact, the first two 'code bundles' are associated with widespread improvements in performance, whereas as we go on, the focus for improvement is narrowed somewhat.

Build Your Own Structure

Several codes are relevant here. *Plan how to tell the story* (Micro4), *Organise the ideas* (Micro7), *Rehearse to check whether what is planned is logical and clear* (Meta4). They have in common that the speaker imposes some organisation on what is to be said. This is particularly interesting given the independent strand of task research (see Skehan and Shum [2014] and Wang and Skehan [2014]) which argues that tasks containing structure lead to higher performance (Skehan, 2014c; Chapter 10, this volume). Equally interesting is that, consistent with the task structure literature, many aspects of performance are involved, including accuracy, complexity, and AS-boundary pausing, a powerful combination. One assumes that having a clearer structure makes it more likely that the speaker can be 'ahead of the game', as it were, and create on-line planning opportunities, enabling errors to be avoided, more ambitious language used, and also, with favourable conditions building on favourable conditions, more effective clause boundary pausing to be possible, which in turn enables easier marshalling of resources during speech.

Avoid Trouble, and Be Realistic

Again, a number of codes are relevant. *Choose to use simple words* (LexGram3), *Have no or little concern about vocabulary* (LexGram11), *Have no or little concern about grammar use* (LexGram14), *Rehearse* (To be Accurate—Meta2: Fluent—Meta3, Logical or Clear—Meta4), with these being positive relationships with performance, and then *Plan general* (Micro2), a negative relationship, versus *Plan small details* (Micro3), a positive relationship, and *Plan how to express better* (Micro5), a negative relationship, *Lexical choice—appropriate words* (LexGram2)—a negative relationship, *Use accurate words* (LexGram8) which was positive with accuracy, but negative for complexity and fluency, and *Plan how to express better* (Micro5) a negative relationship with accuracy and complexity. When one reflects on the positive and negative influences here, the common thread seems to be better performance on the occasions when speakers use planning time to prepare simpler things and to work within their limited abilities. The negative relationships reflect the ways a speaker can go wrong and overdo things, and thereby create trouble for themselves. So speakers who give themselves reasonable challenges (plan small and simple, don't worry about grammar or vocabulary, rehearse), and do not plan their way into trouble (plan general, plan how to be better, and to use more appropriate words), do better. Most interesting of all, this strategy for using planning time seems to raise accuracy, complexity, and both aspects of fluency.

Handle Trouble When It Occurs

Of course, for second language speakers, trouble is likely to be inevitable, and so an important positive attribute is to be able to deal with that trouble when it arrives. One aspect of this connects with the first construct proposed above, 'build your own structure'. Skehan (2014c) proposes that one of the benefits of structure is that it enables the speaker, after there has been difficulty, to rejoin the discourse thread that the structure makes possible. So, rather than fall behind further, the speaker can find a new starting point, and in that way, and perhaps with a bit of luck, recover a parallel mode of processing, as opposed to the serial mode that is provoked by a mental lexicon giving the speaker retrieval problems (Kormos, 2006). There are other planning codes that are relevant here. LexGram9 (*Lexical compensation*) has a positive relationship with mid-clause pausing, while LexGram10 (*Lexical compensation and circumlocution*), is positive in its effects on AS-boundary pausing. In each case, though, there is also a negative relationship with some aspect of form, so dealing with trouble has some costs, too.

Plan Small or Specific (Versus Plan General)

The main evidence here comes from the Micro codings, Micro2, *Plan general*, which has a negative relationship with subordination, compared to Micro3, *Plan small details*, which is positive in its effects on subordination and pausing, and also *Rehearse General* (Meta1) which has a negative association with lexical sophistication), and Meta2 and Meta3, *Rehearse Accurate* and *Rehearse Fluency*, respectively, which are positive. An issue which perhaps underlies these factors is that of transfer from the planning phase into actual performance. It appears here as though being focussed and specific in what one does (and this also means 'plan small', a further example of avoiding trouble), enables the more limited aims to be converted from the earlier planning phase into the focussed performance that is intended. General planning processes, in contrast, do not seem to endure, and do not have the same sort of impact. One way or another, the impact of planning small, and avoiding more general planning (Micro 2), can impact on pretty much all aspects of performance.

Avoid Grammar Focus

The key codings here are LexGram12 (*General grammar use*), LexGram13 (*Grammar, Tense*), and LexGram14 (*Grammar, no concern*). None of these has any impact upon accuracy or error. In contrast, the first two, implying a concern for grammar, are associated negatively with subordination and fluency, and the third, a negative portrayal of grammar, is positively associated with subordination and fluency. So, the reverse effect is found to what might be expected here, and it suggests that focussing on grammar confers only disadvantages, and no advantages.

Reflecting on these five 'principles' for effective use of planning time, the most notable reaction one is likely to have is how negative they are, and that they seem to convey that we have learned more about how to use planning badly than how to use planning well. There are suggestions of some principles associated with a good use of planning, such as to impose structure, to be led perhaps by ideas and not form, and to plan small and detailed. But in general, it is what *not* to do that emerges more strikingly.

Indeed, the preponderance of the codes where positive relationships are involved are concerned with complexity and fluency. This is consistent with the generally accepted finding in the literature (e.g., Ortega, 2005) that planning has a beneficial effect on complexity and fluency. So it seems as if our results are consistent with the broad quantitative results that have been published (although of course, there are exceptions, such as Ellis [2009] showing that accuracy effects are not at all uncommon). In other words, the range of influences we have just covered are consistent with the findings from the literature, and provided, therefore, some detailed support in terms of what second language speakers say they do when they plan.

To put this another way, the reported behaviours which are associated with raised accuracy and with raised lexical sophistication are not so numerous, which is something of a disappointment. There are some, however, such as *Lexical choice*, *Accurate words*, as well as *General lexical retrieval*, which make intuitive sense, as well as the Micro code of *Connect or structure the pictures*, implying the value of giving a structure to the story for accuracy. But *Rehearsal*, *Fluency*, and *Rehearsal to be logical or clear* are less obviously relevant. So what underlies the association between self-reported planning behaviours and greater accuracy remains a puzzle. In addition, the *Accurate words* coding, while good for accuracy, seems bad for *Complexity and Fluency*, suggesting some degree of trade-off in performance. *Accurate words* is, though, the main positive influence on lexical sophistication, while the other influences in this performance area are the more generalised negative influences of focussing on simple words, and engaging in general rehearsal. We are left, in other words, with few clear and convincing influences on either accuracy or lexical sophistication, which may have some relevance for the less consistent findings in this area. Behaviours generally concerned with rehearsal of specific things seems good, but the avoidance of harmful influences (in general) seems just as important.

The other issue arising from the literature which is worth commenting on is the respective claims of the Trade-off approaches and the Cognition Hypothesis. Basically, the present study has little direct to say on this. But perhaps two points are worth making. First, there is often competition between different performance areas when one looks at the influence of individual coded behaviours, and so raised performance in one area is often associated with lower performance in another. In general, it looks as if complexity and fluency often go together, and do not compete. In contrast, accuracy does seem to compete with other performance dimensions. The Cognition Hypothesis proposes that under certain circumstances complexity and accuracy can both be raised. When one looks at the way influences on these two areas which arise out of planning seem rarely to go together, one can conclude that the present study does not seem particularly supportive for the Cognition Hypothesis. The second point relates to the way task complexity is seen as the driver, in the Cognition Hypothesis, for raising accuracy and complexity jointly. One can see from the present study the existence of influences which cause ideas to predominate and therefore push the speaker to make the task more complex. On these occasions, however, there is no sign that there is a beneficial influence on accuracy as well.

Some of these issues are taken up in Skehan (2014c). Two other chapters (Bui [2014] and Wang [2014]) explore other facets of planning quantitatively. In Skehan (2014c) these different findings are brought together to offer a more general account of the role of planning in second language task performance.

Conclusion

In general, the planning research supports the idea that using planning in pedagogic contexts where a communicative approach is prevalent is a good thing. The literature suggests that it is rare to find studies which suggest that planning is harmful. There are studies which point to its limitations, but it is clear that using planning is far better on most occasions than not using it. But at the same time, we have not made that much progress over the last 25 years in making suggestions as to when planning is most effective, what alternatives are available to the planner, and ultimately, whether effectiveness in planning can be trained. The present study provides no clear answers to any of these issues, but it is suggestive. The differences in reported planning behaviours certainly suggest that not all planners do the same things, and that some behaviours are likely to be more effective than others. The discussion above suggested that planning choices can be most effectively regarded as a set of operating principles (build your own structure, avoid trouble, don't over-extend, handle trouble, plan small, don't be too focussed on grammar). It appears, then, that it would be worth exploring whether these principles are general; whether speakers who do not at first think of using them could be trained to use them (and whether this would then be more effective); and perhaps most ambitiously of all, whether speakers could be induced to use planning behaviours likely to target particular performance dimensions. The research possibilities here are considerable, and they have the important quality that they would seem likely to have considerable pedagogic payoff.

APPENDIX 7.1

Instructions for the Picture Story Telling Task

In this task you will look at a series of pictures, and then you will need to tell the story in these pictures to the other student. When you finish the story, the other student will ask you a question or more than one question.

You will have 10 minutes, ***by yourself***, to plan what you are going to say during the picture story telling. Use the 10 minutes effectively to tell a good and clear story.

If you go first, then you will describe the story in your pictures to the other student. Do not show the pictures you are describing to the other student. The other student does not have these pictures to look at.

If you go second, the other student will describe the story in their (different) pictures to you.

Try to talk for 2 minutes or more.

Instructions When You Are a Listener

Listen to the other student telling the story in their pictures. When they finish, try to ask a question or more than one question.

- Ask a question if you do not understand something.
- Or ask a question if you would like the other student to say more about the series of pictures.

APPENDIX 7.2

Retrospective Interview Prompts

Name: Major: Gender:

General	Prompts
Planning (Self report)	What did you do? How did you plan? Tell me what you did during the time you're planning?
Then (Notes)	Here are your notes. Do they help you remember more about what you did when you planned? Did making notes help in the actual task although you're not allowed to look at them?
General reactions to self report (more focus Qs)	Do you think the planning time was useful? Why or why not?
	Do you think the planning was useful for the general way or for small things? Why?
	What effect did the planning have on the way you did the task?
Emphasis (Self report)	What did you emphasise?
More specific questions on emphasis. (If nothing said on each of the expected area, ask one by one.)	1. WORDS • To remember words that might be useful? • To use words that might be diverse, accurate? 2. GRAMMAR • To remember grammar? • To avoid mistakes (correctness)?

(Continued)

APPENDIX 7.2 (Continued)

General	Prompts
	3. IDEAS
	• To think of ideas?
	• To organise ideas?
	4. STRUCTURE OF THE STORY (*Picture Story Telling Task*)
	• To structure the flow of pictures
	• To use language to show how the pictures are connected and developed
	5. REHEARSE
	• To be accurate
	• To be fluent
	6. To THINK HOW TO SAY things to make it easier and clearer for your partner?

APPENDIX 7.3

Coding Scheme: Planning activities of ESL speakers doing picture story telling task

No.	CODE	Description of Code	Example
(A) Macro planning			
1	Plan sequence: Scan pictures, then describe	Scan all the pictures, understand what the story is about, then think of how to describe the story	I first went through the pictures. After I got a general idea, I began to think how to tell the story in English.
2	Plan sequence: Look at picture one by one, then describe	Look at the pictures one by one and at the same time think about how to describe each picture	I looked at the pictures one by one, and think about how to tell each picture at the same time.
(B) Micro planning			
1	Understand the pictures in detail	Try to understand the pictures in detail and know what the story is about	I first read the instruction, but I had no idea when I saw so many sheep in the grids. I went through the pictures first and then looked at the details.
2	Plan general things	Plan general things, such as describing the general plot of the story	I planned general things. I needed to have a concept first, and the details could be added while I spoke.

(Continued)

APPENDIX 7.3 (Continued)

No.	CODE	Description of Code	Example
3	Plan small details	Plan small details, such as detailed description	I think it was useful for the subtle things. Maybe I could tell the story in a general way right away but I might make it a mess.
4	Plan how to tell the story	Plan how to tell the story in general	During the 10 minutes, I was thinking how to tell the story.
5	Plan how to express better	Plan how to describe the story more vividly, interestingly, or clearly, etc.	Based on the pictures, I considered how to describe them in a better way and I organized my words.
6	Think of ideas beyond pictures	Think of more ideas beyond the pictures	With some time to plan, I could add my ideas if the links were strange or if I couldn't understand the pictures.
7	Organise the ideas developed from the pictures	Try to organise the ideas developed from different pictures to have a clear story plot	Yes, I read it. Then, I turned to the details and figured out how to organize them. I sorted out how many times the sheep was weighted and how many different sports it did, and I also concluded that at last it succeeded to be the same size as the other sheep.
8	Connect the pictures to develop the story plot	Try to connect or structure the pictures to develop the story plot	I emphasized on the plots. I considered how to connect the pictures to make the story better.
(C) Lexical and grammar planning				
1	Lexical: General retrieval	Try to remember the words used in the task	Looking at a picture, I needed to consider and recall the English words to be used for that picture.
2	Lexical choice: Appropriate words	Choose appropriate words for telling the story	I wanted Yuni to know that the tree is very important. I would think about the language of every scene and the appropriate words to the scenes.
3	Lexical choice: Simple words	Choose to use simple words	I considered using simpler words which could be understood most easily.
4	Lexical choice: Connective words	Choose to use some connective words	Secondly, I added some connective words between sentences to connect all the pictures together.
5	Lexical choice: Personification words	Choose to use some personification words	. . . and added some personification words.

No.	CODE	Description of Code	Example
6	Lexical choice: Advanced words	Try to use some advanced words	...and also use some relatively advanced words.
7	Lexical choice: Various words	Try to use various words to talk about the same thing	A little. For example, for the cake... I thought of two words, *tempt* and *attract*.
8	Lexical choice: Accurate words	Try to use accurate words	I tried to use some accurate words to describe the pictures.
9	Lexical compensation: Approximating	Use a word similar in meaning to replace the word which can't be recalled	If I had any words that I didn't know how to express, I tried to replace them with other words.
10	Lexical compensation: Circumlocution	Use a few words or another way to replace a word which cannot be recalled	Secondly, for those words I didn't know or forget how to say, I need time to find other ways to explain them.
11	Lexical: No/Little concern	No or very little concern about vocabulary	No, not particularly think of the use of words.
12	Grammar: General use	Think of general use of grammar	Yes, I considered the use of grammar as grammar plays an important role in story telling.
13	Grammar: Tense	Think of the use of correct tense	I feel it's necessary to consider it. I thought if I should use present, past or continuous tense.
14	Grammar: No/Little concern	No or very little concern about grammar use	For me, sometimes I didn't pay much attention on grammar. Instead, I rely more on my sense of the language and didn't think much about the correctness.
(D) Metacognitive planning			
1	Rehearse: General	Rehearse what is planned to say (and hopefully remember better)	I did not rehearse word by word. I just considered the sequences of what I would say.
2	Rehearse: Accurate	Rehearse to be accurate	At the same time, I think the rehearsal could help me to be more accurate.
3	Rehearse: Fluent	Rehearse to be fluent	I rehearsed as I want to tell a more fluent story.
4	Rehearse: Logical or clear	Rehearse to check whether what is planned is logical or clear	I think the rehearsal could help to check the logic of the story, and to see whether my story is in accordance with the pictures as well as our common way of thinking.

(Continued)

APPENDIX 7.3 (Continued)

No.	CODE	Description of Code	Example
5	Rehearse: Memorisation	Rehearse to help memorising what is planned	The rehearsal could also help me to memorize some of the things I've planned in order to deliver my story more smoothly.
6	Take notes	Take notes to plan the task (although cannot see it when doing the task)	I made some point-form notes on the draft paper. I usually make point-form. I noted down the flow.
7	Take notes: No need	There is no need to take notes	I didn't since the story is short; if it's a long one, I would take notes.
8	Memorisation	Try to memorise what is planned before doing the task	Finally, I went through my notes, referring to the pictures; and memorize the points planned.
9	Aware of listener's understanding	Try to make the listener understand the story, such as using simple grammar or words	Because the task has no words but just pictures, the planning time could help me think about how to say things to make my partner more easily understand.
10	Lexical: Planned but not used/correctly used	During planning, lexical is considered, but it is not used or not correctly used when doing the task	Though I did think about the word, when I was telling the story, I forgot these things and just said whatever in my mind.
11	Grammar: Planned but not used/correctly used	During planning, grammar is considered, but it is not used or not correctly used when doing the task	Yes, I've thought about grammar, but I didn't pay much attention on it when actually doing the task.

8

LEXICAL PERFORMANCE BY NATIVE AND NON-NATIVE SPEAKERS ON LANGUAGE-LEARNING TASKS

Introduction

The last 20 years or so has seen a vast increase in research into second language learning tasks. A series of articles has been published by this author and co-researchers taking a cognitive approach to task performance (Foster, 2001a; Foster & Skehan, 1996a, 1999; Skehan & Foster, 1997, 1999, 2005, 2007). This chapter reports on a meta-analysis of these studies, (and see also Skehan & Foster, 2007), but it does so with two additional foci. First, most research with tasks has focussed only on second language learners. As a result, it is difficult to disentangle whether performances which are reported are the result of the different variables which are being manipulated (e.g. task characteristics, task conditions) or simply the second language speakerness of the participants. One needs baseline native-speaker data, of the sort reported in Foster (2001a) to enable a better perspective on the results to be obtained.

A second shortcoming of the research is that it has used a restricted set of performance measures. These have been *complexity*, generally measured through an index of subordination which is based on Analysis of Speech (AS) units, roughly equivalent to clauses (Foster, Tonkyn, & Wigglesworth, 2000); *accuracy*, measured usually as error-free clauses; and *fluency*, measured variously through pausing-based indices (e.g. Foster & Skehan, 1996a), repair indices such as reformulation,

---

Originally published as: Skehan P. (2009b). Lexical performance by native and non-native speakers on language-learning tasks. In B. Richards, H. Daller, D. D. Malvern, & P. Meara (Eds.), *Vocabulary studies in first and second language acquisition: The interface between theory and application* (pp. 107–124). London: Palgrave Macmillan. Reproduced with permission of Palgrave Macmillan.

false starts, and so on (Foster & Skehan, 1996a); speech rate (Tavakoli & Skehan, 2005); or length of run (Skehan & Foster, 2005). A major area of omission concerns the lexical aspects of task performance. There have been occasional attempts at measures here. Foster and Skehan (1996a), for example, did explore measures of lexical variety, and Robinson (2001a) reports values for what he terms the token-type ratio, but in the main the lexical area has not been well served.

A brief word is necessary in this section also on the meta-analytic nature of the research reported here. The research is based on a series of linked studies, six in total, which will be detailed below. The present research therefore is an attempt to establish patterns which emerge across larger datasets. It is hoped that this approach will produce more robust and generalisable results (Norris & Ortega, 2006).

Measures of Lexical Performance

The literature on lexical performance generally distinguishes between text-internal and text-external measures (Daller, Van Hout, & Treffers-Daller, 2003). The main text-internal measure which is widely used is the type-token ratio. However, the basic measure is extremely vulnerable to a text length effect (Malvern & Richards, 2002), and typical correlations between text length and type-token ratio are negative and in the order of −0.70 (Foster, 2001b). A series of responses to this problem have been developed and these are reviewed in Tidball and Treffers-Daller (2007), Van Hout and Vermeer (2007), and in Jarvis (2002). The different corrections for length have strengths and weaknesses, but for the present research, the measure which was used is D, obtained through the use of the VOCD sub-routine within CLAN (and CHILDES: MacWhinney, 2000). In a series of publications, Malvern and Richards (2002; Richards & Malvern, 2007) have demonstrated the reliability and validity of this measure, which is based on mathematical modelling. McCarthy and Jarvis (2007) propose that there are measurement-related flaws in the use of D. However, it is clear that the value that D delivers correlates very highly indeed with other measures which are proposed and so there seems no reason not to use it as the most effective lexical diversity measure available.

The next question, of course, is to ask what such a measure measures. At this point, things become a little less clear. At one level, the answer is simple: D provides an index of the extent to which the speaker avoids the recycling of the same set of words. If a text has a lower D, it suggests that the person producing the (spoken or written) text is more reliant on a set of words to which he or she returns often. This naturally raises the questions as to which factors influence the values for D. The problem is that there are multiple possible factors involved here. These include:

- The development of greater vocabulary size and so the capacity to choose from a wider range of words where previously there was a smaller repertoire.

One might predict therefore that age for first language learners, or proficiency level for second language learners would be associated with higher values of D.
- The possession of a better-organised lexicon, with the result that a greater range of words can be easily drawn on.
- Performance conditions, for example, written versus spoken performance would allow more time for lexical retrieval, generating higher values of D.
- A repetitive style, which might be an individual difference factor, could be important here. The contrast would be with a style which tries to achieve what might be termed elegant variation, where the speaker attempts to avoid recycling in order to convey an impression of composed, created language. (This influence will not be pursued here, since it does not connect with the present research design.)
- There may be task influences in that when topics in conversation change with regularity, this may lead to new 'sets' of words being accessed leading to lower opportunities for lexical recycling over the text as a whole.

Clearly the problem here is the existence of what is only a laundry list of influences, reflecting underlying lexicon, communication style, and task influences. The difficulty is disentangling which of these influences is most operative. The present study will begin to address these issues.

A contrasting class of lexical measures uses some external yardstick to evaluate a different construct of lexical variety. Essentially, a measure is computed of the extent to which the speaker draws upon more varied words, referenced by some external criterion. This has been termed lexical sophistication (Read, 2000). Two issues are immediately apparent. First, there is the question of what 'varied words' might mean. Second, there is the problem of how an index is computed which reflects putative variety.

The standard approach to defining variety has been through word frequency. A performance is then judged in terms of its tendency to draw upon less frequent words. One of the most influential methods, the Levels Test (Laufer & Nation, 1999) uses word lists based on generalised written corpora, including specialist corpora for academic words. The test provides information on the number of words in a text drawn from the 1000 word level, the number drawn from the 2000 word level and so on, enabling a judgement to be made regarding the 'penetration' in the text of less frequent words. The ensuing judgement therefore is profile based and gives a complex but interesting perspective on the extent to which very frequent words are less relied upon.

An alternative measure also exists, though, which, like D, uses a mathematical modelling procedure. Meara and Bell (2001) have devised a procedure, P-Lex, which divides a text into ten-word chunks, and then computes the number of infrequent words in each ten-word chunk. For example, one might have the distribution shown in Table 8.1 for a 300 word text.

There are 30 ten-word chunks to work with in Table 8.1 (hence the numbers in the second row add up to 30). One can then explore how many ten-word chunks contain no infrequent words, how many contain just one, and so on. The distribution from the set of scores shown in the table suggests a text where ten-word chunks with no or only one infrequent word predominate, with nine of each. Intuitively, this (hypothetical) distribution suggests a text with mainly fairly frequent words. Meara and Bell (2001) demonstrate that distributions such as that shown in Table 8.1 can be modelled by the Poisson Distribution, a distribution particularly appropriate for data with infrequent events. The method is to estimate the value, lambda, which generates a Poisson distribution which approximates the actual pattern of scores with most accuracy. P-Lex has been widely researched and it has been demonstrated (Bell, 2003) that it is an effective measure for texts which are longer than about 100 words. Table 8.2, where the examples are drawn from the datasets covered in this chapter, provides some examples of actual score distributions, and the associated lambda values.

Clearly, the first two speakers have more ten-word chunks which contain infrequent words, that is to say, the penetration of infrequent words goes further to the right in each set of scores, while Speaker Three produces a preponderance of ten-word chunks with no infrequent words, or only a small number of such words. The lambda values reflect these distributions, and show that, the higher the lambda, the more infrequent words are being used.

The original computer program, P-Lex, needed some slight modifications for the datasets used in the present meta-analyses. The rewritten program was referenced from the British National Corpus spoken component, and so drew upon a corpus of 10 million words (Leech, Rayson & Wilson, 2001, and also the Lancaster corpus linguistics group website). The reference list was lemmatised (and in fact could be used to generate lambda values either in lemmatised or unlemmatised forms). Files of task-specific words were compiled to enable words to be temporarily defined as easy, adaptable for different runs of the program. Finally a cut-off

TABLE 8.1 Distribution of Ten-Word Chunks With Infrequent Words

No. of infrequent words per ten words	0	1	2	3	4	5	6	7
No. of word chunks	9	9	6	4	1	1	0	0

TABLE 8.2 Example Distributions and Associated Lambdas (λ)

No. of infrequent words per 10 words	0	1	2	3	4	5	6	7
(Native) Speaker: personal task: $\lambda = 1.50$	4	6	2	2	2	0	0	0
(Non-native) Speaker: narrative task: $\lambda = 1.54$	6	8	9	3	2	0	0	0
(Non-native) Speaker: decision-making task: $\lambda = 0.78$	18	10	6	2	0	0	0	0

value, using the lemmatised reference list, of fewer uses than 150 per million words was used as the basis for defining difficulty, or rarity, the central requirement of the P-Lex program (Meara & Bell, 2001; Bell, 2003). This value seemed to be most effective in producing a good range of discrimination. It might also be regarded as fairly 'generous' in making difficulty decisions. However, spoken language tends to contain notably fewer infrequent words than does written language.

Assuming this provides a valid and reliable measurement option, we still need to discuss what the construct of lexical sophistication represents and what influences it. Earlier, for lexical diversity, a variety of influences were discussed. These were:

- development of vocabulary size and/or organisation;
- performance conditions, such as modality, time pressure, planning opportunities;
- style, whether repetitive or variational;
- task influences.

Interestingly, all of these would also seem relevant for greater lexical sophistication. Greater size and/or organisation of vocabulary should enable greater lexical sophistication. Similarly, favourable performance conditions such as planning versus no-planning, should similarly be associated with a greater capacity to draw on less basic vocabulary. Style is difficult to comment on here, although perhaps this variable is less salient for lexical sophistication than for lexical diversity. Finally, task influences too might well have an impact on performance, although whether these are the same task influences as those which impact upon lexical diversity is an empirical issue. On the face of it, though, a similar set of influences may be operative, and so one might, again at first sight, expect lexical diversity and lexical sophistication to pattern similarly. Exploring their actual interrelationship will be one of the central themes of the present research.

The Research Database

Table 8.3 outlines the six studies which form the basis for the present meta-analysis. The individual studies drew on a range of task types and task characteristics, on the one hand, and task conditions, on the other. Tasks fell into one of three categories: personal information exchange (P); narratives, either based on picture series or on a video (and necessarily more monologic in nature) (N); and decision-making, where, through interaction, pairs or groups of students were required to make decisions (D). Examples of the tasks are as follows:

> *Personal Information Exchange*: 'You are at school and you have an important examination in ten minutes. But you suddenly remember that you have left the oven on in your flat. Ask your friend to help, and give them directions so that they can get to your home (which they have never visited) and then get into the kitchen and turn the oven off.'

Narrative: A cartoon series from the work of the French cartoonist, Sempé, was presented. It showed a story of a woman going to the fortune teller's. While having her fortune told through cards, the fortune teller's telephone rings (situated directly behind the fortune teller). While the fortune teller's back was turned, the client turned up the cards, saw they were not to her liking, and rearranged them. When the fortune teller finished the call, she unsuspectingly turned back round and told the (glowing) fortune based on the rearranged cards.

Decision-making: Participants were given letters supposedly written to a magazine Agony Aunt and were required to agree on appropriate advice. A typical letter (of three presented in total) would be: 'I'm 14 and I am madly in love with a boy of 21. My friends have told him how I feel and he says that he likes me, but he won't take me out because he says I am too young. I'm upset. Age doesn't matter, does it?'

Table 8.3 provides an overview of the results of these studies. The dependent variables (cf. the earlier discussion) are always complexity, accuracy, and fluency. Then a series of independent variables have been explored, including task characteristics, as well as pre-, during-, and post-task conditions. Pre-task planning was generally operationalised through the provision of 10 minutes planning time; during-task operationalisations were either to introduce surprise new information while the task was being done or to vary the time pressure conditions; the post-task condition was either to have to re-do a task, publicly, after the actual task was done, or to have to transcribe one's own performance, post-task. A very brief outline of the results for each study is shown, as is the corpus size for each study, in thousands of words.

For now, we can see that a series of generalisations can be made on the basis of the results reported in Table 8.3 (see Skehan & Foster, 2007, for extended coverage):

- planning has a consistent effect, strongly raising complexity and fluency, and raising accuracy to a lesser extent;
- a post-task condition, for example, a public performance of the same task, or the requirement to transcribe some of one's own performance after the task is completed, leads to raised accuracy, especially with the interactive decision-making task;
- personal tasks based on familiar, concrete information lead to higher levels of fluency and accuracy;
- decision-making tasks produce higher accuracy and complexity;
- narratives appear to be the most difficult task type, with lowest accuracy;
- tasks containing structure such as tasks based on a clear schema, like a restaurant schema, or alternatively a problem-solution schema (Hoey, 1983) lead to raised accuracy;

TABLE 8.3 Overview of the Studies

Study	Focus	Results	Size in Words
1. Foster and Skehan (1996a) (NNS)	P vs. N vs. D Planning	Strong planning effect Selective task effect	25K
2. Skehan and Foster (1997)	P vs. N vs. D Planning Post-task	Strong planning effect Selective task effect Partial post-task accuracy effect (Decision-making task only)	36K
3. Skehan and Foster (2005)	Planning Mid-task surprise Time (5 vs. 10 mins.)	Strong planning effect No effect of mid-task surprise information Strong time effect (5 mins. > 10 mins. on all measures)	18K
4. Skehan and Foster (1999)	Degree of structure (Narrative tasks) Processing load	Structured task was more fluent and sometimes more accurate Simultaneous processing is very difficult	30K
5. Foster and Skehan (2013)	N vs. D Post-task condition	Clear accuracy effect of post-task on both tasks	30K
6. Foster (2001a) (NSs, same design as Study 1)	P vs. N vs. D Planning NS vs. NNS	Strong planning effect with complexity and fluency Native speakers less formulaic when planned, Non-native speakers the reverse	25K

P = Personal task; N = Narrative task; D = Decision-making task; NS = Native speaker; NNS = Non-native speaker

- tasks requiring the transformation, manipulation or integration of information lead to greater language complexity;
- there is a trade-off between the performance areas, with higher performance in one area often being at the expense of other performance areas.

Lexical Performance on Tasks

There are four basic questions to be considered in this section. First, fundamentally, we need to explore how native and non-native speakers differ in their performance. Second, and equally fundamentally, we need to consider how the two measures of lexical performance interrelate. Third, there is the general question as to how the lexical measures relate to other measures—whether, for example, they relate to complexity, or accuracy, or neither. Finally, there is the issue of what influences the lexical measures. We have seen different patterns of influence on complexity and accuracy, as in Table 8.3. Now we need to explore the same question with the lexical measures.

Native Versus Non-Native Speakers

The first comparison to explore is that between native and non-native speakers. This comparison is only possible for Studies 6 (Foster, 2001a) and 1 (Foster & Skehan, 1996a), since it was only in these two studies that participants did exactly the same tasks, and with essentially the same conditions (10 minutes planning versus no planning). The relevant results, based on between-subjects t-tests, are presented in Table 8.4.

The obvious (in both senses of clear, and also predictable) generalisation here is that native speakers produce more impressive lexical performances than do non-native speakers. All significances are at the 0.001 level, and the differences are all very clear indeed. Native speakers, that is, when doing tasks, draw upon less frequent vocabulary, and also pack a greater variety of words into a text they produce. But there are also some interesting task-speaker interactions. Native speakers are most appreciably higher in their lambda scores with the personal and narrative tasks. The difference between the two groups is much less with the decision-making task, and in any case, the lambda scores here are clearly lower for both groups. The situation is different with D, since here the personal task shows the least difference. Once again the narrative task shows a large difference, making this the only task which is consistent in a large advantage for native speakers for both measures. But interestingly, the values for D for the decision-making task show a clear difference between native and non-natives (in contrast to the smaller difference for lambda). The interactive task leads to less recycling with the native speakers: non-native speakers are nothing like as impressive.

We can assume that the two groups differ markedly in both the size and organisation of their mental lexicons. So it seems that the possession of larger, better-organised lexicons does lead to the use of less frequent lexis *and* less recycling of a smaller set of words. In the first case, the larger vocabulary, linked to its greater accessibility, means that the fund of words that is drawn upon is considerably greater and native speakers can react to tasks effectively. In the latter case, it is also clear that native speakers are not reliant on limited word sets which they have to keep using because of the lack of others.

TABLE 8.4 A Comparison of the Lexical Performance of Native and Non-Native Speakers

	λ			D		
	Personal	Narrative	Decision-Making	Personal	Narrative	Decision-Making
NS Mean	1.38	1.68	0.87	45.6	75.2	90.6
(N = 31)	(0.39)	(0.52)	(0.25)	(11.3)	(19.0)	(11.5)
NNS Mean	1.02	1.14	0.65	36.1	46.9	52.9
(N = 29)	(0.33)	(0.37)	(0.27)	(9.7)	(13.4)	(11.9)
Signif.	$p < 0.001$	$p < 0.001$	$p < 0.001$	$p < 0.001$	$p < 0.001$	$p < 0.001$

Standard deviations are given in parentheses

The Relationship Between D and Lambda

The relationship between these two measures is shown in Table 8.5. The table is organised in terms of the different studies which were completed, and also shows the separate tasks where there was more than one task in a study. Each cell gives a correlation coefficient to indicate the nature of the relationship concerned. Significance and marginal significance are shown.

The N sizes in these studies are not large, and so it is difficult to achieve significance. But the basic conclusion is unavoidable—the level of relationship between these two measures is very low at best, and more probably, non-existent. The highest correlations would only account for very low levels of shared variance. This applies to native speakers and non-native speakers alike, and across personal, narrative, and decision-making tasks. We therefore have to draw the conclusion that lexical diversity and lexical variety are independent of one another. Earlier, it was speculated that possessing a larger and better-organised lexicon might raise D, and one might also speculate that this would impact upon lambda also. The evidence is not consistent with this happening. So it may be that the salient influences upon D are not the same as those on lambda. We need to look elsewhere to try to tease out what these contrasting influences might be.

Relationships of Lexical Measures to Complexity (and Accuracy)

The three areas concerned here, lexis, structural complexity, and accuracy, are all part of the formal structure of language. It is interesting to explore, therefore, how they interrelate. Robinson (2001b; Robinson & Gilabert, 2007), for example, proposes that accuracy and complexity should correlate, while Skehan (1998) suggests that limitations in attention means that usually they do not, as non-native speakers prioritise one performance area over the other. It now becomes interesting to throw lexical performance into the mix.

There are interesting differences here in the patterns of relationships between measures for native and non-native speakers. For the non-natives across the range

TABLE 8.5 Pearson Correlations Between D and Lambda in Different Studies

	Personal	Narrative	Decision-Making
Study 6: Native speakers ($N = 31$)	0.19	−0.28	−0.30
Study 1: Non-natives ($N = 29$)	−0.27	0.08	0.32
Study 2 ($N = 40$)	0.35	0.06	−0.11
Study 3 ($N = 64$)	n/a	n/a	0.29 ($p < 0.04$)
Study 4 ($N = 22; N = 24$)	n/a	−0.33; −0.06	n/a
Study 5 ($N = 45$)	n/a	−0.23	0.31 ($p < 0.06$)

Study 6 is placed first, next to Study 1, since the same tasks were done in both, with the difference only being the native vs. non-native speaker status. In addition, for Study 4, two values are shown, since there were two narrative tasks. Where 'n/a' is shown, this indicates that a relevant task type was not used in that study.

of studies, lambda correlates consistently negatively with accuracy, that is to say the greater the lexical sophistication and use of infrequent words, the lower the accuracy. The relationship between lambda and complexity for this same group is not quite such a clear pattern, but the relationship here, too, is mainly negative. Less frequent words, for non-native speakers, are associated with lower complexity. In other words, more varied lexis seems to cause problems for non-native speakers and provokes more error while not driving forward complexity. There seems, in other words, to be something of a toll for those who mobilise less frequent lexical items, in that the syntactic implications of such words derail, rather than build, syntax.

It was considered inappropriate to use accuracy measures with the native speakers in Study 6 in the present datasets. But we can examine the relationship between lambda and syntactic complexity. This is positive, with the three correlations of 0.43 (personal, $p < 0.05$), 0.57 (narrative, $p < 0.001$), and 0.21 (decision-making, not significant), with N sizes of 28, 31, and 33 respectively. In other words, for native speakers, less frequent words seem to push speakers to use more complex language. Native speakers seem able to handle the consequences of lemma retrieval without disruption, presumably accessing information quickly and then acting upon its consequences in real time. Non-natives, in contrast, pay a penalty for more difficult lexical retrieval.

The relationships with D are different. For non-native speakers, lexical diversity tends to be positively related to accuracy: the less recycling of vocabulary there is, the higher the accuracy that is achieved. Possibly, greater recycling is associated with more within-clause repetition of lexical items as speakers are attempting to buy time to deal with the trouble that they have encountered, while non-native speakers who are not experiencing trouble are able to avoid such clause-internal repetition and introduce more variation into their speech. Finally, again for non-native speakers, *D* correlates negatively with complexity in the majority of cases. In other words, speakers who recycle vocabulary most, nonetheless are able to achieve greater complexity. Drawing on the same lexical sets, in other words, seems to provide room for attention which can enable more complex language to be produced. Native speakers, in contrast, show no correlation between *D* and language complexity.

These results give us our first major insight into the nature of speech performance for the two groups. If we relate their performance to Levelt's model of speaking (1989), with its three major stages in speech production of Conceptualisation, Formulation, and Articulation, it appears to be the case here that with native speakers, Conceptualisation delivers a pre-verbal message which makes demands upon the Formulator, but that the Formulator meets these demands very well, in that the lexical choices implied by the pre-verbal message then trigger effective use of syntactic frames. More demanding lexis leads to more complex syntax. With the non-native speakers, in contrast, this does not happen. More demanding lexis implied in the pre-verbal message creates difficulty for the Formulator and disrupts syntactic planning. Lexis does not drive syntax in the same way as with native speakers. (It does, though, need to be borne in mind that the non-native speakers here are at low-intermediate level, and research is certainly needed with higher proficiency levels to explore whether increasing proficiency is associated with a greater correspondence between lexis and syntax). The final point of interest here is the positive association between *D* and accuracy for the non-native speakers. Comfortable non-recycling seems to be a reflection of a non-native speaker being able to devote ongoing Formulator-linked attention to avoiding error. (The relevance of Levelt's model is covered in much greater depth in the Discussion section).

Task Influences on Lexical Measures

We have already had a glimpse of the influence of task types while comparing native and non-native speaker data from Studies 1 and 6. Regarding lambda, these two studies are representative of all the others. The average values across all the studies, now drawing on different examples of personal, narrative, and decision-making tasks are 1.23, 1.49, and 0.66 respectively. In other words, narrative tasks consistently produce the highest values, and so are provoking the greatest use of less frequent words. It would appear that the monologic nature of the narrative, coupled with its non-negotiability, (i.e. the given story which has to be told, with its characters and elements), accounts for this pattern of lexical use. Lambda for personal tasks does not reach this level. Although not monologic, the personal task often did lead to monologic-type turns as people developed a viewpoint, and one of the personal tasks used, the Oven task, was itself close to a narrative, with its unavoidable sequence of actions that has to be followed to give clear instructions to one's partner about getting to one's home. But very strikingly here, and for native as well as non-native speakers, the lowest values for lambda are found with the decision-making task. The previous two tasks are either very strongly input driven (narratives, the Oven personal task), or draw upon familiar, well-organised information. The decision-making tasks, in contrast, require a blend of basic cognitive activity where general principles have to be applied to particular cases, and also improvisation, as the interactive nature of the task is responded to. It may also be that speakers aim at a lower level of what might be termed 'idea density', and are more reliant on time-creating devices. Possibly also there is listener awareness because of the greater obviousness of interactivity. The consequence seems to be a lower tendency to use language which is lexis-driven or in which less frequent lexical elements are drawn on as necessary. The differences in the figures between tasks are striking and consistent.

The task effects on D are interestingly different. The personal tasks are inconsistent, but the figures for the narrative and decision-making are the reverse of those for lambda. For non-native speakers, the decision-making task is consistently higher for D. These differences are not as great as they were for lambda, but are statistically significant for Study 6, the native speakers, and for Studies 2 and 5, with all significance levels at 0.001 (paired subjects t-tests: N sizes respectively at 23, 23, and 36). The comparison for Study 1 approaches significance ($p < 0.08$), with the decision-making D score higher than that for the narrative. It appears that interactivity is associated with an avoidance of recycling, possibly because learners are using one another's words more, and so there is scope for 'on the fly' input, in contrast to the more monologic narratives where learners are more concerned to express their own ideas. In contrast, the focus in the narratives seems to be on selecting and retrieving the appropriate word even if it is more difficult to do so. There is also an important task influence in the decision-making tasks, in that these tasks require pairs of participants to discuss a series of things. In one case this was a series of putative crimes, and in another a series of letters to an Agony Aunt. This means that the topic within the interaction changed at quite regular intervals. It may be that this, too, has a significant effect, with the new topic causing participants to need to use new sets of words. This may then lead to the lower recycling and higher D.

Returning briefly to the native/non-native comparison, it is worth recalling from the last section that the difference between these two groups does not operate at a consistent level. In the main there seems a slightly greater difference between them with D, and this especially for the narrative and decision-making tasks. With lambda it is the narrative which generates the greatest difference, and there is surprisingly little difference for the decision-making task. It would seem that narrative tasks provoke the most consistent difference in lexical performance between the two groups, since native speakers here are able to draw upon much less frequent lexis, and avoid recycling lexis. These effects do not appear jointly so strongly with the other two task types.

The Effects of Planning on Lexical Measures

In order to be able to compare native and non-native speakers, we will restrict discussion here to Studies 1 and 6 because these studies, with the same research design, explored the performance of the two groups. The relevant figures for D are presented in Table 8.6, while the figures for lambda are presented in Table 8.7, where the results of between-subjects t-tests are reported.

The difference between these two tables is striking. Lexical diversity does not seem affected by the opportunity to plan. It seems more an on-line processing issue, which must reflect Formulator operations on a second-by-second basis. In contrast, the values for lambda do show a planning influence, although not everywhere and not all the time. Arithmetically, all planning values are higher than the non-planning values but significance is obtained for only one of the native speaker tasks, the narrative, and for two of the non-native speaker tasks, the personal and the decision-making. The native speakers show an effect of planning

TABLE 8.6 Influence of Planning on D for Native and Non-Native Speakers

	Personal	Narrative	Decision-Making
Study 6: Nat. Sp. Unplanned	46.9	79.8	92.2
Study 6: Nat. Sp. Planned	44.3	67.2	89.0
Significance	ns	ns	ns
Study 1: Non-nat. Sp. Unplanned	37.0	44.7	53.6
Study 1: Non-nat. Sp. Planned	34.6	49.0	51.8
Significance	ns	ns	ns

Study 6: N = 31; Study 1: N = 29

TABLE 8.7 Influence of Planning on Lambda for Native and Non-Native Speakers

	Personal	Narrative	Decision-Making
Study 6: Nat. Sp. Unplanned	1.27	1.46	0.80
Study 6: Nat. Sp. Planned	1.48	1.95	0.93
Significance	ns	0.01	ns
Study 1: Non-nat. Sp. Unplanned	0.94	1.10	0.54
S1: Non-nat. Sp. Planned	1.14	1.18	0.78
Significance	0.05	ns	0.01

Study 6: N = 31; Study 1: N = 29

only on the most monologic task, where the opportunity to plan seems to equip them to draw upon less frequent lexis. There is also the point that these two tasks, given their monologic nature, are inherently more predictable, since there is less scope for interaction to take the conversation in unforeseen directions. Planning, as a result, can have a more dependable impact. Yet the narrative is the one task that does not show a significant difference for the non-native speakers, whereas here the more interactive tasks, especially the decision-making task do see raised performance. The complexity of the narrative retelling, despite perhaps its push towards specific lexis, seems to have defeated the non-native speakers, who seem to have allocated so much attention to wrestling with the ideas that they could not mobilise any less frequent words. This is a curious result. In contrast, they do seem to have been able to channel planning time to using less frequent lexis in the more interactive or more familiar tasks. It seems as if these tasks are within their abilities to a greater degree, and there is enough spare capacity available to enable them to retrieve less frequent vocabulary items.

Discussion

It is striking that the two lexical measures in this study do not correlate and are often affected by different things. The capacity to avoid recycling vocabulary, and the capacity to inject vocabulary richness into performance seem to connect with different aspects of speaking. On this issue, as well, the congruence in results between native and non-native speakers is striking—the two measures do not relate for *either* group. One might think that factors like having a greater vocabulary stock which is more organised and more accessible ought to be a strong fundamental influence. Although this does seem to account for the performance differences between native and non-native speakers, that is as far as it goes. Elsewhere, different patterns for the two measures are more salient. These results are consistent with studies by Daller and Xue (2007) who report a correlation of 0.21 (non-significant) between the two measures for a group of 50 Chinese learners of English doing an oral picture description task; and by Daller and Phelan (2007) who report a correlation of 0.39 (again non-significant) for essays written in an EAP context. In contrast, Malvern, Richards, Chipere, and Durán (2004) do report a significant correlation (0.42; $p < 0.001$) for a large sample of L1 British children writing narratives at Key Stages 1–3. It is possible, however, that written material may be associated with higher levels of correlation, although even here, 0.42 could not be regarded as a very strong level of relationship.

If then the influence of a larger mental lexicon, while important, does not account for many aspects of the results, principally the lack of relationship between lambda and *D*, we need to ask what other factors are at play. First we have the issue of unavoidable lexis. We have seen that the narratives, in general, lead to the highest lambda scores. In narratives, the 'task' is strongly input-driven, and task fulfilment requires engaging with the material which is given. In a sense, therefore, what needs to be said is non-negotiable. This seems to push participants, native or non-native speaker, into retrieving the less common words which are implicated in the task. This influence does not seem to impact upon D to the same extent. Further, interactive tasks, although they make some lexical items salient, seem to allow participants freedom to express themselves without necessarily retrieving these key items if alternative means of expression can be found. There may also be the issue that interactivity can tolerate some degree of vagueness and generality, because speakers anticipate that, if necessary, further interaction can resolve misunderstandings. Narratives, in contrast, may put pressure on the speaker to be more precise and find more exact phrasing.

A second possible factor concerns a tension between interactivity and predictability. Interactive tasks produce higher values of D (i.e. less recycling of words). Clearly, within an interaction there is unpredictability, as a conversation takes the course that it takes. There is also the issue that turns are shorter, usually, and speakers may, as part of what they say, take account of interlocutor needs, including processing needs. As a result, their speech may be more involved and less detached, with the result that a speaker does not focus so much on their own contribution in isolation but may try to incorporate things said by their interlocutor. The result may be that their own speech draws on this interactive input, and as a result pushes up the values of D. In contrast, non-interactive tasks are more likely to put the speaker into a detached, long-turn, self-sufficient mode, leading to more recycling because there are not so many external influences.

There is a third influence which comes into play here, and unfortunately there is something of a confound involved. The monologic tasks tended to be about one thing, for example, narrate a story or describe how to get to your home. In contrast, the interactive tasks tended to have shifting topics, such as judgements on a series of crimes, advice for a series of letters to an Agony Aunt. It may well be the case that there is a strong topic effect on D scores. The arrival of a new 'crime' to discuss, or letter to advise on, may trigger the use of new sets of words. As a result, there is less recycling, but this is an artefact of topic change, rather than an inherent feature of interactive discourse (although of course much interactive discourse does have such topic change as an entirely natural component). So the result is that we cannot distinguish here between interactivity and topic change as possible influences upon the D scores which were obtained. Further, more focussed research designs are needed to explore this issue.

We turn next to attempt to relate the results to a wider model of speaking, whether of first or second language. The Levelt (1989) model of speaking proposes three stages, the Conceptualiser (whose output is the pre-verbal message, and which essentially is concerned with the conceptual content and packaging of what will be said), the Formulator (which accepts the pre-verbal message, and which then engages in processes of lemma selection and consequent syntax-building processes), and the Articulator. Focussing on the first two of these processes is illuminating in relation to the present results. One can propose, from the results presented here, that lambda, and lexical sophistication, relate more to the Conceptualiser stage of the Levelt model, and to the nature of pre-verbal message implications for lemma retrieval. This applies particularly clearly to the native speakers whose lexical systems are richer and more organised, and who therefore can handle the processing implications delivered by the Conceptualiser and integrate lexis effectively to realise the demands that are being made on the Formulator. For them the correlation with (syntactic) complexity is another reflection of the way their syntactic performance can be effectively lexically-driven. This is easier for native speakers, and problematic for non-native speakers. It is also interesting that for non-native speakers, more demanding Conceptualiser operations have bad implications for accuracy. Heavy lexical demands on Formulator operations impair parallel processing (in which the Formulator currently works on previous Conceptualiser operations while the Conceptualiser gets on with new work) since the difficulties experienced by the Formulator have attentional implications which spill over and influence the Conceptualiser. The result is a need for the second language speaker to engage, laboriously, in serial operations (Kormos, 2006).

In contrast, it is hypothesised that lexical diversity, as indexed by D, is more clearly a Formulator factor, perhaps shown by the correlation between D and accuracy. The Formulator is concerned with on-line, moment-by-moment decisions during speaking, but within certain parameters. Digging deep, and retrieving unusual lexical items is not the emphasis (since these are the province of the Conceptualiser and the pre-verbal message it delivers). Making surface level choices is, and so the attention available seems to be concerned with using less demanding words more effectively. It is as if restricted sets of words prime one another, and once available, can be integrated more easily, and help avoid the need for wider, and more disruptive lexical retrieval.

A final thought concerns the applicability of the Levelt model to non-native as well as native speakers. Kormos (2006) argues that it is extendable, and at a general conceptual level, this must be so. All speakers need to organise thought and then marshal linguistic resources to express their thoughts. But the Levelt model, in the native speaker case, operates with certain assumptions. These are that what the Conceptualiser delivers to the Formulator is 'fair game', in the sense that unreasonable demands, given the size and organisation of the mental lexicon, are not being made, and so the Formulator can deal with these demands, in real time. Native language lexicons are rich, comprehensive and well-organised, permitting lemmas to be accessed, and, when particular lemmas are problematic, enabling substitutions to be made (Pawley & Syder, 1983). Now it has to be said that the non-native speakers in all the studies that the present chapter is based on were intermediate level, and low rather than high intermediate. Any claims which are made have to be restricted to this group. But it is clear for these second language speakers that the sorts of relationship one finds for native speakers do not apply clearly, as in the case of the lambda-complexity correlations. The interpretation seems to be that the second language mental lexicons on which they draw are not as extensive or as organised, and that this has major implications for the transferability of the Levelt model to this case. These learners, one assumes, have a Conceptualiser stage which is potentially as effective as that of the native speakers, but the pre-verbal message it delivers to the Formulator makes demands that the more limited Formulator cannot meet. The speaker is then in a race against time, as s/he wishes to produce more language, but is still wrestling with the implications of the previous Conceptualiser pre-verbal message. As a result, strategies of communication become more salient, including avoidance and abandoning messages. It seems clear, therefore, that additional influences upon performance, such as task characteristics and also performance conditions, may be more important as they can ease the processing burden in ways which make the Conceptualiser-Formulator connection less troublesome.

Conclusions

There has been a strong exploratory quality to the research reported in this chapter, since there is relatively little published material on relationships between measures of lexical diversity and lexical sophistication; on lexical comparisons between native and non-native speakers; and on lexical measures related to a variety of task genres completed by the same participants. The emphasis therefore has been on the presentation of data on each of these points. But clearly now the need is pressing for there to be additional research which attempts to resolve some of the puzzles identified here.

First, there is a need to gather data, using measures such as D and lambda, with second language learners at different, and especially higher, proficiency levels. Such data can be very revealing about how the Levelt model becomes appropriate, without modification, as higher proficiency levels are achieved. Second, we need much more research with lexical measures specifically comparing different genres. Most research to this point has been based on only one type of task, rather than on a comparison of different tasks as was the case in the present research. Third, we need to explore more systematically the variables identified post hoc such as topic change, unavoidable lexis, and interactivity. Such research will establish whether plausible interpretations are indeed convincing.

Acknowledgement

The author would like to thank Brian Richards and an anonymous reviewer for their very helpful comments on a previous version of this chapter.

9
REFLECTIONS ON PLANNING

Introduction

The two planning studies reprinted in this section are, once again, a pairing of something early and something relatively recent. Basically, Foster and Skehan (1996a) followed in the footsteps of Ellis (1987) and Crookes (1989). As we saw, Ellis linked planned language to greater accuracy (at least, for regular forms of the past tense), and then Crookes, who critiqued Ellis's research design, used a very different research design and reported no accuracy effect for planning. He did, though, report raised complexity and fluency. A number of factors are at play here. First, there is the issue of accuracy, and whether this is a particularly difficult aspect of performance to raise (as claimed in Chapter 5). Second, there is the issue of second language task performance more generally—what its dimensions are, and how each should be measured. Third, there are broad research design issues as one decides what are the most effective ways of asking research questions, and which variables and methodologies should be used.

Taking the first of these three points, our initial hunch, in Foster and Skehan (1996a), was that an accuracy effect was there to be found, but that perhaps choice of task was very important. We wanted to use what we thought of as more realistic tasks, following the assumption that learners would be able to 'be themselves' more easily while doing the task. We felt that information gap tasks, ubiquitous in task research, were not likely to facilitate more natural language (and raised accuracy). (With hindsight, I would now describe such tasks as non-negotiable.) In addition, we wanted to embed our research in intact classrooms, and indeed the person who actually collected the data, Pauline Foster, worked as a teacher in the school where data was collected, adding to the authenticity of what we were asking participants to do. (Pauline has argued persuasively since that time, e.g. in Foster [1998], that it is desirable for research to have ecological validity of this sort.)

Regarding the second point, we approached the problem of measurement with trepidation. We were persuaded that generalised measures were more likely to capture variance between learners than specific measures would. Even though specific measures might have considerable validity, especially when linked to specific tasks, e.g. pronouns with narrative tasks, generalised measures simply provide more tokens to work with, and so are more likely to detect differences between groups. Subsequent research has confirmed that this was an effective strategy. We followed Crookes in measuring complexity, accuracy, and fluency, and in our case, all of these with generalised indices. What we did has been widely used by others since the article appeared, and indeed Pauline has since then published on the details of measuring complexity (Foster, Tonkyn, & Wigglesworth, 2000) and accuracy (Foster & Wigglesworth, 2015). The next chapter in this book develops measurement issues in more detail.

Finally, we wanted to use a quantitative design (following Ellis and Crookes), but we wanted to complexify the design itself. Hence the use of contrasting tasks (personal information exchange, narrative, decision-making, with all these tasks or at least task types taken from existing coursebook materials—another attempt at ecological validity), and more than one planning condition (with instructions, and without instructions for the planning time). As we will see below, this too has had an influence on subsequent research. I can't resist saying though that I seriously doubt if this research would be publishable now. One of the regrets of the study is the small numbers involved. That alone would torpedo any publication plans because the power of the research design was very low, and it is all the more surprising therefore that we found the significances that we did. The research design also raises another regret: that the study was entirely quantitative. At the time we had nothing whatsoever against qualitative work, but research is time-consuming, and we didn't have enough time to build in a qualitative component. And also, to be candid, we did not realise at that time how important a qualitative dimension actually would have been!

It was, in fact, this sort of concern that pushed me, some time later, to a qualitative study, reprinted here (Pang & Skehan, 2014). This is quite recent, and the result of a RGC grant in Hong Kong, on which Francine Pang worked as co-researcher. More accurately, this study used a hybrid design, since we also collected performance data which was susceptible to quantitative analyses. It's a bit recent as a study to start reflecting on its impact! But it is pleasing that, as is discussed below, other qualitative studies are starting to appear. It was also a study of some surprises to us. The planning literature, where researchers have collected feedback data from participants (more common than the full-on and time-consuming qualitative data collection we did), often reports general approbation for the opportunity to plan, but this is balanced by occasional individuals who say they would have preferred not to have planning time! So when we discovered that planning, some of the time, could be associated with worse performance on the actual task, we had some data that might be relevant to why some participants don't like having the chance to plan: they may have realised that things went wrong. But even though, with hindsight, this makes sense, it was not at all what we were expecting.

In this section I take these two framing studies as the starting point. I discuss the planning literature under several headings: a survey of quantitative research with planning; the other qualitative studies which have appeared; the connection between planning and repetition; some miscellaneous issues such as proficiency level; and then (inevitably) a reexamination of planning through a Leveltian lens.

Quantitative Research With Planning

The two republished planning studies relate to a number of current issues within the task literature. Although there have been a number of on-line planning studies (and more on this below), most quantitative studies in the planning field have followed the Crookes operationalisation: give learners pre-task planning time, and then measure their performance. A body of research now exists which has clarified our knowledge of the effects of planning considerably. The areas that have been researched are:

- time spent planning;
- durability of the effects of planning;
- role of instructions;
- source of planning;
- relationship of planning to proficiency level;
- relationship of planning to task complexity;
- the contrast between pre-task and on-line planning.

Most researchers, with the aim of achieving consistency and comparability of research, have followed Crookes (1989) and given participants 10 minutes pre-task planning time, but of course that particular time interval is arbitrary. Even so, it is worth saying that in two qualitative studies I did with Francine Pang (Skehan & Pang, 2008; Pang & Skehan, 2014), when planners were asked if 10 minutes was too long, and if so what sort of time would have been ideal, the most frequent answer was that 8 minutes (a reduction, obviously, of only 2 minutes), would have been the preferred option. So while 10 minutes might have an arbitrary quality, it turns out to be mostly acceptable to those doing the tasks. In addition, as the Mehnert (1998) study, discussed below, indicates, 10 minutes turns out to be a time period during which interesting things occur.

Even so, different researchers have used different time intervals, such as 1 minute (Wigglesworth, 1997), 3 minutes (Elder & Iwashita, 2005), and 5 minutes (Tavakoli & Skehan, 2005). Two studies have explored planning time more systematically, considering it as an experimental variable in itself. These are Mehnert

(1998) and Li, Chen, and Sun (2015). Mehnert (1998), for example, used 1 minute, 5 minutes, and 10 minutes planning time intervals, and found that there was an implicit set of priorities in what participants did. Accuracy effects emerged after just 1 minute, whereas 5 minutes produced fluency improvement (which continued with the 10-minute condition) while 10 minutes was needed to produce a change in complexity. The results in Li, Chen, and Sun (2015) are partly similar and partly different to Mehnert. The planning time intervals used were slightly different, at 0, 0.5, 1, 2, 3, and 5 minutes. Accuracy is similar, in that 1 minute planning time was needed to give a significant improvement in the errors per AS-measure, with the later planning times not leading to significant additional improvement. In contrast to Mehnert, fluency results were similar to accuracy, in that 1 minute seemed the critical separating value for most of the measures. Complexity did not present a clear picture at all, while lexical diversity did suggest a slight trend to improvement as planning time increased, with 1 minute producing the highest value, but then with lower figures reported. It would have been interesting to see a 10-minute condition here to make comparison with Mehnert easier. An important point to make is that there was a testing context for this study, and indeed, this had an influence on the planning time intervals which were chosen. Other research, e.g. Iwashita, McNamara, and Elder (2001) has reported a levelling effect for planning: it seems that candidates within a testing situation orient themselves towards accuracy, and planning is less of an influence on other areas of performance. We will return to these findings when we consider qualitative studies in more depth below.

Another interesting insight into the effects of pre-task planning, albeit based on only one study, concerns the durability of the effects of planning. Skehan and Foster (2005) report a study intended to explore the effects on planned performance of presenting learners with surprise and slightly discrepant information. This was presented after a task had been running for 5 minutes. The task was 'the Judge' task, where pairs of students were presented with 'crimes' and asked to agree on the length of a custodial sentence, or even an acquittal. After 5 minutes had passed, new information, which somewhat contradicted the original information, was presented. For example, one case concerned a doctor who had given a lethal dose of a painkilling drug to a terminally ill patient who was in considerable pain. The case implied that this was at the request of the patient and with the consent of the patient's family. The participants had to decide if this doctor should be sent to prison, and if so, for how long. Then the additional information, given after 5 minutes, was that it was discovered that the same thing had happened to several of this doctor's patients and that there was no certainty consent had been given on all these occasions. The hypothesis was that planners would be more able to integrate this information into their discourse than would non-planners. This did not work in the slightest: planners did not integrate information better at all!

But an important and somewhat accidental point is that the research design obviously required a control group. Each group, experimental (i.e. with planning) and control (i.e. without planning), had a 5-minute period with the original set of 'crimes' and then 5 more minutes after they were given the discrepant new information. What we found was that the participants, both planners and non-planners, simply deteriorated in performance after the first 5 minutes, and that having been a planner conferred no resistance to this deterioration. The most interesting thing, in other words, is that it appears that the effects of planning are short-lived. We have to confront the worrying issue that second language learners, at least at this intermediate level, do not seem to be able to sustain higher-level performance for any length of time. The boosting effects of planning, in other words, may not be enduring.

A more extensive line of planning research, now with several studies, is to explore what happens when planners are provided with some instructions. Foster and Skehan (1996a) divided their planners into a group which simply had 10 minutes planning time and a group who were given suggestions as to what they might do with the planning time. For all tasks (personal information exchange, narrative, and decision-making) these suggestions covered discourse, ideas, and meaning, as well as basics such as syntax and lexis. For the most interactive task, the decision-making, the participants were also asked to consider what their conversational partner might say and how they might respond. Both planning groups achieved higher-level performance, but the planners with instructions (and it should be emphasised that they were provided with suggestions only but were not compelled in any way to use them) tended to achieve the highest levels of complexity in the study, whereas it was the non-instruction planners who produced the highest levels of accuracy. We were so struck by these results that we redesigned a later study (Skehan & Foster, 2005) to incorporate a comparison between detailed and undetailed planning. Sadly the results didn't hold up. There were supportive trends (and no counter-evidence), but no significances, and so we have to temper our original conclusions quite considerably.

Even so, there have been some other studies exploring guidance in planning, and with mixed results. Mochizuki and Ortega (2008) used a grammar handout, on relativisation, with beginning level Japanese students. These grammar-focussed instructions led to the production of more and more accurate examples of relativisation. There were also generalised measures of complexity and accuracy, and the instructed planning group, compared to a conventional planning group (with 5 minutes planning) produced similar levels on these general measures. In a related study, Park (2010) argues that studies of instructed planning have not distinguished between specific instructions and planning itself, and so she used a 2x2 design, with plus-or-minus planning and plus-or-minus specific instructions. In addition, as a dependent variable, she used Language Related Episodes (LREs), where these related to lexis or morphosyntax (considered separately from one another). The specific instructions were more extensive and detailed than in Foster and Skehan (1996a), and participants were given 5 minutes to work with these before the planning started. In addition, the narrative task, to a set of pictures from Heaton

(1975) was allocated some 20 minutes. There was no clear and distinct effect for the specific planning condition. There were a lot more lexical LREs than morphosyntactic LREs. In addition, planning, in general, led to slightly fewer lexical LREs than non-planning, while specific instructions, whether planned or not, produced fewer lexical LREs. Planning had no clear effect on morphosyntactic LREs, but specific instructions produced more. The study does bring out that distinguishing between specificity and planning is helpful. Otherwise differences in the research design of the study make it difficult to compare with other research (length and detail of the specific instructions, length of time for speaking, different dependent variables). Particularly difficult is the use of LREs. These may tap into constructs which are different from conventional accuracy and complexity measures: engaging in an LRE, for example, may be a consequence of problems rather than the capacity to use language accurately, even though there is the benefit that language is coming into focus.

Two related studies report a different take on instructions: providing pre-task video-based modelling. Kim and McDonough (2011) report that with groups of young, high-beginner to low-intermediate Korean students, providing modelling opportunities is associated with more LREs, and more relevantly, more effective LREs, with appropriate resolution of language points. The general quality of interaction between participants was also better. Kim (2013a) reports the use of pre-task video-modelling which focusses on question formation. In this case, too, the modelling is associated with more progress in question formation as a result of interactions when completing three tasks, as compared to simply planning alone.

The growing literature on planning interventions, then, is broadly encouraging. As we will see below, a major issue for planning in general concerns the extent to which what happens during planning time carries over into the actual task performance. This is particularly relevant for the planning instructions and modelling studies. The interventions do not seem to do any harm (Skehan & Foster, 2005), and there is some evidence that they can do good. The beneficial evidence concerns attention to form, as this is indexed by LREs (Park, 2010; Kim & McDonough, 2011), and also in generalised performance (Foster & Skehan, 1996a), and in some specific aspects of performance (Kim, 2013b). It may be that written instructions alone are not hugely effective, and may have the disadvantage that, if overly complex, they are not understood, or acted upon effectively. Exploring different types of instruction might be a worthwhile undertaking. Modelling, although only on the evidence of (currently) rather slender research, may, through its concreteness, have more to offer. The results so far are encouraging, but there is scope for a lot more research, and such research could have important implications for pedagogy.

We turn next to some related research—a study of what are termed the focus and source of planning (Skehan & Foster, 1999). The study using a decision-making task, the Balloon task, where participants had to decide who had to be thrown out of a sinking balloon (claimed to be the only solution to the survival of those remaining!), and each participant was given a role to defend—that of actor, politician, or EFL teacher. (We could, of course, have filled the balloon with social workers and surgeons and so on, but we took the advice of a colleague, Meic Llewellyn, that 'worthies' of this sort tended to provoke rather boring discussion as to who should get the heave.) Focus concerns whether the planning is 'nudged' towards a concern for meaning or for form, and in a way, this was a form of instruction-giving. Somewhat disappointingly, this had little impact on the language used. Whether planning time was directed at meaning or form did not connect with performance. Since there was no qualitative aspect to this research we do not know whether participants who were meant to focus on meaning did so, and likewise for form. It may well be that participants did whatever they wanted to do, whatever the 'focus' of the instructions. In contrast, source of planning was more associated with significant findings. There were considerable differences in the achievement of the different groups according to this condition. Whatever the role, be it actor, politician, EFL teacher, the group-based planning was the least effective, mainly because groups take time to gel, and this wasn't accomplished in the allocated planning period. A teacher-assisted group was far more effective. Not only did they produce higher-level performance, but they also showed, as a group, improvement in accuracy *and* complexity, a relatively rare combination. The individual planners, the typical condition from most research studies, were clearly better than the group planners, but well behind the teacher-assisted group, and did not show the joint raising of accuracy and complexity either.

Once again, the conclusion has to be that what happens in planning is not monolithic. There is variation. In this case the major effect was through the source of planning. Teachers, in this respect, have more effective ideas as to what is worth planning, how planning should be conducted, and probably, though there is no direct evidence on this, on how a connection can be made between what happens during the planning period and what happens during performance itself. The group-based planners demonstrate that efficiency of using planning time is an issue, and although if they had been given more time they might have come up with excellent and possibly deeper ideas, in the event it was the interaction of the group itself, without instruction as to how to proceed, which diverted them from planning the sorts of useful things they could have used in the actual task. The individual planners avoided the distractions of the group, which was good, but at the same time they did not have the range of experiences and expertise of teachers to make the planning work efficiently.

Given the range of planning studies that now exists, one might have thought that it would be fairly straightforward to link planning effectiveness to proficiency level, so that we have a clear ideas as to whether planning changes in importance as proficiency increases, or whether different types of planning have greater or lesser impact. One possibility would be to generalise on the basis of multiple studies done at different proficiency levels. Alternatively, and even better, one study might vary proficiency systematically to chart the changes that occur. Unfortunately neither possibility, easy in principle, is easy in practice because of lack of evidence. The latter strategy simply has not been popular, perhaps because it is more difficult to develop convincing theoretical reasons for gathering such data. The former is more feasible, but there are not the range of studies one would like to enable comprehensive generalisations to emerge. Doubtless this will change in the future, but for the moment, we have to make the most of what we have got, which are a series of unconnected studies. Three typical studies will briefly be mentioned.

Wigglesworth (1997) explored the effects of pre-task planning with two proficiency levels, and reports that planning was more effective with the advanced group in this comparison. Tavakoli and Skehan (2005) explored two proficiency levels (high beginner and intermediate) and found that planning was effective with both, and even that being a lower level planner was better than being a higher-level non-planner. As a final note on proficiency level, Ortega (2005), as part of a qualitative study (and see below) reports that advanced proficiency students, when they report what they did during pre-task planning time, talk about rehearsal of what they are going to say, but do not emphasise retrieval so much, as though they expect this to look after itself during actual performance. Intermediate-level students, in comparison, talk about rehearsal and retrieval equally. For them, there seems to be a greater priority in needing to prime the contents of the mental lexicon.

Although the range of planning studies with advanced learners is not enormous, we can nonetheless offer some tentative generalisations. First, there seems to be more of an effect of pre-task planning on oral rather than written performance. Second, syntactic complexity is the performance area most consistently affected by this form of planning, with a clear majority of studies showing this effect. Effects for lexical performance, fluency, and accuracy are not so evident, although they are each reported in a small number of studies. Third, it seems that pre-task planning is more Conceptualiser oriented with advanced learners. More Formulator-linked performance features are less affected by planning at this level (Bui, Skehan, & Wang, in press).

I turn next to the issue of task difficulty or task complexity. These are my terms and Robinson's respectively, but we are getting at the same thing—the extent to which a task poses greater demands, irrespective of the individual doing the task. I have argued that the more difficult the task, the greater the contribution of planning. For example, in Foster and Skehan (1996a), three tasks were used: a personal information exchange (give instructions to your home so that an oven can be turned off); construct a narrative based on a number of pictures where there was no obvious storyline; and agree on the appropriate custodial sentence, if any, for a series of crimes. Planning had relatively little effect on the first task, which drew on personal experience. It had its greatest effect on the narrative, which required quite a bit of thought. The decision-making task fell in the middle, but more towards the narrative. Skehan and Foster (1997) used the same three task types, but different exponents in each case, and produced similar results. So it seems as if, when the task is more demanding, planning makes a greater contribution.

Quite distinct from any of the previous research issues is the notion of on-line planning, whose relevance has been consistently advocated by Rod Ellis. In work done with Fangyuan Yuan he distinguishes between what he terms strategic (called pre-task here) planning, the planning which takes place before the task is done, and the focus for this section so far, and on-line planning, the planning which takes place 'on the fly' during planning when the performance conditions are more relaxed and unpressured. In a series of studies (Yuan & Ellis, 2003; Ellis & Yuan, 2004; Ellis & Yuan, 2005), it has been shown that giving participants on-line planning opportunities through unpressured conditions is associated with increases in accuracy. It seems as though putting time pressure on second language speakers means that accuracy is the first performance area to suffer (since complexity and fluency are not affected), whereas under unpressured conditions there is time to channel attention towards accuracy and error avoidance, and participants exploit this opportunity.

A PhD student of mine, Zhan Wang, was a little troubled that this on-line planning research used a slightly loose operationalisation of on-line planning itself (Wang, 2014). Generous time was given to the on-line planners, and less generous time to the pre-task planning condition. But participants in each condition frequently didn't use all the time which was available, which suggested that intended pressure and actual pressure might not be the same. She devised a different operationalisation, in which a slowed video imposed a more standardised rhythm on the nature of the performance—everyone had to follow this speed. When she looked for an accuracy effect under this condition, it was not there. But she had another experimental condition in her study. (Several more, in fact!) Other participants had the slowed video and on-line planning opportunities but they also had the opportunity to watch the video-to-be-narrated before the actual experimental condition. She reasoned that this gave them a pre-task planning opportunity. Interestingly, in this condition, pre-task planning *and* on-line planning, there was raised accuracy (and complexity also). She argues that to raise accuracy what is needed is pre-task planning *coupled with* on-line planning opportunity. In Leveltian terms, the Conceptualiser needs to be involved, and also the Formulator given conditions that allows time for a focus on accuracy in the context that ideas have already been assembled. Both conditions need to apply to generate the raised accuracy.

Actually, proficiency (discussed above) may also be a factor when these studies are compared. Ellis and Yuan's (2005) participants were advanced level, whereas Wang's (2014) participants were intermediate level. So while Wang's argument is that it is the synergy between both types of planning that is vital, it may be the case also that on-line planning effects vary as a function of proficiency level.

Those with higher proficiency, and with, presumably, better mental lexicons, can access lemma information more easily, so that for them, more processing time is enough—they do not need to have engaged in so much Conceptualiser work beforehand since Formulator operations proceed easily and smoothly.

An interesting sub-literature has arisen in recent years on working memory connections to planning, and the contrasting influences on pre-task and on-line planning. The evidence here suggests that differences in working memory do not contribute to greater retention of the effects of planning in the subsequent performance. Wen (2009) found no increase in task performance for those with higher working memory. Similarly Guara Tavares (2013) found no association, and Nielsen (2013) found that giving participants in her study pre-task planning time did not compensate for low working memory. So while it may be the case that other aspects of memory might have a relationship here for the transfer of material from pre-task planning to actual task performance, working memory does not. As a research strategy it may be worth including measures of other aspects of memory to see if they correlate with the effectiveness of the transfer from pre-task planning to actual performance.

In contrast, a series of studies have demonstrated a clear relationship between working memory and performance under on-line planning conditions. Li and Fu (2016), Guara Tavares (2013), and Ahmadian (2012a) have all reported correlations between working memory scores and accuracy under on-line planning conditions. It appears that being able to hold more material in working memory and/or to process this material more effectively facilitates processing when time is available. Working memory can help this more generous time availability to be exploited. And there is greater logic to these results. On-line processing requires simultaneous Conceptualiser, Formulator, and Articulator operation, with these, in the ideal case, functioning in parallel. The more capacity there is while processing is taking place, the more likely it is that Conceptualiser work can proceed, that retrieval of lemma information and syntax building can occur, and that the transition from lemma information to actual sound can take place. Indeed, in the Levelt model the articulatory buffer is an important component, and it appears that for second language speakers, greater working memory can make a difference, in production, and give some flexibility in the operations within this buffer. So this aspect of memory is important, but not to retain the results of pre-task planning, only to enable ongoing operations to proceed more effectively.

Qualitative Research With Planning

The range of studies we have explored so far, all largely quantitative and CALF-oriented, have made considerable progress in advancing our understanding of planning and its effects on performance. As a result of this research there are prospects of inferring what is going on 'inside' planning as a result of the consistencies in the research results. But inferring is rather removed from the reality of what happens in planning, and so it is good that we now have some qualitative studies of both pre-task and on-line planning. The reprinted Pang and Skehan (2014) study, as indicated earlier, was an attempt to contribute to this literature, and this section will try to discuss that study under the wider context that now exists.

The first significant qualitative research was conducted by Ortega (1995, 1999, 2005). She gathered qualitative data from learners at two proficiency levels completing narrative tasks. She used a coding scheme for the retrospective interview comments which was based on O'Malley and Chamot's (1990) scheme for taxonomising learning strategies. Striking in these retrospective accounts was the importance of rehearsal and retrieval as processes that figured prominently in the planning time. Ortega (2005) also reports that the advanced students used planning more for rehearsal rather than retrieval, whereas the lower-proficiency students split their planning time more equally between these two processes. As indicated earlier, it was as though the advanced students had confidence, and self-knowledge regarding their L2 mental lexicons and felt that retrieval could look after itself in actual performance. Rehearsal was something that they thought would contribute more.

The focus of Ortega's work was on what participants (L1 English of L2 Spanish) did while planning, not on performance itself. Pang and Skehan (2014), the article reprinted in this volume, was a qualitative study in which the L1 was Cantonese or Mandarin and the L2 was English. Although present in this volume, it is worth commenting on here because of the way it fits into the flow of the argument. Two research design differences to Ortega's work need highlighting. First, with the coding scheme, the broad intention was to allow categories to emerge from the retrospective interview data, and indeed several passes were made through the data until a reliable coding scheme was established. But as a background influence for this coding, the Levelt model was used. Consequently there was an awareness, as the codes were being developed, of the stages within the Levelt scheme as well as the associated process of monitoring and of how the emerging codes related to these stages and processes. Second, in addition to the retrospective interviews, performance data from the actual task was collected and this was analysed and scored, through CALF measures, in the normal way. The purpose in doing this was to enable connections to be established between the RI coding system and actual task performance, and to explore whether self-reporting planning behaviours were associated with higher or lower performance on the actual task.

The coding scheme, despite the different background influences (O'Malley and Chamot, Levelt) did turn up a number of similarities to what was reported in Ortega (2005). Rehearsal and retrieval emerged in each and functioned similarly. The Pang and Skehan scheme does have some important differences though. The major categories that emerged were Macro (or Discourse) planning, Micro (or Ideas) planning, Lexis and Morphosyntax planning, and Metacognition. Fairly clearly, one can relate micro or idea planning in this system to the Conceptualiser stage and Lexis and Morphosyntax to the Formulator. Macro or discourse planning is also Conceptualiser oriented but interestingly concerned with a larger unit of discourse, and indeed some participants used this form of planning to impose some structure on what they were going to say (Skehan & Shum, 2014), a task feature shown to raise performance. Metacognition does not straightforwardly relate to the Levelt model. What happened is that some participants seemed to be self-aware and have insight about the planning process itself, and were able to look ahead to the actual performance. Perhaps this connects with a point made in Chapter 5—that for second language spoken performance, Conceptualiser foresight of Formulator limitations is helpful. Metacognition, as a category which emerged from the data, might suggest that some people are better at this than others.

One can restate this categorisation (macro, micro, etc.) to three general (and somewhat related) features: scale, focus, and foresight. These features are useful when making a link between self-reported planning behaviours and actual performance. Scale concerns how much is planned, with the attempt to plan a great deal of the upcoming performance contrasting with a focus on planning detail. Focus concerns discourse (macro) or ideas (micro) or lexis or morphosyntax. Finally, foresight concerns the participant's metacognitive awareness of the link between planning and the subsequent performance, with some participants being more aware of this relationship than others. The interesting thing is that these labels are associated with different degrees of effectiveness of planning.

A preliminary point is worthwhile. Fairly obviously, planning precedes performance, and this means that, for planning to make a difference, what has been planned has to be retained and then used in the performance. In turn, this suggests that planning some things may be more susceptible to memory fading than others, or conversely, benefit from more effective retention. Scale is the most complicated in this respect. Generally, planning detail is vulnerable to lack of retention, and so quite a bit of planning effort may be devoted to detail, but this may not then be available for use. Planning at a larger and less detailed scale is more likely to be retained and be effective in the performance. But this takes us on to focus, since scale and focus are interlinked. Planning detail often means retrieval of lexical items and this is the sort of thing which is difficult to retain. Similar factors apply with morphosyntax: if the subsequent performance relies on detail, there is a greater chance that this will be forgotten and, possibly, not remembered at the level of detail that would be useful. In contrast, planning discourse is likely to be at a more general level, and this is likely to be retained. Even beyond that, if the planning introduces some discourse organisation, such as introducing structure to the task (Skehan & Shum, 2014), that may have a considerable positive impact on performance. What seems to happen (and this connects very much with the literature on task structure [Skehan & Shum, 2014]) is that such planning provides a macrostructure for the task performance, and then, while speaking, participants can devote more attentional resources to Formulator operations. The broad shape of what is to be said has been outlined, and the interrelationship of the elements within this outline aids retention, and then the focus in performance can be more directed to the surface of language. Planning ideas has a similar effect, although here the wider organisation of what is to be said may not be so clear. But ideas, especially when interlinked, seem easier to recall than do detailed lexis and syntax, and this translates also into higher-level performance. Obviously the converse also applies: not planning discourse and avoiding ideas and concentrating on detailed lexis and morphosyntax do not work so well, and lead to a lowering of performance.

Finally we have metacognition, self-awareness and foresight on the part of the planner. Again participants in Pang and Skehan (2014) showed variation. Those who could more effectively reflect on their intended performance were more likely to avoid excess ambition in their planning and as a result their performance seemed to benefit from their more limited aims. It also seems likely that such metacognitively aware participants were better at avoiding the pitfalls of planning that doesn't transfer to performance. In other words, they were more likely to plan discourse and ideas, and less likely to devote planning time only to retrieval and rehearsal. These participants, intuitively, seemed to use planning time in ways that would lead to greater payoff, cf. the 'foresight' advantage discussed earlier.

Throughout the previous review of quantitative studies there have been hints as to how the black box of planning can be opened. What has been interesting from the qualitative studies is that many of these hints have been confirmed. Planners, clearly, are autonomous agents who may have clear views as to what might be done during planning time. Ignoring the choices that are available during this time is dangerous. By studying what successful planners do, it may indeed be possible to discover what are the most effective strategies that might be adopted and then demonstrate these strategies to other, less successful planners. The general area of training planning is discussed below. It has considerable potential for promoting more effective second language acquisition and performance.

Different Ways of Being Prepared: The Case of Repetition

Of course a first reaction to this sub-heading might be to wonder what repetition is doing in a chapter on planning. In that regard, Bui (2014) with the notion of 'readiness' and Skehan (2014c) with notions of 'preparedness' try to widen the context in which planning is discussed. In each case the intent is to consider what happens before a task is done that might be relevant to the way that the task is actually done. Pre-task planning is one such factor, but it is not the only one, since one can broaden what can happen earlier considerably. There are a number of other possibilities, and mentioning these briefly brings out that pre-task planning, although the most extensively researched variable in our field, is only one of a range of possibilities.

- *Alternative pre-task activities for 'cold' topics*: A first point here is to bring out what 'cold' means. Essentially this is a topic chosen by the teacher or the researcher. This may well be of interest to the participants in a research study, or a classroom, but the key point is that it is not a development of the speaker's life, but instead chosen by someone else, and has to be responded to. Imagine meeting someone at a party and being told 'You have to agree on custodial sentences for a series of crimes'! The major point here is that having time to plan (over 10 minutes) for such a cold topic is not the only option. Many experienced teachers preface a teaching activity, e.g. with a listening or reading comprehension, with methods of raising consciousness about the topic, of getting learners to foreground what they know that is relevant. In the case of task research similar things could be done, as advocated in Willis and Willis (2007). Mind mapping, foregrounding ideas, brainstorming are all things that attempt to make a transition between what the speaker knows and is interested in, and the topic chosen by the teacher. Abrams and Byrd (2016) took this approach when they explored writing performance with college learners of German. They contrasted two groups, each of whom did pre-tasks, one oriented to grammar and the other to meaning. The first group did a pre-task, focussing on pronouns and subject-verb agreement. The second did a brainstorming activity. There were no differences between the groups for complexity or fluency of the language produced. But the meaning group produced significantly more accuracy and had higher lexical diversity scores. In addition there were substantial differences between the groups, in favour of the meaning group, for global quality, and this was linked to greater lexical accuracy and choice. So in this case, an alternative pre-task activity to planning produced interesting effects.
- *Talking about familiar things*: Although a topic for a task may be chosen by a researcher, it is quite possible that the selection will involve a topic known to be familiar to the participants. This was done by Qiu and Lo (2016) who report that measures of cognitive engagement were higher with familiar topics. Bui (2014) in a thorough investigation of this topic, where performance was measured through CALF indices, reports that familiarity had effects on lexical measures, but surprisingly little effect elsewhere, and generally less than conventional pre-task planning, which was also an independent variable in the study. More broadly, these studies indicate that exploring familiarity and even degrees of familiarity might be a different way into researching preparedness for a task.
- *Talking about things which have been talked about before*: Related to familiarity, but I would argue, distinct from it, is the case of speaking about something

which has been talked about before. Labov (1972) famously uses the prompt of asking respondents to recount an incident where they had a brush with death. Richard Schmidt (personal communication) once mentioned that he hadn't had great success with this prompt, but that asking respondents to recount an incident where they had suffered an injustice worked much more consistently! The purpose of these prompts was to elicit spontaneous speech. My take is slightly different here—in each case it is likely that the same narrative has been produced (possibly many times) before. Of course, this narrative will be familiar, but I want to argue that there is something additional where a story has actually been spoken before. I want to argue that this is a form of preparedness (even involving previous Articulation), and of a particular sort, bundling actual use with familiarity.

The purpose in discussing these alternatives is to bring out that there are different ways of being prepared or ready. Pre-task planning is just one option. These others all enable the speaker to avoid having to deal with a communication topic suddenly and without any 'equipment'. They could therefore each become the basis for interesting research which takes us beyond the sorts of findings already reported by Bui (2014).

The focus of this section, though, is repetition, as a form of indirect preparation. In this case, the original topic is likely to be a 'cold' topic, chosen by the researcher and then presented to participants to get on with. But then a repeated performance can benefit from the first performance since the process of doing a task once will make the participants more prepared for the second (and any subsequent) performance. The topic may need to be worked on from nothing, or at least very little, but the process of engaging with the task will be important in easing and even extending later performances. It then becomes interesting to explore the nature of the psycholinguistic processing that takes place, and the impact on different aspects of performance.

Repetition research with tasks has become a hot area. In the first studies done in a second language task context, Bygate (1996, 2001) explored the impact on the second performance of repeating a narrative some ten weeks after the original performance. He reports that the second performance showed a more dense packing of information and also that language could be elaborated. The time interval in his studies is quite long, but the effects were clearly there. This research did not use a CALF framework to measure the second performance, and the features of language just mentioned are what emerged from the data through a linguistic analysis. Bygate (2001) also reports though that the effects which were found require an exact task repetition: using task *type* repetition (but with different content) was not associated with comparable results. Wang (2009, 2014) also used repetition, also with a narrative, but in this case with immediate repetition, and the performances were assessed through CALF. The participants were intermediate-level L1 Chinese college level learners of English. She reports massively improved structural complexity, accuracy, and fluency, but that lexical aspects of performance did not show particular improvement. For the complexity, accuracy, and fluency measures, though, the effect sizes were very large.

Lambert, Kormos, and Minn (2016) report a remarkable study in which there were six performances (i.e. five repetitions) of the same task by the same people! The participants were Japanese intermediate-level college students. Performance was assessed through CALF-linked measures. Speech rate was taken to be a general index of quality of performance. Clause-final filled pauses were taken to reflect Conceptualiser operations. Mid-clause filled pauses were hypothesised to concern Formulator lexical operations while self-repair was taken to relate to Formulator syntactic operations. (It should be noted that these are not the standard operationalisations of CALF, but that in this study each is reasoned to be an effective measure of the underlying constructs of complexity, accuracy, and fluency. These measures are discussed more extensively in the next chapter, on CALF measures.) What is fascinating from this study is that different measures were influenced by different repetitions in the sequence. Speech rate continued to improve up to the fifth performance, while clause-final filled pauses reduced (i.e. showed more fluency) up to the third performance, and then levelled off. Mid-clause-filled pauses reduced, showing greater fluency, until the fourth performance, while self-repair only 'kicked in' with improvement after the fourth performance. Lambert et al. (2016) interpret this pattern of results as connecting with Leveltian stages. Speech rate is taken as a general, integrated indicator of performance. The other measures are more selective. Following their interpretation, it appears that the Conceptualiser benefits most initially but then this influence diminishes as though the general structure of ideas has been 'firmed up'. But then aspects of Formulator operations continue to benefit from repetition, first with lexical aspects increasing in solidity (leading to fewer filled mid-clause pauses), and then more syntactic aspects of performance, and the capacity to monitor needing to wait until quite late in the repetition sequence. In other words, repetition in this sequence connects with what second language speakers need to address first, second, etc. Most strikingly of all, it appears that it is not simply a case of one repetition being beneficial, but that even several repetitions contribute additional and distinct value (even if one quails at introducing this as a standard pedagogic technique!).

Four other recent studies make distinct contributions to the repetition literature. Fukuta (2016) reports on a qualitative study. From participant reports this suggests that the repeated performance was more concerned with Formulator (specifically, syntactic encoding) factors than Conceptualiser operations. This is slightly consistent with Lambert et al. (2016) but suggests that from the perspective of the participants, Formulator issues come to the fore quickly. Lambert et al. (2016) were concerned with performance, not self-reports, and it may be that what preoccupies the participants takes time to manifest itself in performance itself. Thai and Boers (2016) report on a study where repetition is linked to time pressure. Given the research on the 4–3–2 technique (where a performance is repeated twice, but with progressively less time available), Thai and Boers (2016) wanted to compare the effects on performance of a 4–3–2 minutes retelling time with a constant 3–3–3 minutes. They report that the former leads to increases in fluency but at the expense of accuracy and complexity. The latter leads to a more balanced performance. Kim and Tracey-Ventura (2013) compared exact task repetition and procedural repetition in groups of Korean children learning English. It is difficult to establish the proficiency level, but low intermediate might be the best estimate. In fact, the procedural repetition group were the ones who, in post-tests, produced higher syntactic complexity. Both groups showed improvement for task-induced language features, in this case the past tense. But there were no differences between the groups, and little improvement, for speech rate or generalised accuracy measures. The lack of an advantage for the exact repetition condition is a striking feature of this study, and the clear contrast with Bygate (2001). Qiu and Lo (2016) investigated repetition linked to task engagement and attitudes to repetition. They report positive attitudes to repetition, but found relatively little connection between repetition and engagement, although it is not totally clear how their dependent variables (number of words, time on task, self-repair, and elaborated clauses) are operationalisations of engagement.

There are, of course, problems in drawing conclusions with this literature. Different researchers have had different priorities and have used different independent variables. Above all this has meant that time intervals between original and repeated performance have been different. As yet, therefore, we do not have any clear idea how the benefits of repetition change, either positively or negatively, as the repetition interval changes. This is an area where urgent research is needed, not least because there are disagreements within psycholinguistic research as to the durability of priming effects (Kaschak, Kutta, & Schatschneider, 2010). The lack of standardisation in how performance is measured is also a serious problem, since some studies use the CALF framework (although in varied ways) and others do not do so at all. So finding one's way to generalisations is fraught with difficulty. But at a general level one can conclude that repetition is mostly positive in its effects, that it can influence complexity, accuracy, and fluency, and that, like planning, it is easy and free to implement pedagogically.

So even if the database is incomplete one can start to theorise how repetition can have its beneficial effects, and how it resembles and also differs from conventional pre-task planning. A first point, and a similarity, is that during the second performance the speaker can draw on the first actual performance, just as the pre-task planner can draw upon what is remembered from what has been done during the planning period. The studies we have reviewed suggest that the first repeated performance (and of course this is the only one in most studies) helps Conceptualiser operations, with the result that the ideas to be expressed have been marshalled and even perhaps organised, and this then does not need to be done (so much) during the repeated performance. In turn this means that the repeated performance might be a good basis for more elaborate or reorganised

Conceptualiser work (as in Bygate, 1996, 2001) using the first performance as the foundation. That ideas seem more memorable than the detail of language might connect with the way Bygate (1996) demonstrates an effect even after a ten-week interval. But it may also be the case that the repeated performance does not need to engage in additional Conceptualiser work if the results of the first performance are adequate. In this case the repeated performance can benefit from more attention being available for Formulator operations.

The qualitative planning research has shown that ideas translate into performance more memorably, but that memory from the planning of detail to help Formulation is a little vulnerable. In contrast, processes implicated in repetition (compared to planning) may be a little different. For one thing, the need to retrieve lemmas, driven by the pre-verbal message, is likely to prime a wide range of associated lexical elements and the traces of these primings may smooth the Formulator operations during the second performance. The first performance may have raised their activation level so that later they come more readily to consciousness during performance. More significant is the need to consider what sort of information is contained in a lemma. The first language mental lexicon is likely to contain lemmas which minimally have semantic (meaning-based) information as well as information about syntactic frames. There will certainly be phonological information, so that words can actually be produced (and modified where necessary to take account of the linguistic environment). But there will also be discourse information, and associative network information, and collocational information, and maybe much else besides. When a first language speaker retrieves lemma-based information, most of these things are made available (below the level of consciousness). The key issue is that when the second language speaker engages similar retrieval processes, particularly on first performance, it is likely that 'core' information will be retrieved, but possibly not with the same level of representation as is the case with first language speakers. Equally important, the wide range of information just described may not be retrieved at all, or possibly it will be partially retrieved.

We can now compare what happens during planning and what happens during the process of repetition. Planners, as we have seen, retrieve, particularly at lower-proficiency levels (Ortega, 2005). This is done, presumably, in the hope of being prepared for the actual performance. But it is likely that this retrieval is shallow, maybe consisting of meaning and phonological form elements. When performance is actually required, and assuming the shallow retrieval is recalled, there is still quite a lot more to do. With repetition, in contrast, prior to the repeated performance, the first performance, since it is an actual performance, forces the speaker to confront the functioning of the lemmas which are retrieved. In other words, meaning and general phonological form are not enough. There will be a need to extract relevant information held in the lemma to enable syntax building. It may be that discourse or collocational information is also semi-retrieved and links are made with associated material that feeds into the utterance. These activities are likely to lead to a greater depth of processing, and consequently, a higher likelihood of retention. Then, in the repeated performance, successful operations from the first performance are more likely to become available, and more quickly on this second performance. In addition, it is likely that the first performance will have caused semi-retrieval to occur for less central lemma features. In the second performance these semi-retrievals will be at a heightened state of activation and may be retrieved more fully and more easily. The result will be that the repeated performance can benefit from the greater depth and completeness of the first actual performance, compared, that is, to the sort of preparation that planning can give. In addition, it is likely that the original performance will prime a network of related lemmas, and this too may facilitate the second performance, raising possibilities that did not exist so easily on the first performance. Here too there is a contrast with planning, since it is likely that the shallower processing during planning will rarely go beyond the basic information in the lemma that is retrieved.

The conclusion to draw from this is that depth of processing, long attested as vital in cognitive psychology, is highly relevant to the nature of preparation, and also distinguishes between pre-task planning and repeated performances. The deeper the preparation, the more effective subsequent performance can be. As a result, when preparation opportunities are used, the more that second language speakers can be induced to use deeper processing, the greater the impact on actual performance is likely to be. That is not to say that planning is not effective. It is more that repetition seems to be an alternative and often superior technique.

Remaining Issues: Research Opportunities

The previous sections have put forward a view of preparation which is consistent with the research literature, and which broadens conceptions of how second language speakers' performance can be raised. But it has to be said that the most striking issue is that more research is necessary since the research base on which the section is based is rather slender. This section will discuss areas where more research is needed, and also outline suggestions for pedagogic intervention.

Proficiency Level: Both planning research and repetition research lack systematic investigation of the role of proficiency changes. In each case there are different studies at different proficiencies but the variable of proficiency has not been controlled carefully and in a way that enables precise comparisons. This is a considerable practical omission since the effectiveness of these techniques at different proficiency levels may vary. But there are also theoretical reasons why we would like to know how things change as proficiency changes. If we assume that as proficiency grows, so does the second language mental lexicon, then we need to see how the Conceptualiser-Formulator balance changes as the demands that the Conceptualiser makes can be more readily met by second language mental lexicon resources. With planning we need to know how second language speakers capitalise on planning opportunities differently. Do they manage to use the Conceptualiser stage more efficiently? Or alternatively, do they maintain general Conceptualiser operations, but then achieve higher levels of accuracy and fluency as they respond to demands made at the Formulation stage? With repetition, similarly, do we see a more effective Formulator stage, or do we see released attention devoted to more elaborate Conceptualiser work?

Methods of Improving the Efficiency of Planning: The research on the effects of instruction, and video-modelling, and also the qualitative research studies have shown that planning may be malleable. This hints at considerable promise. There is scope for more research into the effects of using and varying instruction for planning, exploring issues like the detail of instruction, the clarity of different formats of providing instruction, the focus of such instruction, whether language or content. If we regard planning as beneficial, then exploring different instructional options may make for an important bridge between research and pedagogy.

More generally, and not necessarily using only pre-task instructions, there may be scope to train planning. The qualitative research has shown that planning can be beneficial, but it also can lead to problems, such as planning too generally, so that forgetting occurs, and planning over-ambitiously, so that difficulties are encountered. It may well be that we can learn from these insights and lead second language speakers into using planning time more efficiently and more durably. Indeed, the wider issue of practising planning may have considerable potential here. It may well be that as second language learners become more used to being given planning time, they learn to use it better.

Qualitative Research: The qualitative research literature is slender, and perhaps the most important thing to call for is simply more research, with a wider range of L1s, at a wider range of proficiency levels. It would be desirable for this research to routinely collect performance data, and relate the reports of what people did during planning time to variation in performance. But perhaps most important here is that there should be qualitative research with tasks other than narratives. So far the existing research, for perfectly understandable reasons (greater degree of control, largely) has been with narratives. But we need other task challenges, certainly involving interactive tasks, and with a range of objectives (information exchange, opinion-exchange, different types of reasoning). These will give us a much more robust database for understanding what people do during planning, and how different behaviours connect with performance.

Understanding the influences on on-line planning: Initially things were fairly simple here: on-line planning seemed to support accuracy in a selective manner. Things have now become a little more complicated, so that more research is needed. First, we need to make progress on the operationalisation of on-line planning (and perhaps also, how to use qualitative techniques effectively [Ahmadian & Tavakoli, 2014]). Second, we need to explore the circumstances which lead to on-line planning effectiveness. Wang (2009, 2014) is the only study which contained a clear operationalisation of on-line planning and which explored a combined pre-task plus on-line condition, and as we have seen, reported raised performance in different areas, not only in accuracy. We simply need more studies to explore whether, and in what circumstances, on-line planning can work effectively alone, and whether it needs support in some form. Wang (2014) showed how pre-task planning could achieve this. Others, such as Li and Fu (2016) have shown how working memory advantages performance. It may be that other variables, similarly, make on-line planning more, or less effective, with changes in proficiency level being a clear candidate here. Such research could be particularly revealing regarding Formulator operations.

Specific Research on Repetition: In some ways, this is the area that is most in need of research, since the potential lines of inquiry are so great. Fundamental will be systematic research which varies the time interval between the original and the repeated performance. Wang (2014) showed major Formulator-linked influences with an immediate condition (with Conceptualiser advantages also). With the much longer interval of ten weeks, the major focus in Bygate (1996) was towards Conceptualiser influences. The difficulty is that we do not have enough research between these two time intervals, and so even though one may propose that as the time interval increases, the impact on Formulator operations reduces, we do not have the research to back this up. In addition, exploring time intervals such as one day, or (say) three days, or one week and so on could link with notions of how long the advantages that flow from priming or from exploiting partial lemma retrieval might last (Kaschak et al., 2010). We know, from the planning literature, that memory in performance for what has been planned is vulnerable. It would be helpful to have some ideas of the optimum time difference between original and repeated performances for the different psycholinguistic processes that underpin second language speech.

Another area where more repetition research is needed is with proficiency level. The argument made here has been that repetition benefits second language speakers because of shortcomings with the second language mental lexicon. We can assume, though, that as proficiency increases, so the limitations from the second language mental lexicon diminish. One could explore therefore if Formulator operations are eased, and that it becomes more possible to handle the demands of the Conceptualiser and the pre-verbal message more easily. One might even expect that the impact of repetition on the Formulator might diminish, and one might, even with short intervals between original and repeated performance, see an impact on the Conceptualiser, as in Bygate (1996), since the development of the second language mental lexicon might be sufficient to enable accurate and fluent performance on the first occasion. This certainly underscores calls there have been (Ellis, 2011; Bui et al., in press; Skehan, 2014) for native speaker data to be collected as a baseline against which to judge second language performance.

We have also seen interesting results with multiple repetitions (Lambert et al., 2016). This, too, is an area of research well worth expanding, with different tasks, and above all with different dependent measures. If methods can be found for tying particular dependent measures to particular stages in second language speaking, this would contribute hugely to our understanding of the psycholinguistic processes underlying such speaking. Finally, it may be valuable to continue to explore the relationship between repetition of particular tasks and the repetition of task type. Disappointment has been expressed over the lack of generalisation that has generally been found, but the database here is not extensive. It would be worth revisiting this area, and perhaps exploring exactly what 'different' actually means, since there are undoubtedly degrees of difference. In any case, it would be worthwhile to explore whether small changes in the repeated task, compared to the original, might lead to generalisation.

Planning Research, the Levelt Model, and Pedagogy

The final section tries to bring things together, linking a small elaboration of the Levelt model, what we have learned about planning activities, and the way planning research can be reinterpreted. The chapter finishes with a discussion of the implications for pedagogy.

The section starts, almost inevitably, with the Levelt model, but in a way I consider extended in a way that is particularly useful for second language research, and especially planning. The starting point for this is simple—it is to consider the processes of speaking when we are concerned with more than one cycle of the Levelt model. This is schematised in Table 9.1.

Table 9.1 refers to the first four communication cycles, and this is enough to clarify the points that are important. But in reality there are many more than four cycles in most communications. The diagram brings out that the system needs to get started (and begins with a Conceptualiser only cycle, followed by a Conceptualiser-Formulator cycle). Thereafter, though, from Cycle 3 on, all three speaking stages are working together in parallel for each speaking cycle (except, to nitpick, the last two). The key is that the numbers refer to propositions which will be expressed, and that when one gets beyond the first communication cycle, (and

TABLE 9.1 Cycles of Speaking

Communication Cycle	Time 1	Time 2	Time 3	Time 4
1	Conc.1			
2		Conc.2; Form.1		
3			Conc.3; Form. 2; Artic.1	
4				Conc.4; Form.3; Artic.2

Conc. = Conceptualiser; Form. = Formulator; Artic. = Articulator more than one speaking stage is active at the same time), each speaking stage is occupied with a different new proposition. Hence, at Cycle 3, the Conceptualiser has got on to proposition 3, while the Formulator is still occupied with proposition 2, and the Articulator, at this stage, is only dealing with proposition 1. Since, for the native speaker, these stages are encapsulated, this arrangement works well. It is predicated upon each succeeding stage having the wherewithal to deal with what it receives from the preceding stage. In particular, the Formulator needs to be able to respond effectively to the demands implicit in the pre-verbal message.

In the second language case, as discussed in Chapter 4, the Formulator, less resourced as it is, has trouble dealing with the demands of the pre-verbal message, and the result is that it requires more attentional resources than can be provided if parallel functioning is to be maintained. What 'gives' in this system is the maintenance of parallel functioning, and so the smooth functioning of the system outlined in Table 9.1 is not possible. Formulation demands cause the parallel Conceptualisation and Articulation to be put on hold, and instead a more serial mode of communication is used, hopefully only until a parallel mode is restored.

This argument merely repeats what was outlined in Chapter 5. Here the concern is the relevance this analysis has for the place of planning. So far in this section we have been assuming the functioning of ongoing speaking. That is where native speakers manage parallel processing but second language speakers struggle. But when we are dealing with pre-task or strategic planning, we have a different situation to the flow of normal speaking. The opportunity to plan gives the speaker the opportunity to ease the tasks that will be faced by the Conceptualiser and the Formulator when the speaking occurs. The latter, the Formulator, is the easiest to comment on here, and perhaps less important. Retrieval and rehearsal during planning are things that can be done which are intended to prepare the ground for tripwires in Formulation. As we have seen, they are often vulnerable to forgetting. But they are attempts to combat difficulties and they may be effective.

The situation is more complex with the Conceptualiser. A simple (but still important) interpretation would be similar to what happens regarding the Formulator—the planning period can be used to 'seed' the Conceptualiser with relevant ideas, with connections between ideas, and with the organisation of ideas in ways that may be relevant to subsequent speaking. Then, during the actual speaking, the preparatory work (work which it appears, from the qualitative research, is more likely to be recalled) can be drawn on more readily, and lead to improvement in performance.

Table 9.1 implies that the different cycles in communication are such that Conceptualiser work, in the form of the pre-verbal message, is the input to the Formulator, and the 'fit' between Conceptualiser work and Formulator work is complete—they operate at the same scale. In other words, the Conceptualiser, once the Formulator input has been delivered, gets on with the next bit of conceptualisation. But it may well be the case that the span of the two sets of operations is different, and that the Conceptualiser provides input that is only a subset of what has been completed at that stage. In other words, larger Conceptualiser input is packaged to take account of Formulator limits, and there is remaining scope to drive future Formulator cycles.

This is likely to be the case in normal speaking, with native and non-native speakers, even when planning does not take place. In other words, probably as a result of the nature of the task, e.g. a structured narrative, the influence of a particular Conceptualisation stage may extend over several Formulation stages, rather than having totally new Conceptualisation input for each Formulation stage. Importantly, when there is pre-task planning, the time may be spent, in effect, 'loading up' the Conceptualiser, so that preparation is accomplished for numerous cycles of speaking. This may be done through the ideas which are to be expressed, or additionally, it may be done through a clearer sense of discourse development for the speaking. In either case, the subsequent performance will be driven by different fundamental organisation. For native speakers, this may be the norm, even though such an approach may not be important or necessary for them. For non-native speakers, in contrast, it may be of considerable help because the preparation, if effectively done, can sustain them during the pressures of communication, and even be a powerful resource to sustain parallel processing since it makes it more feasible to allocation attention to Formulation without losing the thread of the discourse.

This analysis allows us to look at planning from a slightly different perspective. If planning opportunity is used to prepare the Conceptualiser to work over several cycles, it is likely that this will have an impact on the discourse flow of the performance. The emphasis will be on how a series of utterances are linked, and are driven by a pre-verbal message whose scope extends over more than one utterance. This might be part of the explanation of the subordination complexity effect which is regularly found in pre-task planning studies. It could also be relevant to the fluency effect which is equally common, since the span and range of underlying ideas will drive a series of utterances, and in so doing reduce the likelihood of, for example, end-of-clause filled and unfilled pausing, and also perhaps, raise the speed of communication. The next chapter will explore some empirical consequences of such an insight, and argue that measures of complexity and fluency need to be considered differently from a discourse and a clause-based perspective respectively.

It may also be useful, given this analysis, to revisit some of the research areas covered earlier in this chapter, and in so doing gain a wider perspective on planning. First, perhaps, it is useful to review the insights from the qualitative research. This suggested, based on the codings of the self-reports, that, during pre-task planning time, second language learners do five general sorts of things:

- Macro planning: This is planning that has a discourse-oriented quality, where the participant is looking ahead to see how to organise what they are going to say. There is a language emphasis here, but oriented towards the broader

discourse. This clearly foreshadows Conceptualiser operations, and also preparation which will impact over more than one communication cycle.
- Micro planning: This focusses on ideas, their development and their organisation. This too is Conceptualiser oriented but now concerned with the content of the actual ideas. This may have implications beyond one cycle, but would equally be limited to one such cycle.
- Retrieval: Here the focus is on the words, or lemmas, that will be used, and the speaker is trying to bring to mind features of each lemma that might be relevant to communication. This is Formulator oriented.
- Rehearsal: This process is concerned with the detailed building of phrases or even larger units within the utterance, which are prepared, as whole, so that they may be used in actual speaking. This is clearly Formulator oriented.
- Metacognitive activity: This concerns the activity during the planning period which monitors other processes, and also looks ahead to potential difficulties. It might also relate attempts at preparation in the light of the capacity (and limitations) of the speaker. There may often be greater span to such metacognitively influenced preparation.

This list of the things that people report they do during planning provides a framework that facilitates the discussion of the recasting of Conceptualisation provided above, and its linkage to planning. It enables the different areas from the research literature to be re-examined slightly.

Instructions and Modelling: Instructions and modelling can do three things which may help relative to what might be termed solitary planning. They can be more systematic and comprehensive in covering the possibilities that exist. They can expose the speaker to ways of preparing that they might not have thought of. They can organise planning in such a way that it can be retained more effectively for actual performance. Linking this to the five features just mentioned, it seems to be the case that instructed or modelled planning has a much greater chance of producing balanced preparation, across the different possibilities, and that as a result, it is likely that there will be a reasonable amount of Conceptualiser-linked, and more memorable planning. In this way, the planning that takes place can have a more durable effect, and enable Conceptualiser operations within the actual task to have relevance to longer cycles of speaking.

Task Complexity: Necessarily, when tasks are more complex, ideas are going to have greater prominence. Planning time therefore is likely to be strongly allocated to this area, and as a result, to Conceptualiser operations. Such preparation will make it more likely that speakers will have foreseen difficulties that might occur during actual performance. So, in this way, the Conceptualiser emphasis, and Micro planning, is going to be more memorable, and the Formulator operations eased. It may also be the case that Metacognition during planning becomes more important if speakers can anticipate difficulties, and try to think of ways of avoiding these. This in turn is likely to link with Macro (discourse) planning, as speakers try to be more efficient in the Conceptualiser preparation that they undertake.

Proficiency Level: Ortega (2005), as we have seen, reports that more advanced learners rehearse, but tend to avoid retrieval (assuming this is not going to be a difficult operation during performance). It seems likely therefore that Conceptualiser-linked macro and micro planning will become more important (and lead to more memorable preparation), and Formulator-linked planning is de-emphasised. Greater proficiency, in other words, tends to push second language speakers away from Formulator preparation, and towards the more enduring Conceptualiser. Going along with this, the greater responsiveness of the second language mental lexicon can reduce the need for planning which spans several communication cycles.

Time: The research on the length of time for planning suggests that second language speakers first emphasise Formulator-linked processes, and then only in the second half of a 10-minute planning period do they start to focus on Conceptualiser-linked preparation. The qualitative research might imply that this is exactly the wrong way around! The products of planning (rehearsal, retrieval) that seem most vulnerable to fading are, in this way, separated in time the maximum extent from their actual use. This may be a very natural reaction on the part of second language speakers, but it might be worth exploring whether inducing a different sequence might not be more effective as far as Formulator operations are concerned. (This may also, partly, be connected with why Conceptualiser operations are better recalled in actual performance—they are the focus of planning activity most recently in a 10-minute period.) But what actually happens may have some beneficial aspects. Macro and micro planning, if they come last, may be most effective at sustaining actual performance, with longer span impact with Conceptualiser operations in actual performance.

Pre-Task and On-Line Planning: The interesting way to approach this area is to consider what the above analysis has to say if there is only pre-task planning or only on-line planning. As a very broad generalisations, one could claim that pre-task planning emphasises Conceptualisation operations (or at least these are what are retained most effectively) while on-line planning provides more time for Formulator operations to be carried out. In reverse, pre-task planning is not so supportive of Formulator operations (although planners may indeed engage in rehearsal and retrieval, and these activities are likely to be beneficial, if somewhat vulnerable to fading), and on-line planning does not emphasise Conceptualiser work (although, of course, some of the time available in the on-line condition has to be devoted to the ideas which are to be expressed). But the combined condition (Wang, 2014) enables the strengths of each condition to be exploited, and the weaknesses overcome. Conceptualiser work at the pre-task stage, whether macro, micro, or metacognitive in nature, will more effectively drive forward the ideas to be expressed in the actual performance. Formulator work in the on-line condition will provide opportunities to capitalise on any pre-task retrieval and rehearsal processes and in turn provide more attentional availability for a focus on accuracy and monitoring. The result is the balanced improvement in all aspects of performance (except, on the research evidence available so far, lexis).

We see, then, that five areas that have been the focus of a great deal of planning research (instruction and modelling; task complexity; time available for planning; proficiency level; and the relationship of pre-task and on-line planning) all benefit from an analysis in terms of the possible processes named by participants in qualitative research (macro, micro, rehearsal, retrieval, metacognition). In addition, the implications of a Conceptualiser 'loaded up' during pre-task planning in such a way that it functions both within conventional, self-contained Conceptualiser-Formulator-Articulator sequences, and also as a driver of several sequences, and several steps of Formulator-Articulator operations, makes a good deal of sense.

At the same time, I have to accept that a great deal of this argument is speculative, and draws on existing research findings to present a more theoretical account of what happens during planning. But I feel this is necessary. We now have an extensive research literature on planning (pre-task and on-line), but there may be a danger that this literature will fragment into a focus on the sorts of different sub-areas discussed in this section. To counter that, I have felt it useful to propose a more over-arching perspective on these different sub-areas. Inevitably, I have used the Levelt model to try to bring these different areas together to achieve a deeper understanding of planning and of the way the second language speaker uses planning time in different ways from the first language speaker.

10
EMPIRICAL WORK WITH TASKS

Introduction

The third of the empirical chapters in this section is from an edited collection focussing on vocabulary (Richards et al., 2009). The study on which the chapter is based attempted to explore issues of vocabulary, naturally, but also incorporated fluency measures, as well as a native/non-native speaker comparison. The empirical base for the chapter was the data from the series of studies I conducted with Pauline Foster (Skehan & Foster, 2008).

The reason for including the chapter in this volume is that it exemplifies another facet of my work—the details of the measurement of task-based performance. I would claim that what was (relatively) novel were a concern to explore different measures of lexical performance (lexical density and lexical sophistication) as well as their relationship (relatively low!); to examine whether these measures behaved differently with the native and non-native speaker groups (and they did, with lexical diversity distinguishing between the two groups very, very clearly, while lexical sophistication did not); and also, regarding fluency, the importance of the location of silent pauses. Fundamentally the thrust of the article was to question individual measures of lexis and fluency in order to understand the underlying constructs better, and also, perhaps, to raise our understanding of them. The approach, to subject existing measures to some scrutiny, obviously needs to be done more generally, and go beyond lexis and aspects of fluency. That is the main purpose of this reflections chapter.

For the last 30 years or so, complexity, accuracy, lexis, and fluency (CALF) have been the dependent variables of choice in a whole range of studies (although, of course, task-based performance doesn't have to be measured this way). Initially, of course, without clear precedents, individual researchers largely made their own decisions about how to measure each construct, and there was quite a lot of variation. But as time has passed, and with researchers looking to achieve comparability of research studies, a limited degree of consensus has emerged. If, and this is a big 'if', one is concerned with generalised measures, one could propose the following set of operationalisations as being most typical:

- Complexity is measured as the proportion of clauses per AS-unit (where AS refers to the Analysis of Speech unit advocated by Foster, Tonkyn, and Wigglesworth [2000]). In effect this is a measure of the degree of subordination in spoken language. More recently Norris and Ortega (2009) have proposed words per clause as a complementary measure.
- Accuracy is measured as the proportion of clauses which are error free.
- Lexis, a more recent addition to characterising task performance, is typically measured as lexical diversity (essentially a type-token ratio corrected for text length) and lexical sophistication (which indexes the importance in task performance of less frequent words), and as we have seen, these were the focus in the reprinted chapter.
- Fluency, which is generally accepted as having distinct, if related components, is now frequently measured through amounts of pausing (breakdown fluency), repair fluency (as when speakers reformulate or repeat), and speed.

Measures in each of these areas have served us well, and offer the potential (not always taken) of some degree of cross-study comparability. But there are problems. First, unavoidably in a young area, is that of standardisation. Not all researchers use the same measures or the same units (cf. the alternative approaches taken to the AS unit). Second, and relevant in this section, there is the issue of construct validity (Norris & Ortega, 2003). In an ideal world in each performance area, there would be a theoretical and empirical basis for the choice of measure involved. In addition, where a construct needs to be represented by more than one measure, there would be a basis for the combinations of operationalisations that would be used. This is where there is scope for progress. If we are to continue with CALF measures, the time seems ripe to reflect on the alternatives which are available.

From a theoretical point of view, there have been several relevant publications. We have seen a special issue of *Applied Linguistics* (Housen & Kuiken, 2009), and also two volumes dedicated to CALF issues (Van Daele et al., 2008; Housen et al., 2012). But I would argue that the area where we also need to make progress is with the empirical alternatives which are available, and in this area, arguably, less has been said. The database for this endeavour with be a set of studies I was associated with while in Hong Kong. The advantage that these studies have is that I have analysed them with the same computer program, TaskProfile (Skehan, 2014b), which generates exactly the same measures for each. It has also been possible to adapt the program as new insights have become available, so that measures introduced in other studies in the literature can be recalculated for these datasets.

The datasets are also useful because collectively they cover a range of independent variables, so that more can be said than would be true of any individual study. This will become clear through the following descriptions of the datasets, the research design in each case, and the independent variables involved. The dependent variables, i.e. the measures of different facets of performance, will be covered in the discussion to come.

Pang and Skehan (2014): This is a qualitative study of planning (actually reprinted in this volume) and its major achievement is that it developed a coding system for what people said they did when given planning time prior to doing a narrative task. In addition the actual performance data, as indicated in the reprinted article, was transcribed, coded, and analysed. The qualitative aspects of this study are not relevant here. What is relevant is that although Pang and Skehan (2014) only reported on narrative task performance, in fact, each participant completed a decision-making interactive task (the Agony Aunt task: Skehan & Foster, 1997) and this performance data too was analysed. There were 48 participants in the study, making it a viable quantitative study in its own right. The study therefore enables performance comparisons of narrative vs. decision-making and also proficiency level, since two levels (low intermediate and high intermediate) were involved.

Bui (2014): This is a dataset from my PhD student Gavin Bui. The study has two main independent variables. The first is planning, conventionally interpreted as 10 minutes pre-task planning time. The second is specialisation-familiarity. Gavin used two expository-account tasks: (a) explain what happens where there is a virus in the human body, and (b) explain what happens when there is a virus in a computer. He had two groups in his study. The first were medical students, and the second were computer science majors. As a result each group were matched with one of the tasks and mismatched with the other, enabling the effects of familiarity of subject matter to be investigated. (Medical students who knew about computers, and vice versa, were excluded!)

Skehan and Shum (2014): This was a study of the impact of task structure and of speaker status (native vs. non-native), conducted with Sabrina Shum. It was based on narrative retellings based on (edited) Mr. Bean videos. There were four videos and these varied in degree of structure (Tavakoli & Skehan, 2005), ranging from no structure (a story which was little more than a series of events with only a beginning and end) to tight problem-solution solution structure. In addition there was a contrast between native speakers (L1 English) doing this task and non-native (L1 Chinese) speakers. There were 28 participants in each L1 group.

Wang and Skehan (2014): This study manipulated three variables: Time Perspective, Degree of Structure, and Vocabulary Difficulty. This study too was based on Mr. Bean videos (different ones!). Time perspective was a between-subjects variable, and contrasted a Here-and-now condition (participants watched the video and simultaneously narrated the story) and a There-and-then condition (where the video was viewed, and when it was finished, participants narrated the story), following Robinson (2011a). Then, as a within-subjects design, there were two values of structure and two of vocabulary difficulty, arranged in a counterbalanced 2x2 design, so that all four tasks were done by all participants in each of the two groups (Here-and-now and There-and-then).

The four datasets enable a wider perspective when we explore the different performance dimensions. The dependent measures are identical. Between them the studies draw on a range of independent variables. They also duplicate some variables, e.g. task structure, enabling a degree of triangulation. We will look at structural complexity, accuracy, and fluency, in turn, and this will be followed by a brief discussion of style, and whether speakers are consistent in their performance profile scores across tasks. The lexis results will be referred to, as appropriate, but will not be covered so systematically, since they were in focus in Chapter 8.

Structural Complexity

The first area to probe is that of complexity and the first thing to examine is the relationship between the two most frequently used complexity measures, clauses per AS unit (Foster et al., 2000) and words per clause (Norris & Ortega, 2009), through correlation analysis. In Pang and Skehan, the correlation between clauses-per-AS unit and words per clause is −0.37 for the narrative, and 0.06 for the decision-making task. In Bui, the correlation for the medical task is −0.16 and for the computer task −0.21. In Skehan and Shum the correlations for the four tasks for the non-native speaker group are −0.18, 0.21, −0.12, and −0.06 whereas for the native speakers they are 0.48, 0.32, 0.13, and 0.43 (with the first and last of these reaching significance). In Wang and Skehan there are four correlations for the Here-and-now group: 0.08, 0.01, 0.26, 0.00, and similarly for the There-and-then group, which are −0.13, −0.47, 0.05, and −0.17 (with the second of these reaching significance). Inoue (2016) presents very similar results, with close-to-zero correlations between these measures for each of two picture-based narrative retellings. The findings are pretty consistent. There is essentially no correlation between the two measures (except partly with the native speaker group in Skehan and Shum). In other words, for non-native speakers, subordination and words per clause measure different things. Obviously, strong claims can be made for the construct validity of each of these measures separately. These results strongly suggest, however, that such claims are about different constructs.

An additional perspective is provided if the various experimental effects in the different studies are examined. Even if the two measures do not correlate, we can still explore whether different independent variables raise both, raise neither, raise one only or the other only. If that is done some interesting patterns emerge. For example, the narrative format (as opposed to the dialogic, in Pang and Skehan) and the planning condition (as opposed to the non-planners in Bui) lead to higher scores for subordination *and* words per clause. The structure condition in Skehan and Shum is associated with increased subordination only, and this is true also for the There-and-then condition in Wang and Skehan. (I would also argue that the narrative task in Inoue [2013], which produces more subordination, is the more structured task of the two narratives in her study.) There are then a number of separate influences on raising the words-per-clause scores only. These are:

- low (vs. high) proficiency in Pang and Skehan;
- specialisation match (vs. mismatch) in Bui;
- less structure (vs. more structure) in Skehan and Shum;
- Here-and-now (vs. There-and-then) in Wang and Skehan;
- greater vocabulary difficulty (vs. lower vocabulary difficulty) in Wang and Skehan;
- native speaker status (vs. non-native speaker status) in Skehan and Shum.

This mass of detail is represented, hopefully a little more clearly, in Table 10.1.

So we have influences which raise both complexity measures and then others which raise only one of them, and sometimes influences which raise one while lowering the other (structure for subordination, and lack of structure for words per clause). Not only, in other words, do the different complexity constructs/ measures do different things, they are influenced variously by a range of factors.

We only have a small set of studies to base these generalisations on, but they are still very suggestive, and clearly require explanation, even if such explanation can only presently be post hoc and tentative. Inevitably, in my case, the Levelt model

TABLE 10.1 Independent Variables and Structural Complexity

Effect of Variables	Independent Variables	Study
Raise subordination and words per clause	• Narrative (vs. dialogue)	Pang & Skehan
	• Planned (vs. unplanned)	Bui
Raise subordination only	• Structure (vs. unstructured)	Skehan & Shum
	• There-and-then (vs. Here-and-now)	Wang & Skehan
Raise words per clause only	• Low profic. (vs. high proficiency)	Pang & Skehan
	• Specialisation match (vs. mismatch)	Bui
	• Less structure (vs. more structure)	Skehan & Shum
	• Here-and-now (vs. There-and-then)	Wang & Skehan
	• Difficult lexis (vs. easier lexis)	Wang & Skehan
	• Native speaker (vs. non-native speaker)	Skehan & Shum

has to be involved here, with its stages of Conceptualisation and Formulation, especially. We can start with Planning and the Narrative format, the two contexts associated with increases in *both* subordination and words per clause. Pang and Skehan (2014), following the qualitative research of Ortega (2005) explore the connection between self-reported planning behaviour and actual performance. They, consistent with Ellis (2005) report that planning may be directed in various ways. Partly it may be used to develop *and organise* the ideas that are going to be expressed. Partly it may be directed to lexical retrieval and rehearsal. In other words, different aspects of planning may relate to the Conceptualiser (marshalling ideas and their interrelationship) and to the Formulator (retrieving lexis, preparing specific phrases to be used). In this way, some preparatory work is being done which will impact upon the complexity measure of subordination (the Conceptualiser-linked work) and some on words per clause (the Formulator-linked work). Planning does not involve only one thing: the variety of what can be planned is the basis for the joint raising in performance that is involved. Narrative tasks can similarly be viewed in terms of Conceptualiser and Formulator demands. Telling a story (or in Bui's study, providing an account of a virus) is a mixture of dealing with the overall structure, and then dealing effectively with individual scenes or pictures or features or stages. Dealing with the unity of the account, and of the way elements or pictures are related, is likely to push for greater subordination, as compound and complex clauses are used to spell out relationships or causal connections. Then, when working on detail within sections of the narrative or the account, there is a need to develop clarity to address issues of precision and completeness. With many narratives this is often built into instructions when speakers are encouraged to provide as much detail as possible. In summary, then, both planning and narrative structure push speakers to produce language with increased subordination and increased length of clause. There may be no correlation at the individual level, but the different influences are nonetheless operative more generally.

Two influences raise subordination but lower words per clause. These are the There-and-then condition (relative to the Here-and-now condition), and Structured (relative to less structured) tasks. Taking the first of these, it seems that with the Here-and-now condition, in which a lot of input has to be handled, and then rechannelled as a spoken account, the pressure to communicate under these conditions deprives the speaker of attentional availability to be able to engage the Conceptualiser deeply, and to repackage the material that is presented. The speaker is forced to function as a sort of simultaneous interpreter. As a result, there seems to be a 'one clause at a time' quality to performance, and within this, more attention to developing the clause in question, and using more words. Under the There-and-then condition, even though the need to retrieve material may be an issue which does consume attentional resources, there is not the same time pressure, and the result is that repackaging and reorganising are possible, and there is time to bring out the interrelationships of the elements of the story, i.e. the task becomes more negotiable. As a result, there is more subordination. Interestingly, such clausal complexity seems to be the priority, and longer, more developed clauses are not. Structure is interestingly similar. The explanation for the raising of subordination is most plausibly that structure, by its nature, clarifies the relationships between the elements in a narrative, e.g. the link between problem and solution, in such a way that retelling the narrative effectively will need to show what these relationships are, and this, naturally, is likely to support a need to use complex and compound sentences. The lowering of words per clause by structure, or alternatively put, the raising of words per clause by the unstructured condition suggests that lack of structure switches the focus from bringing out the relationship between elements to a mode of narrative retelling in which individual pictures or scenes are highlighted, separately, and then all that is left to do is indicate detail, detail which pushes each clause to be longer since 'doing better' is achieved in a much more localised way. The two very similar influences, then, seem to indicate a tension between a broad discourse emphasis versus a very local and detailed approach to communication. This is exactly the same tension with which the previous chapter on planning finished.

There are four remaining influences which all raise the words-per-clause measure. They fall into two pairs (proficiency level and speaker status: familiarity and vocabulary difficulty). First of all we have proficiency, and the intriguing result that *lower*-proficiency non-native speakers (in Pang & Skehan, 2014) and also native speakers (in Skehan & Shum, 2014) produce higher words-per-clause means. (In passing, it should be recalled that for subordination native speakers do not differ from the non-native speakers in Skehan & Shum.) Native speakers, perhaps, are easier to account for here. While subordination may be strongly influenced by task demands (hence the lack of NS-NNS difference), the native speaker proficiency, and attendant mental lexicon superiority, means that the components of a simple sentence (subject, object, complement, adjunct) can all be developed easily, and so the number of words in a clause has a number of sources of greater length, a greater length which can be easily achieved. What is more interesting is that lower-proficiency students (low intermediate), from Pang and Skehan's research, produce higher words-per-clause means than do the higher proficiency (higher intermediate students). One can only assume here that the lower proficiency means that speakers are struggling to express their meanings, and the result is that as they are floundering, they increase the number of words in a clause to no useful communicative purpose. Using more words is the *consequence* of lower proficiency, and the lack of resources to express meanings concisely.

The remaining pair of influences here are familiarity (and in Bui [2014], the matching of area of expertise and focus of task), and vocabulary difficulty (in Wang & Skehan, 2014), since each raises words per clause only. It may well be that what these two factors have in common is vocabulary itself, and indeed the matched students in Bui's (2014) study had higher lexical sophistication scores. In the Bui study, what the matched participants could do is access more impressive and specialised lexical elements. Then these more sophisticated vocabulary items could function within clauses to require more elaborate clause-based morphosyntax. With the vocabulary difficulty condition in the tasks in Wang and Skehan (2014) it was the pre-selection of tasks which required less frequent vocabulary which produced the same effect. Difficult lexis tasks were those which were rated as requiring more difficult lexis and which had provoked the use of such lexis in a pilot study. So in this study, too, more difficult vocabulary could push for more elaborate clause structure. In both studies, being able to use more challenging lexical items drove speakers to build longer clauses, while the simpler lexical material in the mismatched condition (Bui) or the easier-lexis condition (Wang & Skehan) did not make such demands.

So we see that it is not sufficient to index complexity with only one measure. We also see that the two measures that are currently most used, subordination and words per clause, do clearly different things and are often raised or lowered by different influences (although joint effects are possible). (It may also be the case that additional measures are required to reflect other aspects of performance.) The database for these conclusions is, though, not extensive and further research is obviously required. More variables need to be explored, including task and task condition variables as well as proficiency level. This may provide a clearer understanding of how the two measures make their separate contributions. For now the suggestion seems to be that discourse-oriented and clause-oriented processing may have some level of distinctness from one another. As indicated in the last chapter, there are influences which push, at the Conceptualiser stage, for greater span and elaboration of the relationships between elements, and there are other influences which are more clause-oriented. Sometimes they coincide and sometimes they do not.

Accuracy

There are variations in how generalised measures of accuracy work. Three factors could potentially be at play. These are:

- clause-based accuracy measures;
- error-gravity-based measures, which do not treat all errors as equally serious, and build this into the calculation of an overall error score;
- clause-length based measures, where the index of accuracy is based on the maximum length of clause that can be handled without error. (This variation can, potentially, be linked with error-gravity approaches to measurement.)

In contrast to complexity, where the two measures we have just examined did not correlate, the accuracy measures do inter-correlate, mostly substantially. Typical correlations are in excess of 0.70, and often higher than that. Taking a more multivariate approach, factor analyses consistently generated two-factor solutions.

One factor is almost always clause-based while the other involved length-based measurement. Error gravity does not emerge so clearly in these factor analyses so the major tension seems to be between clause-based and length-based error, although the general levels of correlation suggest that this isn't much of a tension—more a slight contrast. The conclusion one can come to here is the simple one: error is error; accuracy is accuracy. There are no strong contra-indications to this. It does not appear to matter very much which accuracy measure is used—they all deliver the same result. Nor is there any suggestions that different measures generate different results with different independent variables, in contrast to what happened with the structural complexity measures.

There is one exception to this, and it does have its interest. In the Pang and Skehan dataset, there were scores for a narrative picture retelling task and a decision-making interactive task (the Agony Aunt task). The error-free clauses measure (based on all errors) and the Length Accuracy score (based on all errors) all showed the accuracy level to be greater for the decision-making task. However, the Length Accuracy score *ignoring minor errors* showed the narrative task to generate higher accuracy. To obtain this result, what must have happened is that while more errors were made in the narrative task (accounting for the more accurate performance on most indices for the decision-making task), these errors tended to be minor. When these minor errors were allowed to pass, the narrative became the more accurate task! Further research is needed to establish whether this is a freak result, or reflects something more substantial.

Fluency

As we saw earlier, in previous research fluency has been conceptualised in terms of:

- breakdown fluency, indexed largely by silent pauses;
- repair, indexed through reformulations, repetition, false starts, and replacements;
- speed, indexed by values such as words per minute, syllables per minute, or inverse syllable speed (De Jong, Groenhuot, Schoonen, & Hulstijn, 2015).

This view of fluency takes us beyond a monolithic view of what 'smoothness' in language might consist of. But it is now beginning to encounter problems in dealing with the newer data that is available, as will be reported below. There have also been suggestions for the use of slightly revised fluency measures to perhaps capture different ways that smoothness is achieved. Pause location is one such development, and I have argued in the reprinted article (Skehan, 2009b) for the need to measure end-of-clause and mid-clause pauses separately, as they may reflect different psycholinguistic processes. One can also measure filled pauses ('um', 'er', etc.) in distinction to silent pauses. It is an open question as to whether silent and filled pauses fulfil similar or different functions. It is also possible that filled-pause location (end-of-clause and mid-clause) is important to consider. It has also been suggested (Kahng, 2014) that standardised measures of number of pauses (e.g. pauses per 100 words) and total silence should be supplemented by an index of average pause length. We also have what might be termed composite measures of fluency such as length-of-run, or phonation time. Kahng (2014) suggests also using number of cooccurrences: the number of times different dysfluency markers occur at the same point, such as a silent and a filled pause occurring together. Given the datasets that are in focus here, and the variables they include, it seems an opportunity to revisit our understanding of the dimensions of fluency.

To this end, a series of factor analyses were run on the different datasets. Each took an eigenvalue of 1 as the criterion to accept a factor as meaningful, and each was followed by Varimax rotation. As a preliminary point, it should be noted that Pang and Skehan, and Bui used tasks that did not involve video retelling whereas Skehan and Shum, and Wang and Skehan only used such retellings. The former studies, obviously, represent different and less immediate pressures on fluency, whereas the latter two studies, with a video running, are clearly different (although, of course, this did not apply to Wang & Skehan's There-and-then condition). The contrast, as we will see, leads to some revealing comparisons.

Two (related) patterns emerged in the factor analyses. First, in a number of the analyses, almost all based on the non-video studies, three factors emerged. These were:

- silent pausing;
- repair;
- filled pausing.

When there was such a three-factor solution, silent pausing was typically the first factor, and repair and filled pausing swapped place as second or third factors unpredictably. Speed did not emerge as a separate factor (not surprising, given the structure of the dataset), but was generally 'pitted' against either repair or filled pauses but not silent pauses. Silent pausing emerging as a fairly clear first factor is not perhaps surprising, and generally consistent with the literature. Typically, in the solutions in the present analyses *all* silent pause locations (at clause boundaries *and* mid-clause) loaded on this factor. What is interesting then is that repair and filled pauses generated separate factors, from one another and from silent pauses, quite consistently. In other words, pausing seems not to be a general category here. Filled pauses seem to be doing something distinct in the flow of discourse from unfilled silent pauses in these non-video-based studies. Silent pauses may reflect a degree of breakdown as the speaker is fumbling towards some way of continuing. They may be thrust on the speaker, as resources are lacking, and the way is not clear for what could be said next. Filled pauses, in contrast, may reflect a greater degree of engagement, and a floor-holding strategy while a half-formulated plan is brought to fruition, with the speaker having some confidence that the current speaking problem can be solved (as opposed to unfilled pauses, when confidence may not be so high). If this is the case, then silent pausing indicates a serious communication problem while filled pausing and repair reflect speakers trying to keep on track.

But the situation is complicated further when we turn to the two studies based on video-based narrative retellings. Bear in mind that the communicative pressure is greater in these narrative retellings. The consequence of this seems to be that the clarity of the three factors which emerge in the non-video studies is mostly absent, even with the native speaker group in Skehan and Shum. Instead, the first factor which is extracted in the Skehan and Shum (2014) study, with both native and non-native speaker groups, is a mixture, typically of mid-clause silent pauses, mid-clause filled pauses, and repair. In these analyses there is usually a later factor (second or third) based on silent pausing, but this is usually less prominent. So it seems, with greater communicative pressure, what becomes more important, even for the native speakers, is the need to regroup, and to sort out what are often mid-clause and presumably lexically based problems. Interestingly, with the native speakers, there is often a less prominent AS pausing factor, suggesting a discourse mode of planning. The non-native speakers, in contrast, seem more oriented to ongoing Formulator-linked solutions of communication problems.

Wang and Skehan present essentially the same picture, although this is perhaps slightly less clear-cut. The first factor is typically a hybrid, bringing together repair, silent mid-clause pauses, and filled mid-clause pauses. Similarly there is often a factor mostly based on silent pauses. The major difference is that there is also a distinct factor based on the filled pauses. This occurs in five of the eight analyses (Here-and-now vs. There-and-then by four tasks). Sometimes this is a secondary factor, but there is no particular trend for this to be associated with the Here-and-now compared to the There-and-then conditions (and indeed this is a general point in that the two conditions do not have systematic differences).

These analyses do suggest that the three areas of silent pauses, filled pauses, and repair have some distinctness and importance and that therefore we have to talk of four, not three, fluency factors (i.e. these three plus speed). A first point, then, is that they have different functions, and influence dysfluency in different ways. Silent pauses and filled pauses, for example, seem to reflect different sources of difficulty. The first, as suggested earlier, may focus on a more serious level of difficulty where the speaker (native or non-native) needs to regroup in a more serious way. The second may indicate a small degree of confidence that the breakdown is temporary but a recognition that ongoing Formulator work is being disrupted. The filled pauses then function as a floor-holding strategy. Interestingly repair is different from each of these, and may reflect other influences. The difficulty is that we cannot really say what these influences are with any precision. They may reflect an orientation to avoid error and to monitor, so that it is, effectively, a style (and see below). They also may reflect proficiency, both low (as many candidate errors are spotted and worked on) or high (where wider resources become available, and so the scope for repair becomes greater). They may also reflect the discourse vs. clause tension, discussed in the last chapter, and in this chapter relating to structural complexity measures. The greater pressure in the video-based studies seems to make the clause-internal factor (mid-clause silent and filled pauses and repair) more prominent. There is considerable scope for research here.

Style

In Skehan and Shum (2017) as well as Skehan, Foster, and Shum (2016) the issue of style was discussed—that is to say, a predisposition, on the part of the speaker, to prioritise (and conversely, de-emphasise) certain aspects of performance. This raises the question of the extent to which aspects of language task performance are more strongly influenced by personal style, on the one hand, or alternatively by task design and task condition factors, on the other. If the first case, style, applies then there should be high correlations across tasks and conditions, and also, possibly, lack of experimental effects. If the second interpretation (task effects) prevails, then the cross-task correlations may be low or at least lower, but experimental effects should be prominent. And of course there can be situations where there are high (style) correlations and also experimental effects (as well, logically, as low correlations and no experimental effects, though this, obviously, won't be pursued!). High correlations and experimental effects do indicate style and research design working together. High scorers would still be high scores relative to low scorers, but everyone would have shown that they are influenced by the task and the way it was done.

One final point in these preliminary remarks is that one can also explore the same tension regarding style vs. experimental effect in terms of native speaker groups. Once again we are back to using native-speaker groups as a touchstone, so that we have a better understanding of any findings with non-native speaker groups. Two variant designs are possible. One could study the very same people performing in their L1 and their L2 to see if there is cross-language consistency in different performance features. This was done by Derwing, Munro, Thomson, and Rossiter (2009) and De Jong et al. (2015). One can also study different groups of native speakers and non-native speakers doing the same tasks, particularly where there are multiple tasks, to tease out where there is consistency of performance across task, and compare that with consistency of experimental effects because of the research designs involved. Both research strategies have been used, but in the present case, it is the latter that will be used, as in Skehan and Shum (2017).

Table 10.2 below shows, for the different studies we have been examining in this section, the different performance measures which generated sizable cross-task correlations. In Pang and Skehan this is simply the correlation between the narrative and the decision-making tasks, and in Bui it is the correlation between the computer virus account and the medical virus account. For Skehan and Shum there are four narrative tasks involved, generating six inter-task correlations. In this

TABLE 10.2 Cross-Task Correlations Across Four Studies

	P+S	Bui	S+S_NS	S+S_NNS	W+S_HnN	W+S_TnT
90				Mid-filled 0.96 Repetition 0.90	Mid-silence 0.90	Repetition 0.90
80			Mid-filled 0.87 Mid-silence 0.84 Repetition 0.83 AS 100 0.81	AS 100 0.80	Mid-filled 0.83 Repetition 0.83 PrunWPM 0.83	Mid-filled 0.84
70	Repetition 0.79 Mid-filled 0.72	Mid 100 0.76 Mid-filled 0.73 EFC 0.70	Wds Clause 0.74 Lex.Soph: 0.72	D 0.78 Mid 100 0.78 Reform. 0.77 Replacement 0.71 AS filled 0.70	AS 100 0.76 Mid 100 0.70 Wds Clause 0.73	Mid-silence 0.78 PrunWPM 0.75 Mid 100 0.77 D 0.74
60		Repetition 0.68 Mid-silence 0.65 Mid Aver 0.61	D 0.69 Fal Start 0.67 Mid 100 0.61 AS filled 0.60	EFC 0.66 Mid-silence 0.66	EFC 0.66 Lex.Soph: 0.63 D 0.63 Replace 0.60	
50	Mid-silence 0.51	PrunWPM 0.58 Subord 0.56 AS 100 0.53	Subord 0.57 Replace 0.56 Formality 0.50	Wds clause 0.52	Reform 0.59 Fal Start 0.55 Subord 0.51	EFC 0.56
40						AS 100 0.46 Reformul. 0.44

P+S = Pang and Skehan (2014); Bui = Bui (2014); S+S_NS = Skehan and Shum (2014) native speaker group; S+S_NNS = Skehan and Shum (2014) non-native speaker group; W+S_HnN = Wang and Skehan (2014), Here-and-now; W+S_TnT = Wang and Skehan (2014), There-and-then.

case the median correlation is shown, for native and non-native speaker groups separately. With Wang and Skehan, again with four tasks, the same approach is taken: median correlations, shown separately for the Here-and-now and There-and-then groups, (the between-subjects aspect of the research design). The correlations are given next to each variable, and all correlations that are shown were significant. The different rows show the correlations above 0.90, 0.80 etc., to give some degree of scale.

The first focus here is on the different levels of correlation for each of the tasks. It is clear that the two video-based narratives (Skehan and Shum, and Wang and Skehan) show more evidence of style, with clearly more median correlations that are at higher levels. This applies to each of the two groups in each of these studies, the native speaker vs. non-native speaker contrast in Skehan and Shum, and the time perspective contrast in Wang and Skehan (Here-and-now and There-and-then). The least evidence of cross-task style comes from Pang and Skehan, where the correlation is between a (picture-based) narrative and a dialogic, decision-making task. The expository account of viruses in Bui comes somewhere between these other studies with clearly more substantial cross-task correlations than Pang and Skehan, but fewer than the other two studies.

Skehan and Shum (2017), in a similar analysis of style effects but based only on the Skehan and Shum dataset, argued that style effects are considerable, especially regarding fluency. They also linked style to the different Leveltian stages, and argued that Formulator linkages are the most convincing source of style effects, and that such effects are likely to be diminished when Conceptualiser and Monitoring become more prominent. The present results, based as they are on a larger database (though including the Skehan and Shum data) suggest that this conclusion is not totally inaccurate, but at the same time, a little too strong. What seems to emerge, regarding the generality of style, is that narratives, and possibly particularly video-based narratives, are fertile ground for style effects to emerge. As the other tasks in this review of four studies differ more than they did from one another in Skehan and Shum, the prominence of style effects diminishes. This is somewhat true with Bui, and very clearly true with Pang and Skehan. Providing accounts about different things, as in Bui, or speaking monologically as opposed to dialogically, seems much less fertile ground for style, and more likely to be associated with task effects. The database here is slender, but this conclusions seems justified—we need more research!

Turning to the detailed patterns of correlation across the various studies, things become slightly clearer, and more insightful perhaps. With each task, when the inter-task correlations are ranked in magnitude, as they are in Table 10.2, the highest values derive from what might be called a 'within-clause problem' factor. This implicates mid-clause silent pauses, mid-clause filled pauses, and repetitions. These three areas emerge consistently and clearly. It seems as if speakers (and this is equally true for the native speaker group in Skehan and Shum) are consistent across tasks in having difficulties within a clause, and then responding to such difficulties in the same way. They depend upon silent pauses to give them time to regroup mid-clause; they rely on filled pauses in the same way. And they repeat. So the intriguing generalisation is the response to within-clause problems and the consistency for individuals in this regard.

Two additional points are worth making here. First, I would argue that repetition functions similarly to pausing within a clause, perhaps especially similarly to filled pauses. Repetition indicates that the speaker is still 'active', and filling time with nothing much of any additional meaning while something more substantial is being formulated. In this respect it is different to reformulation (where something syntactic or morphological is changed) or replacement (a lexical change) or a false start (since a false start implies a new plan will follow the abandonment). All of these are forms of repair, whereas repetition is simply buying time, as is the case with mid-clause silent and filled pausing. Second, although silent and filled pauses appear to have similar functions for second language speakers, the choice of which to use itself seems to be stylistic, as evidenced by the lack of correlation between these two devices. It seems speakers prefer to choose one rather than the other, thus accounting for the prominent position of each, but their relative lack of relationship in frequency, if not in function. Even so, as argued earlier, there may be the possibility that silent pauses may indicate a greater degree of problematicity, and filled pauses a floor-holding strategy.

There is also a degree of cross-task consistency with the measures of form, both complexity, (through subordination and words per clause), and also accuracy, principally through error-free clauses. This does not occur with quite the same consistency, or level, of the fluency measures. Three of the six datasets show moderate correlations for subordination and words per clause, and four out of five (not six, because the native speaker group are not seen as relevant here) for the error-free clauses measure of accuracy. So it seems to be the case that there is some degree of overlap in complexity and accuracy cross-task. It remains to be determined if this is the result of style or simply level of proficiency—the moderate levels of correlation are consistent with both possibilities.

Two measures of lexis were also investigated, and they show some evidence of style. Lexical measures (D [the text-length-corrected type-token ratio], and lexical sophistication) are not available for the Bui study, but do exist for all others. The correlations and median correlations above 0.40 are shown in Table 10.2 (and if nothing is shown, it is because any correlations are below this level). D shows fairly consistent evidence of style, with fairly high values for both groups in Skehan and Shum (2017) and both conditions in Wang and Skehan (2014). (The inter-task correlation [narrative with decision-making] in Pang and Skehan [2014] is only 0.38.) So the capacity to avoid recycling the same set of words is remarkably consistent—those who do this do it pretty much, all the time. Lexical sophistication also shows some evidence of style. This is with the native-speaker group in Skehan and Shum (2014) and the (non-native) Here-and-now group in Wang and Skehan (2014). Skehan and Shum (2017) propose that lexical sophistication reflects the ideas to be expressed (whereas they propose that D links more with Formulator processes). It appears that native speakers are more consistent across tasks in the way they draw upon their mental lexicon—those who use less frequent words do so regularly. This is less the case with second language speakers, who seem more buffeted by the lexical demands of the particular task. The exception here is the Here-and-now condition in Wang and Skehan (2014), where there is some consistency in this area, even with second language speakers.

Two final points are worth making. First, repair did not emerge as having strong stylistic components. In other words, there do not seem to be second language speakers (or first language speakers come to that) who are predisposed to repair, to monitor, or as a more speculative claim, to engage in on-line planning, since any of these should lead to more consistent reformulation, or replacement, or false starts. Second, it is worth saying that if there are strong stylistic elements, as for example indexed by repetition with correlations typically at the 0.80 level, then one has to think carefully about research designs which attempt to influence this area. It may be very difficult to demonstrate an influence when the power of general communication style may leave very little variance to work with.

Conclusions

There are two parts to this conclusion section. The first simply re-presents the major findings and claims from the chapter. This sets the scene for the second part, which brings together the disparate mentions of a Discourse vs. Clause contrast, and explores what significance this might have for second language task research.

A summary of the findings here is fairly straightforward:

- Two measures of complexity were explored, measures of subordination, most commonly clauses-per-AS unit, and words per clause. These are the most commonly used measures of structural complexity. Interestingly, they often do not correlate and they are often affected differently by different independent variables. There are occasions when they are both affected in the same way, as with pre-task planning and the use of a narrative format. But there are many others where one is raised and the other is unaffected or even lowered. At the very least, any study which needs to measure structural complexity should measure each of them. As is argued below, this is evidence for a distinction between discourse and clause processing.
- In contrast, accuracy simply seems to be accuracy. Attempts to tease out different facets of accuracy (such as error gravity, or a linkage between accuracy and the length of clause which could be used without error) did not yield anything of great interest. One measure of accuracy is pretty much like any other. This, at least, simplifies the task of researchers.
- Broadly, fluency seems to have four factors: silent pausing, filled pausing, repair, and speed. This is slightly different to previous formulations, and, come to that, is not invariant! The important points are first, that filled pausing seems to have a slightly different function to unfilled pausing, and needs to be considered as distinct from it. Second, some of the time a discourse vs. clause-based fluency is important, and for this, distinguishing between different pause locations (AS-boundary vs. mid-clause) is very important. So while the above four-part structure is important, there are times when a general

clause-based factor (drawing together mid-clause silent pauses, mid-clause filled pauses, and some indices of repair) assumes greater importance.
- There is clear evidence of style when one looks for consistency across tasks (and see Skehan, Foster, & Shum, 2016; Skehan & Shum, 2017). The clearest evidence of style comes from repair indices, and there is also strong evidence from filled and unfilled pauses. All of these implicate clause-based processing. The evidence for style at a discourse level is not so strong, but is present, as indexed by AS pausing and also subordination. The existence of style is important to gain a greater sense of realism as to what to expect with experimental manipulations.

These various findings are very interesting, and suggest that there are generalisations which now take us beyond characterising performance simply as complexity, accuracy, and fluency (and lexis also). Measures can be at a subtler level than these broader indices. In that respect, the most exciting prospect is to link the different measures to more underlying psycholinguistic processes, as, for example, Lambert, Kormos, and Minn (2016) attempt.

To develop this approach, it is worth returning to the discourse vs. clause contrast that has been mentioned at various points. Here, as a conclusion to the empirical chapter, the evidence and theory on this contrast will be brought together, linking discussion from Chapter 5, on Theory, Chapter 9, on planning, and the present chapter on empirical work.

From the discussion of planning, two general sources of evidence emerge:

- The qualitative research proposes coding schemes for the self-reports of planning behaviour. In that respect, Pang and Skehan (2014) discuss macro and micro categories, concerned with discourse and ideas, and lexicogrammar planning, linked with the Formulator and the associated processes of retrieval and rehearsal. The first two are clearly concerned with issues above the level of the clause and the latter two with clause-based performance. (This research, which also had a quantitative dimension, suggested that the discourse/ideas aspects were more memorable than the Formulator-linked aspects.)
- The quantitative research suggested that planning is important to help with the way a parallel mode of speaking is sustained, and a serial mode (where attention is taken up entirely at one stage, usually the Formulator) is minimised. We saw that planning can, through 'loading up' the Conceptualiser to handle several cycles of speaking, facilitate this, in that rather than a number of Conceptualiser-Formulator-Articulator sequences, a well-planned Conceptualiser stage can sustain the discourse for longer spans of speaking. (Structured tasks, and even more complex tasks may accomplish the same thing.) The important point here is it is easier to see how a discourse mode

can become important, and operate a little independently of the processes integral to the Formulator. Central to this is that we are dealing with second language speakers. Recall that the Pang and Skehan (2014) study also discussed Metacognition, and this may reflect awareness on the part of the second language speaker of second language mental lexicon limitations. So it may be a good strategy for such a speaker to try to operate at a more robust discourse mode to anticipate the ways the Formulator stage may encounter difficulties and to prepare the ground to overcome them.

From the present chapter, and the discussion of empirical work, there are some parallel sources of evidence:

- Subordination complexity and words-per-clause complexity did not correlate and were frequently affected differently by different independent variables, suggesting that different processes are at work in each case. (In addition, the times when they are affected similarly [planning, narrative task structure] can be understood by these influences affecting both sources of complexity independently.) Subordination complexity seems discourse linked and words-per-clause clause complexity seems more focussed on clause structure itself. Both, indeed, concern complexity, but different aspects of that complexity.
- The evidence on style was interesting. Broadly, the clearest evidence of style concerns the within-clause problem-linked measures (repetition, filled, and unfilled pauses). There was evidence of style for more discourse-linked measures (subordination, AS-boundary pausing) but this was not so marked. So it seems as if clause-based processing may connect with strong style elements, suggesting that this mode of processing has important psycholinguistic reality.
- The factor analyses of the fluency measures may not provide strong evidence for the discourse-clause contrast, but it is there to some degree. This applies particularly clearly if there is any sort of input pressure, as when a video is running which needs to be retold.

Based on this range of evidence, the claim is clear: there is some degree of separation between discourse-level and clause-level processing. This applies to native speakers. But it applies more strongly to second language speakers. Native speakers have the luxury of a well-stocked second language mental lexicon, and can therefore generally handle, at the clause level, the challenges given them in the pre-verbal message. Second language speakers do not have this luxury; the result is that their clause-level processing capacity is more exposed (and is helped if the more discourse-level processing can anticipate these difficulties). Basically, we are dealing here with the Conceptualiser-Formulator implications applied to the second language speaker.

Such an insight can have some important consequences for our field. In research terms, it could have an important influence on the design of research studies. Such studies will need to take into account these different psycholinguistic processes. They will also need to incorporate measures which pick up these different constructs in the performances which are generated. Pedagogically, it could be relevant to the ways second language learners are supported to become more effective second language speakers. Approaching speaking by trying to develop larger-span Conceptualiser work will have a sheltering advantage as far as Formulator operations are concerned. Then specific pedagogic work to nurture clause-based performance may also be justified.

PART III
Testing and Assessment

Introduction

So far in this book the focus has been on tasks and task-use either in a research or a pedagogic context. The goal has been to understand tasks and the conditions associated with them, and to relate them to what we understand about speaking. The one area of application has been, just a little, towards pedagogy. But there is another area where more practical applications are possible, and that is language testing. If tasks are used as an important component of performance testing, and if task researchers can provide insights as to how tasks influence performance, then general task research may be relevant to the choices that testers make.

So, perhaps a little curiously, I will start this introduction with a major qualification to the last paragraph and the potential claims it ends with. It may be that the most effective 'condition' one can use with a task is to tell the task-doer that it is a test! In other words, treating a task as a test may alter the way the task is done. It may, for example, lead to the test taker prioritising accuracy and the avoidance of mistakes, and this at the expense of fluency (or even complexity and more advanced language). In other words, if the goal is to be able to generalise task research findings to test situations, the first hurdle one may have to overcome is the limitation that the basic context will always be different since all candidates realise that tests are important. There is some evidence on this point, but it is rather mixed. Some studies, such as Iwashita, McNamara, and Elder (2001) suggest that generalisations from the task area do not work in a testing context, and other studies, such as Tavakoli and Skehan (2005) suggest that they might. The clearest need here is for more research to establish just how much of a threat to generalisation is operative here. For now, though, I will work with the claim that most of the content in the two reprinted chapters is relevant to actual testing contexts, and that the discussion in this reflections section also applies, even if at a general level, since it is not concerned with direct application of task research findings.

The two reprinted chapters come from 2001 and 2009. The first of these, itself a development of Skehan (1995), tried to offer a model of the testing event when tasks are used for performance assessment. It drew upon the research base available at that time, but was hampered therefore because that research base was not very extensive, or systematic. The proposals, consequently, were at a general level, and tried to re-analyse the testing 'event' with tasks in mind. I argued that if performance is dependent on a test taker completing a task, then one has to be consider that tasks are not neutral devices. The rating of performance that occurs may indeed reflect underlying abilities or competences on the part of the test taker to some extent, but they will also reflect an intruding influence of the task itself, such that different tasks could lead to different ratings.

The second reprinted chapter does not advance the model of task-based assessment in any significant way, but it does try to incorporate what had been learned by 2009 regarding generalisations about task and task condition influences upon performance. It tried to do this through wider categories than specific task characteristics (e.g. task structure) and task conditions (e.g. planning) so that more powerful generalisations could emerge, based on macro-categories such as complexifying, and pressuring. If tests are the basis for generalisation, such wider categories should facilitate the way generalisations can be made more effectively than individual task characteristics. Detailed CALF measures also have importance here, since they are the aspects of task performance which have been most investigated by task researchers as dependent variables. As it happens, CALF measures relate fairly clearly to the analytic categories that are used in ratings of performance on test-tasks, and so the different macro-categories (pressuring, etc.) are being related to performance areas which bear clear relationships to the rating categories already used in testing (accuracy, fluency, range-complexity, lexis-vocabulary). My claim would be that the generalisations that come out of the 2009 article have relevance to testing in a fairly clear way.

There are only two reprinted chapters in this section, and they are also relatively short. The reflections chapter, on the other hand, is quite long. It covers four things. First, there is an analysis of the major theories of second language performance that are relevant to testing (Canale and Swain, Bachman, Hulstijn). Second, there is general updating of the sorts of generalisations covered in the 2009 chapter, and more importantly, a clearer relationship between these updates and the Levelt model. This is used to gain insight into notions of task difficulty, and it is argued that we have to consider Conceptualiser and Formulator influences separately as sources of task difficulty. Third, there is extended discussion of the concept of ability for use, as a mediator between underlying competences and actual performance, subject as this is to pressures from the need to use language under realistic conditions. Essentially, this is my attempt to wrestle with the details of the claim made by Jack Carroll many years ago that testing needs to be done with what he termed the use of integrative language skills. These different sections of the chapter are used for the final area—a slight updating of the model of test-task performance from the 2001 reprinted chapter. This now incorporates this extended analysis of difficulty, and also the discussion of the constructs underlying CALF measures from Chapter 10 as these apply to the rating categories that are used in tasks. We may still have the challenge from earlier in this section, that testing itself introduces a major change in how tasks function. But the extended model that is proposed could be the basis for interesting research to bring together the fields of task research, psycholinguistics, and testing.

I would like to finish this section by discussing one of the basic constructs in testing—washback. This proposes (and there is much research to support this claim) that the format of a test may have a strong influence on the teaching and learning that take place prior to the test. In other words, if there is a mismatch between the teaching approach and the testing approach, learners may not be able to use what they have learned when they are assessed. In such circumstances, and especially if one is dealing with a high-stakes test, something will need to change. Sadly it is usually not the test which changes, but the teaching which leads up to it, as learners (and school administrators as well as ministries of education) want to see progress recorded and their efforts rewarded. This would be washback in action, and even if the teaching is excellent, and the testing is dreadful, it is the teaching approach which is more likely to change!

In other words, if task-based approaches to teaching are not complemented by task-based approaches to testing, they may well come under threat. If, for example, testing is based on linguistic units, with formats used which are not communicative in nature, then teaching is likely to gravitate towards this style. The implication is clear: task-based tests need to become commonplace, and task-based testing techniques need to be widely understood and operable, both with high-stakes proficiency testing and also with classroom-based achievement testing. There is room for a lot of progress to be made in this regard. The purpose of the section, and the reflections chapter particularly, is to play a part in bringing about such a situation.

11
TASKS AND LANGUAGE PERFORMANCE ASSESSMENT

Developments over the last fifteen years or so have suggested that pedagogy can fruitfully be organised by means of tasks that learners transact, and that tasks can be used as the basis for syllabus organisation as well as the unit for classroom activities. As Chalhoub-Deville (2001) points out, however, such developments constitute a source of difficulty for achievement testing. Conventional approaches to testing link with sampling frames which can be organised around some structural organisation for a syllabus. Tasks, in contrast, are centrally concerned with the learner achieving some purpose and outcome, and do not directly require the use of conformity-oriented language (Willis, 1990), of the sort that it would be convenient to engage if a syllabus is to be tested systematically.

A move towards tasks also poses problems for abilities-oriented *proficiency* testing. The most influential approaches of this type (Canale & Swain, 1980; Bachman, 1990; Bachman & Palmer, 1996) posit an underlying structure of the components of competence, and then propose mediating mechanisms by which such competences will impact upon performance. In principle, such an approach might be extremely rewarding, but in practice, the codifying nature of the underlying competence-oriented models has not interfaced easily with effective predictions to real-world performances (Harley, Allen, Cummins, & Swain, 1990; Skehan, 1998). At the most general level, the problem is that underlying and generalised competences do not easily predict across different performance conditions or across different contexts. Moving from underlying constructs to actual language use has proved problematic.

Originally published as: Skehan, P. (2001). Tasks and language performance. In M. Bygate, P. Skehan, & M. Swain (Eds.), *Researching pedagogic tasks: second language learning, teaching, and testing* (pp. 167–185). London: Longman. Copyright © Taylor & Francis. Reproduced by permission of Taylor & Francis.

258 Testing and Assessment

In response to these difficulties, a number of investigators have proposed alternative models of how spoken language might be conceptualised and measured. These models attempt to portray the assessment event in more comprehensive ways which (a) incorporate a larger number of performance elements directly, and (b) clarify how research studies might be organised and integrated more effectively to give an empirical basis for the claims that are made about spoken language assessment. The model shown as Figure 11.1 is based on work by Kenyon (1992), McNamara (1995), and Skehan (1998). It is useful to discuss the various components of this model briefly before turning to the factor which is the main focus of this chapter—the influence of the task itself on assessment procedures. The model in general clarifies the potential fallibility of a test score as an indicator of underlying abilities. The section on tasks explores whether there are systematic influences on the nature of the performance which is elicited arising from task characteristics themselves.

Figure 11.1 shows that a test score is most immediately influenced by the rating procedures which have been used. The oral performance which has been elicited

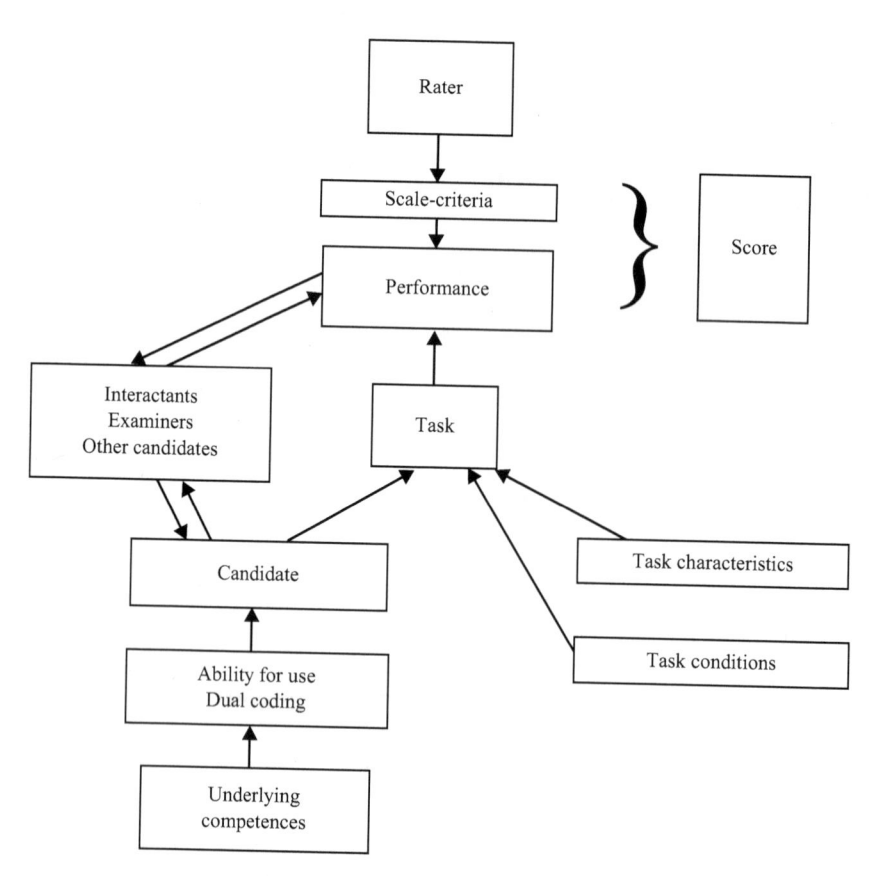

FIGURE 11.1 A Model of Oral Test Performance (Skehan, 1998)

will have been judged by raters. In addition, the performance which is being rated will be filtered through a rating scale. Such scales vary in their origin, in their characteristics, and in their purposes (see Alderson, 1991, and Fulcher, 1996). As a result of these rater and scale factors, we have to consider the possibility that the score assigned to a candidate may not reflect candidate performance only, but may partly be based on biases and limitations arising from raters and scales.

Working systematically through the model, we can identify a number of additional influences on the score which is assigned. These fall into three major headings:

- the interactive conditions under which performance was elicited;
- the relevant abilities of the candidate;
- the task which was used to generate the performance, as well as the conditions under which the task was completed.

The interactive conditions under which performance is elicited have posed problems to oral language assessment which have been recognised for many years. For example, in a conventional assessor-assessed arrangement, the power relations between the participants are manifestly unequal, and the asymmetry which results distorts the language which is subsequently used (Van Lier, 1989). It is also likely that there is important restriction in the functions of language which can be probed in any meaningful way. For these reasons, alternative organisational arrangements for oral testing have been tried in recent years, such as group-based encounters. At the cost of standardisation, they enable a wider range of language functions and roles to be engineered to provide a better basis for oral language sampling with less asymmetry between participants (Van Lier, 1989). At a more theoretical level, the group format enables us to portray the interaction in terms of co-construction, since participants will have some degree of mutual equality, and so the direction the discourse develops will not be preordained and orchestrated by the assessor.

We turn next to the abilities of the candidate. Measuring these, one might say, is the major goal of the actual assessment procedure, so the first value of the dynamic represented in Figure 11.1 is to show how this ability may not have a dominant effect upon the score which is awarded because so many other factors intrude and in potentially unsystematic ways. Again, it is not the focus of the present chapter to cover this area in detail, and so only a brief account will be given here. The model in Figure 11.1 suggests that we need to consider underlying competences *and* ability for use. The former is represented in models such as those proposed by Canale and Swain (1980) and Bachman (1990). Competence-oriented models describe different components of communicative competence, and their interrelationships. They also propose some method by which such underlying competences might influence actual performance. The relevant section of Figure 11.1, however, takes this competence-to-performance linkage further, and proposes the construct of *ability for use* as a set of abilities which mediate between underlying competence and actual performance conditions in systematic ways (Skehan, 1995, 1998). It is then the goal of assessment techniques to devise methods of assessing this construct as well as the underlying competences.

Figure 11.1 describes what is largely a programmatic model. There has been significant research in the area of rater and rating scale influences (Lumley & McNamara, 1995; North, 1996). Further, proposals to describe underlying competences have received considerable theoretical and empirical attention in recent years but the inclusion of interactive conditions and ability-for-use in the model is rather speculative at this point, and unconnected to any testing-oriented evidence. The same has been true of the influence of tasks until recently. The remainder of this chapter will be concerned with relevant research which tries to clarify how the task component of the model is increasingly susceptible to empirical investigation.

Assessing Task Difficulty: Introductory Issues

This section will prepare the ground for a meta-analysis of a number of separate studies of task-based performance. Such an examination of a number of different studies with common features is revealing about the way we might understand the impact of task characteristics on test performance. The section first discusses some measurement issues, and then describes the datasets used in the meta-analysis.

Measuring Task Performance

At the outset, one general issue needs to be clarified concerning the way task performance has been generally measured. Figure 11.1 has shown that it is typical, in assessing spoken performance, to use a rating scale approach. Such scales may be global scales, or they may be more analytic, with separate ratings for areas such as range, accuracy, and fluency. In task-based research, in contrast, such rating scale measures are not typical (but see Wigglesworth, 1997, 2001, for exceptions). Instead, reflecting the different psycholinguistic research tradition to which they belong, researchers into tasks have tended to use more precise operationalisations of underlying constructs.

In general, there is some consensus that measures are required in the three areas of complexity,[1] accuracy, and fluency. These three areas are theorised to have important independent functioning in oral performance (Skehan, 1998).[2] In addition, they enter into competition with one another, with higher performance in one area seeming to detract from performance in others (Skehan and Foster, in press). So, for example, greater accuracy may well be achieved at the expense of greater complexity, and vice versa. Research is ongoing to establish just how these three areas interrelate, but for now it needs to be said that a growing number of investigations into the task-based area are based on carefully computed indices in each of these three areas, and that the competition between them will have an important impact in decisions that are made about task difficulty.

The Datasets for the Present Research

The meta-analysis of task characteristics and their influence on task performance is based on six research studies conducted at Thames Valley University, with Pauline Foster as co-investigator. At the outset, it is essential to give a brief overview of the tasks which were used, and the purpose of the various studies (see Table 11.1).

TABLE 11.1 Overview Description of the Six Studies

Description

Tasks

Study 1: Comparison of the effects of planning on performance on personal, narrative, and decision-making tasks (Foster & Skehan, 1996a)
  (a) *personal*: students[3] have to instruct their partner how to return to their homes, and then turn off an oven which has been left on (Oven task)
  (b) *narrative*: students have to devise a story to a set of pictures: the pictures have common characters, but no obvious storyline (Weave a story task)
  (c) *decision*: students are given a series of "crimes", and have to agree on judicial sentences for these crimes, e.g. woman discovers husband in bed with another woman, and stabs and kills him (Judge task)

Study 2: Comparison of the effects of planning on performance on personal, narrative, and decision-making tasks, together with a comparison of the effects of a post-task and no post-task (Skehan & Foster, 1997)
  (a) *personal*: students have to compare things that surprise them, pleasantly and unpleasantly, about life in Britain (Surprise task)
  (b) *narrative*: students have to tell the story to a cartoon strip of pictures. The pictures have clear structure and an amusing ending (Sempé task)
  (c) *decision*: students have to agree on advice to give letter writers to an Agony Aunt column. Each letter conveys a difficult problem, e.g. father is worried about his child living with mother and new partner in a drug-suspected communal house. How should he act? (Agony Aunt task)

Study 3: Comparison of the effects of planning on a decision-making task, together with comparison of the effects of introducing surprise information mid-task (Skehan & Foster, 2005)
  (a) *decision*: as in Study 1 (Judge task)

Study 4: Comparison of four different conditions for video narrative retelling, with different processing loads. Three conditions require different versions of simultaneous tellings, i.e. telling the story while the video is playing, while the fourth is a delayed condition. Comparison of two tasks, one more structured and one less structured (Skehan & Foster, 1999)
  (a) *unstructured narrative*: Mr. Bean video of Crazy Golf. In this video Mr. Bean plays a round of golf, in which various mishaps occur. The events are an essentially disconnected series (Golf task)
  (b) *Structured narrative:* Mr. Bean video of restaurant meal. Mr. Bean has a restaurant meal in which various amusing events occur, but against the background of a typical restaurant "script" (Restaurant task)

(Continued)

TABLE 11.1 (Continued)

Description
Tasks

Study 5: Comparison of four different planning conditions: teacher-fronted, solitary, group-based, and control (Foster & Skehan, 1999)
  (a) *decision-making*: Balloon debate, with occupants to defend an actor, politician, or an EFL teacher. Students are assigned pre-task groups for teacher and group conditions where particular planning conditions are implemented. Then, students are assigned new groups and have to argue a position as to who should be thrown from the balloon (Balloon task)

Study 6: Comparison of two different experimental post-task conditions (based on the need for participants to complete a transcription of their own recorded task-based performance) and a control group (Skehan and Foster forthcoming)
  (a) *decision-making*: (Agony aunt task, as above)
  (b) *narrative*: Picture cartoon strip (Sempé task, as above)

Assessing Task Difficulty: Task Characteristics and Contrasts

At the beginning of the series of research studies, the conceptualisation of task type was in terms of a contrast between personal, narrative, and decision-making tasks. (These task types were chosen as maximally representative of tasks used in language teaching coursebooks.) As the research programme has developed, however, it has become clear that this contrast between task types, although useful, is not the whole story, by any means. It was originally thought that it would be possible to generate a number of (roughly equivalent) personal, narrative, and decision-making tasks. As the research results accumulated, however, it became clear (somewhat unsurprisingly, in retrospect), that not all exponents of each of these task types were indeed the same as regards the complexity, accuracy, and fluency of the language produced. It became clear, in other words, that other, finer-grained features, operating at a more basic level, were influential. Where there were differences between the more global task types that had been the starting point for the research, this was probably due to the combination of finer-grained factors that happened to be shared.

On the basis of the emerging results, Skehan (1998) proposed the following set of task characteristics which might impinge upon the nature of performance (in each case, the studies from the Thames Valley programme which bear upon the variable in question are indicated):

- *Familiarity of information*: tasks vary as to whether they require information that is familiar to the participants because it is part of their personal experience, compared to tasks which require the assimilation of material presented by the experimenter. Tasks based on familiar information are Study 1a, and Study 2a, where, in each case, the retrieval of personally relevant information, which is well-known to the participants, becomes the basis for completing the task. In Study 1a participants' contributions are based on their route home from college and house layout. In Study 2a participants describe what surprises them about life in Britain, pleasantly and unpleasantly. Both these tasks (and all others) were piloted, and in the piloting performance gave no indications of effortful retrieval—such material as participants wanted to use seemed instantly available to them.

- *Dialogic vs. monologic*: some tasks require interaction, and a discourse style that leads participants to alternate in who holds the floor, compared to others where extended turns are required, with little need to interact, so much as listen and wait for one's turn. A sub-set of monologic tasks are narratives, where one participant tells a story. Clear dialogic tasks are the Judge task (Study 1c and Study 3), and the Agony Aunt task (Study 2c, and Study 6b). Each of these is a decision-making task. There was one other such task, the Balloon debate, (Study 5), but in this case although the task was completed in groups of four, there was little dialogic performance when the learners "took the floor" to defend their different characters—instead learners "declaimed" at some length. The narratives in the research were Study 1b (Weave a Story), Study 2b (Sempé cartoon), Study 4 (both tasks: video-based narratives) and Study 6a (Sempé cartoon). These were completed by pairs of students, with each taking it in turn to tell the narrative and be asked questions.

- *Degree of structure*: some tasks contain a clear macrostructure, with the time sequence underlying the task fairly clearly identifiable. Other tasks do not have this clear over-arching structure. Examples of structured tasks are: Study 1a (personal), Study 2b (narrative), and Study 4b (structured narrative) and Study 6b, the same task as Study 2b. In all these cases, the time line for the information underlying the task is clear and well-organised, with the different stages in each case having a clear relationship with one another.

- *Complex outcomes*: some tasks require only straightforward outcomes, in which a simple decision has to be made. Others require multi-faceted judgements, in which the case or position a learner argues during a task can only be effective if it anticipates other possible outcomes, and other learners' contributions. In the present research, this functions as a sub-category of dialogic tasks, in that the clearest comparison is between the Agony Aunt task from Studies 2 and 6, one the one hand, and the Judge task from Studies 1 and 3, together with the Balloon debate from Study 6, on the other. The Agony Aunt task is the only one which requires joint engagement with the ideas concerned, as opposed to superficial negotiation of appropriate custodial sentences (in the Judge task) or ejection from the Balloon.

- *Transformation*: some tasks do not require participants to operate upon the information which is presented or retrieved, but instead simply to reproduce it. Others require some degree of on-line computation which changes the state or the relationship of the elements in the task. Most of the tasks in the six research studies do not require transformation of this sort, emphasising instead retrieval of information or judgements about material which is presented. An exception is the narrative task from Study 1 where participants had to use their imaginations to "impose" a story structure upon an unrelated series of pictures. In so doing, the shared characters within the given picture set had to be transformed in their relationships with one another. In this respect, it comes close to what Brown et al. (1984) term a dynamic task, except that here the dynamic qualities are derived from the mental operations of the participants themselves, rather than from the unfolding events of a *given* story.

We now have five task characteristics which can be investigated through the six studies in the Thames Valley research. These studies can be used to explore whether these different characteristics have systematic influences upon performance. It has to be admitted, though, that these comparisons were not planned at the outset of this research programme. They are worth pursuing however, since the various studies do share sufficient common features to justify the comparisons which are made. In particular, the scoring of the dependent variables was approached in a fairly consistent manner, so that the scores which are quoted below can be validly related to one another. However, the numbers and nature of the tasks which enter into the comparisons are not so systematic. The generalisations which are offered below should therefore be treated as tentative, and the basis for future, more systematically organised research studies.

Assessing Task Difficulty: Empirical Results

The following section will detail the results for each of the five task characteristics mentioned above. In each case, three sets of measures will be used to assess the various tasks concerned. These are complexity, accuracy, and fluency. Complexity is measured through a subordination index. Data is coded into communication units and clauses (Foster et al., 2000), and then an index is calculated representing number of clauses per c-unit. This has been shown in the research programme to be a sensitive measure of the degree of subordination in spoken language. It is also taken to be a surrogate measure of general language complexity. Accuracy is calculated as the proportion of clauses which are error-free. Finally, fluency is measured by the number of pauses greater than 1 second in duration per 5 minutes of performance. Better performance is therefore indicated by *higher* complexity and accuracy scores and *lower* numbers of pauses.

In the course of the research programme a number of other measures have been explored, such as the range of different syntactic structures that are drawn on; the type-token ratio of the lexis; or dysfluency indicators such as reformulation and repetition. The measures which are actually used in these analyses are those which have proved most sensitive to experimental differences, as well as the most clearly defined for operational purposes. It is not claimed that they are definitive measures (and indeed, reviews such as Wolfe-Quintero, Inagaki, and Kim [1998] are showing what a range of measures can be used in this regard). But they are serviceable and have now been used by the Thames Valley research team, and others (e.g. Wigglesworth, 1997), with encouraging results.

Familiarity of Information

Skehan (1998) hypothesises that familiarity of information will lead to greater fluency and accuracy of performance, since the easy access to information should make only limited demands on attention, allowing material to be assembled for speech more easily, and with greater attention to form. He proposes that there will be no push towards greater complexity as a result of the greater familiarity, since speakers will be likely simply to draw upon well-established language to code familiar events.

The most direct test of this hypothesis is to examine the results from Studies 1 and 2, where in each case, tasks based on familiar information (the two personal tasks) can be compared with tasks which are not. The relevant results are shown in Table 11.2.

In Studies 1 and 2, the personal task does indeed generate higher accuracy than the narrative, but so does the decision task, in each case. It appears, therefore, that while the results are not inconsistent with familiar information leading to greater accuracy, the evidence in support is not strong, since there are alternative routes to achieving greater accuracy of performance. Turning to fluency, the results from Study 1 are supportive of the original hypothesis. The personal task in this case is associated with fewer pauses and greater fluency than the other two tasks. In this case, it does appear that familiar information is associated with less interruption to the speech flow. However, these results are not particularly supported when we look at Study 2. In this case, the personal task produces the *least* fluent performance, with the narrative generating the fewest pauses, and the decision task leading to more fluent performance. Additional analyses were carried out with the planning variable, since it is possible that there might be an interaction with

TABLE 11.2 Familiar Information, Fluency, and Accuracy

		Personal	*Narrative*	*Decision*	*Sig.*
Accuracy	Study 1	0.68	0.62	0.67	0.05
	Study 2	0.66	0.62	0.68	0.01
Fluency	Study 1	14.8	22.2	27.1	0.001
	Study 2	23.1	17.8	21.7	0.04

planning, such that when there is time to prepare, familiar information might be selectively associated with more fluent performance. The results, however, are not supportive of this: the same patterns occur under all planning conditions.

The evidence, therefore, is not strongly supportive of an effect for familiarity of information on either accuracy or fluency. The present results are based on a meta-analysis of studies not intended to make sustained systematic comparisons and so it may be that other correlating variables are obscuring potential relationships. The accuracy achieved from the dialogic decision-making tasks may be a case in point, since, as will be shown below, such tasks independently and consistently generate greater accuracy. The comparison made in Table 11.2 may not therefore be the best one to judge the effects of familiar information on task performance. What we can say, though, is that familiarity does not have such a strong effect on performance that higher accuracy is guaranteed. In other words, the effect seems weaker than was anticipated. Similarly, the effects upon fluency may depend on factors additional to the information itself. In the personal task in Study 2, for example, the need to retrieve information may introduce a strong processing element into performance, such that fluency is disrupted. But this brings us to the point made immediately above: familiar information does not guarantee more attention being available to achieve a higher level of performance.

Dialogic Tasks

Foster and Skehan (2013) propose that interactive tasks are associated with greater accuracy and complexity, but lower fluency. They suggest that such effects are due to:

- *greater accuracy*
  - communication-driven push towards precision
  - "creation" of more time to focus on form, as partner is speaking
  - recycling of partner's language, both with tendency to re-use correct language and to edit and correct it
- greater complexity
  - collective re-interpretation of the task to make it more complex
  - scaffolded elaboration of partner's language
- lower fluency
  - need to accommodate the unpredictability of partner's contributions, i.e. greater need to engage in on-line planning
  - uncertainty of turn-taking, and consequent disruption to fluency

The descriptive statistics for the relevant comparisons are shown in Table 11.3. The comparisons involve:

- *Studies 1 and 2*, where dialogic (decision-making) tasks were contrasted with narrative and personal tasks;
- *Study 6*, where a dialogic (decision-making) task was contrasted with a narrative;
- *Study 5 vs. Studies 1, 2, 3, and 6*, where the comparison was between *different* decision-making tasks, in that Study 5 used a Balloon debate, which was essentially monologic, compared to all other decision-making tasks which were much more interactive in nature.

In the first comparison, for Studies 1 and 2, a one-way within-subjects analysis of variance yields an F value of 5.64, and a significance level of $p < 0.001$. However, the significance is located in the contrast between the narrative task accuracy level of 61% error-free clauses and the decision-making (67%) and personal (68%) tasks. In other words, while the decision-making (dialogic) task yields significantly more accuracy than the narrative task, it is not significantly different from the personal task. The other comparisons, are, however, clearer in their results. In the second comparison, the t-test between the decision-making task (68% accuracy) and narrative tasks (56% accuracy) in Study 6 generates a t-value of 4.14, translating to a significance level of $p < 0.001$. Then, in the third comparison, the between-subjects t-test shows that the more monologic Study 5 decision-making task (61% accuracy), is significantly different from the other (dialogic) decision-making tasks (mean 68% accuracy), with a t-value of 3.56 and a significance value of $p < 0.001$. In a guarded fashion, therefore, and provided other relevant variables do not intrude, it can be claimed that dialogic tasks are associated with fewer errors.

A similar mixed picture emerges with the complexity results. The first comparison, Studies 1 and 2, does generate a significant effect for the dialogic

TABLE 11.3 Accuracy, Complexity, and Fluency on Dialogic vs. Non-Dialogic Tasks

Study	Accuracy (% of error-free clauses)			Complexity (clauses per c-unit)			Fluency (No. pauses per 5 mins.)		
	Decis. making	Nar.	Pers.	Decis. making	Nar.	Pers.	Decis. making	Nar.	Pers.
1 ($N = 32$)	0.67	0.61	0.68	1.32	1.35	1.16	27.1	22.3	14.8
2 ($N = 40$)	0.68	0.62	0.68	1.67	1.31	1.37	21.7	17.8	23.1
3 ($N = 60$)	0.68	–	–	1.41	–	–	22.8	–	–
5 ($N = 66$)	0.61	–	–	1.44	–	–	8.6	–	–
6 ($N = 42$)	0.68	0.56	–	1.47	1.35	–	12.8	10.8	–

decision-making task compared to the narrative and personal tasks ($F = 15.6; p < 0.001$), but this result should be modified in that the complexity mean for Study 1 narrative is actually higher than that for the decision-making task in that study (1.35 vs. 1.32). The second comparison, for Study 6, does produce a clear result. The comparison yields a t-value of 1.84, which is significant at the $p < 0.05$ level (one-tailed test). However, the comparison between the more monologic Study 5 decision-making task and all the other (dialogic) decision-making tasks is not significant. This suggests that, as with the accuracy results, dialogic tasks *tend* to be associated with greater complexity, but this effect is mediated by other factors.

We turn finally to the fluency results. In the first comparison, for Studies 1 and 2, the dialogic task generates less fluency than the other two tasks ($F = 7.93; p < 0.001$). Once again, however, the results are not completely clear-cut, in that the personal task from Study 2 does generate slightly less fluent performance than the dialogic decision-making task from this study. The trend, however, does seem in the direction of lower fluency being associated with interaction. The second comparison, from Study 6, does not yield a significant result ($t = 0.66; p > 0.05$). The third (between-subjects) comparison between the Study 5 decision-making task and all the other decision-making tasks ($t = 8.35; p < 0.001$) is highly significant, with the Study 5 more monologic decision-making task generating much more fluent language than that in the more interactive tasks.

Returning to the rationale for these effects proposed at the beginning of this section, it is clear that the next stage of the research is to return to the transcripts of the different performances to see whether the factors which are proposed to account for the task difference effects can be detected in the actual data. The quantitative results are mixed, and now need to be triangulated from another data source. It is encouraging, though, that the results described here complement those reported in Bygate (2001), especially for complexity and fluency, in relation to the narrative and interactive tasks.

Degree of Structure

Skehan (1998) proposes that this variable has an effect upon the fluency and accuracy of performance. He suggests that tasks which contain clear structure, especially sequential structure, facilitate task performance by clarifying the macro-structure of the speech event. As a result, the lack of need to engage in large-scale planning frees up attentional resources for on-line planning. This additional attention, he proposes, is directed towards the immediate goals of avoidance of error and breakdowns in communicational flow, i.e. accuracy and fluency.

Three tasks, out of the total set used, were identified as containing greater structure. These were the personal task from Study 1 (turn off the oven); the narrative task from Studies 2 and 6 (the Sempé story, i.e. the same task in each study), and the Restaurant task from Study 4. The first source of evidence here comes from within-subjects comparisons from Study 1 where the personal task results can be opposed to those for the other two tasks. Regarding fluency, the within subjects one-way analysis of variance is significant ($F = 16.6; p < 0.001$), with the personal task generating significantly more fluency than the other two tasks. With respect to accuracy, the corresponding analysis also indicates significance ($F = 3.58; p < 0.05$), but the operative contrast is between the personal *and* decision-making tasks, which are significantly more accurate than the narrative. These results provide partial support only therefore.

The findings for the comparison from Study 2 show similar results for fluency, ($F = 4.7; p < 0.04$), with the narrative task (the structured Sempé story) generating significantly fewer pauses than the other two tasks. The results for accuracy from Study 2 are, however, very different. Significance is achieved ($F = 6.2; p < 0.01$), but the significant contrasts are in the reverse direction to those predicted, with the Sempé task associated with *lower* accuracy at 62% error-free clauses. On this occasion, at least, the structured task did not produce greater accuracy. The same two tasks were used in Study 6, where t-tests produced exactly the same results as for Study 2. Fluency was greater in the structured Sempé task, but this difference did not attain statistical significance ($t = 0.66$). Accuracy, however, was clearly greater in the decision-making Agony Aunt task ($t = 4.14; p < 0.001$). No different pattern emerges if these studies are analysed at a greater level of detail by examining the different planning conditions.

The trend towards clearer effects for fluency rather than accuracy is particularly evident in Study 4. Relevant results are shown in Table 11.4.

All the fluency effects shown in Table 11.4 generate significant differences, all beyond the $p < 0.001$ level of significance. It is clear also that when fluency is operationalised in terms of repetition etc.,[4] the structured task generated roughly *half* the amount of disfluency that the unstructured task generated. However, the accuracy effects, although showing a very slight superiority for the structured "restaurant" task, do not remotely approach significance.

We can summarise the results in this section by saying that there is a fairly consistent pattern that tasks based on more structured information seem to be associated with greater fluency. There are some indications that accuracy might also be enhanced, but the evidence is, to say the least, mixed, and so it would be unwise at this stage to make any claims in this direction. If on-line planning and attentional availability are facilitated by structured tasks, these are directed towards fluency.

TABLE 11.4 Structured and Unstructured Narratives

Variable	Golf task (N = 21) (mean)	Restaurant task (N = 24) (mean)
Repetition	39.3	19.1
False starts	29.5	15.5
Reformulations	10.9	4.8
Replacements	8.2	5.2
Accuracy	47%	50%

Complexity of Outcome

This contrast is restricted to the decision-making tasks, and opposes the tasks which are susceptible to minimal interpretation for outcome, enabling low-level negotiation of consensus, (Judge and Balloon), and those which require engagement and careful examination of the different facets of a decision (Agony Aunt). The results in this case are clear cut. Skehan (1998) predicts selectively for complexity here, and the differences found are indeed confined to this area. The relevant data are presented in Table 11.5.

Given that these comparisons are based on large groups (of 82 and 157 participants respectively), they represent powerful evidence that the complexity of task outcome is a major influence upon the complexity of the language which is produced in a task. The less easily the consensus is achieved in a decision-making task, the more participants have to engage in subtler dialogue and the more extending is the language that is likely to be used.

Transformations of Task Material

The one task which required material to be transformed, on-line, was the narrative from Study 1. Skehan (1998) predicts that transformations will be associated with greater complexity, as learners have to wrestle with the need to bring the elements of the task into some sort of meaningful (and non-given) relationship with one another.

When one examines the results from this study, the within-subjects one-way analysis of variance for the complexity scores suggests that there are significant differences, but that the specific contrasts are between the personal task, on the one hand, and both the narrative and decision-making tasks, on the other ($F = 11.3$; $p < 0.001$), with associated mean scores: 1.16, personal, and 1.32 (decision-making), and 1.35 (narrative). This only provides partial support for the hypothesis. However, a more supportive picture emerges if one examines the results when the mean scores for the different planning conditions are examined in more detail. These are shown in Table 11.6.

Comparisons at each of the different levels of planning do not reach statistical significance, but the power of the comparisons is limited by the small sample

TABLE 11.5 Complexity of Outcome and Task Performance

Variable	Mean Score Complex Outcome	Mean Score Simpler Outcome	t-Value	Sig.
Accuracy	0.68	0.65	1.51	0.24
Complexity	1.59	1.41	5.01	0.001
Fluency	17.5	27.7	−0.127	0.90

sizes that result when such fine-grained comparisons are made. What is striking, however, is that the task requiring transformations always generates the highest level of complexity under planning conditions, and that *this advantage grows as the planning condition changes*. In other words, as the planning becomes more directed (Foster & Skehan [1996a] discuss this in terms of the task being interpreted as more challenging) there is an interaction with the complexity measure, such that the task requiring transformation benefits most from this opportunity to plan. In other words, requiring learners to handle tasks requiring transformations immediately does not produce significantly greater complexity. When, though, planning time is given to enable them to respond to the *potential* complexity of the task, they are able to meet the challenge more effectively and the complexity of their language is greater.

Summary of the Task Results

It is easier now to try to summarise the results which have been obtained for each of the characteristics by representing the data in tabular form. The summary is shown in Table 11.7.

TABLE 11.6 Complexity Measures for Tasks Requiring Transformation and Tasks Not Requiring Transformation Under Different Planning Conditions

	Narrative	Personal	Decision-Making
Unplanned	1.22	1.11	1.23
Undetailed planners	1.42	1.16	1.35
Detailed planners	1.68	1.26	1.52

TABLE 11.7 Summary of the Effects of Task Characteristics on Complexity, Accuracy, and Fluency

Task Characteristic	Accuracy	Complexity	Fluency
Familiarity of information	No effect	No effect	Slightly greater
Dialogic vs. monologic tasks	Greater	Slightly greater	Lower
Degree of structure	No effect	No effect	Greater
Complexity of outcome	No effect	Greater	No effect
Transformations	No effect	Planned condition generates greater complexity	No effect

Limitations of the Meta-Analysis

The existence of the six related datasets has enabled analyses to be performed which have the advantage of linking a range of different variables. The generalisations which are then possible can be more wide-ranging in their applicability. But there are serious limitations to this approach. The meta-analysis has had an inevitable opportunistic quality. The six datasets in question are related, since they derive from a common research framework, but they were not *designed* to ensure principled and systematic comparisons between the range of variables involved. Where it is possible to make broader-based but still clear comparisons (e.g. the large samples underlying the *complex outcomes* comparison), the conclusions made can have some force. On occasions, the comparisons have a rather tentative character. For example, the structured tasks are a personal and a narrative, and these from different studies. These tasks then enter into contrasts with a whole range of "non-structured" tasks. Clearly, the designation "structured" was not by original design, but through post hoc analysis. This must inevitably limit the force of the claims which are made. On many other occasions, the variables under investigation can only be partially disentangled. For example, one of the predictions concerned accuracy. Structured tasks were predicted to generate greater accuracy. Hence the (structured) narrative in Study 2 would be predicted to be more accurately done. But it was also proposed that dialogic tasks (which narratives clearly are not) are also associated with greater accuracy. Hence, when the (structured) narrative in Study 2 was compared with the decision-making task from Study 2 (which may have been unstructured, but which was dialogic) it was not possible to make an absolutely clear comparison because of the confound of variables. Other examples of this occur in the data, and clearly would suggest that the insights obtained so far should feed into the design of a more systematic study in the future. Still, the data that exists is all that can be analysed. Provided that the limitations of the dataset are understood, it is possible to draw the sort of tentative conclusions that have been proposed here, and extract some value from them.

Implications for Testing

It is useful now to relate the findings shown in Table 11.7 to the model of oral language assessment presented in Figure 11.1. It was argued earlier that while model components from Figure 11.1 such as underlying competences and rater effects have benefitted from relevant empirical work, components such as interaction conditions, ability for use, and the role of tasks have not. It has been the goal of the present chapter to explore how this situation may be redressed by reviewing what contribution a particular set of research studies into tasks can make.

Recalling that task fulfil an important mediating function which shapes the nature of the performance which will be the basis for the ultimate rating of the candidate score, we can see that the task itself is hardly a constant in this equation. The five task characteristics which have been explored show that systematic (and potentially uncontrolled and undesirable) effects are likely to follow from any task selection decision. In other words, there may be significant consequences when one task is chosen rather than another. Or to spell this out even more directly, if candidate performances are compared after having been elicited through the use of different tasks, the performances themselves may be very difficult to relate to one another. Different candidates, in other words, might be disadvantaged or advantaged by the particular task that they might have taken as part of their test, and so their performance may not be directly comparable to the other candidates.

Take, for example, the case of one candidate who was required to do a dialogic task compared to another candidate who had a narrative based test. The above results suggest that the first candidate may well have been predisposed to achieve higher levels of accuracy and complexity than would otherwise have been the case, but lower fluency. The situation for the candidate taking a narrative test-task is exactly the reverse. The scores assigned these two candidates might then vary spuriously, even if the candidates were of a similar ability level. Public examination bodies are often attracted by narrative formats to assess spoken language since they seem to contain useful standardisation potential: the present conclusions suggest that such an approach might inadvertently introduce another set of dangers.

In slight contrast, consider a situation where one candidate took a test containing clear sequential macrostructure, and another took a task in which transformations of input material were required. Assume further that in both cases there was some time for planning. The above research-based generalisations would lead us to expect an advantage in the first case for greater fluency and in the second, an advantage for complexity. If we relate these outcomes in performance to the rating scales which are used and/or the predispositions of the raters, we can see that there is even further scope for arbitrary score decisions. These may derive from the particular aspects of performance the rating scales and raters prioritise in importance, linked to the tasks which the candidates were required to do. The potential for inaccuracy is therefore magnified.

In short, to require spoken performances which will be the basis for scoring to be based on tasks which vary in the sort of language that they favour may well introduce error into spoken language assessment. Unless we are able to combat this through research-based studies which inform test design decisions, we are likely to treat candidates unfairly. Or to put this another way, there is a strong need for research programmes which explore just how the range of factors which impact upon the scores assigned in spoken language tests operate in systematic ways. Unless this is done, incorrect decisions are likely to be made.

Notes

1 The construct of complexity is close to what testers mean by range, in that both focus on a willingness to use a greater variety of syntactic forms.
2 They figure in other chapters in Bygate et al. (2001), e.g. Bygate, Foster. In this section the focus is away from acquisition and towards measurement issues themselves.
3 All studies were completed with students working in pairs, except for Study 4, where groups of four students were involved.
4 The task required simultaneous retelling of a video-based narrative. For this reason, since the speed of the video tape influenced the performance, it was decided that measures of pausing-based fluency were inappropriate. Hence the use of alternative measures.

12
MODELS OF SPEAKING AND THE ASSESSMENT OF SECOND LANGUAGE PROFICIENCY

Introduction

Within applied linguistics, the assessment of oral second language proficiency has been explored in a way which is surprisingly detached from developments in a range of related areas, including second language acquisition, psycholinguistics, and our understanding of what is involved in the speaking process. It is the purpose of this article to explore the relevance for such proficiency assessment of theory in the area of first (and second) language speaking, and empirical findings in task-based performance. It will be argued that these two ancillary areas have much to contribute to how we design and evaluate oral assessment procedures.

Models of Speaking

The dominant model of first language speaking is that of Levelt (1989, 1999); Kormos (2006). This model proposes that there are three general stages in speech production, as shown in Table 12.1.

The first stage, Conceptualisation, is concerned with developing and organising ideas to be expressed, in a particular situation, and with a particular emphasis and stance. The second stage, Formulation, involves lexical selections to match the pre-verbal message, triggering lemma retrieval from the mental lexicon, and then

---

Originally published as: Skehan, P. (2009c). Models of speaking and the assessment of second language proficiency. In A. G. Benati (Ed.), *Issues in Second Language Proficiency* (pp. 202–215). London: Continuum. Reproduced by permission of Bloomsbury Publishing Plc.

TABLE 12.1 The Levelt Model of First Language Speech Production

Conceptualisation (Message Level of Representation)
- involves determining what to say;
- speaker conceives an intention and adopts a stance;
- speaker selects relevant information in preparation for construction of an intended utterance;
- the product is a pre-verbal message.

Formulation
- involves translating the conceptual representation into a linguistic form;
- includes the process of lexicalisation, where words that the speaker wants to say are selected;
- includes the process of syntactic planning where words are put together to form a sentence;
- involves detailed phonetic and articulatory planning;
- includes the process of phonological encoding, where words are turned into sounds.

Articulation
- involves retrieval of chunks of internal speech from buffer;
- involves motor execution.

syntax building from the information retrieved through this retrieval. The third stage is concerned with transforming this form of representation of ideas, lexis, and syntax into actual speech.

Fairly obviously, if we are dealing with native language speech, certain assumptions are made. Most central for present purposes is that the Conceptualiser delivers challenges to the Formulator which the Formulator is able to meet, since the driving force for its operation is the mental lexicon, which is extensive, well-organised, and contains rich entries, with semantic, syntactic, collocational, and phonological information. It is the capacity to retrieve such rich information very quickly that enables speech production to be so smooth, without requiring consciousness, and with parallel operations. The Conceptualiser can be working on one stage of operation, while the Formulator is dealing simultaneously with previous Conceptualiser operations, as language is being assembled, just as the Articulator can be working on previous Formulator operations.

When we turn to second language speaking, things are very different. The 'driver' for the Levelt model is the mental lexicon, which is the repository of considerable information about each lemma, information which underpins the production of native language speech in real time. With second language speakers, this mental lexicon is:

- smaller, so that many lemmas required by the pre-verbal message, will not be available
- incomplete, so that where many lemmas are part of the mental lexicon, they are only partially represented, so that for example, limited semantic information may be available, or limited syntactic implication information is available, or no collocational information, etc.;

- less organised, so that connections between lemmas do not prime one another, or alternative forms of expression are less available;
- less redundantly structured, in that collocational chunks are less available, so that speech production has to be done more often 'from first principles' on the basis of rule-generated language.

The result of all these omissions is that during speech production, the pre-verbal message, however impressive, encounters considerable difficulty at the Formulator stage. The smooth process of speech production is disrupted, as second language speakers have to try to find alternative methods of expressing their meanings, or to find ways of using the resources that they have sufficiently quickly so that 'normal' communication can proceed. This is likely to present serious difficulties for the modular, parallel operation of the Levelt model, so that some of the time, this ideal set of interlocking processes is severely impaired.

Task Research

The preceding discussion has been general, and data-free. It has assumed that second language speakers, of different proficiency levels, will encounter difficulties, and that it is meaningful to express these difficulties in terms of the Levelt Model. What is necessary to take the discussion further is some empirical method of characterising difficulty. To this end, we will next review findings from the literature on task-based performance. This literature provides a wide range of generalisations regarding the way task characteristics and the conditions under which tasks are done might have an impact on different aspects of second language performance. These findings can take us beyond the programmatic statements in the previous section.

Broadly, the task findings can be portrayed in terms of the information that tasks are based on, the operations that tasks require to be performed on this information, and the conditions under which tasks are done. These three headings organise the findings which have emerged in the task literature. Regarding information, we can say that:

- the scale of the information (e.g. the number of elements, the number of participants) has an impact on performance, with more information leading to performance that is more complex (Michel, Kuiken, & Vedder, 2007a);
- the type of information has a strong influence, with concrete information being easier to handle than abstract information which in turn is easier to handle than dynamic information (Brown, Anderson, Shilcock, & Yule, 1984), and also with there being a tendency for concrete information to advantage fluency and accuracy in performance;
- greater familiarity with the information is associated with higher levels of accuracy and fluency (Foster & Skehan, 1996a);
- greater organisation and structure in the task information leads to performance which is also more accurate and more fluent (Tavakoli & Skehan, 2005).

There are interesting theoretical issues which relate to this range of findings. For now, we will simply say that these are a set of empirically based generalisations which have relevance for any development of a model of second language spoken performance. In any case, we move on to consider the operations which are carried out on the information in tasks. Here another set of generalisations can be offered, contrasting simple and complex operations. Simple operations, e.g. listing, enumerating (Willis & Willis, 2007), or retrieving (Foster & Skehan, 1996a), or simply describing are associated with higher fluency and accuracy in performance. In contrast, more demanding operations on information, such as sequencing (Willis & Willis, 2007), or reorganising (Foster & Skehan, 1996a), or integrating information (Tavakoli & Skehan, 2005), or reasoning (Robinson, 2001b; Robinson & Gilabert, 2007) are associated with greater language complexity. As these different influences suggest, there is something of a contrast here between the performance areas of complexity, on the one hand, and accuracy and fluency, on the other. Complex operations seem to drive greater language complexity, while simpler operations are more likely to be associated with higher fluency and accuracy.

The final area to consider here is the conditions under which tasks are done. This has provoked considerable research effort. Robinson (2001b) reports higher levels of accuracy in his there-and-then condition, i.e. input absence, contrasted to a here-and-now condition (input presence). A whole series of studies has examined the effect of pre-task planning on performance. The results suggest that such planning is consistently associated with greater complexity and fluency, with these generating sizable effects, while accuracy is generally advantageous, but not to the same degree (Ellis, 2009; Foster & Skehan, 1999a). Yuan and Ellis (2003) have reported that opportunity for on-line planning, i.e. more relaxed time conditions during performance, are associated with greater accuracy. Skehan and Foster (1997, submitted) have proposed that requiring second language speakers to do post-tasks which emphasise language form leads selectively to increases in accuracy. Finally, Skehan (in press) proposes that tasks which contain unavoidable and more difficult lexis are associated with lower levels of accuracy and complexity.

Applying the Levelt Model

The generalisations about second language task-based performance provide the basis for examining the relevance of the Levelt model in accounting for the second language case. An initial assessment would suggest that it has to be applicable. Essentially, the model proposes that thought precedes language, and that the functioning of the model is essentially concerned with how Formulator operations, and associated resources, such as the mental lexicon, can enable the thoughts embodied in the pre-verbal message to be expressed through externalised language. One is drawn into saying that anything other than this would not be satisfactory on general, logical grounds. Communication requires ideas, and the ideas, if they are to be transmitted effectively, require language.

The difficulty, of course, is that first language speakers are able to function in this way because they have mental lexicons which are extensive, elaborate, analysed, and accessible. Pre-verbal message demands can therefore be met, and ongoing speaking in real time is possible. In particular, the different modules within the Levelt model can function in parallel, i.e. the Conceptualiser may be working on the next pre-verbal message, while the Formulator is working on the current one, even while the Articulator is giving voice to the previous. This is possible because the different modules can handle the demands which are placed upon them in real time, and smoothly, such that successive cycles of communication proceed, if not totally effortlessly, at least fairly so.

Problems occur when a second language speaker attempts the same ideas-to-language mapping, but is equipped with a much more limited mental lexicon. The result is, as Kormos (2006) argues, that parallel processing below the level of consciousness is replaced by serial, effortful, and conscious attempts to deal with pre-verbal message demands on the mental lexicon—demands which are either beyond it, or which require considerably greater allocation of attention. Messages may then be assembled slowly, or communication strategies used, or messages may be modified or even abandoned (Faerch & Kasper, 1983). This is turn brings us back to the question of the applicability of the model. What is argued here is that the model is still relevant (for the general reasons proposed earlier), but that it is inappropriate to regard the model as an 'all or none' affair. The generalisations from the previous section show that performance is systematically influenced by a range of information, operation, and condition influences, and that these impact upon complexity, accuracy, and fluency aspects of performance. Broadly, it is argued that what we have learned from this research is the conditions which facilitate the relevance of the Levelt model and those that do not. So the question needs to be recast so that we explore not whether there is a simple positive or negative answer to applicability, but rather the influences which make the model a more useful explanatory account and those which suggest that its potential for second language speakers is limited.

So far, in reviewing empirical work, we have presented research in the terms which are typical for task-based performance, distinguishing between information, operations, and conditions, as independent variables, and complexity, accuracy, and fluency, as the dependent variables. To examine the relevance of the Levelt model, though, it is necessary to consider an alternative perspective, and to organise the findings which have reviewed in a way more consistent with the model, and transparent in terms of its functioning. This is shown in Table 12.2.

Two introductory points are helpful here. First, the table is organised around the central 'spine' which shows the relevant stages of the Levelt model. There is a section which focusses on the Conceptualiser, and then a separation between

TABLE 12.2 The Levelt Model and Task Performance

Complexifying/Pressuring	Levelt Model Stage	Easing/Focussing
• planning: extending • complex cog. operations • complex info. type • infrequent lexis • non-negotiable task • time pressure • heavy input pressure • monologic	*Conceptualiser* *Formulator: Lemma retrieval* *Formulator: Syntactic encoding*	• concrete, static information • less information • easier cog. operations • planning: organising • dialogic • planning: rehearsing • structured tasks • dialogic • post-task condition

the two Formulator stages of lemma retrieval (and access to the mental lexicon) and syntactic encoding (which is driven by the information made available when lemmas are accessed). These three stages organise the presentation of the information from the task-based performance literature. Second, the outer columns are concerned with four general influences on performance, two which indicate difficulty (complexifying, pressuring) and two which are more focussed on achievement (easing, focussing).

Complexifying focusses on performance influences which make the message to be expressed more demanding, elaborate, or extensive. These influences are mostly relevant for Conceptualiser operations. Pressuring concerns influences which make performance more difficult, but are not connected with differences in the complexity of the message. In contrast, they are concerned with the time under which a task is done, or the amount or nature or inflexibility of the material which is involved. Easing is, in a sense, the reverse of Complexifying, and entails the ways in which the pre-verbal message can be arrived at in a more direct manner. Finally Focussing (which is not the reverse of Pressuring), concerns the way in which performance conditions themselves introduce some level of Focus-on-Form, thereby privileging performance areas such as accuracy and complexity. This framework is useful for re-presenting the results from the task literature in ways which bring out more clearly how the findings we have can illustrate the differing degrees of applicability of the Levelt model to the second language speaker case. We will explore each of them in more detail.

There are three clear influences on Complexifying. The first involves planning. At the outset, it needs to be said that planning appears more than once in Table 12.2, reflecting the different things that can happen during planning. Here the facet of planning time which is focussed on is when preparation is associated with making the ideas in a task more complex than they otherwise would be. It is clear (Skehan & Foster, 1999; Ortega, 2005; Skehan & Pang, 2008) that this happens some of the time. Speakers use planning time to explore the ideas in a task, and consequently approach the task as more challenging than it otherwise would be. For example, in an Agony Aunt task, planning may be used to generate more complex advice to the writer of a problem letter, or in a narrative it could be used to develop the connections in a picture story series.

A second influence here could be the more complex operations which a task inherently requires if it is to be completed properly. These might be to reorganise the input which is provided, e.g. Foster and Skehan's (1996a) narrative task, where a story had to be invented from a series of pictures, rather than a pre-existing storyline simply narrated. Or there might be the need to integrate information to tell a story effectively, as in Tavakoli and Skehan's (2005) task where background and foreground elements had to be connected to one another. There might also be a greater need to use reasoning, as in Michel et al.'s task (2007c) involving selection of a cell phone where there are many features which influence the eventual decision.

The third kind of influence concerns the type of information which is involved. Brown et al. (1984) showed that dynamic information, e.g. relating to a changing scene, is more difficult to deal with abstract information, which in turn is more difficult to deal with than static information. It seems that the greater difficulty in dealing with such information types is more demanding of memory resources, and where there are also more complex operations involved, this adds to task complexity. It is assumed that all three influences here concern the Conceptualiser stage of speech production, and the nature of the cognitive activity implicated in producing the pre-verbal message.

We turn next to a series of influences which increase the pressure on the operation of the Formulator stage. Regarding the lemma retrieval stage, the first influence is the infrequency of the lexis which is involved in a task. It appears that when less frequent lexis is required, this has damaging implications for the complexity and accuracy of the language which is produced (Skehan, in press). This contrasts with native speaker performance, where lexical infrequency is positively correlated with language complexity—less standard lemmas seem to drive more complex syntax in a harmonious way. So tasks which push learners to need more difficult lexis seem to give them lemma retrieval problems which spill over, because of their attentional demands, into other aspects of performance. Lemmas are retrieved slowly and imperfectly, and the additional effort required for this disrupts the parallel processing of the material for speaking.

Similarly, non-negotiable tasks (Skehan & Foster, 2007) also cause pressure. Native speakers, when generating language, are able to draw upon a range of alternative choices relatively effortlessly. So during speech production they can make a range of selections as they are producing an utterance (Pawley & Syder, 1983). Non-native speakers do not have the luxury of such choices, and as a result are less able to adapt if a first lexical or syntactic choice is unavailable in the mental lexicon. Where tasks are negotiable, such speakers can adapt and revise the pre-verbal message so that it meshes more easily with resources which are available. When tasks are non-negotiable, however, as with narratives where the input is given, this is not possible, and disruption of performance results.

These two pressure-inducing factors are concerned with the nature of the meanings that are required for a task. The remaining pressuring influences are, in one way or another, simply associated with time. Most obviously, requiring tasks to be done under timed conditions is going to add to the speaker's problems. Ellis (2005b) has reviewed these studies and shown that on-line planning is a possibility when time pressure conditions are relaxed, with the result that greater accuracy is obtained. When there is greater time pressure, in contrast, the result is that accuracy is lowered. But a related issue concerns whether a task is monologic or dialogic. Monologic tasks are consistently more difficult (with lower accuracy, and sometimes, lower complexity; Skehan & Foster, 2007). What seems to happen here is that the speaker, being responsible for keeping the discourse going, has to plan, execute, monitor, and continue speaking without any respite. The result is performance is lowered, because on-line planning opportunities are less frequent. In contrast, a more dialogic condition does enable one speaker to have a break while interlocutors are speaking. As long as the other speakers' contributions are processed sufficiently, there may be spare capacity available while listening to enable a speaker to plan upcoming conversational contributions, as well as potentially use something said by interlocutors if it is appropriate to his or her own contribution. Monologic tasks do not give any easy natural breaks. Dialogic tasks do and so reduce the pressure, overall (Skehan, in press).

We turn next to factors which ease performance. Some of these can simply be dealt with as the reverse of the effects we have already covered on complexifying or pressuring. For example, regarding information, we can say that tasks based on concrete, static information (Foster & Skehan, 1996a); tasks involving less information (Brown et al., 1984); and tasks which require simpler operations, such as listing (Willis & Willis, 2007), are likely to be easier, and as a result, Formulator-based aspects of performance (accuracy, fluency) are likely to be raised. Similarly, task conditions which reduce pressure, such as a dialogic task, also make the task easier, as more time is available to plan on-line. But there are other influences which are not mirror images of what has been said before. For example, planning figures here, but now in different ways. If planning is directed to organising what will be said, actual performance is eased (Pang & Skehan, 2008). The planning, effectively, handles the wider plan of what will be said, so that during actual performance, major ideas do not have to be developed and the speaker can focus on the surface of language. Similarly, if a task is structured (Tavakoli & Skehan, 2005), speakers are more likely to be able to exploit the macrostructure of the task, and not need to engage in deeper planning. They too can focus on the surface, and are able to mobilise Formulator resources more effectively, and thereby achieve higher levels of accuracy and fluency. Returning to planning, in addition to the functions of extending ideas, which complexifies, and organising, which eases, planning may be directed to rehearsing language for actual performance (Ortega, 2005). This too eases, but on the assumption that what is rehearsed is both remembered and is actually useful during performance. If these conditions are met, the result is that performance is eased.

So far, we have been looking at the interplay of ideas and their realisation through language. Following much of the task literature, we have conceptualised performance in terms of language complexity, accuracy, and fluency, and have tacitly assumed in information-processing perspective based on limited attentional resources. So the assumption has been that speakers have limited capacities, and that task difficulty, as well as eased performance conditions, influence performance priorities (Skehan, 1998). Performance, in this view, is a reflex of other influences. But there are also studies which suggest that second language speakers, with their limited attentional capacities, may choose to prioritise particular performance areas. We have seen this slightly with the way planning time can be directed towards rehearsal, where speakers use the preparation time in order to be ready with specific language, and as a result target accuracy, or sometimes, particularly complex structures. But there are other ways in which the same selective effect can occur, always with a focus on some aspect of form, either directed towards accuracy or complexity. We have already seen how interactive tasks can help speakers since they provide on-line planning opportunities (Foster & Skehan, 1996a; Skehan & Foster, 1997). But the effects of such tasks may be wider. Dialogic tasks make salient the existence of an interlocutor, and it may be that speakers increase their focus on accuracy precisely because they want to be understood and try to avoid misunderstandings by selectively attending to accuracy and avoiding error (Pang & Skehan, 2008). In this way, they prioritise attentional focus through awareness of their interlocutor's comprehension needs.

These claims, though, are based on interpretations of research studies with different research foci. Two studies, though, specifically examine how speakers may have the capacity to prioritise particular performance areas. Skehan and Foster (1997) showed that using a post-task condition (requiring speakers, post-task, to engage in a public performance) led to higher levels of accuracy on a decision-making task (although not on narrative or personal information exchange tasks). It had been hypothesised that foreknowledge of this post-task condition would lead learners to selectively prioritise accuracy during their task performance. Subsequently, Foster and Skehan (submitted 2009) used a different post-task condition, hypothesised to be stronger. They required learners to transcribe 1 minute of their task performance, a more personally relevant and language-focussed condition, and hypothesised that this would have a stronger effect specifically on accuracy. This prediction was borne out, not only for a decision-making task, as in Skehan and Foster (1997) but also for a narrative task. In addition, for the decision-making task, complexity, too, was also significantly raised. These results suggest that effective task conditions can lead speakers to focus on particular aspects of performance, despite the attentional limitations which prevail.

Task Research and Proficiency Assessment

The analysis and review of research presented so far suggests that attentional limitations are vital in understanding performance on second language tasks and that one can categorise the range of different influences as follows:

- Complexification, in that factors such as extension planning, information type and operations upon information push speakers to express more complex ideas. This set of influences impacts on Levelt's Conceptualiser stage.
- Easing, with factors such as the reverse of the last set and which therefore simply reduce the work the Conceptualiser has to do, coupled with other factors, e.g. organising or rehearsal planning, dialogic conditions, or structured tasks which give speakers clear macrostructure for what they want to say, or provide more on-line planning opportunities. The consequence in all these cases is that Formulator operations are eased.
- Pressuring, where input conditions or performance conditions mean that speakers have less opportunity to regroup while speaking, and are deprived of on-line planning opportunities. This too is a Formulator influence.
- Focussing, where selective aspects of performance are privileged, and so a focus-on-form is injected into task performance so that attention is directed in particular ways, towards accuracy or complexity. Once again this is a Formulator influence.

These are a set of factors which influence what is going to be said and how it is going to be said. What is central to this analysis is the balance between Conceptualiser pressure (or lack of it) and Formulator pressure (or lack of it), and how these two sets of pressures work themselves out during ongoing performance. Complexification gives a limited attentional system more things to do, depriving other areas of resources. Easing has the reverse effect, where ideas are manipulable or packageable more easily, thus releasing attention for use in other aspects of speech performance. Pressuring has the general effect of depriving all other areas of performance of time that would be useful. Finally, Focussing operates differently in that it prioritises attention allocation, whatever is going on elsewhere.

We now need to switch and try to consider how this analysis might have relevance for the assessment of second language spoken proficiency. Here it is useful initially to revisit some of the basics of language testing—that testing concerns the ways we use the information elicited through tests in order to sample, to make judgements, and to generalise about real-world performance. One approach to doing these things is to provide learners with tasks to do, of increasing levels of difficulty, and then observe what is the maximum level of difficulty that can be successfully handled. (This is like treating language proficiency as similar to a weightlifting contest.) This approach makes the unidimensionality assumption—that increasing proficiency means getting better along only one dimensions (as when the bar gets heavier in weightlifting). Sampling, in this view, means assessing learners along this one-dimensional scale of difficulty. But it can be argued that anything interesting enough to be worth measuring is likely to be multi-dimensional (Skehan, 1984), with the result that sampling has to be directed at probing the different dimensions that are important (whatever they may be) and then decisions have to be made about how strengths and weaknesses in performance across these dimensions can be combined to yield an overall judgement of proficiency.

The major insight from the analysis presented in this chapter is that for spoken language performance we have to analyse test tasks first in terms of the influences covered in Table 12.2, and particularly in terms of the demands they make on Conceptualiser and Formulator stages in speaking respectively. What influences the Conceptualiser appears to be different from what influences the Formulator and so Conceptualiser difficulty is not the same as Formulator difficulty. In a sense, it is what the Conceptualiser does that shapes the overall difficulty of the ideas which are expressed in a task, and the influences on the Formulator are then constrained by challenges set by the Conceptualiser, although this stage too is affected by a range of influences. The problem is essentially one of sampling, and what the above analysis does is clarify the basis on which sampling needs to take place. It is a truism of testing that one-item tests are non-functional, and so if we apply this to the assessment of spoken language performance, this means that a series of tasks will be necessary for any effective assessment to be made. The matrix in Table 12.2 helps clarify how a range of tasks and a range of performance conditions can be sampled as the basis for language testing. Different Conceptualiser influences and different Formulator influences need to be drawn on if any rounded estimate of ability for use is to be provided.

This approach interacts with how performance itself is measured (Pollitt, 1991). Language use, being complex and multi-dimensional, is not susceptible to simple counting. There needs to be a more complex rating of performance, and this in turn means that one has to decide what areas of performance should be represented in the different rating scales which are used. We have seen that Conceptualiser work is reflected in language complexity, and so this aspect of performance requires valid and reliable rating in what is often termed Range in language assessment, i.e. use of syntax and vocabulary. But Formulator activity is associated with greater fluency and accuracy, other areas where rating scales exist, with precisely these headings. In other words, a Leveltian analysis of performance suggests that we need separate ratings of language complexity (range), accuracy, and fluency if we are to obtain any satisfactory overall assessment of the quality of a second language speaker's performance. Only with such information will we be able to make effective predictions about how second language speakers will use language in the real world.

13
REFLECTIONS ON ASSESSMENT

Introduction

The 2001 chapter, looking back, made three main contributions. First, it brought out clearly that using tasks in assessment is not neutral. Although, when tasks are used, the outcome will be a judgement, a rating, which might take account of the task that has been set, and accommodate to it, essentially the central point is that performance may be partly dependent on the choice of task and the choice of task conditions. Tasks do not considerately hold up language for display in automatically useful ways. Task and condition choices potentially intrude. The result of this is that comparing performance across two task-based tests becomes complicated, and potentially unfair. What the rater has to work with, the language generated by the task, or the task outcome, may not provide a comparable baseline to other performances. The second point is simply that it follows therefore that task research is relevant to testing and assessment, and the findings from the task literature need to be taken seriously by testers. The focus for task researchers may be performance and acquisition, but the implications spill over into assessment. The third point is that *ability for use* needs to be a central construct in task-based performance and assessment. A task-based approach has no problem with underlying competences being important in actual performance (and even that measurement of such underlying competences can be relevant to predicting task-based performance to some extent). But the 2001 chapter argued that the manner by which such underlying competences are mobilised into actual performance is an additional and distinct area and worthy of study. There may be systematicities, in other words, as to how particular second language speakers might differently exploit very similar underlying competences, with the result that their performances might be distinctly different from one another. The capacity to mobilise competences for performance (across different tasks and different task conditions), and to solve communication problems, is what is implicated in ability for use.

I feel that these three points still have importance, and the 2009 chapter was essentially a progress report on what had been achieved in addressing them. It concentrated on bringing out the ways that task-based research had made contributions which were relevant for assessment, and so drew on the task research literature, as it explored CALF measures, and clarified the ways tasks and task conditions mean that using a task-based approach to assessment is not neutral. But it did two additional things. First, it organised the research in terms of the Levelt model, distinguishing between Conceptualisation, and Formulation, and in the latter stage distinguishing between lemma retrieval and then syntax building. In this way, it tried to provide a psycholinguistic basis for looking at speech production, and so this was an attempt to introduce mainstream theory into characterising ability for use. Second, the chapter attempted to categorise the different influences in ways that might be relevant for assessment. Hence the terms complexifying, easing, pressuring, and focussing. These four categories emerge reasonably naturally from the task literature. But they also have relevance to testing. Complexifying, clearly, is concerned with influences which make a task more involved and demanding, probably because more thinking and memory operations are required, or because little support is provided. Easing, conversely, is concerned with the opposite—making a task less demanding of thinking and memory, either because there are fewer steps, or the information is easier to deal with or more accessible, or because support materials are available. Pressuring is concerned with performance conditions, such as the amount of information integral to the task or the speed at which input is received, or output is expected. Finally, focussing is where the task or the conditions push speakers to prioritise particular performance areas. Most typically, this would be accuracy (and this is closest to the task literature findings), but it could involve the other performance areas of complexity (structural or lexical) or fluency.

As the two chapters themselves have explained, testing consists of sampling behaviour so that decisions can be made about language ability, decisions which are essentially the basis for generalisations as to how language will be used in a range of real-world situations. The sampling then needs to be done in the most efficient, reliable, and valid way to enable such generalisations to be made. Testing time is almost always limited, and so needs to be used as efficiently as possible. To sample narrowly compromises and limits the generalisations that can be made. But to sample excessively may go beyond the bounds of what is feasible in terms of resources for assessment.

What the analysis in terms of complexifying, pressuring, easing, and focussing does, essentially, is provide a framework for the sampling that might take place within assessment. Implicit in this is the claim that sampling with one task under one set of conditions cannot be sufficient. To do so would risk an inadequate database which cannot sustain generalisations which might be made. The question then concerns how much data collection, i.e. testing, needs to take place to form an effective basis for decision-making and generalisation. In other words, we need to build into a communicative, task-based assessment battery some variation in:

- degree of complexity;
- factors which lead to greater pressure;
- factors which ease performance;
- any factors which push learners to use language of a particular sort.

On this basis we could design tests which gather more robust information which could then be used to make decisions about level of language ability.

Current Models of Language Assessment

Of interest now is to consider how these proposals relate to existing models of spoken language assessment. As we will see, the three approaches to be considered here all wrestle with the problem of relating underlying competences to actual performance. First of these, historically, is the Canale and Swain (1980) approach. Originally it was portrayed as having a three-competence structure for communicative competence (linguistic, sociolinguistic, and strategic) and then Canale (1983) reconfigured the framework as linguistic, sociolinguistic, *discourse*, and strategic competences (although this extension is not the major issue here). The important aspect is the functioning of strategic competence. While the other competences were indeed competences, and underlying in nature, strategic competence, in contrast, had an action element, and was intended to come into play when the other competences were lacking. So there was simultaneously a competence element (representing a basic underlying set of things which were typically done when problems were encountered) as well as a capacity for action when communication was taking place and needed some level of improvisation. (There were even possibilities that use of such a strategic competence could be the basis for development and acquisition.) However, this conceptualisation of strategic competence, while important and a significant step forward, was still limited, since it was not implicated in what might be termed 'normal' communication, but instead reserved for what people did, 'on the fly' when problems were encountered.

A more elaborate attempt to account for underlying competences *and* actual language use is represented in Lyle Bachman's work (1990; Bachman & Palmer, 1996). First of all he reorganised underlying competences (his Language Competence) into Organisational Competence (basically underlying linguistic competences, in morphosyntax, lexis, and phonology) and Pragmatic Competence (discourse and sociolinguistic competence from Canale [1983]). Given that this was partly motivated by empirical considerations, this was a significant change.

Even more important, though, is the reanalysis and repositioning of strategic competence. In the Bachman model, this is now central to communication, and not restricted to being problem-oriented or connected with improvisation. It is seen more as a marshalling competence, which draws upon Language Competence, and also Topical Knowledge, Personal Characteristics, and Affective Schemata, and then is organised into three metacognitive processes of Goal Setting (deciding what needs to be, or should be said), Assessment (searching for and gathering relevant resources), and Planning (integrating the various sources of relevant information). This viewpoint has the considerable strengths that it incorporates a clear place for language knowledge, and it then, effectively, provides an account of ability for use, as strategic competence draws upon other areas to actually communicate. As we will see below, there are ways in which it is consistent with the Leveltian approach taken here, while providing detail about an area which is weaker in the present approach—which underlying competences we need to be concerned with.

The final model of language performance to be considered is that of Hulstijn (2015). This model proposes two distinctions, first between what are termed Basic and Higher Language Cognition, and the second between Core and Periphery. Basic Language Cognition concerns language abilities which are shared by all the native speakers of a language, and represents a generalised knowledge store (of lexis, morphosyntax, phonology, etc.). These are achieved simply by maturation, and exposure to input, within the ages defined by critical period studies. Higher Language Cognition concerns language knowledge and capacity for use which are not guaranteed in any native speaker population but which are dependent on particular exposure to language, integrally connected with education, and likely associated with greater cognitive ability. This second distinction, interesting though it is, does not concern us here. More relevant is Hulstijn's distinction between Core and Periphery. The Core overlaps considerably with Basic Language Cognition, but is not exactly the same. As Hulstijn puts it, it concerns:

- Linguistic cognition (knowledge and speed) in the phonetic-phonological, morpho-phonological, morpho-syntactic, and lexical/pragmatic domains, and includes pragmatic knowledge, sociolinguistic knowledge, and knowledge of discourse organisation.

Complementing the Core is the Periphery, and this contains (at least):

- interactional ability;
- strategic competences: how to perform under adverse conditions, e.g. time constraints, and also with limited linguistic knowledge;
- metalinguistic knowledge: explicit knowledge of grammar;
- knowledge of the characteristics of various types of oral and written discourse.

The Core-Periphery distinction brings us much closer to the proposals from Canale and Swain (1980) and Bachman (1990). Linguistic cognition, first of all, seems reasonably close to the framework of competences that each of these proposes, except that it also includes speed (something we will return to), possibly reflecting Hulstijn's interest in usage-based accounts of language development and use. Then his notion of what is included in the periphery essentially subsumes and extends what is included in the earlier formulations, and brings a greater level of precision. Interestingly, though, strategic competence does not seem to involve the 'normality' of Bachman's formulation, but instead retains Canale and Swain's improvising, dealing-with-problems character and extends it to include dealing with time pressure.

We see, then, that each of the proposals (Canale and Swain, Bachman, Hulstijn) are based on a competence-organised substrate and then abilities related to action, to converting the underlying substrate into actual speech. The competence proposals that each proposal makes are not identical, but they do have a great deal in common. There are competences for linguistic elements, and a concern for discourse and sociolinguistic competences. So there is a commitment in all cases to underlying and generalisable competences which, one assumes, are drawn on in communication and are foundational. Hulstijn's inclusion of speed is the one thing that stands out as qualitatively different in these different accounts.

But then all three approaches also provide components which are concerned with translating these underlying competences into actual performance and communication. Canale and Swain (1980) have strategic competence, and this consists of the underlying and generalised resourcefulness skills which will enable the solution of problems in actual performance. It is problem-oriented, in other words. Bachman (1990) is far more general in how he characterises strategic competence. It is distinct from the other competences in positioning within the model, even having a role in marshalling these other competences in 'normal' communication, and includes other knowledge sources (about the world) and the processes of Assessment, Goal Setting, and Planning, with these relevant for all ongoing communication. Hulstijn is broader and more detailed about the components of his periphery. Only one part of this may be labelled strategic competence, but the periphery more generally does have resemblances to the two other proposals. Interactional ability figures (and for Hulstijn speech is primary, since most aspects of literacy are covered in his Higher Language Cognition analysis), and so, I find slightly curiously, *knowledge* of various types of oral and *written* discourse (italics added). In addition there is metalinguistic knowledge.

But if we ignore the differences, the common features to Canale and Swain, Bachman, and Hulstijn, are:

- underlying competences;
- factors which influence how these competences respond to communication demands and are used, in turn, in communication.

Looking at things this way means that any attempt to assess language needs to have methods of assessing underlying competences *and* methods of assessing the activation/use factors. The interest then switches to how these challenges are met within testing procedures, and going along with this, how they are met for proficiency testing, achievement testing, and diagnostic testing.

If we focus on Bachman's approach (since it is well established, influential, and clear), this means having (a) some methods of sampling linguistic competence, including language competence (morphosyntax, lexis) and organisational competence (discourse, sociolinguistic), and then (b) methods of sampling what happens in the operation of strategic competence—effectiveness of accessing relevant knowledge, and of the processes of assessment, goal setting, and planning. Possibly for the first of these, sampling competences, the challenge is clearer (since there is some degree of precision in the characterisation of these competences) and so the content area is more well-defined. In addition, the testing methods and formats are more well established, since item-based testing is more feasible and the heavy artillery of traditional test analysis is available. Construct validity, content validity, statistical analysis are all likely to make contributions. For the latter, mobilising competences in actual communication, the course of action is considerably murkier. It is not particularly clear what should be tested, how content and construct validity can be established, and how data could be analysed. Sampling, in other words, has much less of a clear framework to guide it. Perhaps, then, this is the area where a task-based approach to testing has most to contribute.

The Relevance of Task Research

Task research is relevant to testing and assessment in at least four ways. In this section, by far the longest in the chapter, we will consider, first, the general findings that have emerged from task research, second, the relevance of a Leveltian analysis as this potentially relates to the models we have considered of the competence-performance relationship, third, the knotty issue of task difficulty, and fourth, how the measurement dimensions of task research have something to contribute to assessment, especially regarding the rating of performance. In all cases we will be drawing on the earlier chapters in the book.

Task Research Findings

If assessment is to proceed effectively, and address the challenge common to all testing of sampling behaviour in a systematic, valid and reliable way so that effective generalisations and decisions can be made, then the basis of sampling has to be clarified and defended. When one is dealing with competence-oriented linguistic assessment, this may be a lot easier, since item-based formats may be used, and a relatively large number of items included to achieve breadth of sampling. The situation with performance and task-based testing is rather different. The 'space' which needs to be sampled is much less clear, and in addition, gathering data is much more time-consuming since, by definition, such assessment needs to give test takers something worthwhile to do, and this is likely, in the form of test tasks, to require time. How much sampling can then be done with different items (or tasks) becomes a greater challenge.

In earlier sections of this book I have covered findings in the task research literature, and also developed the argument that while task characteristics have delivered some important and interesting results, the impact of tasks has been overshadowed somewhat by the consistency and strength of the findings of task condition research. Even so, both task characteristics and task conditions are relevant to testing. A very brief overview of tasks, task conditions, and their effects is provided in Tables 13.1 and 13.2.

TABLE 13.1 Summary of Task and Task Condition Effects on Performance

Task structure	• Greater accuracy, fluency
	• Sometimes (depending on the structure) greater complexity (subordination) or lower complexity (words per clause)
Information type Familiarity	• Concrete information raises accuracy, fluency
	• Familiar information raises lexis, and sometimes accuracy, fluency
Reasoning operations	• Generally raises complexity
- causal	• Sometimes raises accuracy
- spatial	• Sometimes reduces fluency
- transformative	
Monologic vs. dialogic	• Dialogic, if there is engagement, raises complexity and accuracy, but may lower fluency
Non-negotiability	• Lowers fluency and accuracy

TABLE 13.2 Summary of Task Condition Effects on Performance

Strategic planning	• Raises complexity and fluency consistently
	• Less consistently raises accuracy
On-line planning	• Raises all aspects of performance when combined with strategic planning
Post-task conditions	• Raises accuracy, particularly with decision-making tasks
Repetition	• Raises complexity consistently, and accuracy and fluency usually
Support	• Reduces memory demands, but can raise input pressure. Greater complexity (as words per clause) but lower subordination.
Surprise information	• Has little effect
Time	• Leads to lower level performance generally

Task condition research has suggested a number of generalisations, shown in Table 13.2.

The motivations for task research studies have been various. The two most research-generating approaches, the Cognition Hypothesis and the Limited Capacity Approach, have led to studies which have produced many of the findings shown above. But other researchers have contributed important work also without being influenced by these two particular positions. In fact, none of this matters as far as testing and assessment are concerned. The key point is that a range of systematic findings are now available as to how the performance may be influenced by the particular task and the particular conditions that were used.

This discussion brings out, through the detail of findings in task research, how the publications from 2001 and 2009, which were more programmatic in nature, as well as the extensions described in Chapters 9 and 10, now can feed into decisions regarding the tasks and conditions that make up a test battery. Testing organisations have done this implicitly for many years and testing expertise undoubtedly draws upon this knowledge. Task research now can provide additional insights to make it more likely that these decisions are evidence-based. The difference is that we are beginning to identify macro-categories (complexification, pressuring, easing, focussing) that can make this a more practical possibility. But as the next section shows, exploring these influences through the frame of Conceptualiser-focus and Formulator-focus can be an even better way of doing this.

Applying the Levelt Model to an Assessment Context: Its Relevance for Ability for Use

At the outset to this section it is worth repeating the processes the Levelt model contains.

Conceptualisation subsumes:

- determining what to say;
- forming an intention;
- adopting a stance;
- selecting information in preparation for the construction of an intended utterance;
- generating a pre-verbal message.

It is interesting here that the strictly language dimensions in this stage are not great. There is a strong emphasis on relating what is to be said to the previous conversation and to the context. These influences are seen as vital in shaping what is to be actually said. There is also a strong emphasis on the underlying reasons and motivations for what will be said, given that many things could, of course, be said at any one point, but what is selected to be said is going to reflect how the speaker wants to position themselves, and to develop the conversation (Clark,

1996). After all this is done (the first three bullet points, above) we then reach the need to retrieve information from long-term memory, information which at this stage is not particularly linguistic in nature, but is concerned with ideas and the interrelationship between ideas. Only when this is accomplished do we reach the final Conceptualisation stage, which is the generation of the pre-verbal message, the foundation, still largely non-linguistic, for what will actually be said.

Clearly, effective speaking requires that there has been effective Conceptualisation, (and the reverse applies to poor conceptualisation). Yet nothing so far has overtly implicated linguistic knowledge itself. It follows from this analysis that we have to consider this contribution of Conceptualisation to be part of an ability for use. And it is striking that much of what has just been said complements the proposals in Bachman's strategic competence and Hulstijn's periphery. The former discusses Assessment, Goal setting, and Planning, while the latter includes Interaction Ability and Knowledge of the characteristics of types of written and spoken discourse. These stages (Bachman) or components (Hulstijn) fit nicely into what is being covered within the Conceptualisation stages in Levelt. Despite the different labels which are used by different authors, I would consider them to be important parts of Ability for Use.

When we move to the Formulation stage in speech production, linguistic factors become more prominent. The basic function of this stage is to translate conceptual representation into linguistic form. This involves:

- lemma retrieval, as triggered by the pre-verbal message;
- syntactic planning, driven by the information contained in lemmas as well as issues of stance from the Conceptualisation stage;
- similarly lemma-driven development of phonology.

Lemma retrieval, as indicated earlier in this book, involves issues of:

- speed of access;
- clarity and accessibility of syntactic information;
- clarity and accessibility of phonological information;
- clarity and accessibility of discourse information;
- second language mental lexicon organisation:
  - connections with other lemmas, and scope for priming;
  - knowledge of collocates;
  - knowledge of formulaic alternatives which can be used.

Lemma access is important, indeed central, because it then drives the rest of message generation, first with syntax building and then with phonological realisations. If we are dealing with performance and task-based testing, as opposed to item-based relatively decontextualised tests, then when linguistic factors are important, it is the functioning of the second language mental lexicon to underpin Formulator operations that is at play. So rapid access to range of information stored in the lemma is crucial.

So far we have examined the two stages of Conceptualisation and Formulation in isolation, but of course they, together with Articulation and Monitoring, are part of a cycle of communication (as indicated in Chapter 9) where each stage works in an encapsulated and parallel manner, with one moment's Conceptualisation becoming the next moment's Formulation and then Articulation. So it is not simply the second language mental lexicon that is vital—it is also important exactly how the Formulation stage plays a part in the cycle of ongoing communication. In this respect the central issue, for the second language speaker, is the extent to which the Formulator stage, with its reliance on a limited second language mental lexicon, means that the parallel functioning of the stages in speaking is derailed, and moves to a more serial mode of communication, as the attention required to handle the problems that originate in the second language mental lexicon spillover to the other processes and stages in communication.

We have covered these issues elsewhere in the book. Their relevance here is in how they relate to language testing, and in particular to the different models we explored earlier in this chapter. Bachman (1990) as we have seen discussed the concept of Strategic Competence in terms of Assessment, Goal setting, and Planning. This seems to echo many of the aspects of Conceptualisation in Levelt's model. Canale and Swain (1980) and Hulstijn focus on Strategic Competence as resourcefulness, and this seems to fit into Formulation, with some connections also with Monitoring. (In addition, Hulstijn includes dealing with adverse production conditions, principally time pressure, as part of Strategic Competence. This too would have to be regarded as part of Formulator operations.) Hulstijn also discusses, as part of the Periphery, factors such as interactive ability, knowledge of characteristics of oral and written discourse (the first of which has to be close to interactive ability), and metalinguistic knowledge. It seems to me that these have to be closer to decisions that are made, explicitly or implicitly, within the Conceptualiser stage, since they impact on such things as the assessment of the communicative situation, the development of what to say and the stance to take towards it, and then also the information that is selected.

It is interesting, therefore, that attempts to characterise Strategic Competence, as well as Hulstijn's Periphery can be fairly naturally related to Leveltian stages. In some ways they extend this model as it is applied to the second language case. In addition, though, there are aspects of the Levelt model (developing stance, retrieving information, generating a pre-verbal message, and exploiting the second language mental lexicon) which are not clearly captured in these different formulations of second language use. But I would want to argue that:

- it is fruitful to consider all these processes within the general heading of Ability for Use;

- it is worth conceptualising Ability for Use as an important component of task-based testing;
- there is an urgent need for research in this area.

Conventional, linguistic-knowledge-oriented testing focusses, essentially, on the second language mental lexicon and its richness and organisation, and the way this has generality and power in predicting language test scores. This endeavour is, of course, entirely worthwhile and indeed unavoidable. But there is more to communication than having a mental lexicon, at whatever level. Essentially, ability for use is concerned with, precisely, individual differences in the capacity to *mobilise* that second language mental lexicon. Accordingly, any attempt to develop effective formats for task-based tests needs to focus on the way Ability for Use has scope to show itself, and the sampling that is involved in the development of any such test needs to devise ways to enable the different facets of Ability for Use to be relevant.

Task Difficulty

Pollitt (1991) makes an interesting distinction, for language testing, between counting and judging. Conventional testing procedures, which are item-based, lend themselves to counting, and the range of statistical procedures that follow from this. But Pollitt also discusses testing procedures which are not item-based because performance is multi-dimensional and complex. Performances in this approach do not generate item-based additive scores, but instead usually need to be *judged*, normally through the use of a rating scale, whether generalised or analytic. Pollitt argues that such scores are likely to be somewhere in a range not much greater than 1–7, i.e. raters, effectively, cannot make limitless discriminations, and seven categories is something of a maximum.

Item-based procedures appear to have far more potential scores (1–100, for example, is fairly conventional) and to enable finer discriminations. The difficulty is in determining what the different scores in such tests, detached from actual performance as they are, actually mean. In this respect, an important feature in the item-based testing armoury is the scope there is to calibrate the difficulty of individual items, and then to explore the scalability of those items. (Scalability means that the items have relationships to one another which are consistent, and enable them to be located on a scale of lower to higher performance.) Item response theory and the associated software is now commonplace and holds out the hope of being able to develop statistically satisfactory scales. An aspect of this is that any particular item can be shown to have a fairly precise difficulty level, since it can be shown to be at a particular point on an easy-to-difficult cline.

Obviously, if you believe what is to be tested can be itemised, this is the way to go! The problem is that any commitment to task-based testing will regard performance as infinitely more complex than an item-based approach is appropriate for. An item-based approach is essentially reductionist, whereas task-based performances are multi-dimensional and complex. Yet the central claim, that tests (and tasks-as-tests) vary in difficulty is an important one and relevant to task-based testing equally. Earlier we discussed the way task research and the range of findings it has generated can be an important input to decisions about what sampling needs to take place in a task-based test. But perhaps even beyond this, the Holy Grail would be to have some sense of the comparative difficulty of different tasks-as-tests, so that not only would there be sampling across a range of task characteristics and task conditions, but there would also be a scale of measurement built in to the tasks which were used. This would also provide a framework such that tasks could be used to test, effectively, at different proficiency levels. It would also have importance in the development of achievement tests, as well as those to assess proficiency.

How then can we address the issue of difficulty in task-based testing? Note that Robinson's proposals on task complexity are not directly relevant here. These proposals are linked to syllabus issues and to ways of promoting a focus on language. There is relevance, if resource-directing variables impact upon language complexity and accuracy and these performance areas figure in ratings of performance. But these are not the focus of Robinson's ideas on how tasks influence performance. He does, in fact, discuss the concept of task difficulty, but the meaning of this term for him is quite different, since it is concerned with how difficult a particular individual finds a task, and this in turn depends on individual difference factors, not simply the task itself.

So the notion of task difficulty is, indeed, a difficult one. If one takes proposals such as those made in Norris et al. (1998) and then Brown, Hudson, Norris, and Bonk (2002), there are prospects of using rating schemes to assess the difficulty of tasks (within reason of course, in six levels), rating each task on a number of criteria and then totalling the ratings to get an index of difficulty. For example, one task in Norris et al. (1998) required searching a newspaper for full-time and part-time jobs, in a certain sector, and then ranking them for highest to lowest paid. This was rated 2 (out of 6). Then another task required two résumés to be written for a client (matching two different jobs), based on the input from an interview tape. This was rated 5. This may be a promising approach in principle. However, attempts to use rating schemes to establish task difficulty do have serious problems. As a starting point they require some sort of analytic framework, and as yet, we do not have a definitive one available. (Norris, Brown, Hudson, and Yoshioka [1998] used a scheme loosely based on my 1996 article in *Applied Linguistics*!) There are potentially applicable systems, but these often change as research results develop (as this book has, hopefully, demonstrated). Perhaps more serious is the point that there can be many interpretations of a particular task. Different test takers may respond differently depending on their interpretation of a task and specific background knowledge and skills. A shallow interpretation of a test task can make it fairly easy whereas a more challenging interpretation of the very same task can change difficulty markedly. (This is essentially the same point that was made in Chapter 5—tasks often do not generate the performances that were predicted.)

I would propose that many of the problems in trying to work with task difficulty are the result of a fundamental tension in what happens in a task, and that this tension can be understood more effectively in terms of the Levelt model. In a nutshell, it seems to me that there are two major and fairly distinct sources of task difficulty, and these derive from the Conceptualiser and the Formulator. For that reason, it seems to me more effective if one tries to develop a notion of difficulty purely in relation to Conceptualiser demands, and then a separate notion of difficulty which derives from Formulator operations. Both have to be explored, but also held distinct. Then, if any attempt is made to assess proficiency through task-based testing procedures, both sources of task difficulty have to be sampled separately.

My 2009 publication is relevant for this, both in detail and programmatically. It provided an analysis, in relation to Levelt stages, of complexifying and pressuring, and then easing and focussing, with these presented as two pairs. It would perhaps be an improvement to think of them not as two pairs, but more clearly in relation to Levelt's stages, as shown in Table 13.3. Complexifying relates to the

TABLE 13.3 Types of Influence on Second Language Task Performances

	Influences on Speaking	
Conceptualisation	*Complexifying* • planning: extending • complex cognitive operations • reasoning • transformation • complex information type • structure • dialogic	
Formulation: General: Lemma retrieval and syntactic encoding	*Pressuring* • Monologic • Time pressure • Heavy input pressure • High memory demands • Non-negotiable task	*Easing* • Dialogic • Opportunity for on-line planning • Limited input • Low memory demands
Lemma retrieval	• Less frequent lexis	• Planning: organising
Syntactic encoding	• More advanced syntax	• Planning: rehearsal • Structured tasks
Monitoring	*Focussing* • post-task conditions • testing conditions	

Conceptualiser stage, and then Pressuring and Easing, almost two sides of the same coin, are important at the Formulation stage. Where relevant these are separated into the lemma retrieval and syntactic encoding stages, but there are various factors here which are of general importance for Formulation, and are shown first. Then Focussing is linked with Monitoring, rather than any of the specific stages of the model.

Undoubtedly, as more research results accumulate, the details of this table will change, partly by being extended, as new features come to be included, and partly by change, as perhaps some of the influences are repositioned or reinterpreted. But the point for now is that the distinctions between complexifying, pressuring, easing, and focussing can be defended as capturing what we know so far, and also defended as linking with a model of speaking, devised for the first language case but extended to the second.

Now we can return more directly to issues of testing. I would argue that there is something of a split between the Conceptualiser influences and the Formulator influences. Bear in mind, first of all, that it is the essence of a task-based approach to testing that any task that is used should be worthwhile, and have some meaning to the test taker. It cannot be an obvious language display task, and so criteria such as meaning-based, outcome-evaluated, real-world conditions, and so on (Skehan, 1998) will apply. The first set of influences respond to aspects of this. The task is likely to involve ideas, and doing something which might have a real-world connection. This relates to the sorts of processes covered earlier under Conceptualisation, and to the thinking and the organisation of ideas that underlies performance. With the Formulation-linked influences, we are dealing with a different set of considerations. Ideas need to be translated into language, and that requires access to the second language mental lexicon and the syntax and phonology building that follows from that. Here the influences are, broadly, concerned with pressure versus ease, with difficulty in accessing the second language mental lexicon versus relaxed conditions. The emphasis is less on the ideas to be expressed, (although of course these are not unimportant), and more on how language can be built, given the circumstances which are operative. We are dealing largely with the importance of conditions of performance, and how people will vary when conditions are difficult compared to when conditions are more supportive. So one can imagine very different scenarios, whatever the earlier Conceptualisation influences, if the Formulator influences vary.

Centrally, the issue is that what determines difficulty at the Conceptualisation stage is different from what determines difficulty at the Formulator stage. One can imagine Conceptualiser-demanding tasks-as-tests which are very distinct from Formulator-demanding tasks-as-tests. In the former case difficulty is likely to be dependent on the more demanding mental operations that are involved. In the latter, difficulty is likely to be influenced by more pressured conditions. Table 13.4 below brings this out:

TABLE 13.4 Level of Difficulty Linked to Conceptualiser and Formulator Influences

	Conceptualiser Easy	*Conceptualiser Difficult*
Formulator easy	• Unpressured communication • Familiar, structured information only requiring recall	• Unpressured, small-scale communication • Extending, planning, reasoning, and transformation
Formulator difficult	• Pressured communication, heavy input, monologic, non-negotiable • Familiar structured information, emphasis on retrieval	• Pressured communication, heavy input, monologic, non-negotiable • Extending, planning, reasoning, and transformation

There is an old adage in testing. You would always like tests which are cheap, fast, and good. But reality means that the best you can do is get two out of three (and often not even that!). One solution to the above matrix would be extensive assessment sampling of each of the four cells that are shown. That might be a defensible way to achieve 'good' but it certainly would not meet any criteria for fast or cheap! But at least the matrix makes clear what would be ideal: systematic variation in the tasks-as-tests that are used to draw upon each combination here. Obviously that won't be feasible in the normal case, but the range of what might be done could guide what actually is done, so that there is a clearer understanding of what hasn't been sampled, and what, therefore, may limit the generalisations that are possible.

Perhaps the best strategy is first to return to the notion of task difficulty. What the above analysis makes clear is that Conceptualiser-based difficulty is different from Formulator-based difficulty. If one would like, as is typical in testing, to build in tasks-as-tests which can be located on a scale of difficulty, what this means is that the sorts of factors (see Table 13.4 above) which impact upon Conceptualiser-based difficulty will be different to the sorts of factors that impact upon Formulator-linked difficulty. Sampling and decisions on which tasks to include in assessment will have to start with this consideration, and not mix up the two senses of difficulty.

But the analysis now does allow several relevant observations to be made regarding the nature of assessment. Some years ago, the great J. B. Carroll (1961) argued that tests of isolated competences were not enough, and that effective testing needed to take account of integrative language use. The difficulty that followed from this was, of course, how to set up the best integrative testing formats. It seems to me that a task-based approach to testing has gone a long way to addressing these concerns. By studying the impact of task characteristics and task conditions on performance, we now have a better idea as to what needs to be covered when integrative approaches are used, particularly those integrative approaches that we would now regard as tasks. We are now well beyond thinking of the term 'integrative' in an unfocussed way, and can point to ways that tasks-as-tests can be developed to cover a wide range of integrative language uses.

Another important point concerns the purposes for which tests are used. One of the many contributions that Bachman (1990) has made to testing is the distinction between Interactive-ability tests and Real-life tests. The former attempt to come up with a generalised, and ability-oriented estimate of what a candidate can do with the language, in general. A Real-life approach, in contrast, uses testing procedures to estimate how well someone will perform in particular situations, perhaps with vocation-linked or academic discipline performance. Of course, this is an extreme contrast. Many testing situations are a mixture of the two approaches, depending on the particular situation involved. But the first does emphasise assessing generalised abilities which may be drawn in whatever situations are encountered, and the latter has in mind some specific context, such that generalised abilities may be less relevant whereas specific subsets of skills may come to the fore (Skehan, 1984).

Distinguishing between Conceptualiser-linked and Formulator-linked influences for Interactive-ability tests and Real-life tests may be illuminating. In the case of Interactive-ability tests, the purpose may be to identify tests which make low-to-medium Conceptualiser demands, since the focus is not on the challenging thinking that might underlie performance so much as the way underlying proficiencies can be mobilised. Then, Formulator influences can be varied, but even here, if the purpose is to get some measure of basic language functioning, the case may be strong not to increase the difficulties too much, because the purpose may be, in Swain's memorable phrase, to bias for best. If an estimate of proficiency is made when the Formulator conditions are not particularly demanding, additional assessment might be carried out with more demanding conditions. But in all these cases, the purpose in using task-linked information is to enable underlying proficiencies to manifest themselves, in integrative communicative situations without undue interference from Conceptualiser-based demands.

The situation with Real-life tests is very different. Here the purpose is not to get an estimate of generalisable abilities, of maximum predictive power in a range of situations, but rather to do a specific job, making predictions about the capacity to handle the demands in a specific, real-life situation. In some ways this simplifies the task, and indeed, many EAP and occupational tests reflect this. They conduct careful analyses of the target performances that will be required, and then devise testing formats that simulate these as effectively as possible (Long, 2015). Many such tests exist and they do an excellent job. But the analysis presented earlier is still relevant. First of all, the Conceptualiser-Formulator distinction is still important in bringing clarity to the testing formats which are used. The actual content will be integral to real-life tests, and this will have important implications for the sorts of Conceptualiser operations that are involved. This will shape the sorts of tasks that are devised to build up a test. Then there will be real-life conditions which will be relevant to Formulation, including the time pressure that will be involved, the acoustic conditions, the nature of the input, the interactant relationships, the degree of negotiability, and so on. Trying to be systematic as these are associated with Formulator operations will help in the design of better tests.

But while the emphasis here is on testing to deliver in a relatively specific situation, the specificity is not absolute. Most real-life tests of this sort have to deal with a range of situations, such as the variety of language-use contexts in EAP situations, or the range of duties of someone in a particular form of employment. So generalisation does have a role to play, since there is variation in the conditions for language use. In this respect, the range of task research, and the claims that can be made about the impact of different variables would have a major input potential to test design. If one wants to predict how someone will perform not in just one circumscribed role, but in a number of related roles, then being systematic in how variation in Formulator influences particularly are built into test design could be very useful. So once again, a psycholinguistic underpinning to how tests are developed is useful, and takes us well beyond, through principle and through evidence, the broader and vaguer claim that integrative testing is required.

Rating Performance

Earlier Pollitt's (1991) proposal was mentioned that scores in testing, broadly, are based on counting or judging. It follows that with the complexity of performance that is involved in task-based testing, judging is far more appropriate than counting. In effect, this means that the performances that are elicited by tasks-as-tests need to be judged, and the conventional method of achieving this is to use rating scales, which, indeed, abound in performance testing. The problems then shift to how to design rating scales so that they are as reliable and as valid as possible.

Typically rating scales are either generalised or analytic. I will focus on the latter here. Generalised scales are distilled versions of the analytic scales, so what is said about the analytic scales is also relevant for to the generalised scales. Analytic scales vary, of course, but there is, nonetheless, a fair degree of agreement about which areas justify a separate scale. A fairly common arrangement would be to use scales of:

- range;
- vocabulary;
- accuracy;
- fluency;
- task fulfilment.

Obviously there are strong resemblances here between the analytic scales which are used in testing and the dimensions that are common as dependent variables in task-based performance. Some preliminary remarks can help to clarify this. Range concerns the candidate's ability to draw upon a wide repertoire of language structures. This most resembles what is intended in task-based measures of structural complexity. Vocabulary likewise is concerned with the quality of the words which are used in a task, and maps onto the lexical measures which are used to capture task-based performance—diversity and sophistication. Accuracy in a testing context is clearly similar to accuracy as measured when tasks are done, and the same, at a general level, could be said for fluency. So all of these headings for analytic rating scales map onto fairly equivalent performance areas with tasks, as well as the underlying constructs. This is less true of the final heading: task fulfilment. Although there are quite a few publications with the task-based area which explore the notion of task fulfilment (Revesz, Ekiert, & Torgersen, 2015), and which strongly voice the argument that task fulfilment should be central in task research, the quantity of research that is derived from this idea is significantly less. Within testing, though, task fulfilment figures strongly, and is even seen as the key analytic scale, especially with a real-life approach to testing. However, apart from this particular scale, the others do have links to task research, and exploring those links is interesting. The findings from task research have the potential to make some sort of contribution to each, although it has to be said, more with some than with others!

Structural complexity, as we saw in Chapter 10, is mostly measured as the amount of subordination and as the number of words per clause. Occasionally researchers also incorporate a measure of range of structures (Foster & Skehan, 1996a). What we saw in Chapter 10 is that subordination and words per clause, while they sometimes overlap in influences upon them (planning or narrative tasks, for example, raising both) often diverge in what has an impact. Task structure and time perspective are good examples of this. It would seem, from this research, that analytic scales of range might benefit if they included descriptive phrases which refer to these separately. In addition, at the test design stage, it might be worth including sub-tasks which differ in the way complexity is raised, to gain a broader sampling of performance.

Lexis: Two main measures have been used in task-based performance research—lexical diversity (the extent to which a given set of words are recycled or not) and lexical sophistication (the extent to which less frequent words are drawn on). Three features of this research are important. First, the association between text length and lexical diversity is a very strong one, hence the need for some sort of correction. Second, lexical diversity and lexical sophistication have, possibly surprisingly, a fairly low relationship to one another—high lexical diversity scores tell you surprisingly little about what a participant's lexical sophistication scores will be (Skehan, 2009b). Third, lexical diversity shows strong style qualities—second language speakers are remarkably consistent across tasks in their lexical diversity. In an ideal world, vocabulary-based rating scales would be able to incorporate insights from task research and reflect what we have learned about these two aspects of lexical ability. The second of these, lexical sophistication, might indeed be possible, so that raters could capture the extent to which less frequent words are used, and how this might reflect a more extensive mental lexicon. Lexical diversity would be difficult to build in to a rating scale, unfortunately. This is indeed a pity since this measure does show more signs of reflecting differences in active general proficiency (Skehan & Shum, 2014; Inoue, 2013), and certainly the task research shows how native speakers achieve very clearly higher lexical diversity scores. As it is, however, this seems currently to be more of a research instrument not susceptible to easy rating and requiring careful computation. Possibly in the future it can be used on (typed) written task performance.

Accuracy: Surprisingly, perhaps, task research may not have so much to contribute here. The research reviewed in Chapter 10 suggested that, broadly, accuracy is a fairly general construct. Research which has explored different measures (clause based; standardised measures of error per number of words; error gravity; error linked to length of clause) all deliver more or less the same result. In this case, rating scales seem to have a fairly straightforward task to accomplish, since whatever choice is made, a valid measure of accuracy results. There was only one exception discussed: in Pang and Skehan (in preparation) decision-making tasks generated higher accuracy scores than narratives, except when one considered narrative tasks with longer clauses with minor errors ignored. It appeared that narratives pushed participants to make more errors, but that these were often of a minor nature. Still, this is only one finding, and possibly not all that central. We come back to the generalisation: accuracy is accuracy, and rating scales simply need to reflect this.

Fluency: The situation is different with fluency, and this may be the area where task-based research has most to contribute. There is, of course, the starting point that fluency, as Freed (2000) has noted, may be in the ear of the listener, and so in rating language performance for fluency, the ultimate criterion might need to be the impression conveyed rather than the objective measures (a point that is relevant to the other performance areas also). But the objective measures do have some relevance and possibly better understanding of them might have a relevance for the training of judges of spoken language performance.

We saw, then, that analysis of the different fluency measures did suggest that it could be broken down into the components of:

- discourse-linked dysfluency, indexed largely by silent pauses at clause boundaries;
- clause-linked dysfluency, indexed by silent and filled mid-clause pauses, as well as the number of repetitions;
- repair, indexed by reformulations, false starts, and replacements, and taken to reflect the amount of monitoring taking place;
- speed, measured as words or syllables per minute.

These components have some distinctness from one another, logically and empirically. At first sight, one might have the impression that there is little that is new being said here. But I would argue that that is not completely the case. The discourse vs. clause distinction, the detail of the clause-based dysfluency, and the independence of repair as a factor, with this having a positive aspect in a relationship to monitoring, suggest a greater understanding of the factors which contribute to dysfluency, and how these might be represented in fluency rating scales. Bundling anything together may misrepresent slightly the different facets of fluency.

In sum, it appears that the efforts that have been made to measure second language task performance may, at least some of the time, illuminate the sorts of considerations that underlie rating scales for test-based performance. There is a lot more to do here, not least in relating these different insights and measures to different levels of proficiency, so that scales can be used more effectively to discriminate between levels. But the potential is there, and the two areas, task-based performance research and rating scale construction, have the potential to assist one another.

Extending a Model of Second Language Task-Based Testing

The 2001 chapter offered a fairly primitive model of task-based testing. Centrally it proposed that tasks are not neutral testing instruments, that they fit into a wider context, and that the way they can be used in testing is complex. The 2009 chapter then tried to offer generalisations as to how task characteristic and task condition factors might have systematic influences on performance, highlighting complexification, pressuring, easing, and focussing as vital processes. The chapter also made more explicit the connections with the Levelt model. Essentially this commentary on these two chapters has only continued this attempt to clarify the relevance for testing of task-based second language performance research.

But we are now in a position to extend the model that was presented in that earlier publication. The revised model is presented as Figure 13.1. In the model underlying competences are mediated through an ability for use into actual performance, and this is then influenced further by task and task condition choices. The performance, finally, is rated, and so the score ultimately assigned may reflect rater and rating scale influences also.

Obviously, in general, the model is basically similar to that which was presented in 2001. But I would argue that there are three important differences: these are (a) the greater understanding we now have of tasks and task conditions; (b) the clearer connection that exists between task research and rating scales to evaluate performance; and (c) the way ability for use mediates the connection between underlying competences and actual performance. We will look at each component of the model, highlighting, where appropriate, these three areas of difference.

Fundamental to this model are the *underlying competences*. I will say little about these. For conceptual clarity, if not strong empirical support, I incline towards Bachman's views. They have a place for several different underlying components,

Underlying Competences

Organisational Competence
Pragmatic Competence

Ability for Use

Conceptualiser processes
General knowledge base
Working memory
Compensation ability
- monitoring
- resourcefulness
Second language mental lexicon
- speed and access skills
- range of formulaic language
Metacognition
- recovery ability
- foresight, trouble avoidance

Conceptualisation

- more complex
- less complex

Task

- information, input
- operations
- outcome

Formulation

- more pressured
- less pressured
- focussed

Performance

Rating

- raters
- rating scales

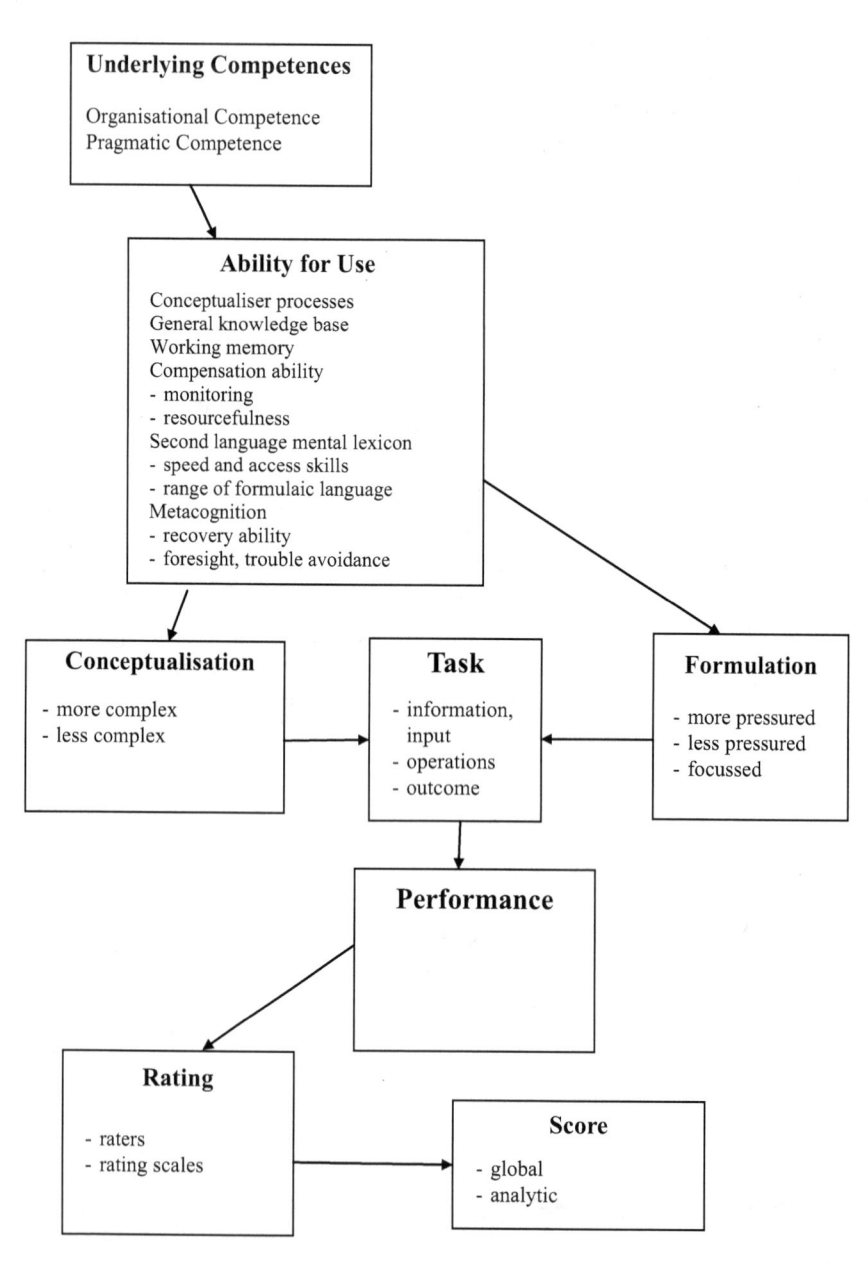

Score

- global
- analytic

FIGURE 13.1 A Model of Task-Based Spoken Language Testing

and since I am not totally convinced by usage-based approaches, I am drawn to the attempt to specific component competences. These certainly involve underlying syntactic and lexical competences. Even so, locating these within the second language mental lexicon seems the most psycholinguistically plausible. But there are attractions also in considering pragmatic competence, as a reflection of connections between language and context, through ease of handling different discourse domains, and sociolinguistic issues. These are pervasive underlying competences which represent the potential for communication. They are also an important goal for testing, particularly in relation to Bachman's Interactive-ability type of test (Bachman, 1990).

But next in the model we have ability for use, and the characteristics and constructs which need to be assessed in this area. These are concerned with individual differences in the skill with which underlying competences are mobilised in performance. If we follow Carroll's (1961) admonition, effective testing has to involve integrative skills, and what the construct of ability for use does is to try to clarify what skills, in addition to basic competences, are involved in any such integrative performance. This is the area, one way or another, that concerned Canale and Swain, and then Bachman, in the way they characterised strategic competence, and also what Hulstijn was concerned with as the Periphery in terms of language skills. All of these proposals will be drawn on here, and then extended slightly.

I would propose something like Bachman's account of Strategic Competence as central. He suggested component stages of Assessment, Goal setting, and Planning, and this is remarkably close to an account one could give based on Levelt, of assessing the situation, deciding what to say, assembling ideas, choosing a stance, and generating the pre-verbal message. I prefer the account based on Levelt, but broadly the two approaches are doing the same sort of thing. This is how normal, routine communication is seen to proceed. Levelt provides more emphasis on the ideas and their relation to context that are the foundation for speaking, whereas Bachman is really trying to encompass all the stages of speaking. But they are agreed that before actual speech comes into the frame, there needs to be thinking, and assessment about the ideas/propositions to be expressed. Bachman ends with planning, which seems to bundle together the pre-verbal message and what, in a Leveltian account, would be seen as Formulator operations. So I would like to add, to both sets of views of what are effectively Conceptualiser operations, the operation of the Formulator, and with it access to the second language mental lexicon and its processes (of lemma retrieval, of syntactic-frame building, of phonological preparation). All of these processes in speech production seem to me to be what ability for use is centrally concerned with, in the normal case. If there are individual differences in these, quite apart from individual differences in proficiency, then they need to be involved in any testing system. In a perfect case they, and the other aspects of ability for use to be covered below, should be separately assessed. In more realistic cases, it is more probable that the best that can be done is to devise testing formats which make their use unavoidable.

So if the basic part of ability for use concerns the processes that underlie speaking, their efficiency and their speed, the next question concerns what supporting abilities might be involved. One such is likely to be the general knowledge base that can be drawn on. The Conceptualiser is concerned with ideas, and so what is known (about the world, about interaction, about previous conversations, and so on) is likely to be relevant, since it provides the input to the general assessment of the situation, and the move to developing a reason for speech. Differences in this general knowledge base will be relevant to the effectiveness of speaking. This will apply to Interactive-ability testing and also, very clearly, to Real-life testing where frequently one may be dealing with the need to predict to specific, real-world context for language use.

A second contributing area to general speaking processes is that of Metacognition, as this applies to second language speaking. In other words, speakers have knowledge about speaking. When communication is effective and ongoing, there may be little need to engage metacognitive processes, as is mostly the situation with native speakers. But speakers do have knowledge about speaking, and this, if engaged, may influence how current speaking is carried out. Speakers may know what causes them difficulty, and pre-empt such difficulties. Part of their metacognition may involve knowledge of different discourse contexts, and so they can mobilise this knowledge to be more effective, such as in specialist scientific discourse, or negotiation in business. Later versions of the Levelt model also suggest that there may be some foreknowledge, in the Conceptualiser, of mental lexicon resources, and this may influence Conceptualiser choices that are made. In addition, Pang and Skehan (2014), in their study of pre-task planning, report that speakers, with that potential advantage, draw upon metacognitive strategies, which suggests that second language speakers engaged in communication may attempt to do the same, even when planning time is not available. Fundamentally, metacognition may reflect a speaker's capacity to have learned from previous communications and experiences in ways which enable a given underlying language-knowledge base to be used more effectively.

This, in turn, leads to the obvious relevance of one particular cognitive ability: working memory, whether here we are concerned with overall working memory size, or its speed of operation (Wen, 2009). Given that speaking involves Conceptualisation, Formulation, and Articulation (together with the associated process of monitoring), and given that these stages, in an ideal case, are meant to operate in parallel, in modular fashion, there are significant demands on attentional resources in general and on working memory, in particular. Working memory really has a foundational role in the entire system working smoothly, and in the way that underlying competences can be used within actual performance. This applies to all communication conditions, but it obviously applies particularly strongly when there are difficult conditions, especially those where there is time pressure. It has to be considered, therefore, as an important component of ability for use. Evidence in support of this comes from a number of studies of planning which have appeared in recent years. As we saw in Chapter 9, we need to distinguish between pre-task planning and on-line planning. The generalisation that emerges when working memory measures have been used in planning studies is that there is a negligible relationship between working memory scores and performance under pre-task planning conditions, but there is a fairly consistent and moderate relationship in the on-line planning studies. This is interesting supportive evidence of the role that working memory plays as part of ability for use, with second language speakers. If speaking involves an articulatory buffer, as a sort of holding area when speech is being assembled (Levelt, 1989), then greater working memory resources constitute a clear advantage.

So far we have simply taken unproblematically the nature of underlying competences, and assumed that ability for use mediates their use in actual performance in very important ways. But it is also important to peek inside these underlying competences to consider whether there might be factors which indicate different levels of preparation for actual performance. A traditional view of these competences would suggest that a rule-based system drives the generation of an infinite potential number of utterances, following, for example, Universal Grammar accounts of competence and actual performance. This is consistent with the Conceptualiser-to-Formulator sequence, since it could be argued that the material held in the mental lexicon (for the native speaker at least) is founded upon such a rule-governed system, and so lemma-driven syntactic-frame building would conform to this underlying system. This assumes a parsimoniously structured system, where rules are filled out through lexical elements.

But of course there have been persistent arguments that actual performance relies much more on memorised chunks of language (Bolinger, 1975; Pawley & Syder, 1983; Sinclair, 1991; Skehan, 1984, 1998). In other words, the (native) speaker can draw upon a vast range of formulaic language, either specific language, or language frames within which small change can take place even though the rest of the frame is invariant. The argument is that within communication, retrieving language chunks of this sort simplifies ongoing processing, and reduces memory load since such chunks are retrieved as wholes, and do not require any internal computation (Skehan, 1996). As a result attention is freed up to focus on other things. The more there is such a repertoire of formulaic language, the more the speaker can concentrate on more demanding aspects of the message. That is not to say that such chunks cannot be analysed—it is just that, if available, as wholes, they do not have to be. So in the mental lexicon the same 'word' can exist more than once. It can be a lemma, connected to other lemmas, or it can be a component of a chunk, in what I have called dual-coding (Skehan, 1996). To make this clear, this goes well beyond the 'stitch in time' view of idioms as somewhat unusual and fixed locutions. I argue that 'idioms' or prefabricated chunks are pervasive and fundamental (Sinclair, 1991), and central for normal, ongoing communication. Native speakers are adept at exploiting such resources to ease communication.

What this means is that not all underlying competences are created equal. If a speaker can draw upon a range of formulaic language, then the demands on the Formulator are reduced. Of course, this more naturally applies to the native speaker. Recent work (Granena & Long, 2013; Bolibaugh & Foster, 2013) has shown that developing a range of formulaic language is very difficult for second language speakers. But if it can be done, the advantage, provided that its use can be orchestrated effectively, is that more time and attention are available to focus on the rest of the message being communicated. One study provides an interesting insight into this. Foster (2001a) designed a study which compared native and non-native speakers doing a task under planned and unplanned conditions. What she found was that native speakers without planning time used more formulaic language than they did when they had planning time. It was as though, deprived of planning time, they relied on the processing 'crutch' that formulaic language provides. Non-native speakers, in contrast, were the reverse. With planning time, they used more formulaic language, and without planning time, less. It was as though they needed the help of planning time to enable them to exploit the benefits that formulaic language can provide. To conclude the discussion of dual-coding and the use of formulaic language, it seems to me that ability for use has to involve the potential to use, more generally, time-creating devices, and more specifically formulaic language, to make the general task of generating messages simpler. Since there are likely to be individual differences in this area, we need to think about the impact of this skill in being more efficient at communicating.

The final part of ability for use to be considered is the compensatory role of strategic competence. This is highlighted by Canale and Swain (1980) and Hulstijn (2015). Each of these authors draws attention to the way second language speakers will encounter difficulties in communication, and then need to address these difficulties. They are proposing, essentially, that there are individual differences in how well different second language speakers do this. There are, it is clear, two parts to this. First there is the importance of spotting the problem, which involves monitoring, and second there is the resourcefulness of the speaker to overcome the problem. The monitoring, following the Levelt model, is feasible at the end of the Conceptualiser stage (when shortcomings in the pre-verbal message may become apparent), or at the end of the Formulator stage, when lemma retrieval difficulties have become apparent, or when errors have been noticed, and then finally after Articulation, when any of the above may apply, as well as difficulties with the phonology that has been produced. Perhaps overlaid on this could be Krashen's (1985) notions of heavy or light monitor users. Whatever the origin, the assumption here is that some people will be more likely to detect problems (shortcomings of lemma access, difficulties in syntax building, or plain mistakes) and that this will have an impact on communication.

But assuming that a problem or shortcoming has been identified, there is still the problem of what to do with it. Here we are dealing with a mixture of reConceptualisation or reFormulation or reArticulation. It is possible second language speakers who are good at one of these are good at the others. But it may well the case that this is not so. ReConceptualisation will require developing a different pre-verbal message, and this may rely simply on flexibility in thinking, capacity to reassess a situation, and to take a different stance. ReFormulation will require flexibility in the way the (second) language mental lexicon is used, as it assessed whether synonyms can be found, so that no major change in Formulation is required. This would contrast with situations where serious underlying deficiencies have been revealed, and the capacity to change may well go back to the Conceptualiser. But in addition to these types of reaction, others too are important. Quick decisions could be made about abandoning a message. Possibly resourcefulness in using dysfluency markers to gain time could be important (repetition, filled and unfilled pauses). There is also the issue of avoidance. It is possible that there is realisation, even at Conceptualiser stage, that problems lie ahead, and that avoidance may be the best strategy. Finally, there is the issue of recovery. It is inevitable that there will be serious problems in communication for the non-native speaker. To an extent, the discussion so far has implicitly emphasised solving problems at the within-clause level. But of course problems can be more extensive than this, if the general discourse flow is derailed. It may be that the skills to relaunch such discourse are a little different. We saw, with structured tasks, that one of the advantages of such tasks may well be that discourse flow can be regained and relaunched because the structure of the task creates what might be termed natural break points, and so the speaker, although diverted by a breakdown in communication, can find a 'restart' point more easily, just as a musician may be able to restart practice at the beginning of a bar or section. It may be that second language speakers vary in how naturally they can find potential restart points. Pang and Skehan (2014), for example, report that some such speakers, when given planning opportunities, impose structure on the task they are doing, and in this way create their own restart points. So this too may be part of the compensatory aspect of strategic competence.

Tasks and Task Conditions: This section does not need to be anything like as extensive as the previous one! Essentially it only recapitulates what has been covered already. The essential point is as before: the task that is done, and the conditions under which it is done are not neutral. Decisions about alternative tasks and alternative conditions are likely to influence, possibly strongly, the performance that is produced. Consequently, if tasks-as-tests are not the same in different test batteries or administrations, or if the generalisations that are to be made from test to real-life performance are dependent on particular tasks or particular conditions, then a research-basis is necessary if one is to avoid dangers of lack of validity and lack of comparability.

Earlier it was argued that it is useful to separate Conceptualiser and Formulator influences on task performance, and that within each of these it is also useful to consider task characteristics and task conditions separately. This is shown in Figure 13.1. In addition, it is useful to consider processes of complexification, pressuring, easing, and focussing. The discussion here does not need to be exhaustive. Instead, examples will be provided which bring out how task and task condition decision can influence performance.

Regarding Conceptualisation and task characteristics, a clear example would be the reasoning demands that the task makes. Robinson (2011a), albeit in terms of the construct of task complexity, has discussed this extensively as a resource-directing characteristic. Here I will consider it as a factor that adds to the difficulty of working with the ideas that underlie a task, and the attention that is required to work with those ideas. (Other examples could concern transformation of the ideas in a task, or the degree of abstraction in the information that is required.) The reasoning that is integral to the task then needs to be worked on before any effective Formulator work can be embarked on.

Regarding Conceptualisation and task conditions, the strongest empirical base here is for planning. In passing, it should be recalled that planning can lead to different sorts of processes. Here the focus is on planning as dealing with the ideas in a task, where the speaker thinks about the development of these ideas, even possibly transforming the task along the way. The result of this planning-as-extending is to push the task to a greater level of Conceptual complexity, and consequent difficulty. (Non-negotiability in a task would have similar complexifying effects, as would the related influence of time perspective in the there-and-then condition.) In designing test tasks and test-task conditions, then, thought needs to be given regarding the potential influences on Conceptualisation. This applies to the sampling frame that might be used for different components of the test, and it also applies to comparisons across tests.

With Formulation and task characteristics, arguably the most researched variable is task structure. This has been shown, fairly consistently, to raise accuracy and fluency. Two processes seem to be at work. On the one hand, the clarity of the macrostructure means that less attention is required for ongoing planning (on-line planning, in effect) since the broad discourse development is already clear. Then, more attention is available for clause-level processing and a greater attention to the surface of language. On the other hand, the existence of structure means that there are slightly more natural 'pick up' points that can be the focus for regaining discourse flow if there has been any problem. So the nature of the task influences particular aspects of task performance. (Familiarity of information similarly influences Formulator operations, with this manifesting itself through lexical differences.)

Task condition influences on Formulator operations are extensive, and two examples will be given. Time perspective is interesting. This variable, much investigated in Cognition Hypothesis studies, contrasts a here-and-now condition, where a task is done with visual support (a map to be drawn when directions are given) or without visual support. The former case is hypothesised to be simpler, since memory demands are lower, whereas the latter is analysed as more complex, since memory demands are higher. But I have argued that the contrast is more complex. In my view, the here-and-now condition, while it does reduce immediate demands on memory, nonetheless involves a considerable amount of input to consider and provides little flexibility for the participant, i.e. it is less negotiable. The there-and-then condition, while making memory demands, eases performance because the speaker can be more selective in what is said, and the message can be repackaged, rather than being input-dominated. The result is different types of performance in each case. On this Cognition Hypothesis proponents and Limited Attention Capacity proponents can agree, even if they do not about the details. But the wider point is that a condition of how to operationalise a variable is likely to have a large effect on performance, and how the Formulator, in particular, operates. Another important variable here is time pressure, as represented in the on-line planning studies. These have shown advantages for accuracy in the performance which is obtained when time conditions are relaxed.

So, working through the components of Table 13.3, we now see that the task literature suggests many influences upon performance. The broad issue, as mentioned earlier, is that this brings out that tasks are not neutral, and that the performance which results may partly be dependent on the task and task conditions that have been used, with these impacting on the different stages of speech production. On the one hand, tasks need to be used in testing if integrative processes are to be involved. On the other, using tasks in this way introduces difficulties since they have the potential to be intrusive with respect to the performance data which is elicited.

An obvious, if time-consuming solution, is to use multiple tasks and multiple conditions (and even combinations of these). Then the overall estimate of effective ability (which is a combination of underlying proficiency and ability for use) can be most validly and reliably estimated, based on this range of data. Such an approach would go some way to being representative, to allowing different underlying proficiencies to show themselves, and to sampling the range of factors which are part of ability for use. At the other extreme one might have one single task without variation in conditions either. To follow this strategy would mean that generalising would be difficult, from an interactive-ability perspective or from a real-life perspective. In the former case, not enough scope would be present to gain any sort of valid and reliable estimate of underlying proficiencies or ability for use. In the latter, the basis for generalisation to real life would be slender indeed.

So some sort of middle course is required, where the sampling of tasks and conditions does not lead to exhaustive coverage of conditions, but on the other hand it goes beyond a single task-condition combination. And it is here that research findings come in. Any task-based test battery needs to contain a range of tasks and conditions, building in a degree of Conceptualiser influences and Formulator influences, ideally sufficiently separately to give a distinct estimate of task difficulty for each. Then, there needs to be a range of complexifying, pressuring, easing, and focussing factors to provide a broader-based foundation for any estimate of effective language ability. So there needs to be variation in the nature of the information used, the need for computation versus the simpler need only to retrieve, and a need to build in different amounts of reasoning. There is also scope to vary the pressure for communication, and perhaps the amount and speed of input. Using both less negotiable and more negotiable tasks would also be useful.

Clearly there can be different emphases for Interactive-ability and Real-life tests. The balance of test tasks in the first case needs to be such that general underlying competences are implicated, as well as ability for use factors. The sorts of variations just discussed in the range of tasks used would be relevant. In the second case, while there must still be a range of tasks and conditions, the orientation to the needs-analysed based account of the actual real-life use can be more focussed. But even then, though the settings may be less varied, there is still importance in trying to vary Conceptualisation and Formulation demands in a focussed way. In either case, Interactive Ability and Real-life, there needs to be a range of elicitation devices. Only then can robust predictions be made about likely real-life integrative performances.

Rating Scales: The task and the task conditions lead to performance being elicited. The next stage is that the performance needs to be rated, and the likelihood is that this will be done by raters, using general and analytic rating scales. There have been interesting attempts to use what is known about actual performance to feed into rating scales so that the wording of scales reflects actual performance and differences between high and low proficiencies (Fulcher, 1996, 1997). But task research, through its interest in performance measurement, can make a distinctive contribution to the final parts of the model shown in Figure 13.1. As we saw in an earlier section, the focus on the performance dimensions of structural and lexical complexity, accuracy, and fluency is providing some insights as to what should be highlighted in these rating scales. So while this may not be a major contribution of task-based research, it may be relevant at this final stage where the performance that is elicited is given some numerical measure to indicate lower- and higher-level performance. Most broadly of all, the discussion in Chapter 10 on the discourse-clause tension may be relevant, since this suggests that performance in each of these broad domains needs to be distinguished from one another. The characterisation of structural complexity in task research in terms of subordination-based measures and words per clause, and the fact that these sometimes correlate but often do not, indicates that rating scales need to be sensitive to the distinction in question (as well as this being important for the sampling of tasks that is used to elicit performance).

Then, regarding fluency, the same discourse-clause contrast is relevant. We have seen that pause location (at AS-boundaries vs. mid-clause boundaries) is an important issue. Similarly, the different role that filled pauses seem to have compared to unfilled pauses may be relevant for the wording of rating scales (and research into them). A background issue here is also the importance of style. The evidence on style, where clause-linked fluency measures is concerned, looks strong, so it may also be the case that it is important not to penalise second language learners for aspects of performance which is linked with style, and which may be similar in the L1 (although a lot of research is needed to establish the strength and relevance of this insight).

The final measurement-linked issue concerns lexis, in the shape of D, as a text-length-corrected measure of lexical diversity, and lexical sophistication, the extent to which the speaker is able to draw on less frequent words. In a sense, lexical sophistication is simpler, and perhaps links with existing vocabulary scales, at least partly. They mostly incorporate mention of quality of lexis, and so rating this area of performance is already fairly standard. D is a more complex issue. It does appear to be a sensitive measure, capturing differences between native and non-native speakers, and very probably, between different proficiency levels. But there are two complications. First, there is strong evidence of style here, so using D would need to be done carefully to avoid penalising speakers for what is a preference in approach to vocabulary use. Second, it would be very difficult to implement. In Pollitt's terms, D means counting, and it is difficult to see either the way rating scales would be developed to capture variation in this area, or to see how there could be any actual measurement, given the time constraints of assessing speaking and the way performances are not routinely transcribed so that computer analysis could be attempted. It is, for now, an intriguing area, and one which may need to wait for advances in technology if it is to be used.

Broadly, then, the conclusion is that task research findings, particularly in relation to measures of second language performance, have a lot to contribute to the detailed wording of analytic rating scales. If this research is drawn on, more effective ratings may be possible which relate to details of actual performance, and how different levels can be distinguished from one another.

Conclusions

After these extensive discussions of the relevance of task research for assessment, this chapter will conclude with a small number of propositions about testing and the relevance of task research:

- assuming there are underlying competences but that it is important to measure them in actual language use, a key challenge is how to conceptualise what additional processes are involved when integrative language skills are used;
- the notion of ability for use is central. This is the ability which draws on component competences and then uses this knowledge base in actual language use. In some ways, this is a relabelling of an expanded view of strategic competence (Bachman, 1990) but it also brings in a more psycholinguistically plausible underpinning, based on Levelt, and on the functioning of a second language mental lexicon organised to enable dual-coding in language processing;

- tasks and task conditions are not neutral. It is clear from task research that task characteristics and task conditions have systematic influences upon performance. This means that it is dangerous, for comparability and for fairness, to use tasks and task conditions which have not been researched in terms of their effects on the dimensions of performance. If this is not done unforeseen effects on the language that is elicited will occur;
- the sampling of performance that takes place within testing needs to be representative in terms of what is known about task and task condition effects. In particular, task difficulty needs to be considered separately in relation to Conceptualiser and Formulator influences;
- insights from task research, particularly the discourse-clause contrast, and the structure of fluency, may have much to contribute to rating scale construction and rating scale use;
- Interactive-ability and Real-life tests require different emphases in test construction, and so the nature of the testing may be different in detail. But more generally the above principles apply equally forcefully to both types of test.

REFERENCES

Note that references to reprinted articles and chapters may have contained 'in press' or 'forthcoming' or 'manuscript' dates. Such references may now contain signposts to the updated publication, or even have two dates given, e.g. (in press; 2001).

Abrams, Z., & Byrd, D. (2016). The effects of meaning-focused pre-tasks on beginning-level L2 writing in German: An exploratory study. *Language Teaching Research*, 1–20.

Ahmadian, M. J. (2012a). The relationship between working memory capacity and L2 oral performance under task-based careful online planning condition. *TESOL Quarterly*, 46(1), 165–175.

Ahmadian, M. J. (2012b). The effects of guided careful online planning on complexity, accuracy, and fluency in intermediate EFL learners' oral production: The case of English articles. *Language Teaching Research*, 16, 129–149.

Ahmadian, M. J., & Tavakoli, M. (2014). Investigating what learners do and monitor under careful online planning conditions. *Canadian Modern Language Review*, 70(1), 50–75.

Alderson, J. C. (1991). Bands and scores. In J. C. Alderson & B. North (Eds.), *Language testing in the 1990s* (pp. 71–86). Oxford: Modern English Publications and the British Council.

Alvarez-Ossario, L. (1996). *The effect of planning in L2 Spanish narratives*. Unpublished manuscript, University of Hawai'i at Manoa.

Anderson, A., & Lynch, T. (1987). *Listening*. Oxford: Oxford University Press.

Anderson, J. R. (1989). Practice, working memory, and the ACT* theory of skills acquisition: A comment on Carlson, Sullivan, and Schieder. *Journal of Learning, Memory, and Cognition*, 15, 527–530.

Anderson, J. R. (1995). *Learning and memory*. New York: John Wiley.

Aston, G. (1986). Trouble-shooting in interaction with learners: The more the merrier? *Applied Linguistics*, 7, 128–143.

Bachman, L. F. (1990). *Fundamental considerations in language testing*. Oxford: Oxford University Press.

Bachman, L. F., & Palmer, A. S. (1996). *Language testing in practice*. Oxford: Oxford University Press.

Baddeley, A. (2007). *Working memory, thought, and action*. Oxford: Oxford University Press.

Baddeley, A. (2015). Working memory in second language learning. In Z. Wen, M. B. Mota, & A. McNeill (Eds.), *Working memory in second language acquisition and processing: Theories, research, and commentaries* (pp. 17–28). Clevedon, Avon: Multilingual Matters.

Baralt, M. L. (2010). *Task complexity, the cognition hypothesis, and interaction in CMC and FTF environments*. Unpublished PhD dissertation, Georgetown University.

Bates, E., Bretherton, I., & Snyder, L. (1988). *From first words to grammar*. Cambridge: Cambridge University Press.

Bei, X. (2010). *The effects of topic familiarity and strategic planning in topic-based task performance at different proficiency levels*. Unpublished PhD Thesis, Chinese University of Hong Kong.

Bell, H. (2003). *Using frequency lists to assess L2 texts*. Unpublished PhD thesis, University of Swansea.

Berwick, R. (1993). Towards an educational framework for teacher-led tasks. In G. Crookes & S. M. Gass (Eds.), *Tasks and language learning: Integrating theory and practice* (pp. 118–133). Clevedon, Avon: Multilingual Matters.

Bialystok, E. (1994). Analysis and control in the development of second language proficiency. *Studies in Second Language Acquisition, 16*, 157–168.

Bolibaugh, C., & Foster, P. (2013). Memory-based aptitude for nativelike selection: The role of phonological short-term memory. In G. Granena & M. H. Long (Eds.), *Sensitive periods, language aptitude, and ultimate L2 attainment* (pp. 205–230). Amsterdam: John Benjamins.

Bolinger, D. (1975). Meaning and memory. *Forum Linguisticum, 1*, 2–14.

Breen, M. (1984). Processes in syllabus design. In C. Brumfit (Ed.), *General English syllabus design* (pp. 47–60). Oxford: Pergamon.

Breen, M. (1987). Contemporary paradigms in syllabus design (Parts 1 and 2). *Language Teaching, 20*, 91–92 & 157–174.

Brock, C. (1986). The effects of referential questions on ESL classroom discourse. *TESOL Quarterly, 20*, 47–59.

Brown, G., Anderson, A., Shilcock, R., & Yule, G. (1984). *Teaching talk: Strategies for production and assessment*. Cambridge: Cambridge University Press.

Brown, J. D., Hudson, T., Norris, J., & Bonk, W. J. (2002). *An investigation of second language task-based performance assessments*. Honolulu, HI: University of Hawai'i Press.

Brumfit, C. (1984). *Communicative methodology in language teaching*. Cambridge: Cambridge University Press.

Bui, G., Skehan, P., & Wang, Z. (in press). Task condition effects on advanced level foreign language performance. In P. Malovrh & A. Benati (Eds.), *Handbook of advanced proficiency in second language acquisition*. New York: Wiley.

Bui, H. Y. G. (2014). Task readiness: Theoretical framework and empirical evidence from topic familiarity, strategic planning, and proficiency levels. In P. Skehan (Ed.), *Processing perspectives on task performance* (pp. 63–94). Amsterdam: John Benjamins.

Bygate, M. (1987). *Speaking*. Oxford: Oxford University Press.

Bygate, M. (1988). Units of oral expression and language learning in small group interaction. *Applied Linguistics, 9*(1), 59–82.

Bygate, M. (1996). Effects of task repetition: Appraising the developing language of learners. In J. Willis & D. Willis (Eds.), *Challenge and change in language teaching* (pp. 136–146). London: Heinemann.

Bygate, M. (2001). Effects of task repetition on the structure and control of oral language. In M. Bygate, P. Skehan, & M. Swain (Eds.), *Researching pedagogic tasks: Second language learning, teaching and testing* (pp. 23–48). Harlow: Longman.

Bygate, M. (2006). Areas of research that influence L2 speaking instruction. In E. Uso-Juan & A. Martinez-Flor (Eds.), *Current trends in the development and teaching of the four language skills* (pp. 159–186). The Hague: Mouton De Gruyter.

Bygate, M., & Samuda, V. (2009). Creating pressure in task pedagogy: The joint roles of field, purpose, and engagement within the interactional approach. In A. Mackey & C. Polio (Eds.), *Multiple perspectives on interaction* (pp. 90–116). New York: Routledge.

Bygate, M., Skehan, P. & Swain, M. (2001). (Eds.), *Researching pedagogic tasks: Second language learning, teaching and testing*. Harlow: Longman.

Canale, M. (1983). On some dimensions of language proficiency. In J. Oller (Ed.), *Issues in language testing research* (pp. 333–342). Rowley, MA: Newbury House.

Canale, M., & Swain, M. (1980). Theoretical bases of communicative approaches to second language teaching and testing. *Applied Linguistics, 1*, 1–47.

Candlin, C. (1987). Towards task-based language learning. In C. N. Candlin & D. Murphy (Eds.), *Lancaster practical papers in English language education*, Vol. 7. *Language learning tasks* (pp. 5–22). Englewood Cliffs, NJ: Prentice Hall.

Carr, T., & Curren, T. (1994). Cognitive factors in learning about structured sequences: Applications to syntax. *Studies in Second Language Acquisition, 16*(2), 205–230.

Carroll, J. B. (1961). Fundamental considerations in testing for English language proficiency of foreign students. In *Testing the English proficiency of foreign students* (pp. 30–40). Washington, DC: Center for Applied Linguistics.

Chalhoub-Deville, M. (2001). Task-based assessments: Characteristics and validity evidence. In Bygate, M., P. Skehan, & M. Swain (Eds.), *Researching pedagogic tasks: Second language learning, teaching, and testing* (pp. 210–228). Harlow: Longman.

Cheng, P. W. (1985). Restructuring versus automaticity: Alternative accounts of skill acquisition. *Psychological Review, 92*, 414–423.

Clark, H. H. (1996). *Using language*. Cambridge: Cambridge University Press.

Clark, H. H., & Clark, E. (1977). *Psychology and language*. New York: Harcourt, Brace, Jovanovitch.

Cook, V. J. (1994). *Linguistics and second language acquisition*. London: Macmillan.

Corder, S. P. (1981). *Error analysis and interlanguage*. Oxford: Oxford University Press.

Coughlan, P., & Duff, P. (1994). Same task, different activities: Analysis of a SLA task from an activity theory perspective. In J. Lantolf & G. Appel (Eds.), *Vygotskyan approaches to second language research* (pp. 173–193). Norwood, NJ: Ablex.

Cowan, N. (2015). Second-language use, theories of working memory, and the Vennian mind. In Z. Wen, M. B. Mota, & A. McNeill (Eds.), *Working memory in second language acquisition and processing: Theories, research, and commentaries* (pp. 29–40). Clevedon, Avon: Multilingual Matters.

Crookes, G. (1986). *Task classification: A cross-disciplinary review*. Technical Report, No. 4, Center for Second Language Research, Social Science Research Institute, University of Hawai'i at Manoa, Honolulu.

Crookes, G. (1989). Planning and interlanguage variation. *Studies in Second Language Acquisition, 11*, 367–383.

Crookes, G., & Gass, S. M. (1993a). *Tasks and language learning: Integrating theory and practice*. Clevedon, Avon: Multilingual Matters.

Crookes, G., & Gass, S. M. (1993b). *Tasks in a pedagogical context: Integrating theory and practice*. Clevedon, Avon: Multilingual Matters.

Daller, H., & Phelan, D. (2007). What is in a teacher's mind? The relation between teacher ratings of EFL essays and different aspects of lexical richness. In H. Daller, J. Milton, & J. Treffers-Daller (Eds.), *Modelling and assessing vocabulary knowledge* (pp. 234–245). Cambridge: Cambridge University Press.

Daller, H., Van Hout, R., & Treffers-Daller, J. (2003). Lexical richness in the spontaneous speech of bilinguals. *Applied Linguistics, 24*(2), 197–222.

Daller, H., & Xue, H. (2007). Lexical richness and the oral proficiency of Chinese EFL students. In H. Daller, J. Milton, & J. Treffers-Daller (Eds.), *Modelling and assessing vocabulary knowledge* (pp. 150–164). Cambridge: Cambridge University Press.

Davies, A. (2003). *The native speaker: Myth and reality* (2nd ed.). Clevedon, Avon: Multilingual Matters.

De Bot, K. (1992). A bilingual production model: Levelt's "Speaking" model adapted. *Applied Linguistics, 13*, 1–24.

De Jong, N. H., Groenhuot, R., Schoonen, R., & Hulstijn, J. (2015). Second language fluency: Speaking style or proficiency? Correcting measures of second language fluence for first language behaviour. *Studies in Second Language Acquisition, 36*, 223–243.

De Jong, N. H., Steinel, M. P., Florijn, A., Schoonen, R., & Hulstijn, J. (2012). Facets of speaking proficiency. *Studies in Second Language Acquisition, 34*, 5–34.

De Jong, N., & Vercelotti, M. L. (2015). Similar prompts may not be similar in the performance they elicit: Examining fluency, complexity, accuracy, and lexis in narratives from five picture prompts. *Language Teaching Research, 19*, 1–18.

Derwing, T. M., Munro, M. J., Thomson, R. I., & Rossiter, M. J. (2009). The relationship between L1 fluency and L2 fluency development. *Studies in Second Language Acquisition, 31*, 533–557.

Doughty, C. (1991). Second language instruction does make a difference: Evidence from an empirical study on SL relativization. *Studies in Second Language Acquisition, 13*, 431–469.

Duff, P. (1986). Another look at interlanguage talk: Taking task to task. In R. Day (Ed.), *Talking to learn* (pp. 147–181). Rowley, MA: Newbury House.

Elder, C., & Iwashita, N. (2005). Planning for task performance: Does it make a difference? In R. Ellis (Ed.), *Planning and task performance in a second language* (pp. 219–237). Amsterdam: John Benjamins.

Ellis, D. (2011). *The role of task complexity in the linguistic complexity of native speaker output*. Qualifying Paper, PhD in Second Language Acquisition program, University of Maryland, College Park, MD.

Ellis, R. (1987). Interlanguage variability in narrative discourse: Style shifting in the past tense. *Studies in Second Language Acquisition, 9*(1), 1–19.

Ellis, R. (1994). *The study of second language acquisition*. Oxford: Oxford University Press.

Ellis, R. (Ed.). (2005a). *Planning and task performance in a second language*. Amsterdam: John Benjamins.

Ellis, R. (2005b). Planning and task-based performance: Theory and research. In R. Ellis (Ed.), *Planning and task performance in a second language* (pp. 3–36). Amsterdam: John Benjamins.

Ellis, R. (2009). The differential effects of three types of task planning on fluency, complexity, and accuracy in L2 oral performance. *Applied Linguistics, 30*, 474–509.

Ellis, R., & Shintani, N. (2014). *Exploring language pedagogy through second language acquisition research*. London: Routledge.

Ellis, R., Tanaka, Y., & Yamazaki, A. (1994). Classroom interaction, comprehension, and the acquisition of L2 grammar. *Language Learning, 44*, 449–491.

Ellis, R., & Yuan, F. (2004). The effects of planning on fluency, complexity, and accuracy in second language narrative writing. *Studies in Second Language Acquisition, 26*(1), 59–84.

Ellis, R., & Yuan, F. (2005). The effect of careful within-task planning on oral and written task performance. In R. Ellis (Ed.), *Planning and task performance in a second language* (pp. 167–192). Amsterdam: John Benjamins.

Faerch, C., & Kasper, G. (Eds.). (1983). *Strategies in interlanguage communication*. London: Longman.

Farahani, A. A. K., & Meraji, S. R. (2011). Cognitive task complexity and L2 narrative writing performance. *Journal of Language Teaching and Research, 2*, 445–456.

Foster, P. (1994). *Discoursal outcomes of small-group work in an EFL classroom*. Working Papers in English Language Teaching No. 2, Thames Valley University, London.

Foster, P. (1998). A classroom perspective on the negotiation of meaning. *Applied Linguistics, 19*(1), 1–23.

Foster, P. (2001a). Rules and routines: A consideration of their role in the task-based language production of native and non-native speakers. In M. Bygate, P. Skehan, & M. Swain (Eds.), *Researching pedagogic tasks: Second language learning, teaching, and testing* (pp. 75–93). Harlow: Longman.

Foster, P. (2001b). *Lexical measures in task-based performance*. Paper presented at the AAAL Conference, Vancouver, Canada.

Foster, P., & Skehan, P. (1994). *The influence of planning on performance in task-based learning*. Paper presented at the British Association of Applied Linguistics Annual Conference, Leeds.

Foster, P., & Skehan, P. (1996a). The influence of planning and task type on second language performance. *Studies in Second Language Acquisition, 18*(3), 299–324.

Foster, P., & Skehan, P. (1996b). *The effects on accuracy and complexity of planning and mid-task manipulation*. Manuscript in preparation (Appeared as Foster & Skehan 2005).

Foster, P., & Skehan, P. (1999). The influence of source of planning and focus of planning on task-based performance. *Language Teaching Research, 3*, 185–214.

Foster, P., & Skehan, P. (2009, submitted). The effects of post-task activities on the accuracy and complexity of language during task performance (Appeared as Foster & Skehan, 2013).

Foster, P., & Skehan, P. (2012). Complexity, accuracy, fluency and lexis in task-based performance: A synthesis of the Ealing research. In A. Housen, F. Kuiken, & I. Vedder (Eds.), *Dimensions of L2 performance and proficiency: Complexity, accuracy, and fluency in SLA* (pp. 199–220). Amsterdam: John Benjamins.

Foster, P., & Skehan, P. (2013). The effects of post-task activities on the accuracy of language during task performance. *Canadian Modern Language Review, 69*, 249–273.

Foster, P., & Skehan, P. (in press). Modifying the task: The effects of surprise, time and planning type on task based performance. *Thames Valley Working Papers in Applied Linguistics*, Vol. 5, Thames Valley University (Appeared as Foster & Skehan, 2005).

Foster, P., & Tavakoli, P. (2009). Lexical diversity and lexical selection: A comparison of native and non-native speaker performance. *Language Learning, 59*(4), 866–896.

Foster, P., Tonkyn, A., & Wigglesworth, G. (2000). Measuring spoken language: A unit for all reasons. *Applied Linguistics, 21*(3), 354–375.

Foster, P., & Wigglesworth, G. (2015). Capturing accuracy in second language performance: The case for a weighted clause ratio. In A. Mackey (Ed.), *Annual Review of Applied Linguistics, 36*, 98–116.

Freed, B. (2000). Is fluency, like beauty, in the eyes (and ears) of the beholder? In H. Riggenbach (Ed.), *Perspectives on fluency* (pp. 243–265). Ann Arbor, MI: The University of Michigan Press.

Fukuta, J. (2016). Effects of task repetition on learners' attention orientation in L2 oral production. *Language Teaching Research, 20*(3), 321–340.

Fulcher, G. (1996). Testing tasks: Issues in task design and the group oral. *Language Testing, 13*(1), 23–52.

Fulcher, G. (1997). Does thick description lead to smart tests? A data-based approach to rating scale construction. *Language Testing, 13*(2), 208–238.

Garcia-Mayo, M. P. (2007). *Investigating tasks in formal language learning.* Clevedon, Avon: Multilingual Matters.

Gilabert, R. (2007a). The simultaneous manipulation of task complexity along planning time and [+/- here-and-now] effects on L2 performance. In Garcia-Mayo (Ed.), *Investigating tasks in formal language learning* (pp. 44–68). Clevedon, Avon: Multilingual Matters.

Gilabert, R. (2007b). Effects of manipulating task complexity on self-repairs during L2 oral production. *International Review of Applied Linguistics, 45*, 215–240.

Givon, T. (1985). Function, structure, and language acquisition. In D. Slobin (Ed.), *The crosslinguistic study of language acquisition* (Vol. 1, pp. 1008–1025). Hillsdale, NJ: Lawrence Erlbaum Associates.

Granena, G., & Long, M. H. (2013). Age of onset, length of residence, language aptitude, and ultimate L2 attainment in three linguistic domains. *Second Language Research, 29*(3), 311–343.

Grice, H. P. (1975). Logic and conversation. In P. Cole & J. Morgan (Eds.), *Syntax and semantics 3: Speech acts* (pp. 41–58). New York: Academic Press.

Guara Tavares, M. da G. (2013). Working memory capacity and L2 speech performance in planned and spontaneous conditions: A correlational analysis. *Trabajas Linguisticas Aplicadas,* Campinas, *52*(1), 9–29.

Harley, B., Allen, J. P. B., Cummins, J., & Swain, M. (1990). *The development of second language proficiency.* Cambridge: Cambridge University Press.

Harmer, J. (1991). *The practice of English language teaching* (2nd ed.). London: Longman.

Harrison, A. (1986). Assessing text in action. In M. Portal (Ed.), *Innovations in language testing* (pp. 72–96). Windsor, UK: National Foundation for Educational Research.

Heaton, J. (1975). *Beginning composition through pictures.* London: Longman.

Hill, L. A. (1960). *Picture composition book.* London: Longman.

Hoey, M. (1983). *On the surface of discourse.* London: George Allen and Unwin.

Housen, A., & Kuiken, F. (2009). Complexity, accuracy, and fluency in second language acquisition. *Applied Linguistics, 30*(4), 461–473.

Housen, F., Kuiken, F., & Vedder, I. (2012). *Dimensions of L2 performance and proficiency: Investigating complexity, accuracy, and fluency in SLA.* Amsterdam: John Benjamins.

Hulstijn, J. (2015). *Language proficiency in native and non-native speakers.* Amsterdam: John Benjamins.

Hunt, K. (1966). Recent measures in syntactic development. *Elementary English, 43,* 732–739.

Inoue, C. (2013). *Task equivalence in speaking tests.* Bern: Peter Lang.

Inoue, C. (2016). A comparative study of the variables used to measure syntactic complexity and accuracy in task-based research. *The Language Learning Journal, 1,* 1–18.

Ishikawa, T. (2007). The effect of manipulating task complexity along the +/- here-and-now dimension on L2 written narrative discourse. In M. del P. Garcia-Mayo (Ed.), *Investigating tasks in formal language learning* (pp. 136–156). Clevedon, Avon: Multilingual Matters.

Iwashita, N., McNamara, T., & Elder, C. (2001). Can we predict task difficulty in an oral proficiency test? Exploring the potential of an information-processing approach to task design. *Language Learning, 51,* 401–436.

Jackson, D. O., & Suethanapornkul, S. (2013). The cognition hypothesis: A synthesis and meta-analysis of research on second language task complexity. *Language Learning, 63*(2), 330–367.

Jarvis, S. (2002). Short texts, best fitting curves, and new measures of lexical diversity. *Language Testing, 19*(1), 57–84.

Jarvis, S., & Daller, M. (Eds.). (2013). *Vocabulary knowledge: Human ratings and automated measures*. Amsterdam: John Benjamins.

Kahnemann, D. (2011). *Thinking, fast and slow*. London: Penguin.

Kahng, J. (2014). Exploring utterance and cognitive fluency of L1 and L2 English speakers: Temporal measures and stimulated recall. *Language Learning, 64*(4), 809–854.

Karmiloff-Smith, A. (1986). From meta-processes to conscious access: Evidence from children's metalinguistic and repair data. *Cognition, 23*, 95–147.

Kaschak, M. P., Kutta, T. J., & Schatschneider, C. (2010). Long-term cumulative structural priming persists for (at least) one week. *Memory and Cognition, 39*, 381–388.

Kellerman, E. (1991). Compensatory strategies in second language research: A critique, a revision, and some (non-) implications for the classroom. In R. Phillipson, E. Kellerman, L. Selinker, M. Sharwood-Smith, & M. Swain (Eds.), *Foreign/second language pedagogy research* (pp. 142–161). Clevedon, Avon: Multilingual Matters.

Kenyon, D. (1992). *An investigation of the validity of the demands of tasks on performance-based tests of oral proficiency*. Paper presented at the Language Testing Research Colloquium, Vancouver, Canada.

Kess, J. E. (1992). *Psycholinguistics*. Amsterdam: John Benjamins.

Kim, Y. (2013a). Effects of pre-task modelling on attention to form and question development. *TESOL Quarterly, 47*(1), 8–35.

Kim, Y. (2013b). Investigating learners' cognitive processes by using stimulated recall methodology in task-based research. In A. Revesz & R. Gilabert (Organizers), *SLA methodological advances in TBLT research: Measurement of task demands and processes*. Colloquium presented at American Association for Applied Linguistics 2013 conference, Dallas, TX.

Kim, Y., & McDonough, K. (2011). Using pretask modelling to encourage collaborative learning opportunities. *Language Teaching Research, 15*(2), 183–199.

Kim, Y., & Tracey-Ventura, N. (2013). The role of task repetition in L2 performance development: What needs to be repeated during task-based interaction? *System, 41*, 829–840.

Klein, W. (1986). *Second language acquisition*. Cambridge: Cambridge University Press.

Kormos, J. (2006). *Speech production and second language acquisition*. Mahwah, NJ: Lawrence Erlbaum.

Kormos, J. (2011). Speech production and the cognition hypothesis. In P. Robinson (Ed.), *Second language task complexity: Researching the cognition hypothesis of language learning and performance* (pp. 39–60). Amsterdam: John Benjamins.

Krashen, S. D. (1985). *The input hypothesis: Issues and implications*. New York: Longman.

Kuiken, F., & Vedder, I. (2007). Task complexity and measures of linguistic performance in L2 writing. *International Review of Applied Linguistics in Language Teaching, 45*, 261–284.

Kuiken, F., & Vedder, I. (2008a). Cognitive tasks complexity and written output in Italian and French as a foreign language. *Journal of Second Language Writing, 17*, 48–60.

Kuiken, F., & Vedder, I. (2008b). *Task complexity and linguistic performance in L2 writing and speaking: The effect of mode*. Paper presented at the AAAL Conference, Washington, DC, March.

Labov, W. (1972). *Sociolinguistic patterns*. Philadelphia, PA: University of Pennsylvania Press.

Lambert, C., Kormos, J., & Minn, D. (2016). Task repetition and second language speech processing. *Studies in Second Language Acquisition, 38*, 1–30.

Lancaster corpus linguistics website. Retrieved from ucrel.lancs.ac.uk.

Larsen-Freeman, D., & Long, M. (1991). *An introduction to second language acquisition research.* London: Longman.

Laufer, B., & Nation, P. (1999). A vocabulary-size test of controlled productive ability. *Language Testing, 16*, 33–51.

Leech, G., Rayson, P., & Wilson, A. (2001). *Word frequencies in written and spoken English.* London: Longman.

Levelt, W. J. (1989). *Speaking: From intention to articulation.* Cambridge: Cambridge University Press.

Levelt, W. J. (1999). Producing spoken language: A blueprint of the speaker. In C. Brown & P. Hagoort (Eds.), *Neurocognition of language* (pp. 83–122). Oxford: Oxford University Press.

Levkina, M., & Gilabert, R. (2012). The effects of cognitive task complexity on L2 oral production. In A. Housen, F. Kuiken, & I. Vedder (Eds.), *Complexity, accuracy, and fluency in second language use, learning, and teaching* (pp. 171–198). Brussels: Univ. of Brussels Press.

Li, L., Chen, J., & Sun, L. (2015). The effects of different lengths of pretask planning time on L2 learners' oral test performance. *TESOL Quarterly, 49*(1), 38–66.

Li, Q. (2014). Get it right in the end: The effects of post-task transcribing on learners' oral performance. In P. Skehan (Ed.), *Processing perspectives on task performance* (pp. 129–154). Amsterdam: John Benjamins.

Li, S., & Fu, M. (2016). Strategic and unpressured within-task planning and their associations with working memory. *Language Teaching Research*, 1–24.

Littlewood, W. (1981). *Communicative language teaching: An introduction.* Cambridge: Cambridge University Press.

Logan, G. D. (1988). Towards an instance theory of automatisation. *Psychological Review, 95*, 492–527.

Long, M. H. (1985). A role for instruction in second language acquisition: Task-based language teaching. In K. Hyltenstam & M. Pienemann (Eds.), *Modelling and assessing second language development* (pp. 77–99). Clevedon, Avon: Multilingual Matters.

Long, M. H. (1989). Task, group, and task-group interaction. *University of Hawaii Working Papers in English as a Second Language, S*(20), 1–26.

Long, M. H. (1996). The role of the linguistic environment in second language acquisition. In W. Ritchie & T. Bhatia (Eds.), *Handbook of second language acquisition* (pp. 413–468). New York: Academic Press.

Long, M. H. (2015). *Second language acquisition and task-based language teaching.* New York: Wiley.

Long, M. H., & Crookes, G. (1991). Three approaches to task-based syllabus design. *TESOL Quarterly, 26*, 27–55.

Long, M. H., & Crookes, G. (1993). Units of analysis in syllabus design: The case for task. In G. Crookes & S. Gass (Eds.), *Tasks in a pedagogical context: Integrating theory and practice* (pp. 9–54). Clevedon, UK: Multilingual Matters.

Loschky, L., & Bley-Vroman, R. (1993). Grammar and task-based methodology. In G. Crookes & S. M. Gass (Eds.), *Tasks in a pedagogical context: Integrating theory and practice* (pp. 123–167). Clevedon, UK: Multilingual Matters.

Lumley, T., & McNamara, T. (1995). Rater characteristics and rater bias: Implications for training. *Language Testing, 12*, 55–71.

Lynch, T. (2001). Seeing what they meant: Transcribing as a route to noticing. *English Language Teaching Journal, 55,* 124–132.

Lynch, T. (2007). Learning from the transcripts of an oral communication task. *ELT Journal, 61,* 311–320.

MacWhinney, B. (2000). *The CHILDES project: Tools for analysing talk: Volume 1: Transcription format and programs* (3rd ed.). Mahwah, NJ: Lawrence Erlbaum.

Malicka, A., & Levkina, M. (2012). Measuring task complexity: Does L2 proficiency matter? In A. Shehadeh & C. Coombe (Eds.), *Task-based language teaching in foreign language contexts: Research and Implementation* (pp. 43–66). Amsterdam: John Benjamins.

Malvern, D. D., & Richards, B. J. (2002). Investigating accommodation in language proficiency interviews using a new measure of lexical diversity. *Language Testing, 19*(1), 85–104.

Malvern, D. D., Richards, B. J., Chipere, N., & Durán, P. (2004). *Lexical diversity and language development: Quantification and assessment.* Basingstoke: Palgrave Macmillan.

Markee, N., & Kunitz, S. (2013). Doing planning and task performance in second language acquisition: An ethnomethodological respecification. *Language Learning, 4,* 629–664.

Matthews, R. C., Buss, R. R., Stanley, W. B., Blachard-Fields, F., Cho, J. R., & Druhan, B. (1989). Role of implicit and explicit processes in learning from examples: A synergistic effect. *Journal of Experimental Psychology: Learning, Memory, and Cognition, 15,* 1083–1100.

McCarthy, P. M., & Jarvis, S. (2007). VOCD: A theoretical and empirical investigation. *Language Testing, 24*(4), 459–488.

McLaughlin, B. (1990). Restructuring. *Applied Linguistics, 11,* 113–128.

McNamara, T. (1995). Modelling performance: Opening Pandora's box. *Applied Linguistics, 16*(2), 159–179.

Meara, P., & Bell, H. (2001). P_Lex: A simple and effective way of describing the lexical characteristics of short L2 texts. *Prospect, 16*(3), 5–19.

Mehnert, U. (1998). The effects of different lengths of time for planning on second language performance. *Studies in Second Language Acquisition, 20,* 52–83.

Meraji, S. R. (2011). Planning time, strategy use, and written task production in a pedagogic vs. a testing context. *Journal of Language Teaching and Research, 2,* 338–352.

Michel, M. C. (2011). Effects of task complexity and interaction on L2 performance. In P. Robinson (Ed.), *Second language task complexity: Researching the cognition hypothesis of language learning and performance* (pp. 141–174). Amsterdam: John Benjamins.

Michel, M. C. (2013). The use of conjunctions in cognitively simple versus complex oral L2 tasks. *The Modern Language Journal, 97,* 178–195.

Michel, M. C., Kuiken, F., & Vedder, I. (2007a). Effects of task complexity and task condition on Dutch L2. *International Review of Applied Linguistics, 45*(3), 241–259.

Michel, M. C., Kuiken, F., & Vedder, I. (2007b). The influence of complexity in monologic versus dialogic tasks in Dutch L2. *International Review of Applied Linguistics in Language Teaching, 45,* 241–259.

Michel, M. C., Kuiken, F., & Vedder, I. (2007c). *The interaction of task condition and task complexity in the oral performance of Turkish and Moroccan learners of Dutch.* Paper presented at the 2nd International Conference on Task-Based Language Teaching, Hawaii.

Miller, G. (1956). The magical number 7, plus or minus 2: Some limits on our capacity for processing information. *Psychological Review, 63,* 81–97.

Miyake, A., & Shah, P. (1999). *Models of working memory: Mechanisms of active maintenance and executive control.* Cambridge: Cambridge University Press.

Mochizuki, N., & Ortega, L. (2008). Balancing communication and grammar in beginning level foreign language classrooms: A study of guided planning and relativization. *Language Teaching Research, 12*, 11–37.

Mohammadzadeh, M. A., Dabaghi, A., & Tavakoli, M. (2013). The effects of simultaneous use of pre-planning along +/-Here-and-Now dimension on fluency, complexity, and accuracy of Iranian EFL learners' written performance. *International Journal of Research Studies in Language Learning, 2*, 49–65.

Naittinger, J. R., & De Carrico, J. S. (1992). *Lexical phrases and language teaching*. Oxford: Oxford University Press.

Nelson, K. (1981). Individual differences in language development: Implications for development and language. *Developmental Psychology, 17*, 170–187.

Nielsen, K. B. (2013). Can planning time compensate for individual differences in working memory capacity? *Language Teaching Research, 18*(3), 272–293.

Norris, J. M., Brown, J. D., Hudson, T., & Yoshioka, J. (1998). *Designing second language performance assessments*. Honolulu, HI: University of Hawai'i Press.

Norris, J. M., & Ortega, L. (2003). Defining and measuring SLA. In C. Doughty & M.H. Long (Eds.), *The Handbook of Second Language Acquisition* (pp. 717–761). Oxford: Blackwell.

Norris, J. M., & Ortega, L. (2006). *Synthesising research on language learning and teaching*. New York: John Benjamins.

Norris, J. M., & Ortega, L. (2009). Towards an organic approach to investigating CAF in instructed SLA: The case of complexity. *Applied Linguistics, 30*, 555–578.

North, B. (1996). *The development of a common framework scale of language proficiency based on a theory of measurement*. Unpublished PhD thesis, Thames Valley University.

Norusis, M. (1990). *SPSS PC User's Manual, Version 4*. Chicago: Statistical Package for the Social Sciences.

Nunan, D. (1989). *Designing tasks for the communicative classroom*. Cambridge: Cambridge University Press.

Nunan, D. (1993). Task-based syllabus design: Selecting, grading, and sequencing tasks. In G. Crookes & S. M. Gass (Eds.), *Tasks in a pedagogical context: Integrating theory and practice*. Clevedon, UK: Multilingual Matters.

O'Malley, J. M., & Chamot, A. U. (1990). *Learning strategies and second language acquisition*. Cambridge: Cambridge University Press.

Ortega, L. (1995). *The effect of planning in L2 Spanish narratives*. Research Note 15, University of, Hawai'i Second Language Teaching and Curriculum Center, Honolulu, HI.

Ortega, L. (1999). Planning and focus on form in L2 oral performance. *Studies in Second Language Acquisition, 21*, 109–148.

Ortega, L. (2005). What do learners plan? Learner-driven attention to form during pre-task planning. In R. Ellis (Ed.), *Planning and task performance in a second language* (pp. 77–109). Amsterdam: John Benjamins.

Oxford, R. (1990). *Language learning strategies: What every teacher should know*. Rowley, MA: Newbury House.

Pang, F., & Skehan, P. (2006). *What do learners do when they plan: A qualitative study*. Paper presented at St. Mary's University College, Twickenham.

Pang, F., & Skehan, P. (2008: ms.: See 2014). *Using a model of speaking to explore second language learners use of planning time*. Hong Kong: Chinese University of Hong Kong.

Pang, F., & Skehan, P. (2014). Self-reported planning behaviour and second language performance in narrative retelling. In P. Skehan (Ed.), *Processing perspectives on task performance* (pp. 95–128). Amsterdam: John Benjamins.

Pang, F., & Skehan, P. (in prep). *Self-reported planning and its connection with dialogic task performance*. Manuscript, Macao Polytechnic Institute.

Park, S. (2010). The influence of pretask instructions and pretask planning on focus on form during Korean EFL task-based interaction. *Language Teaching Research*, 14(1), 9–26.

Pawley, A., & Syder, F. H. (1983). Two puzzles for linguistic theory: Nativelike selection and nativelike fluency. In J. C. Richards & R. Schmidt (Eds.), *Language and communication* (pp. 191–226). London: Longman.

Peters, A. (1983). *The units of language acquisition*. Cambridge: Cambridge University Press.

Peters, A. (1985). Language segmentation: Operation principles for the perception and analysis of language. In D. Slobin (Ed.), *The crosslinguistic study of language acquisition: Vol. 2: Theoretical issues* (pp. 1029–1067). London: Erlbaum.

Pica, T., Kanagy, R., & Falodun, J. (1993). Choosing and using communicative tasks for second language instruction. In G. Crookes & S. M. Gass (Eds.), *Tasks and language learning: Integrating theory and practice* (pp. 9–34). Clevedon, UK: Multilingual Matters.

Plough, I., & Gass, S. (1993). Interlocutor and task familiarity. In G. Crookes & S. Gass (Eds.), *Tasks and language learning: Integrating theory and practice* (pp. 35–56). Clevedon, UK: Multilingual Matters.

Pollitt, A. (1991). Giving students a sporting chance: Assessment by counting and judging. In J. C. Alderson & B. North (Eds.), *Language testing in the 1990s* (pp. 46–59). London: Macmillan.

Prabhu, N. S. (1987). *Second language pedagogy*. Oxford: Oxford University Press.

Qiu, X., & Lo, Y. Y. (2016). Content familiarity, task repetition and Chinese EFL learners' engagement in second language use. *Language Teaching Research*, 1–18.

Read, J. (2000). *Assessing vocabulary*. Cambridge: Cambridge University Press.

Reber, A. (1989). Implicit learning and tacit knowledge. *Journal of Experimental Psychology: General*, 118, 219–235.

Revesz, A. (2009). Task complexity, focus on form, and second language development. *Studies in Second Language Acquisition*, 31(3), 437–470.

Révész, A. (2011). Task complexity, focus on L2 constructions, and individual differences: A classroom-based study. *The Modern Language Journal*, 95, 162–181.

Revesz, A. (2014). Towards a fuller assessment of cognitive models of task-based learning: Investigating task-generated cognitive demands and processes. *Applied Linguistics*, 35(1), 93–98.

Revesz, A., Ekiert, M., & Torgersen, E. N. (2015). The effects of complexity, accuracy, and fluency on communicative adequacy in oral task performance. *Applied Linguistics*, 37(6), 828–848.

Revesz, A., Sachs, R., & Hama, M. (2013). Eye tracking as a means of investigating task-based cognitive *processes*. In A. Revesz & R. Gilabert (Organizers), *SLA methodological advances in TBLT research: Measurement of task demands and processes*. Colloquium presented at American Association for Applied Linguistics 2013 conference, Dallas, TX.

Revesz, A., Sachs, R., & Mackey, A. (2011). Task complexity, uptake of recasts, and L2 development. In P. Robinson (Ed.), *Second language task complexity: Researching the cognition hypothesis of language learning and performance* (pp. 203–235). Amsterdam: John Benjamins.

Richards, B., Daller, M. H., Malvern, D. D., Meara, P., Milton, J., & Treffers-Daller, J. (2009). (Eds.). *Vocabulary studies in first and second language acquisition: The interface between theory and application*. London: Palgrave Macmillan.

Richards, B., & Malvern, D. (2007). Validity and threats to the validity of vocabulary measurement. In H. Daller, J. Milton, & J. Treffers-Daller (Eds.), *Modelling and assessing vocabulary knowledge* (pp. 79–92). Cambridge: Cambridge University Press.

Rivers, W. (1981). *Teaching foreign language skills.* Chicago: University of Chicago.
Robinson, P. (2001a). Task complexity, task difficulty, and task production: Exploring interactions in a componential framework. *Applied Linguistics, 22*(1), 27–57.
Robinson, P. (2001b). Task complexity, cognitive resources, and syllabus design: A triadic framework for examining task influences on SLA. In P. Robinson (Ed.), *Cognition and second language instruction* (pp. 287–318). Cambridge: Cambridge University Press.
Robinson, P. (2008). Re-thinking-for-speaking and L2 task demands: The cognition hypothesis, task classification, and sequencing. Plenary address at the Second International Conference on Task-based Language Teaching, Hawaii.
Robinson, P. (Ed.). (2011a). *Second language task complexity: Researching the cognition hypothesis of language learning and performance.* Amsterdam: John Benjamins.
Robinson, P. (2011b). Second language task complexity, the cognition hypothesis, language learning, and performance. In P. Robinson (Ed.), *Second language task complexity: Researching the cognition hypothesis of language learning and performance* (pp. 3–38). Amsterdam: John Benjamins.
Robinson, P. (2015). The cognition hypothesis, second language task demands, and the SSARC model of pedagogic task sequencing. In M. Bygate (Ed.), *Domains and directions in the development of TBLT* (pp. 87–122). Amsterdam: John Benjamins.
Robinson, P., Cadierno, T., & Shirai, Y. (2009). Time and motion: Measuring the effects of the conceptual demands of tasks on second language production. *Applied Linguistics, 28*, 533–554.
Robinson, P., & Gilabert, R. (2007). Task complexity, the cognition hypothesis, and second language learning and performance. Special Issue of *International Review of Applied Linguistics for Language Teaching, 45*(3), 161–176.
Robinson, P., Ting, S. C.-C., & Urwin, J. J. (1995). Investigating second language task complexity. *RELC Journal, 26*, 62–79.
Robinson, P. J., & Ha, M. A. (1993). Instance theory and second language rule learning under explicit conditions. *Studies in Second Language Acquisition, 15*(4), 413–438.
Samuda, V. (2001). Guiding relationships between form and meaning during task performance: The role of the teacher. In M. Bygate, P. Skehan, & M. Swain (Eds.), *Researching pedagogic tasks: Second language learning, teaching, and testing* (pp. 119–140). Harlow: Longman.
Sanders, A. (1998). *Elements of human performance.* Mahway, NJ: Lawrence Erlbaum.
Sasayama, S. (2011). Cognition hypothesis and second language performance: Comparison of written and oral task performance. *Second Language Studies, 29*, 107–129.
Sasayama, S. (2014). *Measuring cognitive task complexity from the learners' perspective.* Presentation at TBL in Asia Conference, Osaka, Japan.
Sasayama, S. (2015). *Validating the assumed relationship between task design, cognitive complexity, and second language task performance.* Unpublished PhD Dissertation, Georgetown University.
Sasayama, S. (2016). Is a 'complex' task really complex? Validating the assumption of cognitive task complexity. *Modern Language Journal, 100*(1), 231–254.
Sasayama, S., & Izumi, S. (2012). Effects of task complexity and pre-task planning on EFL learners' oral production. In A. Shehadeh & C. Coombe (Eds.), *Task-based language teaching in foreign language contexts: Research and implementation* (pp. 23–42). Amsterdam: John Benjamins.
Schachter, J. (1974). An error in error analysis. *Language Learning, 24*, 205–214.
Schiffrin, R. M., & Schnieder, W. (1977). Controlled and automatic information processing II: Perceptual learning, automatic attending, and general theory. *Psychological Review, 84*, 127–190.

Schmidt, R. (1983). Interaction, acculturation and the acquisition of communicative competence: A case study of an adult. In N. Wolfson & E. Judd (Eds.), *Sociolinguistics and second language acquisition* (pp. 137–174). Rowley, MA: Newbury House.

Schmidt, R. (1990). The role of consciousness in second language learning. *Applied Linguistics, 11*, 17–46.

Schmidt, R. (1992). Psychological mechanisms underlying second language fluency. *Studies in Second Language Acquisition, 14*, 357–385.

Schmidt, R. (1994). Deconstructing consciousness: In search of useful definitions for applied linguistics. *AILA Review, 11*, 11–26.

Schur, E. (2007). Insights into the structure of L1 and L2 vocabulary networks: Intimations of small worlds. In H. Daller & J. Treffers-Daller (Eds.), *Modelling and assessing vocabulary knowledge* (pp. 182–204). Cambridge: Cambridge University Press.

Sheen, R. (1994). A critical analysis of the advocacy of a task-based syllabus. *TESOL Quarterly, 28*(1), 127–151.

Sinclair, J. McH. (1991). *Corpus, concordance, collocation*. Oxford: Oxford University Press.

Skehan, P. (1984). Issues in the testing of English for specific purposes. *Language Testing, 1*(2), 202–220.

Skehan, P. (1992). *Strategies in second language acquisition*. Working Papers in English Language Teaching No. 1, Thames Valley University, London.

Skehan, P. (1994). Foreign language learning ability: Cognitive or linguistic? *Thames Valley University Working Papers in English Language Teaching, 2*, 151–191.

Skehan, P. (1995). Analysability, accessibility, and ability for use. In G. Cook & B. Seidlehofer (Eds.), *Principle and practice in applied linguistics* (pp. 91–106). Oxford: Oxford University Press.

Skehan, P. (1996a). A framework for the implementation of task-based learning. *Applied Linguistics, 17*(1), 38–62. Oxford: Oxford University Press.

Skehan, P. (1996b). Implications of SLA research for language teaching methodologies. In D. Willis & J. Willis (Eds.), *Doing task-based teaching* (pp. 17–30). Oxford: Oxford University Press.

Skehan, P. (1998). *A cognitive approach to language learning*. Oxford: Oxford University Press.

Skehan, P. (2001). Tasks and language performance. In M. Bygate, P. Skehan, & M. Swain (Eds.), *Research pedagogic tasks: Second language learning, teaching, and testing* (pp. 167–185). London: Longman.

Skehan, P. (2007). Task research and language teaching: Reciprocal relationships. In S. Fotos (Ed.), *Form-meaning relationships in language pedagogy: Essays in honour of Rod Ellis*. Oxford: OUP.

Skehan, P. (2009a). Modelling second language performance: Integrating complexity, accuracy, fluency and lexis. *Applied Linguistics, 30*, 510–532. Oxford: Oxford University Press.

Skehan, P. (2009b). Lexical performance by native and non-native speakers on language-learning tasks. In B. Richards, H. Daller, D. D. Malvern, & P. Meara (Eds.), *Vocabulary studies in first and second language acquisition: The interface between theory and application* (pp. 107–124). London: Palgrave Macmillan.

Skehan, P. (2009c). Models of speaking and the assessment of second language proficiency. In A. G. Benati (Ed.), *Issues in second language proficiency* (pp. 202–215). London: Continuum.

Skehan, P. (2012). *Researching tasks: Performance, assessment, pedagogy*. Shanghai: Shanghai Foreign Language Education Press.

Skehan, P. (2013). Nurturing noticing. In J. Bergsleithner, S. N. Frota, & J. K. Yoshioka (Eds.), *Noticing and second language acquisition: Studies in honor of Richard Schmidt* (pp. 169–180). Honolulu, HI: National Foreign Language Center.

Skehan, P. (2014a). *Processing perspectives on task performance*. Amsterdam: John Benjamins.
Skehan, P. (2014b). The context for researching a processing perspective on task performance. In Skehan, P. (Ed.), *Processing perspectives on task performance* (pp. 1–26). Amsterdam: John Benjamins.
Skehan, P. (2014c). Synthesising and applying task research. In P. Skehan (Ed.), *Processing perspectives on task performance* (pp. 211–260). Amsterdam: John Benjamins.
Skehan, P. (2015). Limited attentional capacity and cognition: Two hypotheses regarding second language performance on tasks. In M. Bygate (Ed.), *Domains and directions in the development of TBLT: A decade of plenaries from the international conference* (pp. 123–155). Amsterdam: John Benjamins.
Skehan, P. (2016). Tasks vs. conditions: Two perspectives on task research and its implications for pedagogy. In A. Mackey (Ed.), *Annual Review of Applied Linguistics, 24*, 34–49.
Skehan, P., Bei, X., Li, Q., & Wang, Z. (2012). The task is not enough: Processing approaches to task-based performance. *Language Teaching Research, 16*(2), 170–187.
Skehan, P., & Foster, P. (1996). *The influence of post-task activities and planning on task-based performance*. Working Papers in English Language Teaching No. 3, Thames Valley University, London.
Skehan, P., & Foster, P. (1997). The influence of planning and post-task activities on accuracy and complexity in task based learning. *Thames Valley University Working Papers in English Language Teaching, Vol. 3*.
Skehan, P., & Foster, P. (1997). The influence of planning and post-task activities on accuracy and complexity in task based learning. *Language Teaching Research, 1*, 185–211.
Skehan, P., & Foster, P. (1999). Task structure and processing conditions in narrative retellings. *Language Learning, 49*(1), 93–120.
Skehan, P., & Foster, P. (2005). Strategic and on-line planning: The influence of surprise information and task time on second language performance. In R. Ellis (Ed.), *Planning and task performance in a second language* (pp. 193–216). Amsterdam: John Benjamins.
Skehan, P., & Foster, P. (2008). Complexity, accuracy, fluency and lexis in task-based performance: A meta-analysis of the Ealing research. In S. Van Daele, A. Housen, F. Kuiken, M. Pierrard, & I. Vedder (Eds.), *Complexity, accuracy, and fluency in second language use, learning, and teaching* (pp. 207–226). Brussels: University of Brussels Press.
Skehan, P., & Foster, P. (2013). *Using post task analytic activities to promote accuracy*. Manuscript, Thames Valley University.
Skehan, P., Foster, P., & Shum, S. (2016). Ladders and snakes in second language fluency. *International Review of Applied Linguistics, 54*(2), 97–111.
Skehan, P., & Pang, F. (2008). *Planning, task comparisons, and native vs. non-native speakers: A qualitative study*. Paper presented at the 2nd St. Mary's Conference, St. Mary's University, Twickenham, Middlesex.
Skehan, P., & Shum, S. (2014). Structure and processing condition in video-based narrative retelling. In P. Skehan (Ed.), *Processing perspectives on task performance* (pp. 197–210). Amsterdam: John Benjamins.
Skehan, P., & Shum, S. (2017). What influences performance? Personal style or the task being done. In L. L. C. Wong & K. Hyland (Eds.), *Faces of English education: Students, teachers, and pedagogy* (pp. 28–43). London: Routledge.
Stern, H. H. (1983). *Fundamental concepts for language teaching*. Oxford: Oxford University Press.
Strauss, A., & Corbin, J. (1990). *Basics of qualitative research: Grounded theory procedures and techniques*. Newbury Park, CA: SAGE Publications.

Swain, M. (1985). Communicative competence: Some roles of comprehensible input and comprehensible output in its development. In S. Gass & C. Madden (Eds.), *Input in second language acquisition* (pp. 235–253). Rowley, MA: Newbury House.

Swain, M. (1995). Three functions of output in second language learning. In G. Cook & B. Seidlehofer (Eds.), *Principle and practice in applied linguistics* (pp. 125–144). Oxford: Oxford University Press.

Tarone, E. (1983). On the variability of interlanguage systems. *Applied Linguistics, 4*, 143–163.

Tarone, E. (1985). Variability in interlanguage use: A study of style-shifting in morphology and syntax. *Language Learning, 35*, 373–403.

Tavakoli, P. (2009). Investigating task difficulty: Learners' and teachers' perceptions. *International Journal of Applied Linguistics, 19*(1), 1–25.

Tavakoli, P., & Foster, P. (2008). Task design and second language performance: The effect of narrative type on learner output. *Language Learning, 58*(2), 439–473.

Tavakoli, P., & Skehan, P. (2005). Planning, task structure, and performance testing. In R. Ellis (Ed.), *Planning and task performance in a second language* (pp. 239–276). Amsterdam: John Benjamins.

Tavares, M. G. G. (2009). The relationship among pre-task planning, working memory capacity, and L2 speech performance: A pilot study. *Linguagem & Ensino, 12*, 165–194.

Thai, C., & Boers, F. (2016). Repeating a monologue under increasing time pressure: Effects on fluency, complexity, and accuracy. *TESOL Quarterly, 50*(2), 369–393.

Tidball, F., & Treffers-Daller, J. (2007). Exploring measures of vocabulary richness in semi-spontaneous French speech. In H. Daller, J. Milton, & J. Treffers-Daller (Eds.), *Modelling and assessing vocabulary knowledge* (pp. 133–149). Cambridge: Cambridge University Press.

Towell, R. (2002). Relative degrees of fluency: A comparative case study of advanced learners of French. *International Review of Applied Linguistics, 40*(2), 117–150.

Towell, R., & Dewaele, J-M. (2005). The role of psycholinguistic factors in the development of fluency amongst advanced learners of French. In J. M. Dewaele (Ed.), *Focus on French as a foreign language: Multidisciplinary approaches* (pp. 210–239). Clevedon, Avon: Multilingual Matters.

Towell, R., Hawkins, R., & Bazergui, N. (1996). The development of fluency in advanced learners of French. *Applied Linguistics, 17*(1), 84–115.

Trevise, A., & Noyau, C. (1984). Adult Spanish speakers and the acquisition of French negation forms: Individual variation and linguistic awareness. In R. W. Andersen (Ed.), *Second languages* (pp. 165–189). Rowley, MA: Newbury House.

Van Daele, S., Housen, A., Kuiken, F., Pierrard, M., & Vedder, I. (2008). (Eds.). *Complexity, accuracy, and fluency in second language use, learning, and teaching*. Brussels: University of Brussels Press.

Van Hout, R., & Vermeer, A. (2007). Comparing measures of lexical richness. In H. Daller, J. Milton, & J. Treffers-Daller (Eds.), *Modelling and assessing vocabulary knowledge* (pp. 93–115). Cambridge: Cambridge University Press.

Van Lier, L. (1989). Reeling, writhing, drawling, stretching, and fainting in coils: Oral proficiency interviews as conversation. *TESOL Quarterly, 23*, 489–508.

Van Patten, B. (1990). Attending to content and form in the input: An experiment in consciousness. *Studies in Second Language Acquisition, 12*, 287–301.

Van Patten, B. (1994). Evaluating the role of consciousness in SLA: Terms, linguistic features, and research methodology. *AILA Review, 11*, 27–36.

Van Patten, B., & Cadierno, T. (1993). Explicit instruction and input processing. *Studies in Second Language Acquisition, 15*, 225–243.

Wang, Z. (2009). *Modelling speech production and performance: Evidence from five types of planning and two task structures*. Unpublished PhD thesis, Chinese University of Hong Kong.

Wang, Z. (2014). On-line time pressure manipulations: L2 speaking performance under five types of planning and repetition conditions. In P. Skehan (Ed.), *Processing perspectives on task performance* (pp. 27–62). Amsterdam: John Benjamins.

Wang, Z., & Skehan, P. (2014). Structure, lexis, and time perspective: Influences on task performance. In P. Skehan (Ed.), *Processing perspectives on task performance* (pp. 155–186). Amsterdam: John Benjamins.

Wells, G. (1985). *Language development in the pre-school years*. Cambridge: Cambridge University Press.

Wen, Z. (2009). *Effects of working memory capacity on L2-based speech planning and performance*. Unpublished PhD Dissertation, Chinese University of Hong Kong.

Wickens, C. D. (2007). Attention to the second language. *International Review of Applied Linguistics, 45*, 177–191.

Widdowson, H. G. (1983). *Learning purpose and language use*. Oxford: Oxford University Press.

Widdowson, H. G. (1989). Knowledge of language and ability for use. *Applied Linguistics, 10*(2), 128–137.

Wigglesworth, G. (1997). An investigation of planning time and proficiency level on oral test discourse. *Language Testing, 14*(1), 85–106.

Wigglesworth, G. (2001). Influences on performance in task-based oral assessments. In Bygate, M., Skehan, P. & Swain, M. (Eds.), *Researching pedagogic tasks: Second language learning, teaching and testing* (pp. 186–209). Harlow: Longman.

Willis, D. (1990). *The lexical syllabus: A new approach to language teaching*. London: Collins.

Willis, D. (1993). Syllabus, corpus, and data-driven learning. In C. Kennedy (Ed.), *Plenaries from the 1993 IATEFL Conference*, Swansea, Wales.

Willis, D., & Willis, J. (2007). *Doing task-based teaching*. Oxford: Oxford University Press.

Willis, J. (1996). *A framework for task-based learning*. London: Longman.

Willis, J., & Willis, D. (1988). *Collins COBUILD English course: Book 1*. London: Collins.

Wilson, D. (1994). Relevance and understanding. In G. Brown, K. Malmkjaer, A. Pollitt, & J. Williams (Eds.), *Language and understanding* (pp. 35–58). Oxford: Oxford University Press.

Winter, E. (1976). *Fundamentals of information structure: A pilot manual for further development according to student need*. Hatfield Polytechnic, English Department.

Wolfe-Quintero, K., Inagaki, S., & Kim, H-K. (1998). *Second language development in writing: Measures of fluency, accuracy, and complexity*. Technical Report No. 17, Second Language Teaching and Curriculum Center: University of Hawaii.

Yuan, F., & Ellis, R. (2003). The effects of pre-task and online planning on fluency, complexity, and accuracy in L2 monologic oral production. *Applied Linguistics, 24*, 1–27.

Yule, G., Powers, M., & Macdonald, D. (1992). The variable effects of some task-based learning procedures on L2 communicative effectiveness. *Language Learning, 42*(2), 249–277.

INDEX

ability for use 4, 6, 17, 24, 114, 117, 254, 258–259, 272, 285–287, 289, 294–296, 305–310, 313–315
anticipation 8–9, 67, 78, 91, 101, 118
articulation 58–59, 75. 88, 93–94, 114, 158, 199, 220, 228, 276, 295, 309, 311
articulator 58–59, 70, 75, 92–94, 100, 114, 203, 215, 227–228, 232, 249, 276, 279, 309
articulatory buffer 215, 309
attentional demands 45, 90–92, 94, 281
attentional limitations 35, 37, 46, 48, 53, 68, 85, 284
authenticity 15, 206
automatisation 8, 38, 114, 127
avoiding error 8–9, 91, 101–102, 199, 283

background information 42, 45, 47, 62
breakdown 38, 81, 100, 118, 135, 242–243, 268, 311
breakdown fluency 64, 234, 242

CAF 35–37, 39, 45, 51–53, 63, 81, 86–87, 131, 266
CHAT 160
CHILDES 190
CLAN 39, 190
clause boundary pausing 172, 178
clause-linked dysfluency 304, 314
coding scheme 156–158, 161–162, 175–176, 216, 249

Cognition Hypothesis 10, 11, 17, 45–49, 53, 68–82, 86–89, 91, 100, 104, 106, 110, 119, 122, 155, 180–181, 293, 312–313
cognitive complexity 27, 29–30, 32
cognitive familiarity 27, 29
cognitive processing 27, 29, 147
communication cycles 227, 231
communicative competence 259, 288
communicative language teaching (CLT) 2, 14, 27, 33, 55
complexifying 50, 61–62, 64, 87, 120–121, 254, 280, 282, 287, 298–299, 312–313
complexity of outcome 270–271
complex outcomes 263, 272
Conceptualiser-Formulator balance 95–96, 101–102, 113–114, 119, 224
consciousness 17–18, 20–21, 93–94, 101, 219, 223, 276, 279
consciousness-raising 29, 32, 133
Core 289–290
counting 296, 302, 315
c-unit 134–135, 140, 142–144, 148, 264, 267

D 39, 40, 190–191, 196–198, 201, 203–205, 245, 247, 315
degree of structure 44, 59, 235
detailed planning 136, 139, 142–147, 149, 150–151, 210
directed attention 90, 92

discourse-clause 250, 314, 316
discourse organisation 217, 289
dual-mode 18–19, 24, 26, 28

EAP 1, 202, 301–302
easing 4, 16, 29, 42, 51–52, 61, 65, 72, 88, 109, 119–121, 126, 130, 137, 199, 207, 220–221, 260, 280, 284–285, 287, 293, 298–299, 305, 312–313
effect size 40, 63, 66, 73, 98, 221
emerging rule-governed system 19, 132, 309
encapsulated 58, 59, 94, 228, 295
end-of-clause pausing 229, 241–242
error free clauses 47, 81, 134, 141–142, 145, 150, 166–168, 189, 241, 247, 267, 269
error gravity 81, 248, 304
exact task repetition 220, 222
exemplar-based 18, 21, 23, 84
exemplars 17–19, 24
extended pedagogic sequences 3, 8, 10, 14, 26, 30, 33, 55, 83–85, 105, 131–132, 152, 158, 176, 181, 221–222, 224, 251, 253

false starts 38, 135, 190, 241, 248, 304
familiarity 60, 62, 115, 131, 141, 153, 219, 235, 219
feedback 55–56, 77, 93, 130, 207
fluency 21, 29, 35, 57, 86, 103–104, 134, 140, 143, 160, 179–180, 241, 265, 267, 269–271, 304
focus-on-form 85, 284
foreground information 47, 106
formulaic language 18, 24, 58, 195, 294, 306, 309–310

goal-setting 288, 290–291, 294–295, 307
group-based planning 46, 212, 262

here-and-now 50, 63, 65, 70, 76–77, 235–238, 243, 245–247, 278, 312–313
Higher Language Cognition 289–290
Hong Kong 2, 54, 126–127, 157, 208, 234

idiom 24, 134, 309
information gap tasks 77, 206
information integration 47, 69
input domination 77. 82
input pressure 62–63, 66, 250, 280, 292, 298

instructed planning 210, 230
intake 20, 21
interactional 14, 70, 130, 289–290
Interaction Hypothesis 7, 55, 84, 86
interactive ability 295, 314
interactive tasks 36, 46, 51, 91–92, 111, 202–203, 225, 266, 268, 283
interlanguage 7, 10, 15–26, 30, 32–34, 71, 86, 130, 133, 135, 145, 152
item-based approach 291, 294, 296–297

judging 296, 302

LAC 56–59, 68–70, 72–75, 77–81, 88–90, 106, 119
Lambda 40–43, 161, 166, 175, 192, 196–205
Language Competence 288–289, 291
lemma retrieval 41, 43–45, 50–51, 58, 64–66, 92, 98, 102, 117–119, 198, 204, 226, 275, 280–281, 287, 294, 299, 307, 310
length of run 38, 166–167, 190, 242
less frequent vocabulary 196, 202, 240
Levelt model 10–11, 41, 43, 45, 50, 52–53, 61, 75, 77, 79, 87–88, 90, 92, 94, 96, 99, 112, 114, 120, 124, 157, 165, 176, 204–205, 215–217, 227, 232, 237, 254, 276–280, 287, 293, 295, 298, 305, 308, 310
lexical demands 45, 59, 64, 111, 118, 204, 247
lexical density 134, 233
lexical diversity 87, 104, 190, 193, 197–198, 201, 204–205, 209, 219, 233–234, 303–304, 315
lexicalisation 23, 30, 276
lexical retrieval 41, 156, 165, 180, 191, 198, 204, 238
lexical sophistication 39–40, 52, 62, 87, 161, 166–167, 175–176, 179–180, 191, 193, 198, 204–205, 233–234, 239, 247, 303–304, 315
lexical variety 15, 39–40, 190–191, 197
limited attentional capacity 47, 55, 60, 79, 82, 87–88, 121–122
LREs 210–211

macrostructure 27, 43–44, 51, 99, 109, 115, 117, 119, 217, 263, 268, 273, 282, 284, 312
meaning-focussed 129, 132

memory demands 60, 76, 292, 298, 312–313
metacognition 216–218, 230, 232, 250, 306, 308
metacognitive planning 162, 164–165, 176, 187
metacognitive strategies 176, 308
mid-clause pausing 39, 43, 168, 171, 173–174, 177, 179
modality 27–28, 30, 32, 84, 105, 106, 122, 132, 135, 140, 193
models of speaking 83, 158, 275–285
modular 53, 58–59, 93–94, 100, 277, 308
monitoring 52, 58, 75, 90–91, 96, 101–102, 112, 114, 119, 156–157, 165, 176, 216, 232, 246, 295, 298, 304–306, 308, 310

native and non-native speakers 39, 127, 189, 196–197, 201–202, 205, 229, 310, 315
negotiability 49–50, 60, 65–66, 84, 109–110, 112–113, 123, 199, 292, 302, 312
negotiable tasks 62–63, 116, 119, 281, 314
negotiation of meaning 56, 70, 130
non-negotiability 49–50, 66, 199, 292, 312
non-negotiable 62–63, 74, 109, 116, 119–120, 123, 203, 206, 280–281, 299–300
noticing 8, 9, 18, 20, 71, 129, 132
nudged 90–91, 105, 212

on-line computation 27, 115–116, 122–123, 264
on-line planning 39, 46, 50, 60–61, 65, 67–68, 78, 95–96, 99, 112, 119–120, 122, 126, 178, 208, 214, 231–232, 248, 266, 268–269, 278, 282–284, 292, 298, 309, 312–313
Organisational Competence 34, 288, 291, 306
outcome-evaluated 129, 299

parallel functioning 228, 295
parallel processing 43, 45, 49, 53, 59, 61, 75, 94, 100, 102, 114, 118, 120, 204, 228–229, 279, 281
pause location 39, 241–242, 248, 314
pedagogic activity 55, 83, 85
pedagogy 3, 6, 8, 9, 25, 34, 57, 97, 121–123, 130, 211, 225, 227, 254

Periphery 289–290, 294–295, 307
personal information exchange 36, 91, 125, 136–137, 139, 152, 193, 207, 210, 213, 283
planning-as-extending 63, 72, 312
planning-as-rehearsal 46, 65, 66
post-task activities 23, 31, 85, 132–133, 152
post-task activity 8, 47–48, 52, 54, 67, 78, 101, 132
post-task conditions 67, 113, 120, 127, 194, 262, 292, 298
post-task stage 8, 9, 78, 85, 123, 152
practice 9, 14, 25–26, 32, 57, 111, 139, 141–142, 213, 257, 311
Pragmatic Competence 34, 288, 306–307
preparedness 96–98, 218–220
pressuring 49–50, 52, 61–62, 77, 100, 120–121, 254, 280, 282, 284, 287, 293, 298–299, 305, 312–313
pre-task planning 36, 51, 59–60, 63, 66, 68, 75, 86, 97, 194, 208–209, 213–215, 218–220, 222, 224, 226, 229, 231–232, 235, 248, 278, 308–309
pre-verbal message 43–45, 51, 54, 58–59, 68, 75, 80, 92–93, 115, 117, 119, 165, 199, 203–205, 223, 226, 228–229, 250, 275–276, 278–282, 293–295, 307, 310–311
prime 51, 57, 98, 115, 119, 204, 213, 223–224, 277
problem-solution structure 62, 72, 76, 99–100, 109, 194, 235
proceduralisation 16, 19, 23–24, 26
processing capacity 19, 22, 57, 147, 250
psycholinguistic processes 68, 226–227, 241, 249, 251
public performance 8, 29, 31–32, 37, 67, 85, 91, 133, 152, 194, 283

qualitative data 107, 110, 155, 157, 161, 167, 207, 216
qualitative research 97, 115, 215–216, 225, 228–229, 231–232, 238, 249

rating scales 273, 285, 302–306, 314–315
Real-life 301–303, 308, 311, 313–314, 316
reasoning demands 73, 127, 312
reduced time pressure 117, 119
reformulation 23, 38, 135, 140, 143, 160, 189, 241, 247–248, 264, 269, 304, 310–311

336 Index

rehearsal 32, 46, 60, 65–66, 97–99, 112, 116–118, 120, 156, 165, 175–177, 180, 188–189, 213, 216, 218, 228, 231–232, 238, 249, 283–284, 298
repair 38, 43, 45, 59, 81, 135, 160, 189, 221–222, 234, 241–244, 247–249, 304–305
replacement 38, 43, 135, 140, 142–143, 149, 241, 245, 247–248, 269, 304
resource directing 69–74, 77–80, 88–89, 100, 104–106, 121, 297
resource dispersing 70–72, 88, 100, 104
restructuring 17–19, 21–26, 28–32, 85, 133
retention 98–99, 215, 217–218, 224
retrospective interviews 156–157, 160–161, 163, 216
revision 67, 73, 162–163
rule-based system 18–19, 24, 26, 309

schema 30, 92, 194
schematic 27, 29, 44
second language mental lexicon 58–60, 65, 68–69, 75, 80, 89, 93–94, 96, 98, 102, 114, 117–118, 205, 224, 226, 231, 250, 294–296, 299, 306–307, 315
selective attention 96, 101–102, 112
self-reported planning behaviours 97, 165, 167, 180, 217
serial processing 59, 61, 76, 100
silent pauses 127, 233, 241–243, 246–247, 249, 304
source of planning 208, 211–212
speech rate 23, 190, 221–222
speed 8, 28, 38, 68, 81, 84, 95, 98, 102, 214, 229, 234, 241–243, 248, 274, 287, 289–290, 294, 304, 306, 308, 314
stakes 27, 28, 30, 32, 84, 122
strategic competence 24, 288–291, 294–295, 307, 310, 311, 315
strategic planning 95–96, 98–99, 112, 117, 119, 154, 228, 292
structural complexity 8, 10, 41, 45, 48–49, 52–53, 60, 62–64, 67, 72, 81, 87, 91, 99–100, 103–104, 106, 167, 197, 221, 236, 241, 244, 248, 303, 314
syllables per minute 38, 241, 304
syllabus 13, 25–26, 30–32, 129–130, 257, 297
syntactic encoding 43, 49–51, 62, 66–69, 221, 280, 298–299
System 1, 2 108, 113

task characteristics 5, 8, 14, 36–37, 52, 57, 64, 79, 108, 111, 113–114, 122, 127, 189, 193–194, 205, 254, 258, 260–262, 264, 271, 273, 277, 292, 297, 300, 311, 312, 316
task condition factors 69, 244, 305
task conditions 5, 8, 9, 15, 36–37, 52, 53, 64, 67, 69, 78–79, 83, 85–86, 88, 90, 111–113, 120, 127, 132, 141, 154, 189, 193–194, 254, 258, 262, 282, 284, 286–287, 292, 297–298, 300, 305, 311–314, 316
task engagement 79, 110–111, 222
task repetition 62, 98, 220, 222
task sequencing 27, 85
task structure 47, 54, 57, 69, 72–73, 76, 99, 102, 111, 117, 127, 171, 178, 217, 235–236, 250, 254, 292, 303, 312
task types 36, 153, 193, 199–200, 207, 214, 262
test-task 123, 254, 273, 312
there-and-then 50, 63, 65, 69, 74, 76–77, 106, 235–258, 242–243, 245, 278, 312–313
time-creating devices 143, 200, 310
time perspective 58, 63, 69, 71, 74, 76, 77, 79, 81–82, 88, 154, 235, 246, 303, 312
time pressure 17, 24, 27, 50, 56, 60–62, 67, 84, 108, 112, 117–120, 122, 149, 193–194, 214, 221, 238, 280, 282, 290, 295, 298, 302, 308, 313
total silence 142–143, 147–149, 242
trade-off 10, 36–37, 45–46, 48–49, 52–53, 56, 88, 147, 149, 152, 154–155, 180, 195
Trade-off Hypothesis 36–37, 41, 45, 53, 87
transcription 37, 48, 67, 78, 160–161, 262
transformation 14, 51, 59, 116, 122, 195, 263–264, 270–271, 273, 298, 300, 312
type-token ratio 39, 87, 190, 234, 247, 264

unavoidable lexis 42, 118, 202, 205
undetailed planning 139, 141–147, 150–151, 210

words per clause 73, 81, 234, 236–240, 247–248, 292, 303, 314
working memory 3, 35, 49, 54, 56–57, 60, 74, 77–78, 115, 215, 226, 308–309